INTERNET PROTOCOLS
HANDBOOK

Dave Roberts

CORIOLIS GROUP BOOKS

Publisher *Keith Weiskamp*
Senior Project Editor *Scott Palmer*
Copy Editor *Jenni Aloi*
Proofreader *Kathy Dermer*
Cover Art *Gary Smith*
Cover Design *Anthony Stock*
Interior Design *Michelle Stroup*
Layout Production *Rob Mauhar*
Indexer *Lenity Mauhar*

The Coriolis Group
7339 E. Acoma Drive, Suite 7
Scottsdale, AZ 85260
Phone: (602) 483-0192
Fax: (602) 483-0193
Web address: www.coriolis.com

ISBN 1-883577-88-8 : $39.99

Printed in the United States of America

10 9 8 7 6 5 4 3 2 1

To my wife, Dawn

Acknowledgments

First, thanks to all the great men and women of the IETF that have worked hard to design, build, and deploy the largest network in the world. This book is merely a rephrasing of the technical content of the RFCs they have written to document their progress.

Second, thanks to the editors and production people at the Coriolis Group for once again making a super book: Keith Weiskamp, Scott Palmer, Jenni Aloi, Megan Hartl, Michelle Stroup, and all the rest of the team.

Contents

Introduction

We stand on the brink of a new age. Yes, I know, everyone says that all the time, and when you look outside, everything seems to be the same as it has always been. Nevertheless, this time, it's true.

Computer networks have finally migrated out of the laboratories and into popular culture. It seems that nobody can produce a television commercial anymore without listing an Internet Web address. As the world moves forward, computer networks—and in particular, the Internet—will become part of most people's daily lives.

In addition to the primitive surfing content that exists on the World Wide Web today, we will see a host of traditional daily activities now being networked over the Internet. The financial world has already started its transition; the Internet is now the best place to receive timely financial information, ranging from simple stock quotes to corporate news releases.

This trend will only accelerate and *no industry will be left untouched.* In the same way that the touch-tone telephone revolutionized the customer service departments of traditional business and created a host of new phone-access-only businesses, the Internet will do it all again.

There are plenty of applications and protocols left to be engineered and deployed. This book serves as an aid to that process by providing a reference for those protocols already developed, and in many cases already in daily use, on today's Internet.

Who Should Buy This Book

This book is not for everybody. It isn't an end-user book and won't teach you how to use a particular protocol. It isn't an introductory technical book that teaches you about the various Internet protocols, though it may serve as a helpful adjunct to one. But this book *is* for any person who needs to deal with Internet protocols at a technical level. That includes:

- Network protocol implementers
- Network hardware designers
- Network applications programmers
- Network and system administrators
- Students and professors

Objectives

The objectives of this book are simple:

- Provide detailed, comprehensive information about a variety of common Internet protocols
- Provide this information in a reference format
- Provide the corresponding official standards documents online to backup the printed material and allow quick access to additional information

All the information contained in this book is also available from a number of different sources. The official Internet Requests for Comment (RFCs, see Appendix A) provide the definitive description of each protocol, and many other good books provide a more tutorially-oriented approach to the material.

This is a reference work, not a teaching or explanatory work. Like Joe Friday in Dragnet, this book is, "Just the facts." This books serves the reader who is already familiar with a particular Internet protocol and needs to look up something quickly. This may be a network programmer implementing the protocol or a system administrator trying to diagnose a problem by decoding a frame on a network analyzer.

In short, this book is what is left over when you take all the RFCs of interest, stack them up, and then remove all the expository text. You'll find frame formats, commands and response codes, state machines, protocol identification codes, and so forth.

Having said that, there is nothing more frustrating than thinking you understand a protocol, looking up a fact in a reference book, and then not being able to interpret that fact because you find out you really didn't understand the protocol at all. This book provides detailed source information to assist a reader in gaining more information about a protocol. Typically, this is a reference to an Internet RFC that describes the protocol in detail. All the available Internet RFCs (at the time of publication) are available on the companion CD-ROM, to assist a reader in finding the desired information or explanation.

Inclusion Philosophy

The Internet is a very dynamic system. Just as the content and services available on the Internet change daily, so to do the protocols that must be developed to support the new content and services. New Internet standards are being produced at an incredible rate to serve a rapidly-increasing user base with an increasingly large set of requirements.

At any one time, there are many documents describing Internet standards in various states of preparation. Some are well specified, standards-track proposals with strong support from the Internet engineering community. Others are nothing more than the fancies of their writers. Still others were proposed long ago, and may have been in great use, but are now nothing more than historical curiosities.

With only limited time and pages available for this book, this leads to a natural question: Which protocols make the cut, and which don't? I have adopted the following inclusion philosophy:

- Include the most widely used protocols. This favors the application protocols over such things as routing protocols. Application protocols are of more use to more people. Routing protocols, though terribly important to the Internet, are typically the province of the router vendors themselves, and their technical staffs already know them very well. Including the most widely used protocols first also favors protocols that are new and "hot" as opposed to those that are falling into disuse.
- Favor information from official RFCs over Internet Drafts. Internet Drafts are works-in-progress and, thus can radically change in the blink of an eye. RFCs are more stable. Note that this rule includes cases where the protocol may be defined by an RFC but an in-progress Internet Draft exists which is attempting to correct or clarify the language of the original RFC. Only information from the original RFC is included in this book. In some cases, when it is clear that the Internet engineering community is clearly behind the revisions, I have used some Internet Draft information. Such cases are noted and the reader is encouraged to consult the latest version of the Internet Draft or the equivalent RFC if it has been issued.

- Make exceptions where necessary. Some protocols are widely implemented and widely used but are still in Internet Draft status at the time of this writing. Such protocols are documented when there is significant reason to do so. Again, the reader should note that Internet Drafts are subject to major revision, and is thus encouraged to find the most recent copy of the draft, rather than relying solely on the information in this book.

About the Material

The information in this book is compiled from many RFCs and other resources. In many cases, the material was extracted directly from the RFCs themselves. For instance, the RFC 822 grammar is reprinted directly from the RFC. This was done to ensure that no errors were introduced during the compilation of the material.

Entry Format

The format of data entries is designed to deliver the maximum amount of information in the least amount of space. The objective is to allow you to find the critical information you need without having to wade through pages and pages of textual description. If you wanted to do that, you'd read the original RFCs, not this book.

Each entry is broken up into a number of fields. The fields describe the name of the entry, where you can find its original specification, a more detailed description of the protocol operation, and finally, the relevant frame formats and commands and responses used by the protocol.

Not all entries use the same fields. Many entries do use similar fields, however, and these fields are roughly described as follows:

- **Name.** The Name field describes the name of the protocol entry.
- **Abbreviation.** The Abbreviation field describes the abbreviation typically assigned to the protocol. For instance, the Simple Mail Transport Protocol is often abbreviated as SMTP.
- **Status.** The Status field describes the state and status assigned to the protocol by the IESG. More information about the various possible states and statuses can be found in Chapter 4.
- **Specifications.** The Specifications field lists the various specifications, typically RFCs, that describe the protocol. You can use the information in the

Specifications field to retrieve the corresponding RFCs from the companion CD-ROM if you need more information about the protocol than is provided in the entry.

In some cases, I have combined the material from multiple RFCs into a single entry. In such cases, the Specifications field will list multiple original data sources.

In cases where the protocol is defined in an Internet Draft, the title of the Internet Draft is listed in the Specifications field. When an Internet Draft is listed in the Specifications field, you should be wary of the information contained in the rest of the protocol entry. As noted elsewhere, an Internet Draft has no formal status as an Internet specification document. Internet Drafts are volatile and subject to rapid change. Before using the information contained in the entry, the reader is encouraged to download the latest version of the Internet Draft or corresponding RFC, as explained in Appendix A.

- **Abstract.** The Abstract field gives a short description of the protocol. If you are looking for a protocol that performs a given function and you don't know the name of the protocol, scan the Abstract field to determine whether a listed protocol fits your needs.
- **Related Specifications.** Often, a protocol is related to other protocols in some fashion. The Related Specifications field lists other protocols that are closely related to the protocol entry. For instance, ICMP is closely related to IP. The IP entry lists ICMP in its Related Specifications field.
- **See Also.** The See Also field lists protocols and their associated RFCs that might be of interest. In general, these are specifications that are not as closely related to the protocol as those listed in the Related Specifications field. For instance, TCP and UDP typically use IP as their underlying network layer. The IP entry lists TCP and UDP in its See Also field.
- **Comments.** The Comments field provides commentary on the protocol. This might include small facts or commentary that is related to the protocol but is not contained in the protocol definition.
- **Description.** The Description field provides a short description of the protocol. This field often contains information that can't easily be classified as belonging to any of the other fields.
- **Transport Information.** Application layer protocols such as NNTP and SMTP run over transport protocols such as TCP. The protocol server listens

for connections from clients on well-known port numbers. The Transport Information field lists the port numbers assigned to the protocol server and the type of transport protocol used to make contact.

- **Commands.** Many application protocols use a command/response protocol design. The Commands field lists the commands used by the protocol and a short description of each.
- **Responses.** The Responses field lists the possible protocol responses to the commands described in the Commands field.
- **Protocol State Machine.** Some protocols are modeled using a state machine. In such cases, the State Machine field contains a state machine drawing.
- **Grammar.** Some protocols or format descriptions involve a regular grammar. In such cases, the Grammar field contains a description of the grammar. In most cases, the grammar field has been copied directly from the defining RFC. This means that the grammar format is the same as that used by the RFC. No attempt has been made to normalize all the various grammars into a standardized format. Fortunately, most Internet RFCs use a pseudo-standard form of augmented BNF.
- **Frame, Packet, or Message Formats.** Many of the network layer and datalink layer protocols define standard frame, packet, or message formats for the exchange of information. The Frame, Packet, or Message Formats field shows the appropriate formats and provides a description of the various fields in the format.

State Machine Format

The state machines, contained in the protocol entries, all follow a common format. The basic format is shown in Figure I.1

States are shown as rounded rectangles. The name of the state is shown in the center of the rounded rectangle.

State transitions are shown as arcs or lines with arrows leading from the original state to the final state. The state transitions are labeled with the stimulus that causes the transition to be taken. For instance, Figure I.1 shows "Stimulus 1" causing a transition from State 1 to State 3.

A transition may have an output associated with it. The output may be an action taken by the module implementing the state machine or a message sent to the

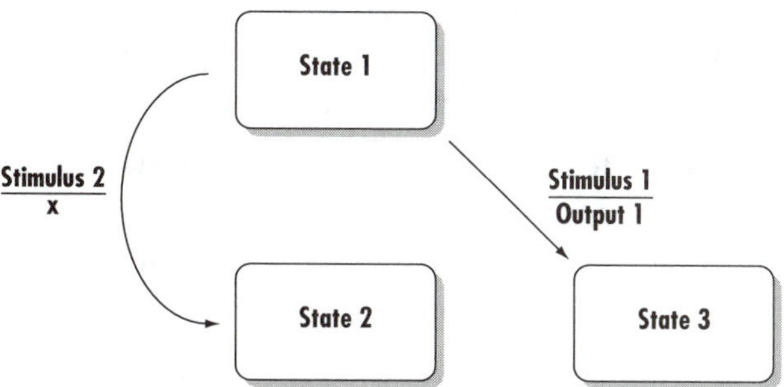

Figure I.1
The state machine format.

other party involved with the protocol. Outputs are shown below a line separating the action from the stimulus associated with the transition. Figure I.1 shows Output 1 associated with the transition leading from State 1 to State 3. When there is no output associated with a transition, the output is either shown as "x," as shown in the transition from State 1 to State 2, or is omitted entirely.

In general, only transitions which lead from a state to another state are shown. Transitions leading from a state back into itself are implied and are not shown. All stimuli which do not cause the state machine to transition to another state are simply ignored.

Grammar Format

Many Internet protocols use a grammar to specify the format of messages or commands and responses. Although there is no standard for grammar specifications, many Internet RFCs use a form of augmented BNF to specify their grammars. This section gives an overview of the augmented BNF form used by many RFCs.

- **Literals.** Literals are enclosed in quotes. For example, a comma would be specified by ",".
- **Rule Naming.** In general, rules are given simple names. Simple rules are given uppercase names. Examples of names include: "specials", "CR", and

"LF". In some cases, rule names are enclosed by "<" and ">" where an ambiguity might result.

- **Alternative Elements.** Alternative elements are separated by "/". In such cases, either of the elements, but not both, may appear.
- **Grouping Elements.** Elements can be grouped by surrounding them with "(" and ")". When grouping occurs, the group is considered as a single element for the purpose of the grammar. Other forms can occur within a group. For instance, "(elem1 (elem2 / elem3) elem4)" describes either: "elem1 elem2 elem4" or "elem1 elem3 elem4".
- **Optional Elements.** Optional elements are shown surrounded by "[" and "]". This implies the element can appear once or not at all.
- **Repetition.** Repetition of elements can be specified by the following notation: <m>*<n>element. This notation specifies that the element can appear at least <m> times and at most <n> times. The default value for <m> is zero and for <n> is infinity. Thus "*element" means that element can appear any number of times. "1*element" means the element must appear at least once. "1*5element" means the element must appear at least once and no more than five times. Note that "*1element" is equivalent to "[element]".

  A special form of the repetition syntax is "<n>element". This is equivalent to "<n>*<n>element" and specifies that the element must appear exactly <n> times. Thus "2DIGIT" specifies that DIGIT must appear twice.
- **Lists.** Since comma separated lists of elements are a common construction, a special syntax is used to describe them. The syntax "<m>#<n>element" is similar to the "*" notation used in specifying repetition except that the elements are separated by a ",". Thus, '(element *("," element))' is equivalent to 1#element. As with the "*" notation, the default values for <m> and <n> are zero and infinity.
- **Comments.** Comments are shown to the right side of the rules, separated by a semicolon. Comments typically give additional information about the rule or describe the semantics of the rule.

Network Byte Order

The byte order for multi-byte quantities in message format drawings is not always specified. All multi-byte quantities are assumed to be transferred in network byte order unless specified otherwise. Network byte order specifies the big-endian ordering convention. Implementers working on little-endian computer architectures, Intel architectures in particular, must keep network byte order in mind when manipulating multi-byte quantities in structures describing message formats.

Command/Response Conventions

Many Internet application protocols, such as SMTP and NNTP, use textual commands and replies. In general, most Internet protocols use the NVT-ASCII character set and the CRLF end-of-line convention (ASCII carriage return followed by ASCII line feed). It is important for implementers to recognize that the CRLF end-of-line convention may differ from the local end-of-line convention. In particular, the C programming end-of-line convention will correspond to the local end-of-line convention which may not be the same as CRLF. Programmers writing portable programs will want to explicitly send the CRLF pair rather than relying on the local end-of-line convention.

Suggesting New Topics For This Book

Almost by definition, this book is incomplete. That's because new Internet protocols are constantly being developed. New editions of this book will be published from time to time. If you have a protocol that you would like include—either one that missed this edition or was developed since it went to press—please let me know about it. Send your suggestions and ideas to "iph-ideas@droberts.com". Of course, not every suggestion will result in protocols being added—there is still only so much room in the book—but it sure helps to know what people consider the most valuable information.

Book Updates From The Web

You can get up-to-the-minute information about this book online. Check out:

http://www.droberts.com

and

http://www.coriolis.com

for more information.

Reporting Errors

Mistakes happen, and I'm hardly immune. While I've tried my best, it is quite likely that errors exist in this book. I hope that they are few and far between and that when they occur, they don't cause you too much trouble. If you find one, I'd like to hear about it so that I can correct it. Please send me a bug report at "iph-bugs@droberts.com."

Contacting The Author

I'm available for comment or questions. If you want to comment on the book or for any other reason, drop me an email at "dave@droberts.com". I get a lot of messages, so I can't promise that I'll answer everything, but I do try.

What's On The CD-ROM

The *Internet Protocols Handbook's* CD-ROM includes the full text of all Internet RFCs (protocol specifications).

The RFCs are organized by document number, with directories on the CD-ROM holding documents in specific ranges. For example, to find the standard for Domain Name System (DNS), you'd look in the directory **\1000** because the document numbers are RFC 1034 and RFC 1035.

Address Resolution Protocol

Name

Address Resolution Protocol

Abbreviation

ARP

Status

Standard (STD 37)

Specifications

RFC 826

Abstract

The Address Resolution Protocol (ARP) provides a method to map Internet Protocol (IP) addresses to datalink addresses (48-bit Ethernet and IEEE 802 addresses, for example). Once this mapping has been established, a host's IP module can directly address an Ethernet or IEEE 802 network frame directly to the appropriate destination node.

Related Specifications

IP-IEEE (RFC 1042), IP-FDDI (RFC 1390)

See Also

RARP (RFC 903), Assigned Numbers (RFC 1700)

Comments

The original ARP specification was developed to support mapping of IP addresses to Ethernet addresses. The specification was general purpose, however, and other RFCs have provided the necessary information for ARP to function with other datalink protocols. Indeed, ARP has become the universal address resolution protocol. Even when IP has been adapted to run over non-broadcast media, such as ATM, the standards have used an ARP-like mechanism to perform the address resolution function.

Description

ARP uses a simple mechanism to map IP addresses to local link addresses: It simply creates a datalink-level broadcast message containing the ARP query. All nodes on the local link receive the message, and the node with the IP address in question generates an ARP response and sends it back to the node that generated the query.

Frame Formats

ARP defines a number of constant values that are used in the ARP request and reply messages. These constants are given the symbolic names shown in Table 1.1.

Table 1.1 ARP Symbolic Constants

Constant Name	Value
ether_type$ADDRESS_RESOLUTION	0x0806
ares_op$REQUEST	1
ares_op$REPLY	2
ares_hrd$Ethernet	1

Note that ARP uses the term "hardware address" rather than "datalink address" or "MAC address," and "protocol address" rather than "network layer address." These terms mean the same thing.

ARP is a generic address resolution protocol and is not specific to either Ethernet or IP. The various ARP fields can be used to map other network address formats to other datalink address formats.

An ARP frame has the following structure:

Ethernet headers (this portion of the frame is replaced appropriately for other datalink protocols):

- 48 bits: Destination address, broadcast for *ares_op$REQUEST*, unicast for *ares_op$REPLY*.
- 48 bits: Source address.
- 16 bits: Ethernet protocol type = *ether_type$ADDRESS_RESOLUTION*.

Ethernet packet data:

- 16 bits: (*ar$hrd*) Hardware address space. For example, *ares_hrd$Ethernet*.
- 16 bits: (*ar$pro*) Protocol address space. For Ethernet hardware, this is from the set of type fields *ether_typ$<protocol>* (0x0800 for IP—see RFC 1700 for more Ethernet protocol types).
- 8 bits: (*ar$hln*) Byte length of each hardware address (Ethernet = 6 or 2).
- 8 bits: (*ar$pln*) Byte length of each protocol address (IPv4 = 4).
- 16 bits: (*ar$op*) Operation code—*ares_op$REQUEST* or *ares_op$REPLY*.
- *n* bytes: (*ar$sha*) Hardware address of sender of this packet (*n* = *ar$hln*).
- *m* bytes: (*ar$spa*) Protocol address of sender of this packet (*n* = *ar$pln*).
- *n* bytes: (*ar$tha*) Hardware address of target of this packet (if known).
- *m* bytes: (*ar$tpa*) Protocol address of target.

A node wanting to obtain a mapping between a protocol address fills in the appropriate fields of the ARP frame and sends it out using MAC layer broadcast mechanisms. The requesting node fills in the *arhrd, arpro, arhln, arpln, arop, arsha, ar$spa,* and *ar$tpa* fields. All receivers on the local network receive the request, because it is addressed to the broadcast address, and examine the various fields to determine whether the request applies to them. If not, the request is simply ignored. A node that supports the requested protocol address space and has been assigned the protocol address in question replies to the query. (There are other checks described in RFC 826 that implementers should use to completely validate the request contents. Implementers should consult RFC 826 for more detail.)

To generate a reply, the node swaps the sender and target address fields, fills in the *ar$sha* field with its hardware address (since it is now the sender), sets the *ar$op* field to *ares_op$REPLY* and sends the reply back to the original requester, using datalink unicast (not broadcast) addressing.

Bootstrap Protocol

Name

Bootstrap Protocol

Abbreviation

BOOTP

Status

Recommended Draft Standard

Specifications

RFC 951, RFC 1497, RFC 1542

Abstract

The Bootstrap Protocol (BOOTP) allows a diskless workstation to discover its IP address, the address of its server host, and the name of its boot image file. Used in conjunction with TFTP, BOOTP allows a diskless node to boot without being manually configured by a user. The client uses TFTP to retrieve the boot file once the necessary names and addresses have been retrieved using BOOTP.

Related Specifications

DHCP (RFC 1541), DHCP-BOOTP (RFC 1533), RFC 1534 (describes the interoperation between DHCP and BOOTP clients and servers)

See Also

RARP (RFC 903), TFTP (RFC 1350, RFC 1782, RFC 1783, RFC 1784)

Comments

DHCP is closely related to BOOTP and uses the same basic infrastructure developed for BOOTP. DHCP extends BOOTP in many ways and obviates the need for BOOTP in most cases. DHCP is much more widely supported than BOOTP.

Description

The Bootstrap Protocol (BOOTP) allows a diskless workstation to obtain its IP address, the IP address of its server, and the name of its kernel image to allow it to boot. Once this information has been learned, a file transfer protocol such as TFTP is used to retrieve the kernel image and continue the boot process.

The protocol uses a very simple two-packet exchange. The client sends out a request packet, and a listening server returns a response packet. The request contains the client's hardware address (an Ethernet address, for instance). The server uses the information provided by the client to supply the client's IP address and the path name of its boot image. The server also returns its own address so that the client can contact it in a later phase of the boot process to retrieve its boot image.

BOOTP uses UDP packets to communicate. A simple UDP/IP stack is small enough to be programmed into a ROM in the booting client. Because the client does not know its own address or the address of its server, the client uses IP broadcast addressing to send its request out to whichever server is listening. The server sends its reply using IP broadcast or by directly addressing the packet to the client using the correct datalink addressing. The most efficient reply form uses unicast addressing, but some clients are unable to receive unicast replies until they are booted. The client may force the server to use a broadcast reply by setting the broadcast bit in the flags field.

The packet format is fixed and is the same for both the request and the reply. A simple operation code distinguishes requests from replies.

A BOOTP server is not required to reside on every subnet where a BOOTP client resides. BOOTP allows routers and other agents to relay BOOTP messages to an appropriate server. This allows one BOOTP server to handle a large group of clients located on different subnets.

Transport Information

BOOTP uses two well-known UDP port numbers: 67 and 68. BOOTP servers listen for boot requests on port 67. Clients listen for the corresponding replies on port 68. Note that this is slightly different than most protocols where the client uses a random port and only the server waits on a well-known port. The client must use a well-known port also because the boot reply message may be broadcast to all nodes on the network. Other nodes using the same random port number for other protocols would become confused when they received a BOOTP reply message.

Message Formats

General Message Format

BOOTP uses a simple message format. All fields are fixed length, and the same format is used for both boot requests and replies. After receiving a boot request, the server can simply fill in the appropriate fields in the message and send it out again.

Table 2.1 describes the fields in the BOOTP message.

Vendor-Specific Information

The BOOTP message contains a vendor information field. This field is used to exchange additional information between the client and server using the basic BOOTP message format. Note that the name of this field is now a bit misleading. While it once served to convey vendor extensions, the field is now used to convey a series of standard options. Indeed, DHCP goes so far as to rename this field entirely.

Table 2.1 BOOTP Message Format

Field Name	Length in Bytes	Description
op	1	Opcode; 1 = boot request, 2 = boot reply
htype	1	Hardware address type; taken from the list of hardware address types used by ARP; 1 = 10 Mbps Ethernet
hlen	1	Hardware address length; 6 for 10 Mbps Ethernet
hops	1	Used by routers to count the number of traversed hops when booting through a router; the client always sets this field to zero
xid	4	Transaction ID. A random number assigned by the client and returned in the reply; this is used by the client to match a reply with a specific request
secs	2	Seconds spent trying to boot; the client sets this field to the number of elapsed seconds since it sent its first request message; the first boot request therefore contains zero in this field
flags	2	Flags; the most significant bit of the field is the broadcast bit. All other bits must be set to zero
ciaddr	4	Client IP address. If the client does know its IP address and is just looking for the name of its boot image, it can specify the address in this field; if the client also needs its IP address, it sets this field to zero
yiaddr	4	"Your" IP address. The server fills in this field with the client's IP address; note that this address might be different than the *ciaddr* field and the client should adopt the address specified in the *yiaddr* field as soon as possible
siaddr	4	Server IP address. Set by the server in the reply so that the client can contact it directly later to retrieve the boot image
giaddr	4	Gateway IP address. Used by forwarding agents when booting across a router and in other forwarding situations (see RFC 1542 for more information); a client must set this field to zero when generating boot requests and ignore it in boot replies
chaddr	16	Client hardware address. Set by the client to its hardware address when generating the boot request; note that the field has a fixed 16-byte length; the actual length of the hardware address in the field is specified in the *hlen* field
sname	64	Server host name. The client may fill this in if it knows the name of its server; other servers will ignore boot requests that do not match. This field is a null-terminated string
file	128	Boot file name. The client can specify a generic boot image type in this field when generating the request ("unix," for example); the server fills in the specific path name to the boot image in the boot reply; this field is a null-terminated string
vend	64	Vendor-specific information

RFC 951 says that the first four bytes of the vendor-specific field should be set to a "magic cookie" value by the client and server to identify the format of the remaining data. RFC 1497 defines a standard cookie value (99.130.83.99 in dotted decimal format) and structure for the following data. While other formats are possible, standard BOOTP clients and servers should use the standard format defined in RFC 1497.

RFC 1542 says that a client should set the vendor-specific area to contain the RFC 1497 magic cookie (99.130.83.99) followed by the end data type code. This alerts the server that the client understands the format described in RFC 1497 without actually transferring any data.

The data following the magic cookie is structured in type-length-value format. Each data fragment is assigned a type code. Using this scheme, clients and servers are not required to interpret every bit of data. They can easily skip over unknown data types using the length field. Tags and lengths are both represented in a single byte. The length field represents only the length of the following data item and does not include the tag and length fields themselves.

There are two exceptions to the type-length-value encoding: pad and end. These data types have no associated data and do not use a length field. They consist entirely of a type byte. All clients and servers must correctly interpret the tag and end type codes. The end type code must always be the last code in the vendor-specific information area.

Note that this information is a compilation of the basic material presented in RFC 1497 along with clarifications from RFC 1533. RFC 1533 describes the DHCP option codes but includes all the BOOTP options as well.

Table 2.2 lists the type codes in RFC 1497.

Table 2.2 BOOTP Vendor-Specific Data Type Codes

Name	Tag	Length	Description
Pad	0	None	The pad type may be used to align subsequent fields to a particular word boundary; it is ignored by processing agents
Subnet Mask	1	4	Contains the subnet client's subnet mask
Time Offset	2	4	Specifies the time offset from Coordinated Universal Time (UTC) for the local subnet; this data is a 32-bit signed integer in network byte order

Continued

Table 2.2 BOOTP Vendor-Specific Data Type Codes (Continued)

Name	Tag	Length	Description
Gateway	3	n	Specifies the IP addresses of n/4 routers for the client's subnet in order of preference; the option length must be a multiple of 4
Time Server	4	n	Specifies the IP addresses of n/4 time servers (see RFC 868) in order of preference; the option length must be a multiple of 4
IEN-116 Name Server	5	n	Specifies the IP addresses of n/4 IEN-116 name servers in order of preference; the option length must be a multiple of 4
Domain Name Server	6	n	Specifies the IP addresses of n/4 RFC 1034 domain name servers in order of preference; the option length must be a multiple of 4
Log Server	7	n	Specifies the IP addresses of n/4 MIT-LCS UDP log servers in order of preference; the option length must be a multiple of 4
Cookie/Quote Server	8	n	Specifies the IP addresses of n/4 RFC 865 quote servers in order of preference; the option length must be a multiple of 4
LPR Server	9	n	Specifies the IP addresses of n/4 Berkeley 4BSD printer servers in order of preference; the option length must be a multiple of 4
Impress Server	10	n	Specifies the IP addresses of n/4 Imagen Impress network servers in order of preference; the option length must be a multiple of 4
RLP Server	11	n	Specifies the IP addresses of n/4 RFC 887 Resource Location Protocol servers in order of preference; the option length must be a multiple of 4
Hostname	12	n	Specifies the client's host name; this name may or may not be a fully qualified domain name
Boot File Size	13	2	Indicates the size of the boot image file in 512-byte blocks; the data is a 16-bit unsigned integer in network byte order
Merit Dump File	14	n	Specifies the path name of the file to which the client should save its core image if the client crashes; the path name uses characters from the NVT-ASCII character set and must have a minimum length of 1
Domain Name	15	n	Specifies the client's domain name
Swap Server	16	4	The IP address of the client's swap server
Root Path	17	n	The path name to mount as a root disk; the data is a character string using the NVT-ASCII character set and must have a minimum length of 1

Continued

Table 2.2 BOOTP Vendor-Specific Data Type Codes (Continued)

Name	Tag	Length	Description
Extensions Path	18	n	The path name of a file retrievable by TFTP that contains extension information; this field can be used to help the client reach additional configuration information formatted as in RFC 1457 that will not fit in the 64-byte vendor specific area in the boot reply message; the specified extension file can be as long as it needs to be, and the client should ignore all references to tag 18 in it; the path name must have a minimum length of 1
Reserved Fields	128-254	n	Specifies additional site-specific information
End	255	None	Indicates the end of information contained in the vendor information field; all octets following the end marker should be set to zero (pad)

3 Computing the Internet Checksum

Name

Computing the Internet Checksum

Abbreviation

-none-

Status

Informational

Specifications

RFC 1071

Abstract

Related Specifications

IP (RFC 791), ICMP (RFC 792), IGMP (RFC 1112), TCP (RFC 793), and UDP (RFC 768) all use the Internet checksum.

See Also

RFC 1141 and RFC 1624 describe the methods for updating the Internet checksum field incrementally rather than recomputing it as various fields, such as the time-to-live field, are adjusted. RFC 1936 describes a method of implementing the Internet checksum algorithm in hardware such that it can be performed in parallel with network DMA operations.

Comments

This chapter does not describe a protocol, but because the Internet checksum is used in so many different RFCs, it makes sense to document it. Additionally, the typical textual description of the checksum given everywhere the checksum is used ("the 16-bit one's complement of the one's complement sum of the 16-bit words in the input...") is almost indecipherable to most of us. I always found myself saying, "Let's see the code that implements this!"

Description

This section gives a small refresher on one's complement arithmetic and its application to the Internet checksum. RFC 1071 describes many other properties of the Internet checksum and should be read thoroughly before implementing any high-performance implementation of the checksum.

One's Complement

Most of us work on machines that implement two's complement arithmetic and not one's complement arithmetic. Most of the confusion surrounding the Internet checksum is related to remembering the properties of one's complement arithmetic.

Remember that the one's complement of a number is the number with each of its bits complemented. For example, the one's complement of 0x01 is 0xFE, using an 8-bit word size. The one's complement of a number represents the negative number of the same magnitude. Thus, if 1 = 0x01, then –1 = 0xFE.

It's important to note that zero is represented by two values: 0 = 0x00 and –0 = 0xFF. This property is one of the reasons that one's complement arithmetic lost favor to two's complement arithmetic. Note that adding a number to its negative results in –0. For instance, 2 + –2 = 0x02 + 0xFD = 0xFF = –0.

Now, one's complement arithmetic is basically like two's complement arithmetic with one important distinction: carries out of the high-order bit are added back into the low-order bit of the same result, rather than being discarded. This is done to handle the fact that there are two zeros in the number system.

For instance, let's examine the case –1 + 2 = 1. Using 8-bit numbers, we have 0xFE + 0x2 = C + 0x00. If we simply discarded the carry as in two's complement arithmetic, we would end up with a result of zero. This is clearly not the case, so we correct by adding the carry back into the sum: C + 0x00 = 0x01. This is the correct result.

Handling the carry is the only annoyance of implementing one's complement arithmetic using a two's complement machine.

Sample Code

The sample code shown in Listing 3.1 implements the Internet checksum algorithm. This code is a modified version of the code from RFC 1071.

The code adds 16-bit unsigned integers into a 32-bit accumulator. After all the bytes have been summed, the 32-bit accumulator is reduced to 16-bits, effectively adding all the previous carries out of the high-order bit back into the low-order bit as one's complement arithmetic demands. Finally, the code complements the final result before returning.

This algorithm is endian independent, except for the addition of the last byte of an odd numbered length. The algorithm will, however, return a different value for the same byte stream on a big endian and little endian processor. The final sum will be swapped, depending on the processor type, but this swap will be undone when the 16-bit value is stored in a checksum field and so the final stored sum will be correct.

Note that this code assumes a short is 16 bits and a long is 32 bits.

Listing 3.1 Implementation of the Internet Checksum Algorithm

```
unsigned short checksum(int count, unsigned short * addr)
{
   /* Compute Internet Checksum for "count" bytes,
   *         beginning at location "addr".
   */
   register unsigned long sum = 0;
```

```
   /* Add 16-bit words */
   while( count > 1 )  {
      /*  This is the inner loop */
      sum += * addr++;
      count -= 2;
   }

   /*  Add leftover byte, if any */
   if( count > 0 )
#if BIG_ENDIAN
      sum += (* (unsigned char *) addr) << 8;
#else
      sum += * (unsigned char *) addr;
#endif

   /*  Fold 32-bit sum to 16 bits */
   while (sum>>16)
      sum = (sum & 0xffff) + (sum >> 16);

   /* Return one's complement of final sum */
   return (unsigned short) ~sum;
}
```

Daytime

Name

Daytime

Abbreviation

DAYTIME

Status

Elective Standard (STD 25)

Specifications

RFC 867

Abstract

The Daytime protocol is a simple protocol that allows a client to retrieve the current date and time from a remote server. While useful at a basic level, the Daytime protocol is most often used for debugging purposes rather than to actually acquire the current date and time.

See Also

TIME (RFC 868)

Description

The Daytime service is available as both a TCP and UDP service. The protocol is extremely simple. In the TCP case, the client simply makes a connection to the server. As soon as the connection is established, the server sends the current date and time in ASCII format and closes the connection. The client does not need to send anything to the server; anything that is sent is ignored by the server.

In the UDP case, the client simply sends a UDP datagram to the Daytime port, and the Daytime server sends back a UDP datagram containing the date and time, in ASCII format, to the client's source port. The server simply uses the request datagram to extract the client's source port information and to act as a request trigger. All data in the request datagram is ignored.

The *Formats* section describes some possible date and time formats that may be returned. Because of the loose formatting restrictions, the Daytime protocol is more suited to diagnostic purposes than to actually acting as a time server. See RFC 868 for more information about the Time Server Protocol, which can be used in such a fashion.

Transport Information

The Daytime service is available on well-known TCP port 13 and well-known UDP port 13.

Formats

The Daytime service can return the current date and time in many different formats, depending on the particular server implementation. RFC 867 describes two popular formats:

- Weekday, Month Day, Year Time-Zone, which would yield a date such as Tuesday, February 22, 1982 17:37:43-PST
- dd mmm yy hh:mm:ss zzz, which would yield a date such as 02 FEB 82 07:59:01 PST

Note that all date and time strings are returned using the ASCII character set.

5 Domain Name System

Name

Domain Name System

Abbreviation

DNS, DOMAIN

Status

Recommended Standard (STD 13, STD 14)

Specifications

RFC 1034, RFC 1035

Abstract

The Domain Name System (DNS) is a global distributed database that keeps the Internet running. In its most familiar role, the DNS allows users to map human readable machine names to IP addresses. Interaction with the DNS is done through a "resolver" program that implements the DNS protocol and interacts with the global database.

Related Specifications

RFC 974

Description

The DNS implements a distributed database. The DNS specifications describe the structure of the database and the protocol for finding information within it. Because no single, unified database residing on a single machine could scale to global proportions, the DNS distributes the total data across the entire system. The data is organized hierarchically and different portions of the hierarchy are administered by different organizations. These delegated portions of the hierarchy correspond to pruned sub-trees of the hierarchy and are called *zones*.

The data within the zone is updated independently of the rest of the system, which greatly simplifies administration complexity. Without this independence, local administrators would have to plan database changes and coordinate them with other portions of the DNS system.

Resolvers

An application program interacts with the DNS using a *resolver*. A resolver is a code module that traverses the DNS hierarchy and returns resource records to the requester. The resolver handles all the protocol interaction between the various DNS servers that contain portions of the DNS database.

The resolver starts by interrogating a local DNS server for the information it wants. If the server has the data locally, it will return it and the query ends. Because many DNS requests are for the names of local machines, this is a common case. If the DNS name describes a more remote resource, however, the query becomes more complex and foreign DNS servers must be consulted. This consultation is done using one of two modes: recursive and non-recursive (or referral).

Recursive mode eliminates a lot of complexity in the host resolver. Using the recursive mode, the local DNS server itself contacts other servers to fulfill the resolver's request. When the server finds the information, it returns it to the resolver. Thus, the resolver only makes one query and the DNS server handles any further complexity. It may be the case that the server contacts another server that is also operating in recursive mode. Several servers may form a recursive chain from the source resolver to the server that holds the requested information.

Servers handling recursive queries may cache the responses obtained from other servers. This speeds access to frequently used foreign names. Each resource record contains a time-to-live (TTL) field that specifies the upper time limit the server may cache the entry before retrieving it from the source again. The TTL field ensures that copies of rapidly changing entries are not cached longer than they should be.

Using the non-recursive, or referral, method, a DNS server that does not contain the information of interest returns a referral to the resolver. The referral indicates that the server does not have access to the information, but lists the name of one or more other servers that are "closer" to the information than the current server. The resolver then contacts these other servers, in order, until it finds the information. The other servers can operate in recursive or referral mode and can either return the information or generate other referrals.

Servers are encouraged to support recursive mode but are not required to do so. Clients can request recursive service from the server using the RD bit in the DNS query. The server indicates the availability (not the use!) of recursive service by setting the RA bit in DNS replies. DNS servers should not use recursive mode unless explicitly requested by the client. Using recursive service when it is not asked for makes it much more difficult to diagnose some types of DNS errors.

RFC 1034 contains a great deal of information about the implementation of servers and resolvers and should be consulted before implementing either.

DNS Names

The hierarchical database structure is described using DNS names. DNS names use a bottom-up hierarchical naming convention; the most specific portion of the name is specified first, then the next most specific, finally ending with the DNS root.

Names consist of a list of labels separated by periods ("machine.foo.edu," for instance). Note that a domain name is very similar to a file name in a hierarchical file system, such as those used in Unix and MS-DOS. The main difference is that DNS names are "backwards" and use "." rather than "/" or "\" to separate hierarchical labels. DNS names are case-insensitive. The *Grammar* section contains a more formal description of DNS naming.

In DNS resource records, DNS names are stored as a sequence of strings, one for each label in the name. Each label is stored as a length followed by the number of octets specified by the length. The length is contained in a single octet. The last label is the root of the DNS name space and is a null string, stored as a length of 0 with no following character octets. The maximum length of any label in the DNS name is 63 characters. This implies that the high-order two bits of the length octet are zero. The high-order two bits of the length octet are used to compress DNS queries and responses, as described in a following section.

Resource Records

Each DNS name describes a logical node in the DNS hierarchical tree. Each node contains one or more *resource records* (RR). An RR describes a particular attribute about the named node. For instance, most DNS nodes contain an address RR that contains the IP address of the host the RR describes. Mapping from a host name to an IP address is simply the process of traversing the DNS database to the node that corresponds to the target host name and retrieving its address RR.

RRs are specified using a DNS name, an RR type, and an RR class. DNS queries specify these parameters to retrieve DNS RRs. Resolvers can also use wildcards in the type and class fields, to return all the RRs of all types or classes associated with a given DNS name.

Note that a given DNS name may have multiple RRs of the same type associated with it. In particular it is fairly common for nodes to have more than one A or MX RR.

Figure 5.1 shows the format of a generic resource record.

The following is a description of the field names shown in the figure:

NAME The domain name to which this resource record belongs.

TYPE The resource record type specified as a 2-octet RR type code.

CLASS The resource record class specified as a 2-octet RR class code.

TTL The time-to-live value associated with the resource record. The TTL field is an unsigned, 32-bit value (in seconds) that specifies the maximum time length the resource record can be cached. After this time period expires, the record must be purged from a cache and the source of the record consulted again. A TTL value of 0 specifies that the record should never be cached.

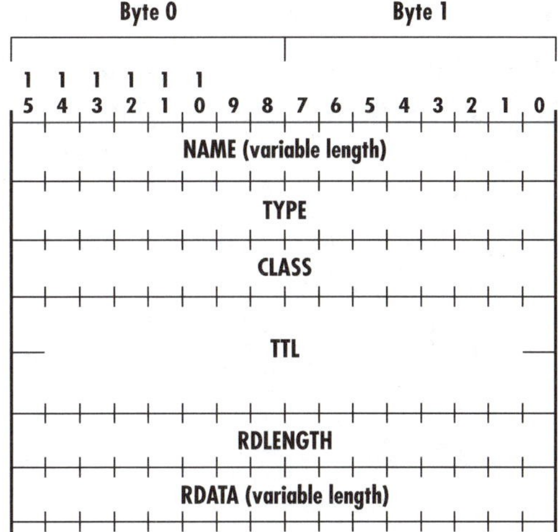

Figure 5.1

Generic resource record format.

RDLENGTH The length of the octets in the RDATA field.

RDATA This field is variable length and contains the resource record data identified by the NAME, TYPE, and CLASS fields.

Table 5.1 shows the values that may be used in the RR TYPE field. Note that some of the values are not used to identify resource record types themselves, but are used in the question portion of a DNS query. Those particular values will never appear as part of the DNS answer. Values in this set are called QTYPEs and are a superset of the TYPE values.

Table 5.2 lists the values that can be used in the RR CLASS field. In general, the most common class is IN, the Internet class. The other classes are used for other types of networking systems and though some may still be in use, they are very rare. Note that some of the class values are not used to identify resource record types themselves but are used in the question portion of a DNS query. Those particular values will never appear as part of the DNS answer. Values in this set are called QCLASSes and are a superset of the CLASS values.

The following sections describe the RDATA format of particular types of RRs. Note that not all RR types are fully described in these sections. Resource record types that are obsolete or experimental are not described. Consult RFC 1035 for more information about the obsolete or experimental types.

The RDATA formats consistently use two particular types of data structures: <domain-name> and <character-string>. A <domain-name> is a series of counted-length labels as previously described in *DNS Names*,. A <character-string> is a counted-length string beginning with a single-octet length and followed by the number of characters specified in the length. The total length of a <character-string> is 256 octets, including the length octet.

Table 5.1 DNS RR TYPE Values

Value	Type	Description
1	A	Host address
2	NS	Authoritative name server
3	MD	Mail destination (obsolete—use MX)
4	MF	Mail forwarder (obsolete—use MX)
5	CNAME	The true, canonical name corresponding to an alias
6	SOA	A marker indicating the starting point of a zone of authority
7	MB	Mailbox (experimental)
8	MG	Mail group member (experimental)
9	MR	Mail rename domain name (experimental)
10	NULL	Null resource record (experimental)
11	WKS	Well-known service description
12	PTR	Domain name pointer
13	HINFO	Host information
14	MINFO	Mailbox or mail list information
15	MX	Mail exchange
16	TXT	Text string
252	AXFR	A zone transfer request (only valid in the question part of a query)
253	MAILB	A mailbox-related records request (requests MB, MG, or MR) (only valid in the question part of a query)
254	MAILA	A request for mail agent RRs (obsolete—use MX) (only valid in the question part of a query)
255	*	Wildcard; requests RRs of all types (only valid in the question part of a query)

Table 5.2 DNS RR CLASS Values

Value	Type	Description
1	IN	The Internet; this class value is used for most queries and resource records
2	CS	The CSNET class (obsolete)
3	CH	The CHAOS class
4	HS	Hesiod
255	*	Wildcard; requests RRs of all classes (only valid in the question part of a query)

A RDATA Format

The A RR type stores the IP address associated with a host. Figure 5.2 shows the format of the A RR RDATA field.

ADDRESS The 32-bit IP address of the RR owner. Hosts with multiple IP addresses will have multiple A records.

CNAME RDATA Format

The CNAME RR type stores the true name corresponding to an alias. That is, if you look up an alias in the DNS, it will contain a CNAME record. The CNAME record contains the canonical name of the resource. If you look up the name given in the CNAME record, you'll find the true RRs associated with the name.

Figure 5.3 shows the format of the CNAME RDATA field.

CNAME The canonical domain name associated with this DNS node. The owner name of this RR is the alias. The CNAME field is specified as a <domain-name>.

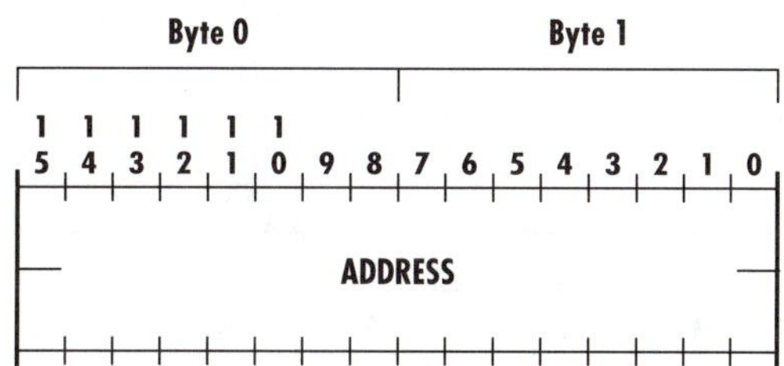

Figure 5.2
The A RDATA field format.

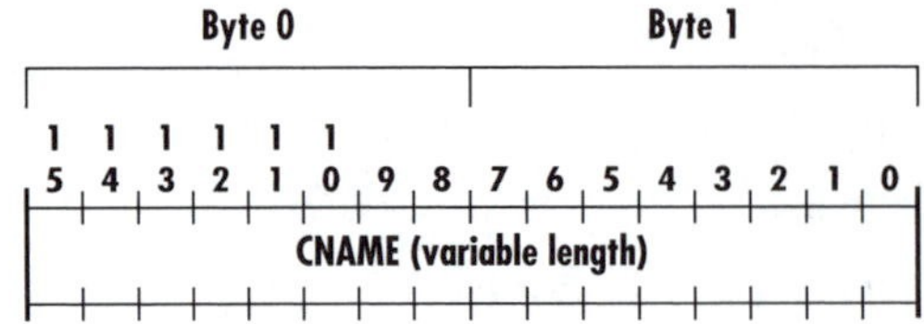

Figure 5.3
The CNAME RDATA field format.

HINFO RDATA Format

The HINFO RR type stores information about the host associated with the DNS node.

Figure 5.4 shows the format of the HINFO RDATA field.

CPU A <character-string> specifying the CPU type of the host corresponding to this node.

OS A <character-string> specifying the operating system used by the host.

MX RDATA Format

The MX RR type stores the name of a host willing to act as a mail exchanger for the owner node. SMTP mailers use MX RRs to forward mail addressed to the owner. A server typically returns A RRs that correspond to the machines indicated in MX RRs in the Additional portion of the DNS reply.

Figure 5.5 shows the format of the MX RDATA field.

PREFERENCE This 16-bit field indicates the preference of this MX record versus other MX records associated with the same owner. Lower PREFERENCE values indicate greater preference.

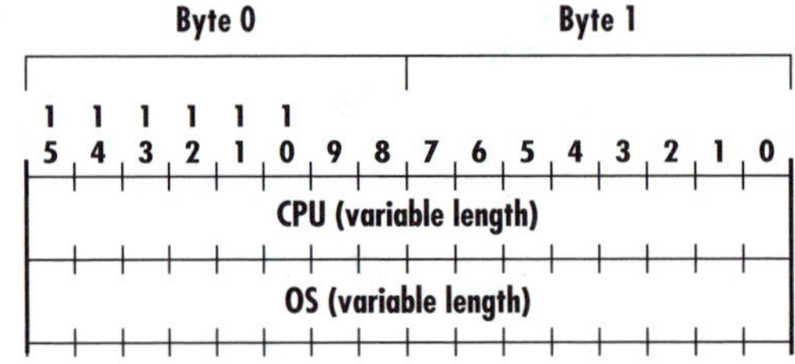

Figure 5.4
The HINFO RDATA field format.

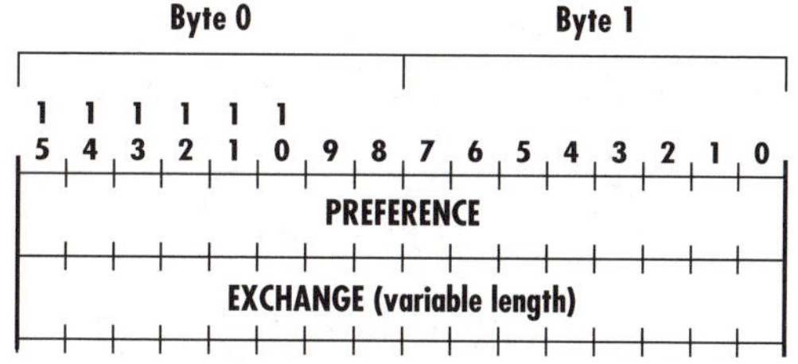

Figure 5.5
The MX RDATA field format.

EXCHANGE The <domain-name> of the host willing to act as a mail exchanger for the owner.

RFC 974 describes the use of MX records in greater detail.

NS RDATA Format

The NS RR type stores the name of a DNS server that is authoritative for a particular portion of the DNS name space. The NS RR is stored in servers that sit "above" the particular name space sub-tree in question and can be used to generate referrals or recursive queries. A server typically returns A RRs that correspond to the machines indicated in NS RRs in the Additional portion of the DNS reply.

Figure 5.6 shows the format of the NS RDATA field.

NSDNAME A <domain-name> indicating the host that should be authoritative for the specified domain and class.

PTR RDATA Format

The PTR RR stores a pointer to another portion of the DNS name space. Although similar in concept to a CNAME RR, a PTR RR does not carry the associated

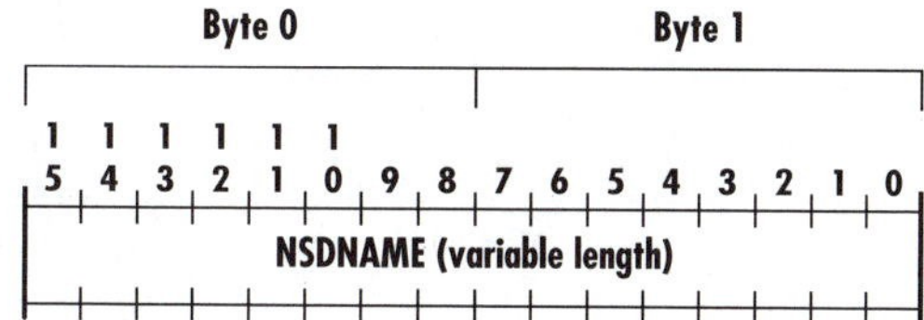

Figure 5.6
The NS RDATA field format.

alias semantics. The PTR RR is typically used to point from nodes in the inverse address lookup name space (IN-ADDR.ARPA) to corresponding nodes in the rest of the DNS name space.

Figure 5.7 shows the format of the PTR RDATA field.

PTRDNAME A <domain-name> that points to some other node in domain name space.

SOA RDATA Format

The SOA RR stores parameters related to a particular zone in the DNS name space. The SOA RR is returned in a response to indicate that the response is authoritative. See RFC 1034 for more information about the use of SOA RRs and caching of DNS responses.

Figure 5.8 shows the format of the SOA RDATA field.

MNAME The <domain-name> of the server that is the primary source of the data in this zone.

RNAME The <domain-name> of the mailbox of the administrator of this zone.

SERIAL The unsigned, 32-bit serial number corresponding to the version of data in this zone. Zone transfers preserve this number. The value wraps around when it reaches its maximum value.

REFRESH An unsigned, 32-bit time interval (in seconds) indicating the time before the zone should be refreshed.

RETRY An unsigned, 32-bit time interval (in seconds) indicating the minimum time that should elapse before a failed refresh should be retried.

EXPIRE An unsigned, 32-bit time interval (in seconds) indicating the maximum time that can elapse before the zone is no longer authoritative.

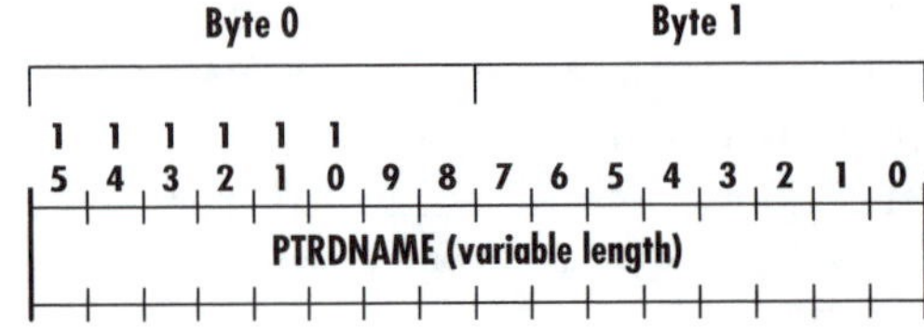

Figure 5.7
The PTR RDATA field format.

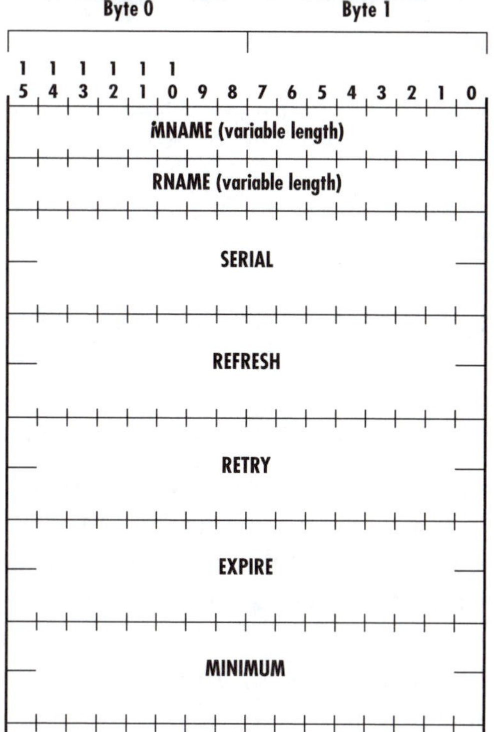

Figure 5.8
The SOA RDATA field format.

MINIMUM An unsigned, 32-bit minimum TTL value that should be used for any RR retrieved from this zone that doesn't otherwise have an individually specified TTL value.

TXT RDATA Format

The TXT RR is used to associate descriptive text with a node in the DNS name space.

TXT-DATA One or more <character-strings>.

Figure 5.9 shows the format of the TXT RDATA field.

WKS RDATA Format

The WKS RR provides information about the well-known services supported by a particular host.

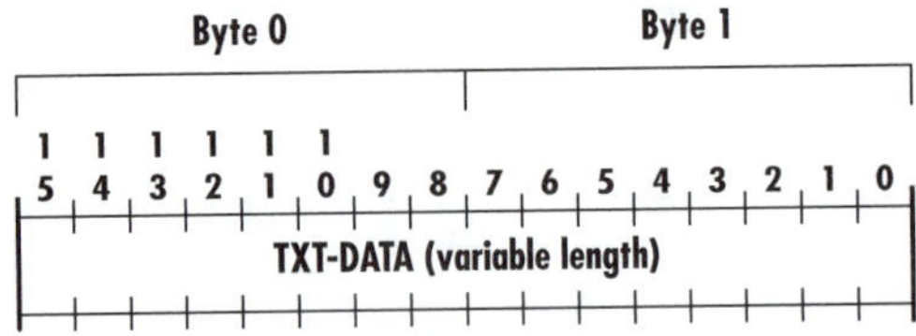

Figure 5.9
The TXT RDATA field format.

Figure 5.10 shows the format of the WKS RDATA field.

ADDRESS A 32-bit IP address.

PROTOCOL An 8-bit protocol number.

BITMAP A bitmap indicating which servers are listening on which well-known ports for the specified PROTOCOL number. For instance, if the WKS RR indicates the TCP protocol (PROTOCOL = 6) and that the 26th bit of the bitmap is set, we know that the SMTP server is running on the owning host because SMTP's well-known port number is 25. The first bitmap bit corresponds to port 0, and the bitmap includes as many octets as are needed for the well-known port numbers corresponding to the services running on the host.

Transport Information

The DNS is accessible using both UDP and TCP. In both cases, well-known port 53 is used to make contact with the server. TCP is typically used only for server-to-server transfers of entire zone resource records. UDP is most commonly used for resolver-to-server communications.

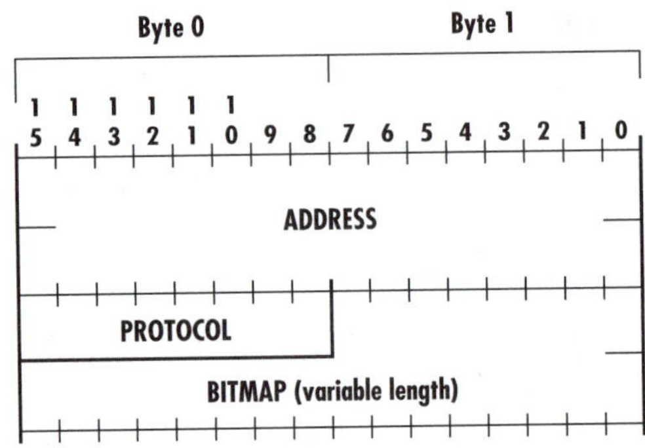

Figure 5.10
The WKS RDATA field format.

See RFC 1035 for more detailed information about using DNS with TCP transport.

Grammar

This section describes the grammar associated with the DNS.

Domain Names

The following grammar describes the structure of a domain name.

```
<domain>        ::=  <subdomain> | " "
<subdomain>     ::=  <label> | <subdomain> "." <label>
<label>:        :=   <letter> [ [ <ldh-str> ] <let-dig> ]
<ldh-str>       ::=  <let-dig-hyp> | <let-dig-hyp> <ldh-str>
<let-dig-hyp>   ::=  <let-dig> | "-"
<let-dig>       ::=  <letter> | <digit>
<letter>        ::=  any one of the 52 alphabetic characters A through Z in
                     uppercase and a through z in lowercase
<digit>         ::=  any one of the ten digits 0 through 9
```

Message Formats

DNS uses a single message format for both DNS queries and responses. The basic message format contains five sections, as shown in Figure 5.11.

The various sections of the message are described in the following sections.

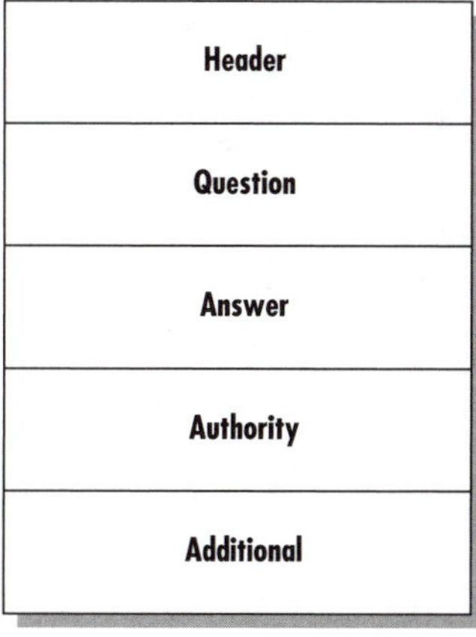

Figure 5.11

Basic DNS message format.

Header

The DNS message header contains some fields that specify which of the other DNS message sections are present, whether the message is a request or a response, and other options. Figure 5.12 shows the format of the DNS message header.

ID The ID field is assigned a unique identifier by the client. This field is simply copied to the reply by the server and can be used by the client to match a reply with an outstanding request.

QR A one-bit field that specifies whether the message is a query (QR = 0) or a response (QR = 1).

OPCODE This field specifies the type of query. Servers copy this field from the query message to the response message. The field can take one of the values shown in Table 5.3.

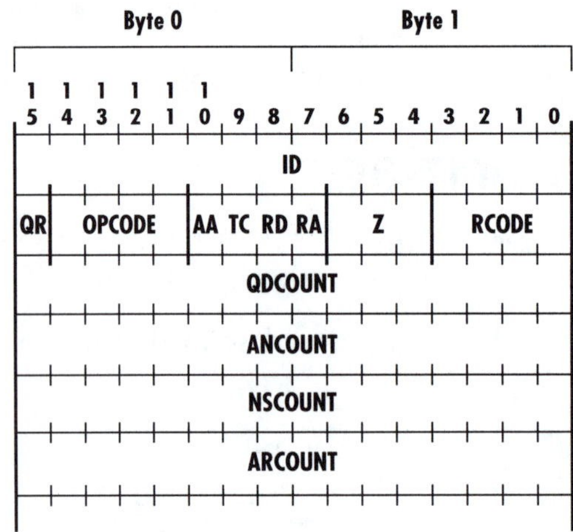

Figure 5.12
The DNS message header section format.

Table 5.3 DNS Header Section OPCODE Values

OPCODE Value	Description
0	A standard query (QUERY)
1	An inverse query (IQUERY)
2	A server status request (STATUS)
3-15	Reserved for future use

AA The AA (Authoritative Answer) bit is set if the responding name server is an authority for the domain name in the query message.

TC The TC (Truncation) bit is set if the DNS message had to be truncated.

RD The RD (Recursion Desired) bit is set if the client wants the server to use recursive queries. The server copies this bit to the response message.

RA The server sets the RA (Recursion Available) bit in responses to indicate that it supports recursive queries.

Z This bit is reserved for future use and must be set to 0.

RCODE The server sets the RCODE (Response Code) field to an error code value. The possible RCODE values are shown in Table 5.4.

QDCOUNT An unsigned, 16-bit integer specifying the number of entries in the question section of the message.

Table 5.4 DNS Header Section RCODE Values

RCODE Value	Description
0	No error
1	Format error; the server detected some problem with the message format or structure
2	Server failure; the server could not process the request because of an internal server problem
3	Name error; this result is given when the server responding to the request is authoritative and the domain name in question does not exist
4	Not implemented; the server does not support the requested operation
5	Refused; the server implements the requested operation but refuses to perform it for the client because of some policy reason (some servers may refuse to perform some operations for all but a trusted set of clients)
6-15	Reserved for future use

ANCOUNT An unsigned, 16-bit integer specifying the number of resource records in the answer section of the message.

NSCOUNT An unsigned, 16-bit integer specifying the number of resource records in the authority section of the message.

ARCOUNT An unsigned, 16-bit integer specifying the number of resource records in the addition records section of the message.

Question

The question section describes the information the client is looking for. This section contains the domain name, class, and type of the requested information. Figure 5.13 shows the format of the question section.

QNAME The domain name of the resource the client is searching for. This field is variable length and may contain an odd number of octets. No padding is used between the QNAME and QTYPE fields.

QTYPE The type of resource record the client is searching for.

QCLASS The class of resource record the client is searching for. Use the IN class for Internet resource records.

Answer, Authority, and Additional

The answer, authority, and additional sections share a similar format. They each contain one or more resource records of the format shown back in Figure 5.1.

The answer section contains the resource record or records that answer the question posed in the DNS query. The authority section contains one or more resource records that point toward an authoritative name server for the question. The

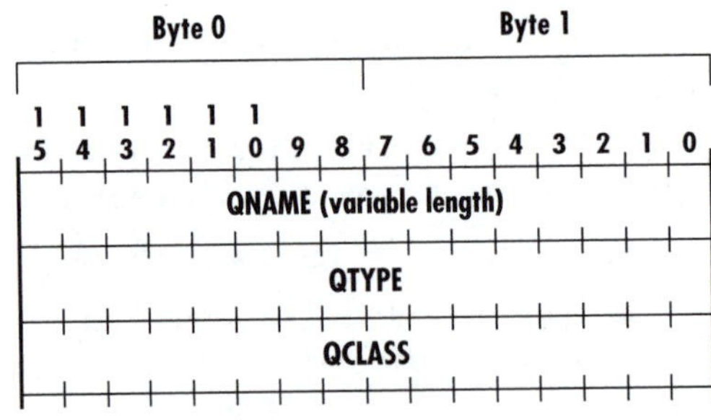

Figure 5.13

The DNS message question section format.

additional section contains one or more resource records that contain additional information related to the query, but not strictly within its scope. Servers return additional records to reduce query traffic in cases when the client will probably ask for these records in the near future. For instance, servers often return A resource records as additional information when the client requests MX resource records because the client will probably want to contact one or more of the servers identified by the MX records in the near future.

Compression

A DNS message containing many resource records can become quite large. DNS uses a simple compression scheme to reduce the size of DNS messages. The compression scheme takes note of the fact that resource records contain the domain name of the resource.

In many query responses, the domain name contained in the set of returned resource records will be identical. DNS compresses the response message by replacing multiple copies of a domain name with a pointer to a previous occurrence of the same domain name. The pointer is a 16-bit value and has the format shown in Figure 5.14.

The pointer can occur anywhere the length octet of a domain name label could occur. The high-order two bits of the first octet are both set to 1, which allows software to determine whether the first octet is the start of a domain name label or is the first octet of a compression pointer. If the two high-order bits are both 0, then the octet is the length octet of a domain name label.

The OFFSET field points to the location of the real domain name labels. The OFFSET field is unsigned and stores the offset of the data from the start of the DNS message.

A pointer does not have to replace a complete domain name. A domain name can begin with a sequence of labels and then conclude with a compression pointer

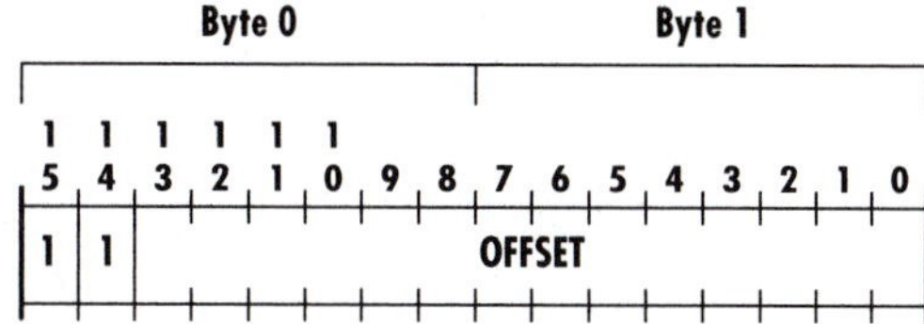

Figure 5.14

The domain name compression pointer format.

representing the final set of labels. Given this property, there are three different ways to represent a domain name in a DNS message:

- As a complete list of domain name labels
- As a single compression pointer
- As an initial set of domain name labels, followed by a compression pointer representing the final portion of the full domain name

DNS clients and servers are not required to use compression, but failure to do so could lead to truncated messages. All clients and servers must be able to parse compressed DNS messages, however, even if they do not generate them themselves.

6 Dynamic Host Configuration Protocol

Name

Dynamic Host Configuration Protocol

Abbreviation

DHCP

Status

Elective Proposed Standard

Specifications

RFC 1541, RFC 1533

Abstract

The Dynamic Host Configuration Protocol (DHCP) allows a client to obtain numerous configuration parameters from a DHCP server. These parameters include the client's IP address, subnet mask, default router, DNS server, and others. Using DHCP, a new host can be added to the network or an old host moved at any time without having to reconfigure the host, which reduces the possibility of configuration errors and leads to plug-and-play network configuration.

Related Specifications

BOOTP (RFC 951, RFC 1497, RFC 1542); RFC 1534 describes the interoperation between DHCP and BOOTP clients and servers

See Also

TFTP (RFC 1350, RFC 1782, RFC 1783, RFC 1784)

Description

DHCP builds on the basic diskless boot protocol provided by BOOTP and greatly extends it. In addition to the basic parameters retrieved by BOOTP clients (IP address, server IP address, and boot image file name), DHCP clients can obtain virtually all their necessary network parameters and boot information.

DHCP uses the same basic message format as BOOTP. As with BOOTP, messages generated by the client include the BOOTREQUEST opcode, while messages generated by the server include the BOOTREPLY opcode. DHCP defines other message types, however, and DHCP messages include a DHCP Message Type option to distinguish between the various DHCP message types.

Most of the information returned to a client using DHCP is supplied in the *options* field (formerly named the vendor-specific field in BOOTP). Because the size of this field is small and fixed length in BOOTP, DHCP extends the maximum size of this field and includes provisions for allowing option data to be carried in the *sname* or *file* fields if there is not enough room in the options field.

Transport Information

DHCP uses two well-known UDP port numbers: 67 and 68. DHCP servers listen for DHCP requests on port 67. Clients listen for the corresponding replies on port 68. Note that this is slightly different than most protocols where the client uses a random port and only the server waits on a well-known port. The client must also use a well-known port because the DHCP reply message may be broadcast to all nodes on the network. Other nodes using the same random port number for other protocols would become confused when they received a DHCP reply message.

The DHCP port numbers are the same port numbers used for BOOTP requests and replies. DHCP servers may interoperate with BOOTP clients and vice-versa.

Protocol State Machine

Figure 6.1 shows the DHCP client protocol state machine. While DHCP servers contain a lot of states associated with leases and the configuration parameters of a given client, they do not need to keep track of the current state of a DHCP protocol exchange.

Message Formats

The following sections describe the message formats used for each DHCP message. Note that DHCP messages use the basic BOOTP message format. All the client DHCP messages use the BOOTP BOOTREQUEST message type, while server messages use the BOOTP BOOTREPLY message type. The exact type of DHCP message is specified as a DHCP option in the options field. This coding

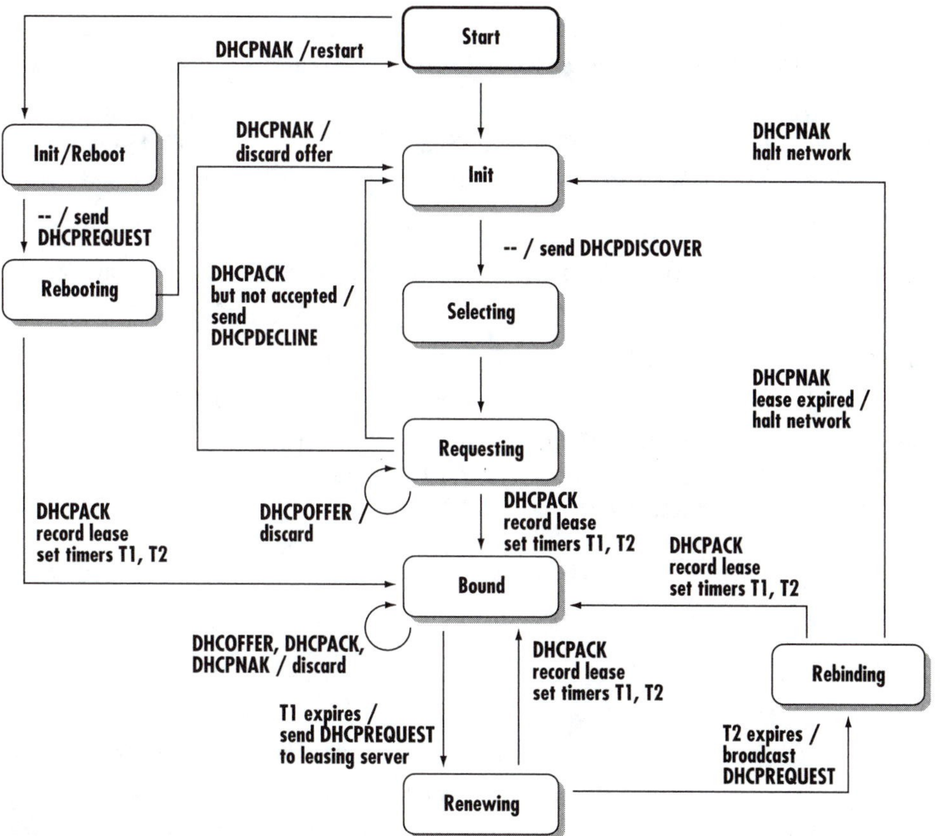

Figure 6.1

The DHCP client state machine.

allows BOOTP server and forwarding agents to interpret the basic DHCP message as a BOOTP message. RFC 1534 describes how DHCP clients and servers can interoperate with BOOTP clients and servers.

Client Messages

Table 6.1 shows the basic format of client request messages. Table 6.2 shows the various DHCP options that may, must, must not, should, and should not be included in each DHCP client message.

Server Messages

Table 6.3 shows the basic format of server reply messages. Table 6.4 shows the various DHCP options that may, must, must not, should and should not be included in each DHCP server message.

Table 6.1 DHCP Client Message Formats

Field	Length in Bytes	DHCPDISCOVER	DHCPREQUEST	DHCPDECLINE, DHCPRELEASE
op	1	BOOTREQUEST	BOOTREQUEST	BOOTREQUEST
htype	1	hardware type	hardware type	hardware type
hlen	1	hardware address length	hardware address length	hardware address length
hops	1	0	0	0
xid	4	selected by client	selected by client	selected by client
secs	2	optional	optional	0
flags	2	Set BROADCAST flag if client requires a broadcast reply	Set BROADCAST flag if client requires a broadcast reply	0
ciaddr	4	0	previously allocated network address	ciaddr
yiaddr	4	0	0	0
siaddr	4	0	0	0
giaddr	4	0	0	0
chaddr	16	client's hardware address	client's hardware address	client's hardware address
sname	64	unused, or options	unused, or options	unused
file	128	generic name, null, or options	generic name, null, or options	unused
options	312	options	options	unused

Table 6.2 Use of DHCP Options by Clients

Option	DHCPDISCOVER	DHCPREQUEST	DHCPDECLINE, DHCPRELEASE
Requested IP address	MAY	MUST NOT	MUST NOT
IP address lease time	MAY	MAY	MUST NOT
Use file/sname fields	MAY	MAY	MAY
DHCP message type	DHCPDISCOVER	DHCPREQUEST	DHCPDECLINE, DHCPRELEASE
Client identifier	MAY	MAY	MAY
Class identifier	SHOULD	SHOULD	MUST NOT
Server identifier	MUST NOT	MUST after DHCPDISCOVER, MUST NOT when renewing	MUST
Parameter request list	MAY	MAY	MUST NOT
Maximum message size	MAY	MAY	MUST NOT
Message	SHOULD NOT	SHOULD NOT	SHOULD
Site-specific	MAY	MAY	MUST NOT
All others	MUST NOT	MUST NOT	MUST NOT

Table 6.3 DHCP Server Message Formats

Field	Length in Bytes	DHCPOFFER	DHCPACK	DHCPNAK
op	1	BOOTREPLY	BOOTREPLY	BOOTREPLY
htype	1	hardware type	hardware type	hardware type
hlen	1	hardware address length	hardware address length	hardware address length
hops	1	0	0	0
xid	4	*xid* from client DHCPDISCOVER message	*xid* from client DHCPREQUEST message	*xid* from client DHCPREQUEST message
secs	2	0	0	0
ciaddr	2	0	*ciaddr* from DHCPREQUEST or 0	*ciaddr* from DHCPREQUEST or 0
yiaddr	4	IP address offered to client	IP address assigned to client	0
siaddr	4	IP address of next bootstrap server	IP address of next bootstrap server	0

Continued

Table 6.3 DHCP Server Message Formats (Continued)

Field	Length in Bytes	DHCPOFFER	DHCPACK	DHCPNAK
flags	4	if request *giaddr* is not 0 then *flags* from client message else 0	if request *giaddr* is not 0 then *flags* from client message else 0	if request *giaddr* is not 0 then *flags* from client message else 0
giaddr	4	0	0	0
chaddr	16	*chaddr* from client DHCPDISCOVERY message	*chaddr* from client DHCPREQUEST message	*chaddr* from DHCPREQUEST message
sname	64	Server host name or options	Server host name or options	(unused)
file	128	Client boot file name or options	Client boot file name or options	(unused)
options	312	options	options	

Table 6.4 Use of DHCP Options by Servers

Option	DHCPOFFER	DHCPACK	DHCPNAK
Requested IP address	MUST NOT	MUST NOT	MUST NOT
IP address lease time	MUST	MUST	MUST NOT
Use file/sname fields	MAY	MAY	MUST NOT
DHCP message type	DHCPOFFER	DHCPACK	DHCPNAK
Parameter request list	MUST NOT	MUST NOT	MUST NOT
Message	SHOULD	SHOULD	SHOULD
Client identifier	MUST NOT	MUST NOT	MUST NOT
Class identifier	MUST NOT	MUST NOT	MUST NOT
Server identifier	MUST	MAY	MAY
Maximum message size	MUST NOT	MUST NOT	MUST NOT
All others	MAY	MAY	MUST NOT

DHCP Options

Although DHCP uses the basic BOOTP message format, most of the information conveyed by DHCP is encoded in the options field (which has been renamed from BOOTP's former vendor-specific information field). Table 6.5 describes the various DHCP options and their format. This information is described in greater detail in RFC 1533.

Because DHCP conveys so much information in the options field, RFC 1541 extends the length of the field to 312 bytes. This brings the minimum DHCP message size to 576 bytes, the minimum IP datagram size that a host must accept. Further, DHCP options can be used to negotiate a larger datagram size or the use of the *sname* and *file* fields to store additional option information.

Table 6.5 DHCP Option Codes

Name	Tag	Length	Description
Pad	0	None	The pad type may be used to align subsequent fields to a particular word boundary; it is ignored by processing agents
Subnet Mask	1	4	Contains the subnet client's subnet mask
Time Offset	2	4	Specifies the time offset from Coordinated Universal Time (UTC) for the local subnet; this data is a 32-bit signed integer in network byte order
Gateway	3	n	Specifies the IP addresses of n/4 routers for the client's subnet in order of preference; the option length must be a multiple of 4
Time Server	4	n	Specifies the IP addresses of n/4 time servers (see RFC 868) in order of preference; the option length must be a multiple of 4
IEN-116 Name Server	5	n	Specifies the IP addresses of n/4 IEN-116 name servers in order of preference; the option length must be a multiple of 4
Domain Name Server	6	n	Specifies the IP addresses of n/4 RFC 1034 domain name servers in order of preference; the option length must be a multiple of 4
Log Server	7	n	Specifies the IP addresses of n/4 MIT-LCS UDP log servers in order of preference; the option length must be a multiple of 4
Cookie/Quote Server	8	n	Specifies the IP addresses of n/4 RFC 865 quote servers in order of preference; the option length must be a multiple of 4
LPR Server	9	n	Specifies the IP addresses of n/4 Berkeley 4BSD printer servers in order of preference; the option length must be a multiple of 4
Impress Server	10	n	Specifies the IP addresses of n/4 Imagen Impress network servers in order of preference; the option length must be a multiple of 4
RLP Server	11	n	Specifies the IP addresses of n/4 RFC 887 Resource Location Protocol servers in order of preference; the option length must be a multiple of 4
Hostname	12	n	Specifies the client's host name; this name may or may not be a fully qualified domain name
Boot File Size	13	2	Indicates the size of the boot image file in 512-byte blocks; the data is a 16-bit unsigned integer in network byte order

Continued

Table 6.5 DHCP Option Codes (Continued)

Name	Tag	Length	Description
Merit Dump File	14	n	Specifies the path name of the file to which the client should save its core image if the client crashes; the path name uses characters from the NVT-ASCII character set and must have a minimum length of 1
Domain Name	15	n	Specifies the client's domain name
Swap Server	16	4	Specifies the IP address of the client's swap server
Root Path	17	n	Specifies the path name to mount as a root disk; the data is a character string using the NVT-ASCII character set and must have a minimum length of 1
Extensions Path	18	n	Specifies the path name of a file retrievable by TFTP that contains extension information. This field can be used to help the client reach additional configuration information formatted as in RFC 1457 that will not fit in the 64-byte vendor-specific area in the boot reply message. The specified extension file can be as long as it needs to be and the client should ignore all references to tag 18 in it; the path name must have a minimum length of 1
IP Forwarding Enable/Disable	19	1	Specifies whether the client should configure its IP module for datagram forwarding; Data value 0 = disable forwarding, 1 = enable forwarding
Non-Local Source Routing Enable/Disable	20	1	Specifies whether the client should configure its IP module to enable forwarding of datagrams with non-local source routes; Data value 0 = disable forwarding such datagrams, 1 = enable forwarding such datagrams
Policy Filter	21	n	This option specifies the policy filters for non-local source routing. The data consists of a list of alternating IP addresses and masks to be used to filter incoming source routes. Any datagram with a next-hop address that does not match one of the filters should be discarded by the client; this option has a minimum length of 8 and must be a multiple of 8 bytes long
Maximum Datagram Reassembly Size	22	2	The data value is a 16-bit unsigned integer in network byte order. It contains the maximum datagram size the client is prepared to reassemble; the minimum legal value for this option is 576 (the minimum IP reassembly buffer size)
Default IP Time-To-Live	23	1	Specifies the default time-to-live value the client should use for outgoing datagrams; the data is a single octet and should have a value between 1 and 255, inclusive

Continued

Table 6.5 DHCP Option Codes (Continued)

Name	Tag	Length	Description
Path MTU Aging Timeout	24	4	The data value is a 32-bit unsigned integer in network byte order; it contains the timeout value in seconds to use when aging path MTU values discovered using the technique described in RFC 1191
Path MTU Plateau Table	25	n	Contains a list of 16-bit unsigned integers used to perform path MTU discovery, as described in RFC 1191. The table is ordered from smallest to largest, and all values must be greater than or equal to 68; the data length of this option must be a multiple of 2
Interface MTU	26	2	The data is a single 16-bit unsigned integer that specifies the MTU size to use on this interface; the MTU value must be greater than or equal to 68
All Subnets Are Local	27	1	Specifies whether the client should assume that all subnets directly connected to the client's subnet use the same MTU size; a data value of 1 specifies that all subnets use the same MTU size, and a data value of 0 specifies that some subnets may have smaller MTU sizes
Broadcast Address	28	4	Specifies the broadcast address to use on the client's subnet; the data is a 4-byte IP address in network byte order; legal values for this option are specified in RFC 1122
Perform Mask Discovery	29	1	Specifies whether the client should perform subnet mask discovery using ICMP; a data value of 1 indicates that the client should use ICMP mask discovery, and a data value of 0 indicates the client should not use ICMP mask discovery
Mask Supplier	30	1	Specifies whether the client should respond to ICMP subnet mask requests; a data value of 1 indicates that the client should respond, while a data value of 0 indicates that the client should not respond
Perform Router Discovery	31	1	Specifies whether the client should perform router discovery as described in RFC 1256; a data value of 1 indicates that the client should perform router discovery, while a data value of 0 indicates that the client should not
Router Solicitation Address	32	4	Specifies the address to which the client should send router solicitation requests; the data is a 4-byte IP address in network byte order
Static Route	33	n	Specifies a list of static routes that the client should install in its routing table. The data is a list of IP address pairs; the first address in the pair is the destination address, and the second address in the pair is the IP address of the router for that destination; the length of option data must be a multiple of 8

Continued

Table 6.5 DHCP Option Codes (Continued)

Name	Tag	Length	Description
Trailer Encapsulation	34	1	Specifies whether the client should negotiate RFC 893 trailers when using ARP; a data value of 1 indicates that the client should attempt to use trailers, while a data value of 0 indicates that it should not
ARP Cache Timeout	35	4	Specifies the timeout period the client should use for ARP cache entries; the data value is a 32-bit unsigned integer representing a time value in seconds
Ethernet Encapsulation	36	1	Specifies the datalink framing that should be used by an Ethernet host; a data value of 0 indicates that RFC 894 framing (Ethernet Version 2) should be used, while a data value of 1 indicates that RFC 1042 framing (IEEE 802.3) should be used
TCP Default TTL	37	1	Specifies the default TTL the client should use for TCP segments; the data is an 8-bit unsigned integer with a minimum value of 1
TCP Keepalive Interval	38	4	Specifies the time interval between TCP keep alive messages; the data is a 32-bit unsigned integer representing a time value in seconds; if the data value is set to zero, the client should not generate keep alive messages unless specifically requested by an application
TCP Keepalive Garbage	39	1	Specifies whether the client should send along a single octet of garbage data with each keep alive message to ensure compatibility with some older implementations; a data value of 1 indicates that a garbage octet should be sent, while a data value of 0 indicates that no garbage octet should be sent
Network Information Service Domain	40	n	Specifies the client's NIS domain for Sun Microsystems Network Information Service; the data is a character string using NVT-ASCII characters; the minimum string length is 1
Network Information Servers	41	n	Specifies a list of NIS server IP addresses in preference order; the option length must be a multiple of 4
Network Time Protocol Servers	42	n	Specifies a list of RFC 1305 Network Time Protocol server IP addresses in preference order; the option length must be a multiple of 4
Vendor Specific Information	43	n	Encodes vendor-specific information; see RFC 1533 for more detail on its encoding and usage
NetBIOS Over TCP/IP Name Server	44	n	Specifies a list of RFC 1001/1002 NetBIOS over TCP/IP name servers (NBNS); the data is a list of 4-byte IP addresses in preference order; the data length must be a multiple of 4

Continued

Table 6.5 DHCP Option Codes (Continued)

Name	Tag	Length	Description
NetBIOS over TCP/IP Datagram Distribution Server	45	n	Specifies a list of RFC 1001/1002 NetBIOS datagram distribution servers (NBDD); the data is a list of 4-byte IP addresses in preference order; the data length must be a multiple of 4
NetBIOS over TCP/IP Node Type	46	1	Specifies the configuration of NetBIOS over TCP/IP clients, as described in RFC 1001/1002; the single data octet can take one of the following values: 1 = B-node, 2 = P-node, 4 = M-node, 8 = H-node
NetBIOS over TCP/IP Scope	47	n	Specifies the NetBIOS over TCP/IP scope parameter described in RFC 1001/1002
X Window System Font Server	48	n	Specifies a list of X Window font servers; the data is a list of 4-byte IP addresses in preference order; the data length must be a multiple of 4
X Window System Display Manager	49	n	Specifies a list of systems running the X Window System Display Manager that available to the client; the data is a list of 4-byte IP addresses in preference order; the data length must be a multiple of 4
Requested IP Address	50	4	Specifies the IP address that the client would like to have assigned to it; this option is used in DHCPDISCOVER messages
IP Address Lease Time	51	4	In DHCPDISCOVER and DHCPREQUEST messages, this option specifies the address lease time the client is requesting. In DHCPOFFER messages, this option specifies the lease time the server is willing to offer; the data is a 32-bit unsigned integer indicating the lease time in seconds
Option Overload	52	1	Specifies that the DHCP message *sname* or *file* fields are being used to carry additional DHCP options; the single data octet can take one of the following values: 1 = the file field holds options, 2 = the sname field holds options, 3 = both file and sname hold options
DHCP Message Type	53	1	Specifies the DHCP message type; the single data octet can take one of the following values: 1 = DHCPDISCOVER, 2 = DHCPOFFER, 3 = DHCPREQUEST, 4 = DHCPDECLINE, 5 = DHCPACK, 6 = DHCPNAK, 7 = DHCPRELEASE
Server Identifier	54	4	Servers include this option in DHCPOFFER messages to allow clients to distinguish between multiple offers. Clients specify the address of the server associated with the accepted offer in DHCPREQUEST messages; the data is the 4-byte IP address of the offering server

Continued

Table 6.5 DHCP Option Codes (Continued)

Name	Tag	Length	Description
Parameter List Request	55	n	Used by DHCP clients to request a list of parameters that the client would like for configuration; the data is a list of 1-byte DHCP option type codes; the list may be in preference order and the server, while not required to do so, should try to return the parameters in the same order
Message	56	n	Servers may include this option in DHCPNAK messages to provide an error message to the client when a failure occurs; clients may include this option in DHCPDECLINE messages to specify the reason for their refusal; the message is a string of NVT-ASCII characters
Maximum DHCP Message Size	57	2	Clients may include this option in DHCPDISCOVER and DHCPREQUEST messages to indicate the maximum DHCP message size that the client is willing to accept; the data is a 16-bit unsigned integer specifying the message length in octets; the minimum length value is 576
Renewal Time Value	58	4	Specifies the time interval for the renewal timer (T1); T1 specifies the time from address assignment until the client transitions to the Renewing state; the data is a 32-bit unsigned integer specifying the T1 value in seconds
Rebinding Time Value	59	4	Specifies the time interval for the rebinding timer (T2); T2 specifies the time from address assignment until the client transitions to the Rebinding state; the data is a 32-bit unsigned integer specifying the T2 value in seconds
Class Identifier	60	n	Used by clients to specify their type and configuration to a DHCP server; the data is a string of octets interpreted by the server
Client Identifier	61	n	Specifies a client's unique identification value. DHCP servers use this value to index a database and return client-specific configuration options to the client. This value must be unique for all clients in the DHCP domain. This value consists of a type-value pair; typically, the type will contain a 1-byte hardware address type defined in the assigned numbers document and the value will indicate the client's hardware address
Reserved Fields	128-254	n	Specifies additional site-specific information
End	255	None	Indicates the end of information contained in the options field; all octets following the end marker should be set to zero (pad)

Echo

Name

Echo

Abbreviation

ECHO

Status

Recommended Standard (STD 20)

Specifications

RFC 862

Abstract

The Echo protocol is a simple diagnostic protocol. The Echo server simply returns the data that is sent to it back to the client. The Echo server provides both TCP and UDP service.

Description

The Echo service can be used to test applications or to diagnose connection problems and such. The service simply returns whatever data is sent to it. Both TCP and UDP service is provided.

In the TCP case, the client opens a connection and sends the server data. The server, in turn, sends all the data back to the client. This continues until the client closes the connection.

In the UDP case, each UDP datagram received by the server simply has its source and destination address and port information reversed, and is returned immediately to the client.

Transport Information

The server provides Echo service on well-known TCP port 7 and UDP port 7.

8 File Transfer Protocol

Name

File Transfer Protocol

Abbreviation

FTP

Status

Recommended Standard

Specifications

RFC 959

Abstract

The File Transfer Protocol (FTP) is used to move files from computer to computer. In the early days of the ARPANET, there were many different kinds of computers and operating systems in use, and FTP was designed to help normalize these differences when moving a file between two dissimilar systems.

Related Specifications

TELNET (RFC 854, RFC 855)

Description

FTP, like many Internet protocols, uses a simple command-response protocol. The FTP client connects to the server at the well-known port number. This initial connection becomes the FTP control connection and is used to send commands and responses. Actual data transfer occurs on a secondary connection, the data connection.

The control connection uses the TELNET protocol to exchange line-oriented commands and replies. Although TELNET is a whole protocol in itself, FTP needs only a subset of the complete TELNET functionality and most TELNET options can be ignored. The main reason for using TELNET on the control connection is that it serves to define a basic character set and end-of-line convention—the default parameters of the network virtual terminal (NVT). In practice, using TELNET for the control channel simply means that the character set is US-ASCII and the end-of-line convention is <CRLF>.

Transport Information

The FTP server waits for clients to establish a control connection on well-known TCP port 21. The data connection can be established on the default data port 20, but this is typically changed using the PORT or PASV commands.

Data Types

FTP is designed to work across a range of heterogeneous computer hardware and operating systems. Because of this, the data that FTP exchanges must be converted to a neutral type for data transport and then back to a local data type at the receiving host. FTP defines four data transfer data types, described in Table 8.1.

Table 8.1 FTP Data Types

Type	Type Code	Description
ASCII	A	NVT-ASCII text
EBCDIC	E	EBCDIC text
IMAGE	I	Raw binary data represented as a series of octets
LOCAL	L	Raw binary data using a variable byte size

The client takes the responsibility of telling the server which data type to use for the data transfer. The client specifies the data type using the TYPE command followed by one of the type codes shown in Table 8.1.

Note that the ASCII type identifies NVT-ASCII text and not US-ASCII text. NVT-ASCII uses an 8-bit character size and a <CRLF> sequence to represent the end-of-line character. See the TELNET specification for more information.

The default data type, unless otherwise specified, is ASCII.

File Structure

Different operating systems store file data in different structures. The FTP specification defines a number of file structures to help move data from one system to another. Table 8.2 shows the defined file structures and the structure codes used with the STRU command.

The default file structure, unless otherwise specified, is File.

Transmission Modes

FTP defines three data transmission modes. These modes are used to specify any additional coding or sequencing that is performed on the data as it is transferred between hosts. Note that the transmission mode is independent of any data type or file structure the data might have. Table 8.3 shows the transmission modes defined in RFC 959.

Commands

FTP commands are short ASCII strings followed by optional parameters depending on the particular command. Table 8.4 lists the complete FTP command set.

Table 8.2 FTP File Structures

Structure	Structure Code	Description
File	F	No internal structure; simply a sequence of bytes
Record	R	A series of records
Page	P	A series of data blocks called "pages"

Table 8.3 FTP Transmission Modes

Mode	Mode Code	Description
Stream	S	The file is transferred as a stream of bytes; if the file has Record structure, the end of file will be sent as a record indication; if the file has File structure, the end of file is indicated by closing the data connection
Block	B	The file is transferred as a sequence of data blocks preceded by header information; block mode allows the restart of an interrupted transfer at an intermediate data block
Compressed	C	The file data has been compressed using a simple run-length encoding; see RFC 959 for the RLE scheme details

Table 8.4 FTP Command Set

Command	Optional/Required	Description
USER	Required	User name: Specifies the user name for access control
PASS	Optional	Password: Specifies the user password, if any, for access control
ACCT	Optional	Account: Specifies additional account information that may be needed on some systems
CWD	Optional	Change working directory: Specifies a new directory on the remote system that the user wants to work with
CDUP	Optional	Change to parent directory: Indicates that the working directory should be changed to the parent of the current directory
SMNT	Optional	Structure mount: Indicates that the user wants to mount a different file system data structure
QUIT	Required	Quit: Informs the server that the client wants to end the FTP session
REIN	Optional	Reinitialize: Restarts the current session at the authentication phase, the same state as when the control connection is first established
PORT	Required	Data port: Specifies the host address and data port that the server should contact when establishing the data connection
PASV	Optional	Passive: Informs the server that the client will contact it when setting up data connections and asks the server to return the port information needed for the connection
TYPE	Required	Data type: Indicates the data type that should be used for subsequent data transfers
STRU	Required	File structure: Indicates the file structure that should be used for subsequent data transfers

Continued

Table 8.4 FTP Command Set (Continued)

Command	Optional/Required	Description
MODE	Required	Transfer mode: Indicates the transfer mode that should be used for subsequent data transfers
RETR	Required	Retrieve: Downloads the specified file from the server
STOR	Required	Store: Uploads the specified file to the server
STOU	Optional	Store unique: Identical to STOR except the server chooses a unique name for the file and returns it to the client
APPE	Optional	Append: Uploads the specified file to the server; if a file of the same name already exists, the uploaded data is appended to the pre-existing file
ALLO	Optional	Allocate: This command is needed on some file systems to preallocate space for a new file; the ALLO command specifies the file size
REST	Optional	Restart: Used to restart an interrupted transfer at a specified point; the REST command indicates the point at which the transfer should resume and should be followed by a data transfer command
RNFR	Optional	Rename from: Specifies the old pathname of a file that is being renamed; this command must be followed immediately by the RNTO command
RNTO	Optional	Rename to: Specifies the new pathname for the file specified by the RNFR command
ABOR	Optional	Abort: Requests the server to abort the last command and any data transfer process associated with it
DELE	Optional	Delete: Deletes the specified file from the server
RMD	Optional	Remove directory: Removes a directory
MKD	Optional	Make directory: Creates a directory
PWD	Optional	Print working directory: Requests the server to return the name of the current working directory
LIST	Optional	Directory list: Requests the server to return a directory listing using the data connection; the returned listing typically contains more information about the files, such as size and modification date, in a system dependent listing format
NLST	Optional	Name list: Requests the server to return a list of file names in the current directory; this function returns a list of file names with no additional information
SITE	Optional	Site parameters: Allows the client to specify site-specific options and parameters

Continued

Table 8.4 FTP Command Set (Continued)

Command	Optional/Required	Description
SYST	Optional	System: Requests the server to return its operating system type
STAT	Optional	Status: Requests the server to return status about the current in-progress file transfer, a specific file, or the general server status
HELP	Optional	Help: Requests help about the commands the server implements or more detailed help about a specified command
NOOP	Required	No operation: Forces the server to respond with a positive reply; NOOP has no effect on any server state

Note that a server is not required to implement the complete command set, only the required commands listed in the table. In practice, a server is not very functional with the minimal command set and most servers typically implement other commands such as LIST, NLST, CWD, MKD, RMD, etc. Few servers implement all the commands listed in RFC 959.

The SYST command returns a registered operating system name. The currently registered system names from the most recent Assigned Numbers RFC (RFC 1700) are shown here:

AEGIS
AMIGA-OS-1.2
AMIGA-OS-1.3
AMIGA-OS-2.0
AMIGA-OS-2.1
AMIGA-OS-3.0
AMIGA-OS-3.1
APOLLO
AIX/370
AIX-PS/2
BS-2000
CEDAR
CGW
CHORUS
CHRYSALIS
CMOS
CMS
COS
CPIX
CTOS
CTSS
DCN
DDNOS
DOMAIN
DOS
EDX
ELF
EMBOS
EMMOS
EPOS

FOONEX
FORTH
FUZZ
GCOS
GPOS
HDOS
IMAGEN
INTERCOM
IMPRESS
INTERLISP
IOS
IRIX
ISI-68020
ITS
LISP
LISPM
LOCUS
MACOS
MINOS
MOS
MPE5
MPE/V
MPE/IX
MSDOS
MULTICS
MUSIC
MUSIC/SP
MVS
MVS/SP
NEXUS
NMS
NONSTOP
NOS-2
NTOS
OPENVMS
OS/DDP
OS/2
OS4
OS86
OSX
PCDOS
PERQ/OS
PLI
PSDOS/MIT
PRIMOS
RMX/RDOS
ROS
RSX11M
RTE-A
SATOPS
SCO-OPEN-DESKTOP-1.0
SCO-OPEN-DESKTOP-1.1
SCO-OPEN-DESKTOP-2.0
SCO-OPEN-DESKTOP-3.0
SCO-OPEN-DESKTOP-LITE-3.0
SCO-OPEN-SERVER-3.0
SCO-UNIX-3.2.0
SCO-UNIX-3.2V2.0
SCO-UNIX-3.2V2.1
SCO-UNIX-3.2V4.0
SCO-UNIX-3.2V4.1
SCO-UNIX-3.2V4.2

SCO-XENIX-386-2.3.2	SCO-XENIX-386-2.3.3
SCO-XENIX-386-2.3.4	SCS
SIMP	SUN
SUN-OS-3.5	SUN-OS-4.0
SWIFT	TAC
TANDEM	TENEX
THE-MAJOR-BBS	TOPS10
TOPS20	TOS
TP3010	TRSDOS
ULTRIX	UNIX
UNIX-BSD	UNIX-V1AT
UNIX-V	UNIX-V.1
UNIX-V.2	UNIX-V.3
UNIX-PC	UNKNOWN
UT2D	V
VM	VM/370
VM/CMS	VM/SP
VMS	VMS/EUNICE
VRTX	WAITS
WANG	WIN32
WYSE-WYXWARE	X11R3
XDE	XENIX

Responses

Each FTP command generates a response from the server. An FTP response consists of a three-digit numeric reply code, followed by a space, followed by text, followed by <CRLF>.

The three-digit numeric code is suitable for driving a client program state machine, while the text can be shown to a human user.

If the text is very long, the server may return a multi-line reply. A multi-line reply begins with a typical one-line response, but replaces the space following the numeric code with a hyphen character. The last line of a multi-line reply has the same format as a single-line reply (a numeric code followed by a space). The numeric code in the last line must match the numeric code given in the first line. All intermediate lines of text can take any form that would not otherwise falsely signal the end of the multi-line reply.

FTP numeric reply codes use an internal structure to convey information to the client FTP process. The first digit of the reply code indicates the general success or failure of the command. Additional digits describe the general functional area of the response and distinguish between fine gradations of the response. Tables 8.5 and 8.6 describe the meanings associated with a reply code's first and second digits.

Table 8.7 lists the complete set of FTP replies in numeric order.

Table 8.5 FTP Reply Code—First Digit

Code	Description
1yz	Positive preliminary reply—The command is being acted upon; expect a final reply code before sending another command
2yz	Positive completion reply—The command was successfully executed; a new command may be sent
3yz	Positive intermediate reply—The command was accepted, but the final result is being delayed because other information needs to be supplied from the client; this reply is used for sequencing command groups
4yz	Transient negative completion reply—The command failed, but the condition is temporary (although there is no indication of how long the condition will persist); the user agent should try again
5yz	Permanent negative completion reply—The command failed and will always fail if given again; the command should not be attempted again

Table 8.6 FTP Reply Code—Second Digit

Code	Description
x0z	Refers to command syntax
x1z	Indicates information returned by commands requesting information such as status or help
x2z	Refers to the state of the control or data connections
x3z	The reply is associated with the login process and accounting procedures
x4z	Reserved for future use
x5z	Refers to the state of the requested file transfer or other file system command

Table 8.7 FTP Reply Codes in Numeric Order

Reply	Notes
110 MARK *yyyy* = *mmmm*	Restart marker reply; *yyyy* is client data stream marker and *mmmm* is server's equivalent marker
120 Service ready in *nnn* minutes	
125 Data connection already open; transfer starting	
150 File status okay; about to open data connection	
200 Command okay	
202 Command not implemented, superfluous at this site	
211 System status, or system help reply	
212 Directory status	
213 File status	
214 Help message	
215 *NAME* system type	Where *NAME* is an official system name from the list in the Assigned Numbers document
220 Service ready for new user	
221 Service closing control connection	Logged out if appropriate
225 Data connection open; no transfer in progress	
226 Closing data connection	Requested file action successful (for example, file transfer or file abort)
227 Entering Passive Mode (h1,h2,h3,h4,p1,p2)	
230 User logged in, proceed	
250 Requested file action okay, completed	
257 "*PATHNAME*" created	
331 User name okay, need password	
332 Need account for login	
350 Requested file action pending further information	
421 Service not available, closing control connection	This may be a reply to any command if the service knows it must shut down
425 Can't open data connection	
426 Connection closed; transfer aborted	
450 Requested file action not taken	File unavailable (e.g., file busy)
451 Requested action aborted: local error in processing	
452 Requested action not taken	Insufficient storage space in system

Continued

Table 8.7 FTP Reply Codes in Numeric Order (Continued)

Reply	Notes
500 Syntax error, command unrecognized	This may include errors such as a command line that's too long
501 Syntax error in parameters or arguments	
502 Command not implemented	
503 Bad sequence of commands	
504 Command not implemented for that parameter	
530 Not logged in	
532 Need account for storing files	
550 Requested action not taken	File unavailable (for example, file not found, no access)
551 Requested action aborted: page type unknown	
552 Requested file action aborted	Exceeded storage allocation (for current directory or data set)
553 Requested action not taken	File name not allowed

Table 8.8 lists the various FTP commands and the possible replies each can generate.

Table 8.8 Possible Responses to FTP Commands

Command Group	Command	Preliminary Responses	Secondary Responses
Connection establishment			
		120	220
		220	
		421	
Login			
	USER		
		230	
		530	
		500, 501, 421	
		331, 332	
	PASS		
		230	
		202	
		530	
		500, 501, 503, 421	
		332	

Continued

Table 8.8 Possible Responses to FTP Commands (Continued)

Command Group	Command	Preliminary Responses	Secondary Responses
	ACCT		
		230	
		202	
		530	
		500, 501, 503, 421	
	CWD		
		250	
		500, 501, 502, 421, 530, 550	
	CDUP		
		200	
		500, 501, 502, 421, 530, 550	
	SMNT		
		202, 250	
		500, 501, 502, 421, 530, 550	
Logout			
	REIN		
		120	220
		220	
		421	
		500, 502	
	QUIT		
		221	
		500	
Transfer parameters			
	PORT		
		200	
		500, 501, 421, 530	
	PASV		
		227	
		500, 501, 502, 421, 530	
	MODE		
		200	
		500, 501, 504, 421, 530	
	TYPE		
		200	
		500, 501, 504, 421, 530	
	STRU		
		200	
		500, 501, 504, 421, 530	

Continued

Table 8.8 Possible Responses to FTP Commands (Continued)

Command Group	Command	Preliminary Responses	Secondary Responses
File action commands			
	ALLO		
		200	
		202	
		500, 501, 504, 421, 530	
	REST		
		500, 501, 502, 421, 530	
		350	
	STOR		
		125, 150	
			(110)
			226, 250
			425, 426, 451, 551,
552			
		532, 450, 452, 553	
		500, 501, 421, 530	
	STOU		
		125, 150	
			(110)
			226, 250
			425, 426, 451, 551,
552			
		532, 450, 452, 553	
		500, 501, 421, 530	
	RETR		
		125, 150	
			(110)
			226, 250
			425, 426, 451
		450, 550	
		500, 501, 421, 530	
	LIST		
		125, 150	
			226, 250
			425, 426, 451
		450	
		500, 501, 502, 421, 530	
	NLST		
		125, 150	
			226, 250
			425, 426, 451

Continued

Table 8.8 Possible Responses to FTP Commands (Continued)

Command Group	Command	Preliminary Responses	Secondary Responses
		450	
		500, 501, 502, 421, 530	
	APPE		
		125, 150	
			(110)
			226, 250
			425, 426, 451, 551,
552			
		532, 450, 550, 452, 553	
		500, 501, 502, 421, 530	
	RNFR		
		450, 550	
		500, 501, 502, 421, 530	
		350	
	RNTO		
		250	
		532, 553	
		500, 501, 502, 503, 421, 530	
	DELE		
		250	
		450, 550	
		500, 501, 502, 421, 530	
	RMD		
		250	
		500, 501, 502, 421, 530, 550	
	MKD		
		257	
		500, 501, 502, 421, 530, 550	
	PWD		
		257	
		500, 501, 502, 421, 550	
	ABOR		
		225, 226	
Informational commands			
	SYST		
		215	
		500, 501, 502, 421	
	STAT		
		211, 212, 213	
		450	
		500, 501, 502, 421, 530	

Continued

Table 8.8 Possible Responses to FTP Commands (Continued)

Command Group	Command	Preliminary Responses	Secondary Responses
	HELP		
		211, 214	
		500, 501, 502, 421	
Miscellaneous commands			
	SITE		
		200	
		202	
		500, 501, 530	
	NOOP		
		200	
		500 421	

Grammar

RFC 959 provides a small grammar to describe the format of the various FTP commands. This grammar is shown in the following sections.

Note <SP> represents US-ASCII space, <CR> represents US-ASCII carriage return, and <LF> represents US-ASCII line feed. <CRLF> represents a carriage return followed by a line feed.

Commands

```
USER <SP> <username> <CRLF>
PASS <SP> <password> <CRLF>
ACCT <SP> <account-information> <CRLF>
CWD <SP> <pathname> <CRLF>
CDUP <CRLF>
SMNT <SP> <pathname> <CRLF>
QUIT <CRLF>
REIN <CRLF>
PORT <SP> <host-port> <CRLF>
PASV <CRLF>
TYPE <SP> <type-code> <CRLF>
STRU <SP> <structure-code> <CRLF>
MODE <SP> <mode-code> <CRLF>
RETR <SP> <pathname> <CRLF>
STOR <SP> <pathname> <CRLF>
STOU <CRLF>
APPE <SP> <pathname> <CRLF>
```

```
ALLO <SP> <decimal-integer> [<SP> R <SP> <decimal-integer>] <CRLF>
REST <SP> <marker> <CRLF>
RNFR <SP> <pathname> <CRLF>
RNTO <SP> <pathname> <CRLF>
ABOR <CRLF>
DELE <SP> <pathname> <CRLF>
RMD <SP> <pathname> <CRLF>
MKD <SP> <pathname> <CRLF>
PWD <CRLF>
LIST [<SP> <pathname>] <CRLF>
NLST [<SP> <pathname>] <CRLF>
SITE <SP> <string> <CRLF>
SYST <CRLF>
STAT [<SP> <pathname>] <CRLF>
HELP [<SP> <string>] <CRLF>
NOOP <CRLF>
```

Arguments

```
<username>  ::=  <string>
<password>  ::=  <string>
<account-information> ::=  <string>
<string>  ::=  <char> | <char><string>
<char> ::=  any of the 128 ASCII characters except <CR> and <LF>
<marker>  ::=  <pr-string>
<pr-string> ::=  <pr-char> | <pr-char><pr-string>
<pr-char> ::=  printable characters, any ASCII code 33 through 126
<byte-size> ::=  <number>
<host-port> ::=  <host-number>,<port-number>
<host-number>  ::=  <number>,<number>,<number>,<number>
<port-number>  ::=  <number>,<number>
<number>  ::=  any decimal integer 1 through 255
<form-code> ::=  N | T | C
<type-code> ::=  A [<sp> <form-code>]
      | E [<sp> <form-code>]
      | I
      | L <sp> <byte-size>
<structure-code> ::=  F | R | P
<mode-code> ::=  S | B | C
<pathname>  ::=  <string>
<decimal-integer>::=  any decimal integer
```

Finger

Name

Finger

Abbreviation

FINGER

Status

Elective Draft Standard

Specifications

RFC 1288

Abstract

The Finger protocol is a simple application protocol that allows a client to find out some information about another user on a remote system. The protocol is useful and very easy to implement.

Comments

The Finger protocol can present security and privacy problems if not administered well. A remote client can find out all sorts of information about a user if system administrators allow information to be given out using the Finger protocol. Administrators are urged to review the information available through Finger on their systems and determine what information is appropriate to give out.

Description

The Finger protocol is extremely simple. The Finger client first makes contact with the Finger server at the well-known port number. The client sends the server a query consisting of a single line of ASCII text followed by a CRLF end-of-line sequence. The server returns one or more lines of text to the client and then closes the connection. After receiving the reply lines, the client closes the connection and the session is finished.

The grammar section of this chapter describes the exact format of a Finger query. Note that the grammar production {Q2} specifies a recursive Finger query. In this case, the Finger server is asked to forward a Finger query to a second server. The "/W" option requests a more verbose reply than would otherwise be returned without the option. A query consisting of just CRLF requests information about all current users of the server system.

The text returned by the server is system dependent but usually contains the user's login name, full name, and some contact information such as an email address or phone number. Many Finger servers refuse to answer specific types of queries such as the {Q2} or {C} query described in the grammar section because of security reasons. In such cases, the text returned is something similar to "Information refused."

Transport Information

The Finger server waits for connections on well-known TCP port 79.

Grammar

The following grammar describes the format of a Finger query:

```
{Q1}    ::= [{W}|{W}{S}{U}]{C}
{Q2}    ::= [{W}{S}][{U}]{H}{C}
{U}     ::= username
{H}     ::= @hostname | @hostname{H}
```

```
{W}        ::= /W
{S}        ::= <SP> | <SP>{S}
{C}        ::= <CRLF>
```

A Finger reply contains lines of ASCII text terminated by CRLF end-of-line sequences.

10 Format of Electronic Mail Messages

Name

Format of Electronic Mail Messages

Abbreviation

MAIL

Status

Recommended Standard (STD 11)

Specifications

RFC 822

Abstract

RFC 822 specifies the format of electronic mail messages. This format is widely used on the Internet and RFC 822 is one of the most widely cited RFCs in existence. For instance, network news messages follow a format similar to RFC 822.

Related Specifications

SMTP (RFC 821), MIME (RFC 1521)

See Also

POP3 (RFC 1725), IMAP4 (RFC 1730)

Description

RFC 822 defines the basic structure of an Internet electronic mail message. Simply, a mail message consists of lines of ASCII characters terminated with CRLF. The first lines of a message are headers. The remaining lines of the message are part of the message body. The message headers are separated from the message body by a single blank line containing just CRLF.

The remainder of this chapter details the RFC 822 grammar that specifies this message format in more detail.

Grammar

The heart of RFC 822 is its grammar. This grammar is reprinted here directly as it appears in RFC 822 itself. No changes have been made. All comments have been left intact. In some cases, this means that that the comments lose a bit of their context and may not make much sense. Consult RFC 822 to understand any ambiguous statements.

Header Field Definitions

```
field       =  field-name ":" [ field-body ] CRLF

field-name  =  1*<any CHAR, excluding CTLs, SPACE, and ":">

field-body  =  field-body-contents
                    [CRLF LWSP-char field-body]

field-body-contents =
                      <the ASCII characters making up the field-body, as
                       defined in the following sections, and consisting
                       of combinations of atom, quoted-string, and
                       specials tokens, or else consisting of texts>
```

Lexical Tokens

```
CHAR = <any ASCII character> ; (  0-177,  0.-127.)
ALPHA   = <any ASCII alphabetic character>  ; (101-132, 65.- 90.)
       ; (141-172, 97.-122.)
```

```
DIGIT   = <any ASCII decimal digit>  ; ( 60- 71, 48.- 57.)
CTL  = <any ASCII control  ; (  0- 37,  0.- 31.)
     character and DEL>  ; (    177,     127.)
CR= <ASCII CR, carriage return>; (     15,      13.)
LF= <ASCII LF, linefeed>  ; (     12,      10.)
SPACE   = <ASCII SP, space>; (     40,      32.)
HTAB = <ASCII HT, horizontal-tab> ; (     11,       9.)
<"> = <ASCII quote mark>  ; (     42,      34.)
CRLF = CR LF

LWSP-char = SPACE / HTAB; semantics = SPACE

linear-white-space  = 1*([CRLF] LWSP-char)  ; semantics = SPACE
   ; CRLF => folding

specials  = "(" / ")" / "<" / ">" / "@"; Must be in quoted-
     /  "," / ";" / ":" / "\" / <">  ;  string, to use
     /  "." / "[" / "]"  ;  within a word.

delimiters  = specials / linear-white-space / comment

text = <any CHAR, including bare  ; => atoms, specials,
     CR & bare LF, but NOT ;  comments and
     including CRLF>  ;  quoted-strings are
        ;  NOT recognized.

atom = 1*<any CHAR except specials, SPACE and CTLs>

quoted-string  = <"> *(qtext/quoted-pair) <">  ; Regular qtext or
        ;   quoted chars.

qtext   = <any CHAR excepting <">, ; => may be folded
     "\" & CR, and including
     linear-white-space>

domain-literal = "[" *(dtext / quoted-pair) "]"

dtext   = <any CHAR excluding "[", ; => may be folded
     "]", "\" & CR, & including
     linear-white-space>

comment= "(" *(ctext / quoted-pair / comment) ")"

ctext   = <any CHAR excluding "(", ; => may be folded
     ")", "\" & CR, & including
     linear-white-space>
```

```
quoted-pair = "\" CHAR  ; may quote any char

phrase = 1*word ; Sequence of words

word = atom / quoted-string
```

Message Syntax

```
message= fields *( CRLF *text ); Everything after
       ;  first null line
       ;  is message body

fields = dates   ; Creation time,
     source ;  author id & one
     1*destination  ;  address required
     *optional-field  ;  others optional

source = [  trace ]  ; net traversals
     originator  ; original mail
     [  resent ] ; forwarded

trace   = return ; path to sender
     1*received  ; receipt tags

return = "Return-path" ":" route-addr  ; return address

received  = "Received"    ":"; one per relay
     ["from" domain]  ; sending host
     ["by"   domain]  ; receiving host
     ["via"  atom]  ; physical path
     *("with" atom) ; link/mail protocol
     ["id"   msg-id]  ; receiver msg id
     ["for"  addr-spec]  ; initial form
     ";"    date-time ; time received

originator  = authentic ; authenticated addr
     [ "Reply-To"   ":" 1#address] )

authentic = "From"       ":"   mailbox ; Single author
     / ( "Sender"     ":"   mailbox  ; Actual submittor
     "From"       ":" 1#mailbox); Multiple authors
       ;  or not sender

resent  = resent-authentic
     [ "Resent-Reply-To"  ":" 1#address] )
```

```
resent-authentic = "Resent-From"      ":"   mailbox
     / ( "Resent-Sender"     ":"   mailbox
     "Resent-From"       ":" 1#mailbox  )

dates   = orig-date ; Original
     [ resent-date ]  ; Forwarded

orig-date = "Date"        ":"   date-time

resent-date = "Resent-Date" ":"   date-time

destination = "To"          ":" 1#address; Primary
     /  "Resent-To"   ":" 1#address
     /  "cc"          ":" 1#address  ; Secondary
     /  "Resent-cc"   ":" 1#address
     /  "bcc"         ":"  #address  ; Blind carbon
     /  "Resent-bcc"  ":"  #address

optional-field =
     /  "Message-ID"        ":"   msg-id
     /  "Resent-Message-ID" ":"   msg-id
     /  "In-Reply-To"       ":"  *(phrase / msg-id)
     /  "References"        ":"  *(phrase / msg-id)
     /  "Keywords"          ":"  #phrase
     /  "Subject"           ":"  *text
     /  "Comments"          ":"  *text
     /  "Encrypted"         ":" 1#2word
     /  extension-field  ; To be defined
     /  user-defined-field ; May be pre-empted

msg-id = "<" addr-spec ">"; Unique message id
extension-field  = <Any field which is defined in a document
     published as a formal extension to this
     specification; none will have names beginning
     with the string "X-">

user-defined-field  = <Any field which has not been defined
     in this specification or published as an
     extension to this specification; names for
     such fields must be unique and may be
     pre-empted by published extensions>
```

Date and Time Syntax

```
date-time = [ day "," ] date time ; dd mm yy
       ;  hh:mm:ss zzz
```

```
day  =  "Mon"   / "Tue" /  "Wed"   / "Thu"
     /  "Fri"   / "Sat" /  "Sun"

date = 1*2DIGIT month 2DIGIT ; day month year
       ;  e.g. 20 Jun 82

month   = "Jan"  /  "Feb" /  "Mar"  /  "Apr"
     /  "May"  /  "Jun" /  "Jul"  /  "Aug"
     /  "Sep"  /  "Oct" /  "Nov"  /  "Dec"

time = hour zone ; ANSI and Military

hour = 2DIGIT ":" 2DIGIT [":" 2DIGIT]  ; 00:00:00 - 23:59:59

zone = "UT"  / "GMT"  ; Universal Time
       ; North American : UT
     /  "EST" / "EDT"  ;  Eastern:  - 5/ - 4
     /  "CST" / "CDT"  ;  Central:  - 6/ - 5
     /  "MST" / "MDT"  ;  Mountain: - 7/ - 6
     /  "PST" / "PDT"  ;  Pacific:  - 8/ - 7
     /  1ALPHA ; Military: Z = UT;
       ;  A:-1; (J not used)
       ;  M:-12; N:+1; Y:+12
     / ( ("+" / "-") 4DIGIT ) ; Local differential
       ;  hours+min. (HHMM)
```

Address Syntax

```
address=  mailbox; one addressee
     /  group  ; named list

group   = phrase ":" [#mailbox] ";"

mailbox=  addr-spec ; simple address
     /  phrase route-addr  ; name & addr-spec

route-addr  = "<" [route] addr-spec ">"

route   = 1#("@" domain) ":"  ; path-relative

addr-spec = local-part "@" domain ; global address

local-part  = word *("." word) ; uninterpreted
        ; case-preserved

domain  = sub-domain *("." sub-domain)
```

```
sub-domain   = domain-ref / domain-literal

domain-ref   = atom ; symbolic reference
```

Alphabetical Listing of Syntax Rules

```
address= mailbox; one addressee
     /  group  ; named list
addr-spec = local-part "@" domain ; global address
ALPHA   = <any ASCII alphabetic character>
        ; (101-132, 65.- 90.)
        ; (141-172, 97.-122.)
atom = 1*<any CHAR except specials, SPACE and CTLs>
authentic = "From"       ":"   mailbox ; Single author
     / ( "Sender"     ":"   mailbox  ; Actual submittor
     "From"        ":" 1#mailbox); Multiple authors
        ;  or not sender
CHAR = <any ASCII character> ; (  0-177,  0.-127.)
comment= "(" *(ctext / quoted-pair / comment) ")"
CR= <ASCII CR, carriage return>; (     15,      13.)
CRLF = CR LF
ctext   = <any CHAR excluding "(", ; => may be folded
     ")", "\" & CR, & including
     linear-white-space>
CTL  = <any ASCII control  ; (  0- 37,  0.- 31.)
     character and DEL>  ; (    177,     127.)
date = 1*2DIGIT month 2DIGIT ; day month year
        ;  e.g. 20 Jun 82
dates   = orig-date ; Original
     [ resent-date ]  ; Forwarded
date-time = [ day "," ] date time ; dd mm yy
        ;  hh:mm:ss zzz
day  = "Mon"  / "Tue" /  "Wed"  / "Thu"
     /  "Fri"  / "Sat" /  "Sun"
delimiters   = specials / linear-white-space / comment
destination = "To"           ":" 1#address; Primary
     /  "Resent-To"   ":" 1#address
     /  "cc"          ":" 1#address  ; Secondary
     /  "Resent-cc"   ":" 1#address
     /  "bcc"         ":"  #address  ; Blind carbon
     /  "Resent-bcc"  ":"  #address
DIGIT   = <any ASCII decimal digit>  ; ( 60- 71, 48.- 57.)
domain  = sub-domain *("." sub-domain)
domain-literal = "[" *(dtext / quoted-pair) "]"
domain-ref  = atom ; symbolic reference
dtext   = <any CHAR excluding "[", ; => may be folded
     "]", "\" & CR, & including
     linear-white-space>
```

```
extension-field  =
     <Any field which is defined in a document
     published as a formal extension to this
     specification; none will have names beginning
     with the string "X-">
field  = field-name ":" [ field-body ] CRLF
fields = dates  ; Creation time,
     source ;  author id & one
     1*destination  ;  address required
     *optional-field  ;  others optional
field-body  = field-body-contents
     [CRLF LWSP-char field-body]
field-body-contents =
     <the ASCII characters making up the field-body, as
     defined in the following sections, and consisting
     of combinations of atom, quoted-string, and
     specials tokens, or else consisting of texts>
field-name  = 1*<any CHAR, excluding CTLs, SPACE, and ":">
group  = phrase ":" [#mailbox] ";"
hour = 2DIGIT ":" 2DIGIT [":" 2DIGIT]
       ; 00:00:00 - 23:59:59
HTAB = <ASCII HT, horizontal-tab> ; (     11,      9.)
LF= <ASCII LF, linefeed>  ; (     12,      10.)
linear-white-space  = 1*([CRLF] LWSP-char)  ; semantics = SPACE
       ; CRLF => folding
local-part  = word *("." word) ; uninterpreted
       ; case-preserved
LWSP-char = SPACE / HTAB; semantics = SPACE
mailbox= addr-spec ; simple address
     /  phrase route-addr  ; name & addr-spec
message= fields *( CRLF *text ); Everything after
       ;  first null line
       ;  is message body
month  = "Jan"  /  "Feb" /  "Mar"  /  "Apr"
     /  "May"  /  "Jun" /  "Jul"  /  "Aug"
     /  "Sep"  /  "Oct" /  "Nov"  /  "Dec"
msg-id  = "<" addr-spec ">"; Unique message id
optional-field =
     /  "Message-ID"        ":"   msg-id
     /  "Resent-Message-ID" ":"   msg-id
     /  "In-Reply-To"       ":"  *(phrase / msg-id)
     /  "References"        ":"  *(phrase / msg-id)
     /  "Keywords"          ":"  #phrase
     /  "Subject"           ":"  *text
     /  "Comments"          ":"  *text
     /  "Encrypted"         ":" 1#2word
```

```
    / extension-field ; To be defined
    / user-defined-field ; May be pre-empted
orig-date = "Date"        ":"   date-time
originator  = authentic ; authenticated addr
    [ "Reply-To"   ":" 1#address] )
phrase = 1*word ; Sequence of words
qtext  = <any CHAR excepting <">, ; => may be folded
    "\" & CR, and including
    linear-white-space>
quoted-pair = "\" CHAR  ; may quote any char
quoted-string  = <"> *(qtext/quoted-pair) <">  ; Regular qtext or
       ;  quoted chars.
received  = "Received"    ":"; one per relay
    ["from" domain]  ; sending host
    ["by"   domain]  ; receiving host
    ["via"  atom]  ; physical path
    *("with" atom) ; link/mail protocol
    ["id"   msg-id]  ; receiver msg id
    ["for"  addr-spec]  ; initial form
    ";"    date-time ; time received

resent  = resent-authentic
    [ "Resent-Reply-To"  ":" 1#address] )
resent-authentic = "Resent-From"      ":"   mailbox
    / ( "Resent-Sender"    ":"   mailbox
    "Resent-From"      ":" 1#mailbox  )
resent-date = "Resent-Date" ":"   date-time
return  = "Return-path" ":" route-addr  ; return address
route   = 1#("@" domain) ":"  ; path-relative
route-addr  = "<" [route] addr-spec ">"
source = [  trace ]  ; net traversals
    originator  ; original mail
    [  resent ] ; forwarded
SPACE   = <ASCII SP, space>; (     40,      32.)
specials  = "(" / ")" / "<" / ">" / "@"; Must be in quoted-
    /  "," / ";" / ":" / "\" / <">  ;  string, to use
    /  "." / "[" / "]"  ;  within a word.
sub-domain  = domain-ref / domain-literal
text = <any CHAR, including bare  ; => atoms, specials,
    CR & bare LF, but NOT ;  comments and
    including CRLF>  ;  quoted-strings are
      ;  NOT recognized.
time = hour zone ; ANSI and Military
trace  = return  ; path to sender
    1*received  ; receipt tags
user-defined-field =
    <Any field which has not been defined
```

```
     in this specification or published as an
     extension to this specification; names for
     such fields must be unique and may be
     pre-empted by published extensions>
word = atom / quoted-string
zone = "UT"  / "GMT"  ; Universal Time
       ; North American : UT
     /  "EST" / "EDT" ;  Eastern:  - 5/ - 4
     /  "CST" / "CDT" ;  Central:  - 6/ - 5
     /  "MST" / "MDT" ;  Mountain: - 7/ - 6
     /  "PST" / "PDT" ;  Pacific:  - 8/ - 7
     /  1ALPHA ; Military: Z = UT;
<">  = <ASCII quote mark> ; (    42,      34.)
```

11 Hypertext Markup Language

Name

Hypertext Markup Language

Abbreviation

HTML

Status

Elective Proposed Standard

Specifications

RFC 1866 (HTML 2.0), draft-ietf-html-tables-06.txt, dated 1-Feb-1996

Abstract

HTML is a simple markup language used to create hypermedia documents used on the World Wide Web. HTML identifies various document features, such as headings and paragraphs, using a set of tags. An HTML browser parses the raw HTML and creates a user-readable version of the document with the various tags removed. Tags can also be used to create hyperlinks to other documents. The browser displays these links using a different color or font. When the user selects a link, the browser displays the document connected by the link.

Related Specifications

HTTP (draft-ietf-http-v10-spec-05.txt, dated 19-Feb-1996)

See Also

There are many Internet Drafts and W3C documents describing extensions to HTML 2.0. At one time, many of these extensions were going to be published as HTML 3.0, but this no longer appears to be the case.

Comments

The currently standardized version of HTML is 2.0, but this means little as the language is evolving at supersonic speeds to keep up with demand for new features. The language evolution is fueled by the World Wide Web browser manufacturers who are constantly trying to add features faster than their competitors.

This chapter describes HTML as defined in RFC 1866 with some additions from recent Internet Drafts where such drafts seem to have overwhelming support throughout the Internet World Wide Web community. By the time you read this, it will certainly be out of date. Be sure to check for newer RFCs, Internet Drafts, and W3C documents updating HTML specifications.

The World Wide Web Consortium (W3C) provides a forum for much of the development work related to HTML. The W3C archive is probably the most up-to-date representation of the current state of HTML. The archive contains specifications, news, and announcements related to the development of HTML. The archive can be found at **http://www.w3.org**.

Description

HTML is an application of ISO Standard 8879:1986 Information Processing Text and Office Systems; Standard Generalized Markup Language (SGML). HTML documents are SGML documents with generic semantics and can be used to represent:

- Hypertext news, mail, documentation, and hypermedia
- Menus of options
- Database query results
- Simple structured documents with in-lined graphics
- Hypertext views of existing bodies of information

RFC 1866, and consequently this chapter, describes a version of HTML in common use before June 1994.

HTML Tags

HTML uses *tags* to identify HTML elements, such as headings, paragraphs, lists, bolded or italicized text, and other similar features. Tags typically appear in pairs (however, there are some prominent exceptions) and surround the text that they apply to. An opening tag appears as "<tag>" while a closing tag appears as "</tag>".

Miscellaneous Tags

Table 11.1 lists some miscellaneous tags.

Document Structure Tags

Table 11.2 lists the tags that apply to documents.

Document Head Tags

Table 11.3 lists tags that may appear in the head portion of the document (surrounded by the <head>…</head> tags).

Table 11.1 Miscellaneous Tags

Tag	Description
<!-- *text* -->	Comment

Table 11.2 Document Structure Tags

Tag	Description
<!DOCTYPE …>	Identifies a document as HTML conforming to RFC 1866 (for example: <!DOCTYPE HTML PUBLIC "-//IETF//DTD HTML 2.0//EN">)
<html>	HTML document; surrounds the entire HTML document text except the <!DOCTYPE …> tag
<head>	Document head
<body>	Document body

Table 11.3 Document Head Tags

Tag	Description
<title>	Specifies the document title
<base>	Specifies a base address for interpreting relative URLs when the document is viewed out of context
<isindex>	Specifies that the user agent should allow the user to search an index by giving keywords
<link>	Specifies a hyperlink used to reference other information like authorship, etc.
<meta>	Specifies meta information that applies to the document; in particular, the HTTP-EQUIV attribute allows the document to specify information that is passed to a user agent in HTTP headers
<address>	Used to specify an address, typically of the document author; this tag may also appear in the document body but is most often used in the head

Body Text Structure Tags

HTML includes a number of tags used to describe the structure of an HTML document. These tags are shown in Table 11.4.

List Tags

HTML provides simple formatting for lists of things using list tags. These tags may be nested to provide multi-level lists. The list tags are shown in Table 11.5.

Phrase Formatting Tags

HTML includes a number of tags for formatting phrases or characters. These tags may appear almost anywhere. Table 11.6 shows the various phrase formatting tags.

Table 11.4 Body Text Structure Tags

Tag	Description
<h1> … <h6>	Headings; six heading levels are defined
<p>	Paragraph; a closing tag is not needed
<pre>	Preformatted text; the text is rendered in a monospace font, and all spacing and line break information is preserved
<blockquote>	Block quote; used to identify a large quotation in which the text is typically rendered as an indented block
 	Line break; a closing tag is not needed
<hr>	Horizontal rule; a horizontal line is drawn across the document

Table 11.5 List Tags

Tag	Description
<li>	List item; identifies an item in most of the list styles (unordered, ordered, directory, and menu); a closing tag is not needed
<ul>	Unordered list; typically rendered as a bulleted list
<ol>	Ordered list; typically rendered as a numbered list
<dir>	Directory list; elements are listed in columns
<menu>	Menu list; typically rendered as a more compact version of an unordered list.
<dl>	Definition or description list; the list consists of a set of terms and definitions or descriptions specified with the <dt> and <dd> tags
<dt>	Data term; specifies a term in a definition list; a closing tag is not needed
<dd>	Data definition or description; specifies the definition or description of the term indicated by the previous <dt> tag

Anchor Tag

The anchor tag is used to specify a hyperlink anchor. Table 11.7 describes the anchor tag and a couple of the most popular anchor attributes. RFC 1866 describes a few more anchor attributes, but these are less commonly used. Consult RFC 1866, section 5.7.3, for more information.

Table 11.6 Phrase Formatting Tags

Tag	Description
<cite>	Book or other citation; typically rendered as italic text
<code>	Source code; used for small sections of source code, which are typically rendered as monospace text; Use <pre> for multi-line code
<em>	Emphasis; typically rendered as italic text
<kbd>	Keyboard entry; indicates text typed by the user, which is typically rendered as monospace text; often used for manuals or other interactive descriptions
<samp>	Sample text; indicates sample text, typically rendered as monospace text.
<strong>	Strong emphasis; typically rendered as bold text.
<var>	Variable; indicates a placeholder, which is typically rendered as italic text.
<b>	Bold
<i>	Italic
<tt>	Teletype
<strike>	Strikethrough

Table 11.7 Anchor Tag

Tag	Attribute	Description
<a>		Hyperlink anchor
	HREF	Specifies a hyperlink destination URI
	NAME	Specifies a named anchor; the named anchor can used by other hypertext links to point to the location of the named anchor *within* a larger document rather than just to the start of the document itself

Image Tag

The image tag is used to include images in HTML documents. Table 11.8 describes the image tag and some of its attributes.

Form Tags

HTML forms provide a flexible method for allowing users to specify data that is sent back to the server. The form tags are shown in Table 11.9.

Table Tags

Table tags allow the tabular layout of HTML data. Table 11.10 describes the various table tags.

Note that this information comes from the draft-ietf-html-tables-06.txt Internet Draft and not from RFC 1866. The information should be treated accordingly. In spite of this, HTML tables are widely implemented in popular user agents and any changes that occur will likely be compatible with the tags described in this section. The full table specification described in draft-ietf-html-tables-06.txt

Table 11.8 Image Tag

Tag	Attribute	Description
<img>		Image
	ALIGN	Specifies the alignment of the image with respect to the current text baseline; options are TOP, MIDDLE, and BOTTOM; popular user agents also implement TEXTTOP, ABSMIDDLE, ABSBOTTOM, BASELINE, LEFT, and RIGHT.
	ALT	Specifies text that can be displayed on user agents that don't have graphic capabilities
	ISMAP	Specifies an image map
	SRC	Specifies the URI of the image content

Table 11.9 Form Tags

Tag	Attribute	Description
<form>		Form
	ACTION	Specifies the action URI for the form which is typically the program or script that will process the form data
	METHOD	Specifies the HTTP method that will be used to process the form data; both GET and POST are legal methods
<input>		A user input field
	TYPE	Indicates the type of user input field; the TYPE attribute can be TEXT, PASSWORD, CHECKBOX, RADIO, IMAGE, HIDDEN, SUBMIT, or RESET
<select>		Specifies an enumerated list of values from which the user can choose
	MULTIPLE	Indicates that more than one item can be selected
	NAME	Specifies the variable name
	SIZE	Specifies the number of visible items
<option>		Specifies an option in a selection list
	SELECTED	Indicates that this option should be selected initially
	VALUE	Indicates the value to be returned if this option is selected
<textarea>		Specifies a multi-line text entry field, similar to <input type=text>
	ROWS	Specifies the height of the field in rows
	COLS	Specifies the width of the field in columns
	NAME	Specifies the variable name

is very complex. This section describes only the most common tags. Consult draft-ietf-html-tables-06.txt or a later version or RFC for more information about some of the less frequently used tags.

Table 11.10 Table Tags

Tag	Attribute	Description
<table>		Specifies a table
	ALIGN	Specifies the horizontal position of the table relative to the current margins; the value may be LEFT, RIGHT, or CENTER
	WIDTH	Specifies the width of the table
	COLS	Specifies the number of columns in the table

Continued

Table 11.10 Table Tags (Continued)

Tag	Attribute	Description
	BORDER	Specifies the width of the border framing the table
	FRAME	Specifies the sides of the table frame to render
	RULES	Specifies where to draw rules within the table
<caption>		Specifies a caption for the table
	ALIGN	Specifies the alignment of the caption relative to the table; the value may be LEFT, RIGHT, TOP, or BOTTOM
<tr>		Specifies the start of a table row
	ALIGN	Specifies the alignment of data within cells in this row
<th>,<td>		The <th> and <td> tags are used to specify table cells; <th> tags specify header cells while <td> tags specify data cells
	NOWRAP	Specifies that text should not be allowed to wrap within the cell
	ROWSPAN	Specifies the number of rows the cell spans
	COLSPAN	Specifies the number of columns the cell spans
	ALIGN	Specifies the alignment of data within the cell

Character Set

Basic Character Set

Table 11.11 shows the basic character set code positions used for HTML. This character set is based on ISO 8859-1.

Table 11.11 Basic HTML Character Set

Reference	Description
� -	Unused
	Horizontal tab
Line feed
-	Unused
Carriage return
-	Unused
	Space
!	Exclamation mark
"	Quotation mark

Continued

Table 11.11 Basic HTML Character Set (Continued)	
Reference	**Description**
#	Number sign
$	Dollar sign
%	Percent sign
&	Ampersand
'	Apostrophe
(	Left parenthesis
)	Right parenthesis
*	Asterisk
+	Plus sign
,	Comma
-	Hyphen
.	Period (fullstop)
/	Solidus (slash)
0 - 9	Digits 0-9
:	Colon
;	Semicolon
<	Less than
=	Equals sign
>	Greater than
?	Question mark
@	Commercial at
A - Z	Letters *A* through *Z*
[	Left square bracket
\	Reverse solidus (backslash)
]	Right square bracket
^	Caret
_	Horizontal bar (underscore)
`	Acute accent
a - z	Letters *a* through *z*
{	Left curly brace
		Vertical bar

Continued

Table 11.11 Basic HTML Character Set (Continued)

Reference	Description
}	Right curly brace
~	Tilde
- Ÿ	Unused
	Non-breaking space
¡	Inverted exclamation
¢	Cent sign
£	Pound Sterling sign
¤	General currency sign
¥	Yen sign
¦	Broken vertical bar
§	Section sign
¨	Umlaut (dieresis)
©	Copyright
ª	Feminine ordinal
«	Left angle quote, guillemotleft
¬	Not sign
	Soft hyphen
®	Registered trademark
¯	Macron accent
°	Degree sign
±	Plus or minus
²	Superscript two
³	Superscript three
´	Acute accent
µ	Micro sign
¶	Paragraph sign
·	Middle dot
¸	Cedilla
¹	Superscript one
º	Masculine ordinal
»	Right angle quote

Continued

Table 11.11 Basic HTML Character Set (Continued)

Reference	Description
¼	Fraction one-fourth
½	Fraction one-half
¾	Fraction three-fourths
¿	Inverted question mark
À	Capital A, grave accent
Á	Capital A, acute accent
Â	Capital A, circumflex accent
Ã	Capital A, tilde
Ä	Capital A, dieresis or umlaut mark
Å	Capital A, ring
Æ	Capital AE dipthong (ligature)
Ç	Capital C, cedilla
È	Capital E, grave accent
É	Capital E, acute accent
Ê	Capital E, circumflex accent
Ë	Capital E, dieresis or umlaut mark
Ì	Capital I, grave accent
Í	Capital I, acute accent
Î	Capital I, circumflex accent
Ï	Capital I, dieresis or umlaut mark
Ð	Capital Eth, Icelandic
Ñ	Capital N, tilde
Ò	Capital O, grave accent
Ó	Capital O, acute accent
Ô	Capital O, circumflex accent
Õ	Capital O, tilde
Ö	Capital O, dieresis or umlaut mark
×	Multiplication sign
Ø	Capital O, slash
Ù	Capital U, grave accent
Ú	Capital U, acute accent

Continued

Table 11.11 Basic HTML Character Set (Continued)

Reference	Description
Û	Capital U, circumflex accent
Ü	Capital U, dieresis or umlaut mark
Ý	Capital Y, acute accent
Þ	Capital THORN, Icelandic
ß	Small sharp s, German (sz ligature)
à	Small a, grave accent
á	Small a, acute accent
â	Small a, circumflex accent
ã	Small a, tilde
ä	Small a, dieresis or umlaut mark
å	Small a, ring
æ	Small ae, dipthong (ligature)
ç	Small c, cedilla
è	Small e, grave accent
é	Small e, acute accent
ê	Small e, circumflex accent
ë	Small e, dieresis or umlaut mark
ì	Small i, grave accent
í	Small i, acute accent
î	Small i, circumflex accent
ï	Small i, dieresis or umlaut mark
ð	Small eth, Icelandic
ñ	Small n, tilde
ò	Small o, grave accent
ó	Small o, acute accent
ô	Small o, circumflex accent
õ	Small o, tilde
ö	Small o, dieresis or umlaut mark
÷	Division sign
ø	Small o, slash
ù	Small u, grave accent

Continued

Table 11.11 Basic HTML Character Set (Continued)

Reference	Description
ú	Small u, acute accent
û	Small u, circumflex accent
ü	Small u, dieresis or umlaut mark
ý	Small y, acute accent
þ	Small thorn, Icelandic
ÿ	Small y, dieresis or umlaut mark

Character Names

HTML defines a set of symbolic names for the non-ASCII characters in the ISO 8859-1 character set. HTML documents can use these symbolic names to reference characters that cannot be easily generated by other means. Table 11.12 shows the symbolic character names.

Table 11.12 HTML Symbolic Character Names

Symbolic Name	Character Code	Description
nbsp		Non-breaking space
iexcl	¡	Inverted exclamation mark
cent	¢	Cent sign
pound	£	Pound Sterling sign
curren	¤	General currency sign
yen	¥	Yen sign
brvbar	¦	Broken (vertical) bar
sect	§	Section sign
uml	¨	Umlaut (dieresis)
copy	©	Copyright sign
ordf	ª	Ordinal indicator, feminine
laquo	«	Angle quotation mark, left
not	¬	Not sign
shy		Soft hyphen
reg	®	Registered sign
macr	¯	Macron

Continued

Table 11.12 HTML Symbolic Character Names (Continued)

Symbolic Name	Character Code	Description
deg	°	Degree sign
plusmn	±	Plus-or-minus sign
sup2	²	Superscript two
sup3	³	Superscript three
acute	´	Acute accent
micro	µ	Micro sign
para	¶	Pilcrow (paragraph sign)
middot	·	Middle dot
cedil	¸	Cedilla
sup1	¹	Superscript one
ordm	º	Ordinal indicator, masculine
raquo	»	Angle quotation mark, right
frac14	¼	Fraction one-quarter
frac12	½	Fraction one-half
frac34	¾	Fraction three-quarters
iquest	¿	Inverted question mark
Agrave	À	Capital A, grave accent
Aacute	Á	Capital A, acute accent
Acirc	Â	Capital A, circumflex accent
Atilde	Ã	Capital A, tilde
Auml	Ä	Capital A, dieresis or umlaut mark
Aring	Å	Capital A, ring
AElig	Æ	Capital AE diphthong (ligature)
Ccedil	Ç	Capital C, cedilla
Egrave	È	Capital E, grave accent
Eacute	É	Capital E, acute accent
Ecirc	Ê	Capital E, circumflex accent
Euml	Ë	Capital E, dieresis or umlaut mark
Igrave	Ì	Capital I, grave accent
Iacute	Í	Capital I, acute accent
Icirc	Î	Capital I, circumflex accent

Continued

Table 11.12 HTML Symbolic Character Names (Continued)

Symbolic Name	Character Code	Description
Iuml	Ï	Capital I, dieresis or umlaut mark
ETH	Ð	Capital Eth, Icelandic
Ntilde	Ñ	Capital N, tilde
Ograve	Ò	Capital O, grave accent
Oacute	Ó	Capital O, acute accent
Ocirc	Ô	Capital O, circumflex accent
Otilde	Õ	Capital O, tilde
Ouml	Ö	Capital O, dieresis or umlaut mark
times	×	Multiplication sign
Oslash	Ø	Capital O, slash
Ugrave	Ù	Capital U, grave accent
Uacute	Ú	Capital U, acute accent
Ucirc	Û	Capital U, circumflex accent
Uuml	Ü	Capital U, dieresis or umlaut mark
Yacute	Ý	Capital Y, acute accent
THORN	Þ	Capital THORN, Icelandic
szlig	ß	Small sharp s, German (sz ligature)
agrave	à	Small a, grave accent
aacute	á	Small a, acute accent
acirc	â	Small a, circumflex accent
atilde	ã	Small a, tilde
auml	ä	Small a, dieresis or umlaut mark
aring	å	Small a, ring
aelig	æ	Small ae, diphthong (ligature)
ccedil	ç	Small c, cedilla
egrave	è	Small e, grave accent
eacute	é	Small e, acute accent
ecirc	ê	Small e, circumflex accent
euml	ë	Small e, dieresis or umlaut mark
igrave	ì	Small i, grave accent
iacute	í	Small i, acute accent

Continued

Table 11.12 HTML Symbolic Character Names (Continued)

Symbolic Name	Character Code	Description
icirc	î	Small i, circumflex accent
iuml	ï	Small i, dieresis or umlaut mark
eth	ð	Small eth, Icelandic
ntilde	ñ	Small n, tilde
ograve	ò	Small o, grave accent
oacute	ó	Small o, acute accent
ocirc	ô	Small o, circumflex accent
otilde	õ	Small o, tilde
ouml	ö	Small o, dieresis or umlaut mark
divide	÷	Division sign
oslash	ø	Small o, slash
ugrave	ù	Small u, grave accent
uacute	ú	Small u, acute accent
ucirc	û	Small u, circumflex accent
uuml	ü	Small u, dieresis or umlaut mark
yacute	ý	Small y, acute accent
thorn	þ	Small thorn, Icelandic
yuml	ÿ	Small y, dieresis or umlaut mark

Hypertext Transfer Protocol

Name

Hypertext Transfer Protocol

Abbreviation

HTTP/1.0

Status

Internet Draft

Specifications

Note: This chapter is based on an Internet Draft. The current Internet Draft describing HTTP, version 1.0, is draft-ietf-http-v10-spec-05.txt, dated 19-Feb-1996. Be sure to check for a newer revision of this document or whether an RFC has been issued based on a version of this document.

Abstract

The Hypertext Transfer Protocol (HTTP) is a simple, application-level protocol used to access hypermedia documents. The protocol is stateless and generic which allows it to be used for many tasks. The primary use of HTTP has been as the basic transport protocol for the World Wide Web.

Related Specifications

HTML (RFC 1866), URLs (RFC 1738, RFC 1808)

See Also

MIME (RFC 1521)

Comments

The World Wide Web has become the "killer application" of the Internet. Its use has exploded and made the formerly text-based Internet an exciting, trendy, pop phenomenon. The explosive increase in Web traffic has driven a rapid evolution for the underlying HTTP protocol. Even before HTTP/1.0 (the version we'll be discussing) was officially documented, many companies actively talked about extensions to the protocol. Several efforts are currently underway to standardize these extensions and fix some performance problems revealed by the rapid increase in Web traffic. See draft-ietf-http-v11-spec-02.txt for more information about HTTP/1.1.

The World Wide Web Consortium (W3C) maintains a large archive of HTTP- and HTML-related technical materials and news at **http://www.w3.org**. Given the quickly evolving nature of the HTTP protocol, this is a good site to keep on your browser hotlist.

Description

An HTTP session is short and sweet. The client opens a connection to the server, sends a request, and awaits a response. When the server receives the request, it generates a response, sends it to the client, and closes the connection. The format of the request and the response messages is described in subsequent sections.

The simple, stateless nature of HTTP allows the creation of proxies. A *proxy* is a server that simply forwards requests from clients or other proxies on to another server or proxy. The second server or proxy sees the original proxy as just another HTTP client. When the proxy receives a response to the forwarded request, it simply returns it to the client. A proxy may implement a cache of recently accessed documents. If the client requests one of these documents, the proxy may return it rather than forwarding the request to the server. Figure 12.1 shows the communication among a user agent, a proxy, and a server.

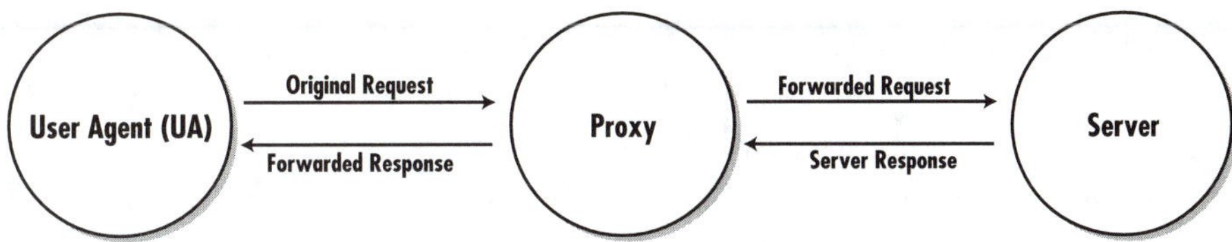

Figure 12.1
HTTP communication among a user agent, proxy, and server.

Transport Information

HTTP servers typically wait for connections on well-known TCP port 80.

Requests

An HTTP client submits requests to an HTTP server. The server responds appropriately by returning a response code and, optionally, the data indicated by the original request.

Each HTTP request includes a request *method.* A method indicates the general operation that the client is requesting the server to perform. Table 12.1 shows the methods defined in HTTP/1.0. HTTP/1.1 includes additional methods not found in HTTP/1.0.

The following sections describe the methods in greater detail.

GET Method

The GET method requests the server to return the information specified by the request URI. In the simple case, the request URI specifies a data file that the server simply includes in the response. The URI may describe data that must be returned by an active process on the server, however.

Table 12.1 HTTP Request Methods

Method Name	Description
GET	Retrieves the information specified by the request URI (Uniform Resource Identifier)
HEAD	Retrieves the header information specified by the request URI, but does not send the entity body
POST	Specifies information that is to be "posted" to the server; the actual action taken depends on the request URI

For instance, the request URI may describe a database query. In this case, the HTTP server would interact with a database engine to return the results of the query in the HTTP response. Another common example is a request URI that indicates that the data to be returned will be generated through a scripting language such as Perl.

If the client request includes the If-Modified-Since header field, the server will treat the request as a *conditional* GET. The server will not return the data if it has not been modified since the data specified in the request. This behavior allows a client to determine whether a cached copy of a URI contains up-to-date data or not. If the data is up-to-date, the client doesn't need the server to resend it.

HEAD Method

The HEAD method functions identically to the GET method except only the response headers are returned; the entity body is not returned. This method is often used to test the validity of hypertext links and to retrieve information about the entity without actually generating additional network traffic by returning the whole entity body.

Note that the If-Modified-Since header is ignored in HEAD method requests. The entity headers are always returned.

POST Method

The POST method is used to send data to the server and requests that it be "posted" appropriately for the resource indicated in the request URI. The POST method is designed to handle cases such as:

- Forms
- Network news (USENET) posting
- Database interaction

The response to the POST method includes status code 201 ("created") along with an entity body that describes the status of the request. Typically, this is a text/HTML entity body that displays a success or failure message for the user.

HTTP/1.0 servers require a valid Content-Length header to accompany all POST method requests.

Responses

The first line of an HTTP response consists of the HTTP version identifier, followed by a three digit status code, followed by a textual description. The status code identifies the result of the method operation to the client. The first digit of the status code indicates the general nature of the result, as shown in Table 12.2.

Table 12.3 describes the currently defined reply codes and their meanings.

Table 12.2 HTTP Reply Code General Descriptions

Code	Category	Description
1xx	Informational	Unused; reserved for future use
2xx	Success	The request was successful
3xx	Redirection	The request requires further action before it can be completed
4xx	Client Error	The request contains a syntax error or cannot be fulfilled
5xx	Server Error	The request was valid but the server cannot fulfill it

Table 12.3 HTTP Reply Codes

Code	Description
200 OK	The request succeeded; the information returned depends on the request method
201 Created	The resource was created by a POST method; the response includes a new URI that can be used to access the new resource
202 Accepted	The request has been accepted for processing but the processing is not yet complete
204 No Content	The server fulfilled the request but there is no new content to send back
300 Multiple Choices	The resource is available in multiple locations: The entity body includes a list of choices from which the user or user agent can select or the server can include a Location header field to indicate a preferred choice
301 Moved Permanently	The resource has been moved permanently; the Location header field indicates the new resource location
302 Moved Temporarily	The resource has been moved temporarily; the client should continue to use the original request URI for future requests
304 Not Modified	This status code is returned if the client issued a GET request with an If-Modified-Since header and the resource has not been modified since the specified date; the response includes the response headers but no entity body

Continued

Table 12.3 HTTP Reply Codes (Continued)

Code	Description
400 Bad Request	The request is malformed in some way an cannot be acted upon
401 Unauthorized	The request requires authorization; the response includes a WWW-Authenticate header field with an authentication challenge
403 Forbidden	The server understood the request but is refusing to fulfill it; authentication will not help
404 Not Found	The server could not find any resource matching the request URI
500 Internal Server Error	The server encountered a condition that prevented it from fulfilling the request
501 Not Implemented	The server does not implement the functionality required to fulfill the request
502 Bad Gateway	The server was acting as a proxy and received an invalid response from the server to which it forwarded the request
503 Service Unavailable	The server is temporarily unable to handle the request because of maintenance or a temporary overload condition

Grammar

The following sections describe the grammar from draft-ietf-http-v10-spec-05.txt. This grammar is taken directly from the text and has not been altered.

Basic Rules

```
OCTET   = <any 8-bit sequence of data>
CHAR = <any US-ASCII character (octets 0 - 127)>
UPALPHA= <any US-ASCII uppercase letter "A".."Z">
LOALPHA= <any US-ASCII lowercase letter "a".."z">
ALPHA   = UPALPHA | LOALPHA
DIGIT   = <any US-ASCII digit "0".."9">
CTL  = <any US-ASCII control character
     (octets 0 - 31) and DEL (127)>
CR= <US-ASCII CR, carriage return (13)>
LF= <US-ASCII LF, linefeed (10)>
SP= <US-ASCII SP, space (32)>
HT= <US-ASCII HT, horizontal-tab (9)>
<">  = <US-ASCII double-quote mark (34)>
CRLF = CR LF
LWS  = [CRLF] 1*( SP | HT )
TEXT = <any OCTET except CTLs,
     but including LWS>
HEX  =  "A" | "B" | "C" | "D" | "E" | "F"
     | "a" | "b" | "c" | "d" | "e" | "f" | DIGIT
```

```
word =  token | quoted-string
token  =  1*<any CHAR except CTLs or tspecials>
tspecials =  "(" | ")" | "<" | ">" | "@"
     | "," | ";" | ":" | "\" | <">
     | "/" | "[" | "]" | "?" | "="
     | "{" | "}" | SP | HT
comment= "(" *( ctext | comment ) ")"
ctext  = <any TEXT excluding "(" and ")">
quoted-string  = ( <"> *(qdtext) <"> )
qdtext  = <any CHAR except <"> and CTLs,
     but including LWS>
```

HTTP Version

```
HTTP-Version= "HTTP" "/" 1*DIGIT "." 1*DIGIT
```

General URI Syntax

```
URI  = ( absoluteURI | relativeURI ) [ "#" fragment ]

absoluteURI = scheme ":" *( uchar | reserved )

relativeURI = net_path | abs_path | rel_path

net_path  = "//" net_loc [ abs_path ]
abs_path  = "/" rel_path
rel_path  = [ path ] [ ";" params ] [ "?" query ]

path = fsegment *( "/" segment )
fsegment  = 1*pchar
segment= *pchar

params  = param *( ";" param )
param  = *( pchar | "/" )

scheme  = 1*( ALPHA | DIGIT | "+" | "-" | "." )
net_loc= *( pchar | ";" | "?" )
query  = *( uchar | reserved )
fragment  = *( uchar | reserved )

pchar  = uchar | ":" | "@" | "&" | "=" | "+"
uchar  = unreserved | escape
unreserved  = ALPHA | DIGIT | safe | extra | national

escape  = "%" HEX HEX
reserved  = ";" | "/" | "?" | ":" | "@" | "&" | "=" | "+"
extra  = "!" | "*" | "'" | "(" | ")" | ","
```

```
safe = "$" | "-" | "_" | "."
unsafe = CTL | SP | <"> | "#" | "%" | "<" | ">"
national = <any OCTET excluding ALPHA, DIGIT,
     reserved, extra, safe, and unsafe>

http_URL = "http:" "//" host [ ":" port ] [ abs_path ]
host = <A legal Internet host domain name
     or IP address (in dotted-decimal form),
     as defined by Section 2.1 of RFC 1123>
port = *DIGIT
```

Date and Time Syntax

```
HTTP-date = rfc1123-date | rfc850-date | asctime-date

rfc1123-date= wkday "," SP date1 SP time SP "GMT"
rfc850-date = weekday "," SP date2 SP time SP "GMT"
asctime-date= wkday SP date3 SP time SP 4DIGIT

date1  = 2DIGIT SP month SP 4DIGIT
     ; day month year (e.g., 02 Jun 1982)
date2  = 2DIGIT "-" month "-" 2DIGIT
     ; day-month-year (e.g., 02-Jun-82)
date3  = month SP ( 2DIGIT | ( SP 1DIGIT ))
     ; month day (e.g., Jun 2)

time = 2DIGIT ":" 2DIGIT ":" 2DIGIT
     ; 00:00:00 - 23:59:59

wkday  = "Mon" | "Tue" | "Wed"
     | "Thu" | "Fri" | "Sat" | "Sun"

weekday= "Monday" | "Tuesday" | "Wednesday"
     | "Thursday" | "Friday" | "Saturday" | "Sunday"

month  = "Jan" | "Feb" | "Mar" | "Apr"
     | "May" | "Jun" | "Jul" | "Aug"
     | "Sep" | "Oct" | "Nov" | "Dec"
```

Character Sets

```
charset= "US-ASCII"
     | "ISO-8859-1" | "ISO-8859-2" | "ISO-8859-3"
     | "ISO-8859-4" | "ISO-8859-5" | "ISO-8859-6"
     | "ISO-8859-7" | "ISO-8859-8" | "ISO-8859-9"
     | "ISO-2022-JP" | "ISO-2022-JP-2" | "ISO-2022-KR"
     | "UNICODE-1-1" | "UNICODE-1-1-UTF-7" | "UNICODE-1-1-UTF-8"
     | token
```

Content Codings

```
content-coding = "x-gzip" | "x-compress" | token
```

Media Types

```
media-type  = type "/" subtype *( ";" parameter )
type = token
subtype= token

parameter = attribute "=" value
attribute = token
value   = token | quoted-string
```

Product Tokens

```
product= token ["/" product-version]
product-version  = token
```

HTTP Message Types

```
HTTP-message= Simple-Request ; HTTP/0.9 messages
     | Simple-Response
     | Full-Request ; HTTP/1.0 messages
     | Full-Response

Full-Request= Request-Line; Section 5.1
     *( General-Header; Section 4.3
     | Request-Header ; Section 5.2
     | Entity-Header ); Section 7.1
     CRLF
     [ Entity-Body ]  ; Section 7.2

Full-Response  = Status-Line ; Section 6.1
     *( General-Header; Section 4.3
     | Response-Header; Section 6.2
     | Entity-Header ); Section 7.1
     CRLF
     [ Entity-Body ]  ; Section 7.2

Simple-Request = "GET" SP Request-URI CRLF
Simple-Response  = [ Entity-Body ]
```

Header Fields

```
HTTP-header = field-name ":" [ field-value ] CRLF
field-name  = token
field-value = *( field-content | LWS )
```

```
field-content  = <the OCTETs making up the field-value
     and consisting of either *TEXT or combinations
     of token, tspecials, and quoted-string>
General-Header = Date ; Section 10.6
     | Pragma  ; Section 10.12
```

Requests

```
Full-Request= Request-Line; Section 5.1
     *( General-Header; Section 4.3
     | Request-Header ; Section 5.2
     | Entity-Header ); Section 7.1
     CRLF
     [ Entity-Body ]  ; Section 7.2

Request-Line= Method SP Request-URI SP HTTP-Version CRLF
Method  = "GET"   ; Section 8.1
     | "HEAD"  ; Section 8.2
     | "POST"  ; Section 8.3
     | extension-method
extension-method = token
Request-URI  = absoluteURI | abs_path
Request-Header = Authorization  ; Section 10.2
     | From  ; Section 10.8
     | If-Modified-Since ; Section 10.9
     | Referer ; Section 10.13
     | User-Agent; Section 10.15
```

Responses

```
Full-Response  = Status-Line  ; Section 6.1
     *( General-Header; Section 4.3
     | Response-Header; Section 6.2
     | Entity-Header ); Section 7.1
     CRLF
     [ Entity-Body ]  ; Section 7.2

Status-Line  = HTTP-Version SP Status-Code SP Reason-Phrase CRLF
Status-Code  = "200"  ; OK
     | "201"; Created
     | "202"; Accepted
     | "204"; No Content
     | "301"; Moved Permanently
     | "302"; Moved Temporarily
     | "304"; Not Modified
     | "400"; Bad Request
     | "401"; Unauthorized
```

```
    | "403" ; Forbidden
    | "404" ; Not Found
    | "500" ; Internal Server Error
    | "501" ; Not Implemented
    | "502" ; Bad Gateway
    | "503" ; Service Unavailable
    | extension-code

extension-code = 3DIGIT

Reason-Phrase  = *<TEXT, excluding CR, LF>

Response-Header  = Location  ; Section 10.11
    | Server  ; Section 10.14
    | WWW-Authenticate  ; Section 10.16
```

Entities

```
Entity-Header  = Allow  ; Section 10.1
    | Content-Encoding  ; Section 10.3
    | Content-Length ; Section 10.4
    | Content-Type ; Section 10.5
    | Expires ; Section 10.7
    | Last-Modified  ; Section 10.10
    | extension-header
extension-header = HTTP-header

Entity-Body = *OCTET
```

Specific Header Fields

```
Allow  = "Allow" ":" 1#method
Authorization  = "Authorization" ":" credentials
Content-Encoding = "Content-Encoding" ":" content-coding
Content-Length = "Content-Length" ":" 1*DIGIT
Content-Type= "Content-Type" ":" media-type
Date = "Date" ":" HTTP-date
Expires= "Expires" ":" HTTP-date
From = "From" ":" mailbox
If-Modified-Since= "If-Modified-Since" ":" HTTP-date
Last-Modified  = "Last-Modified" ":" HTTP-date
Location  = "Location" ":" absoluteURI
Pragma  = "Pragma" ":" 1#pragma-directive
pragma-directive = "no-cache" | extension-pragma
extension-pragma = token [ "=" word ]
Referer= "Referer" ":" ( absoluteURI | relativeURI )
Server  = "Server" ":" 1*( product | comment )
```

```
User-Agent   = "User-Agent" ":" 1*( product | comment )
WWW-Authenticate = "WWW-Authenticate" ":" 1#challenge
```

Authentication

```
auth-scheme = token
auth-param  = token "=" quoted-string
challenge = auth-scheme 1*SP realm *( "," auth-param )
realm  = "realm" "=" realm-value
realm-value = quoted-string

credentials = basic-credentials
     | ( auth-scheme #auth-param )

basic-credentials= "Basic" SP basic-cookie
basic-cookie= <base64 [5] encoding of userid-password,
     except not limited to 76 char/line>
userid-password  = [ token ] ":" *TEXT
```

13 Internet Control Message Protocol

Name

Internet Control Message Protocol

Abbreviation

ICMP

Status

Required Standard (STD 5)

Specifications

RFC 792

Abstract

The Internet Control Message Protocol (ICMP) is used to communicate IP status and error messages between hosts and routers. ICMP messages are sent to inform a host that, for example, a datagram cannot reach its destination, a router is overloaded and doesn't have enough buffering capacity to forward a datagram, or a shorter path exists to the destination host than through this intermediate router.

Related Specifications

IP (RFC 791), IGMP (RFC 1112), RFC 950 (define the Address Mask Request/Reply messages)

Description

ICMP is used to send Internet control messages between destination and source hosts or between an intermediate router and a host. The messages may indicate error conditions that have occurred with datagrams or additional management information. ICMP uses IP to route its messages between hosts. In spite of this property, ICMP is closely tied to IP and is required to be implemented with IP.

Message Formats

ICMP data is carried as the payload of an IP datagram. ICMP specifies additional message formats within this payload area.

Basic ICMP Header

Each ICMP message starts with the same three fields—Type, Code, and Checksum—which are shown in Figure 13.1.

The Type field indicates the basic ICMP message type. It defines the format of the remainder of the message. The Code field indicates why the message is being sent. Each message type defines a number of type-specific code values. The Checksum field is used to guard against errors in the ICMP message data. The Checksum field is the standard Internet checksum, the 16-bit one's complement of the one's complement sum of the message data. The checksum includes the basic ICMP header. For the purposes of the checksum calculation, the checksum field is set to zero.

Figure 13.1

The basic ICMP header fields.

ICMP Message Types

ICMP defines 13 message types, as shown in Table 13.1.

Destination Unreachable Message

Type

3

Code

0 = net unreachable

1 = host unreachable

2 = protocol unreachable

3 = port unreachable

4 = fragmentation needed and DF set

5 = source route failed

6 = destination network unknown

7 = destination host unknown

8 = source host isolated

Table 13.1 ICMP Message Types

Type Code	Description
0	Echo Reply
3	Destination Unreachable
4	Source Quench
5	Redirect
8	Echo
11	Time Exceeded
12	Parameter Problem
13	Timestamp
14	Timestamp Reply
15	Information Request
16	Information Reply
17	Address Mask Request
18	Address Mask Reply

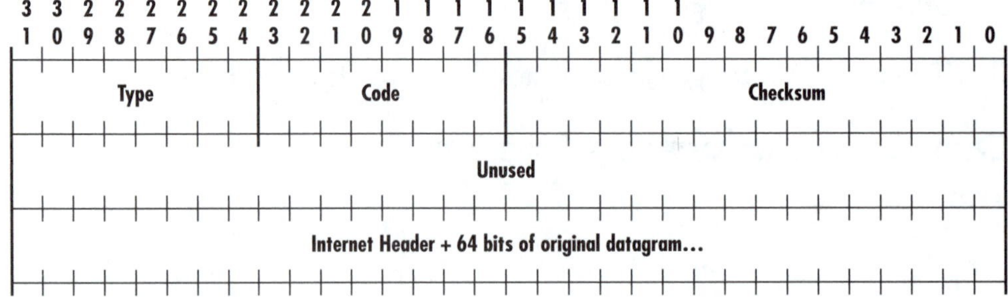

Figure 13.2

Destination Unreachable Message Format.

9 = communication with destination network administratively prohibited

10 = communication with destination host administratively prohibited

11 = network unreachable for type of service

12 = host unreachable for type of service

Internet Header + 64 bits of original datagram

The receiving host uses this data to match the ICMP message to the process that sent the original datagram. In particular, the port numbers used by an upper-layer protocol (UDP or TCP, for example) are assumed to be in the first 64 bits beyond the IP header.

Description

A destination unreachable message is sent to the host that originated a datagram that cannot be delivered because the destination is unreachable. This may occur for one of the following reasons:

- A router may determine that the network on which the host resides is unreachable (the distance to the network in the router's tables may be set to infinity).
- The IP module in the destination host may find the indicated protocol is not available.
- The Don't Fragment bit in the IP header is set, but a router would have to fragment the datagram to continue forwarding it toward the destination.

Codes 2 and 3 are sent by a host.

Source Quench Message

Type

4

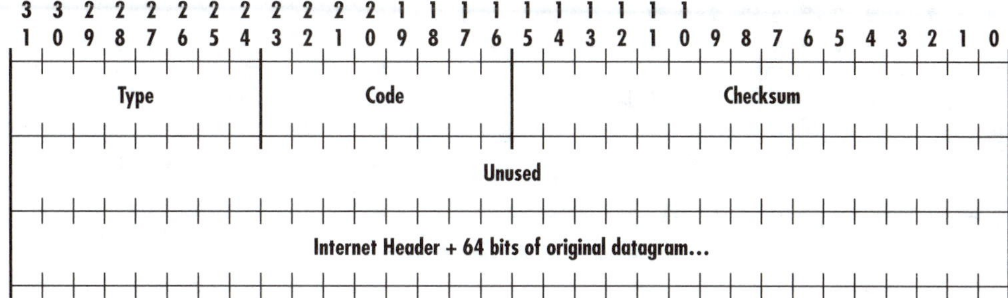

Figure 13.3

Source Quench Message Format.

Code

0

Internet Header + 64 bits of original datagram

The receiving host uses this data to match the ICMP message to the process that sent the original datagram. In particular, the port numbers used by an upper-layer protocol (UDP or TCP, for example) are assumed to be in the first 64 bits beyond the IP header.

Description

The Source Quench message is sent to a host when an intermediate router or the destination host can't keep up with the source host's transmission rate. A Source Quench message may be sent by a router to a datagram source when the router is saturated and it has just dropped a datagram. A receiving host may send a Source Quench message to the source host if its receive buffers are filling. Upon receipt of Source Quench message, the source host should cut back its output rate until it no longer receives Source Quench messages. It may then increase its transmission rate until it again receives Source Quench messages.

Redirect Message

Type

5

Code

0 = redirect datagrams for the Network

1 = redirect datagrams for the Host

2 = redirect datagrams for the Type of Service and Network

3 = redirect datagrams for the Type of Service and Host

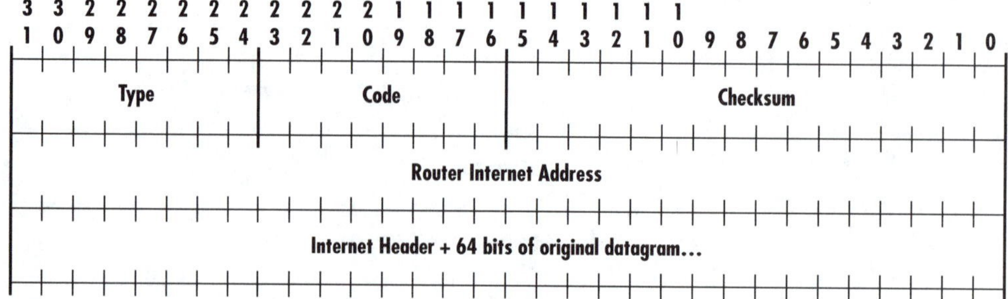

Figure 13.4

Redirect Message Format.

Router Internet Address

This field specifies the address of the router that can better service the network specified in the original datagram. Further traffic should be sent to the specified router instead of the router originating the Redirect message.

Internet Header + 64 bits of original datagram

The receiving host uses this data to match the ICMP message to the process that sent the original datagram. In particular, the port numbers used by an upper-layer protocol (UDP or TCP, for example) are assumed to be in the first 64 bits beyond the IP header.

Description

A router, R1, sends a Redirect message to a host when it determines that a datagram that originated from the host must be forwarded to another router, R2, that is directly reachable from the host. This allows the host to send further datagrams addressed to the original destination directly to the optimal first-hop router, R2, thereby increasing the network efficiency.

Redirect messages are not sent for datagrams that have source routing options, even when a more optimal path exists to the destination.

Echo/Echo Reply Message

Type

8 = Echo

0 = Echo Reply

Code

0

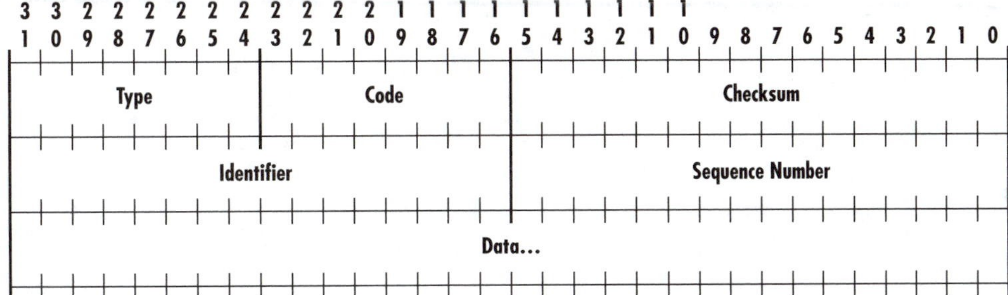

Figure 13.5
Echo/Echo Reply Message Format.

Identifier

A number used to match Echoes with Echo Replies.

Sequence Number

A number used to match Echoes with Echo Replies.

Description

Echoes are used to help determine whether a host is reachable in the network. A host receiving an Echo message forms an Echo Reply message by simply reversing the IP source and destination addresses, setting the ICMP Type field to zero (Echo Reply), and recomputing the ICMP Checksum field. All the data in the original Echo message is returned unchanged in the Echo Reply message.

The Identifier and Sequence Number can be set to anything the Echo sender desires and must be returned unchanged in the Echo Reply. The Identifier field often carries a session number or port identifier. The Sequence Number is often used to detect the loss of an Echo Reply when multiple, sequential Echo messages are sent.

Time Exceeded Message

Type

11

Code

0 = time to live exceeded in transit

1 = fragment reassembly time exceeded

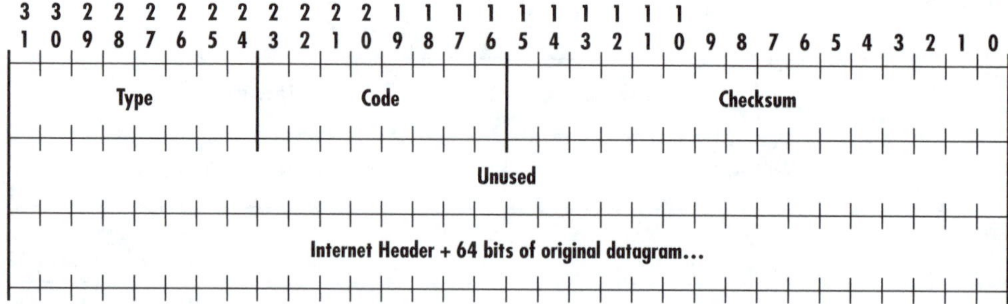

Figure 13.6

Time Exceeded Message Format.

Internet Header + 64 bits of original datagram

The receiving host uses this data to match the ICMP message to the process that sent the original datagram. In particular, the port numbers used by an upper-layer protocol (UDP or TCP, for example) are assumed to be in the first 64 bits beyond the IP header.

Description

A Time Exceeded message is sent to a host under two circumstances:

- A router finds a datagram with the Time to Live field set to zero. The router discards the datagram and sends an ICMP Time Exceeded message back to the source of the datagram with the Code field set to zero.
- A host does not receive all the fragments of a datagram before its local reassembly timer expires. The host discards all the fragments and sends an ICMP Time Exceeded message back to the source of the datagram with the Code field set to 1.

Parameter Problem Message

Type

12

Code

0 = micellaneous parameter problem

2 = required option is missing

Pointer

Identifies the octet where an error occurred.

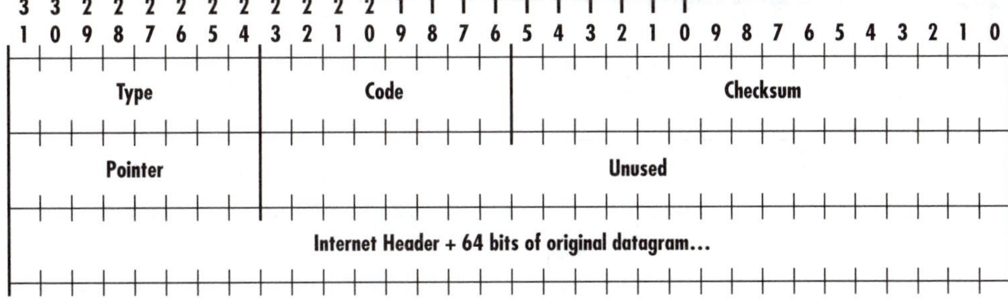

Figure 13.7

Parameter Problem Message Format.

Internet Header + 64 bits of original datagram

The receiving host uses this data to match the ICMP message to the process that sent the original datagram. In particular, the port numbers used by an upper-layer protocol (UDP or TCP, for example) are assumed to be in the first 64 bits beyond the IP header.

Description

The Parameter Problem message is sent to a host when a router or host processing a datagram finds a problem with the information in the IP. This message is only sent if the datagram had to be discarded as a result of the problem. The Pointer field indicates the first octet of data that caused the problem. The Pointer field is zero-based. For instance, 1 indicates a problem with the Type of Service field, while 20 indicates a problem with the first option.

Timestamp/Timestamp Reply Message

Type

13 = Timestamp

14 = Timestamp Reply

Code

0

Identifier

A number used to match Timestamp messages with Timestamp Replies.

Sequence Number

A number used to match Echoes with Echo Replies.

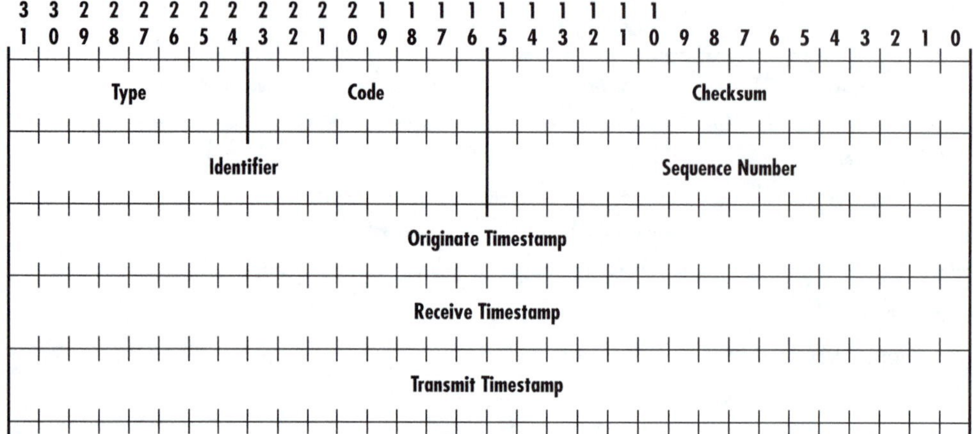

Figure 13.8

Timestamp/Timestamp Reply Message Format.

Description

A Timestamp message is used to determine the latency on the path between the sender and the receiver. The receiver of a Timestamp message forms a Timestamp Reply message by reversing the IP Source and Destination Address fields, setting the ICMP Type field to 14 (Timestamp Reply), updating the Timestamp fields appropriately, and recomputing the ICMP Checksum field.

The Originate Timestamp field is set to the time the sender sent the Timestamp message. The Receive Timestamp field is set to the time the receiver received the Timestamp. The Transmit Timestamp is set to the time the receiver sent back the Timestamp Reply message.

All Timestamp fields are set to the number of milliseconds since midnight UTC. If the host does not have a clock source available that will provide the number of milliseconds with respect to UTC, the host must set the high-order bit of the Timestamp field to indicate the field stores a nonstandard value.

As with Echo/Echo Reply, the Identifier and Sequence Number fields are used to match Timestamp and Timestamp Reply messages.

Information Request/Information Reply Message

Type

15 = Information Request

16 = Information Reply

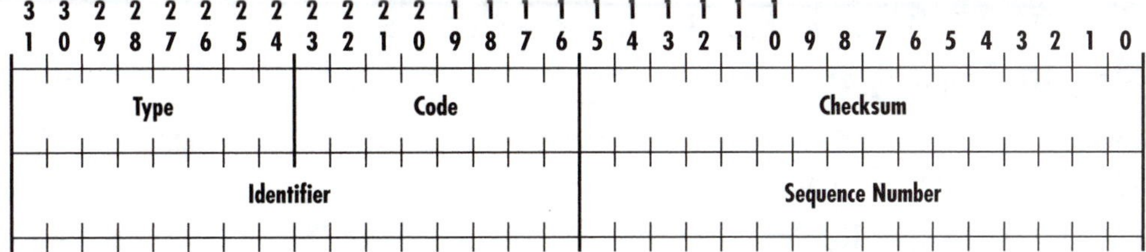

Figure 13.9

Information Request/Information Reply Message Format.

Code

0

Identifier

A number used to match requests with replies.

Sequence Number

A number used to match requests with replies.

Description

The Information Request/Reply messages are used by a host to determine the network number the host resides on. The originating host may set the network portion of the IP source and destination addresses to zero, indicating *this network*. The replying IP module should fully specify the correct network portion of the addresses when it sends the reply.

As with Echo/Echo Reply, the Identifier and Sequence Number fields are set by the originating host to assist it in matching requests with replies. The receiver of a request must not alter the Identifier and Sequence Number fields.

An Information Reply may be formed by simply reversing the IP source and destination addresses (while setting the correct network number information), setting the ICMP Type code to 16, and recomputing the ICMP Checksum field.

The Information Request/Information Reply messages are now obsolete and should not be implemented by hosts. Address discovery mechanisms such as RARP and BOOTP are better suited to perform this function.

Address Mask Request/Address Mask Reply Message

Type

17 = Address Mask Request

18 = Address Mask Reply

Code

0

Identifier

A number used to match requests with replies.

Sequence Number

A number used to match requests with replies.

Address Mask

A 32-bit IP subnet address mask.

Description

Hosts and routers can use the Address Mask Request message to request the subnet address mask of the network on which they reside when they first boot. The host or router generates an Address Mask Request message and broadcasts it on the local network. A router that receives the request message should return the appropriate subnet mask in the reply message.

If the requesting host does not know its own IP address, it should set the source address of the request message to zero. In this case, the responding router will address the reply message to the broadcast address.

Note that this message was defined in RFC 950. Although there are many other ways for a host to learn its subnet mask this method is still supported.

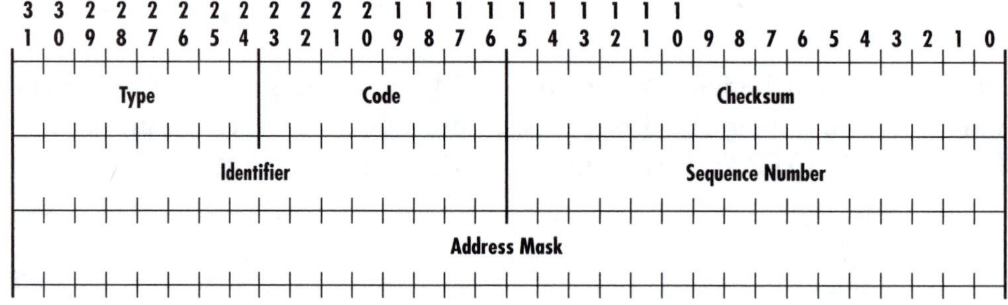

Figure 13.10 Address Mask Request/Address Mask Reply Message Format.

14 Internet Group Management Protocol

Name

Internet Group Management Protocol

Abbreviation

IGMP

Status

Recommended Standard (STD 5)

Specifications

RFC 1112

Abstract

The Internet Group Management Protocol (IGMP) allows an Internet host to participate in IP multicasting services. Using multicast services, a host can send a datagram to group of hosts that have joined a multicast group. Multicasting is similar to broadcasting in that more than one host can receive the datagram. Multicasting, however, is more efficient because only those hosts that join the multicast group and are interested in the data will receive it, rather than all hosts as with broadcasting.

Related Specifications

IP (RFC 791), ICMP (RFC 792)

Description

The Internet Group Management Protocol (IGMP) is used to manage the use of IP multicast groups. IP multicast addressing is used to send a datagram to a group of hosts that may be located on a local subnetwork or anywhere in the world. IP multicast is commonly used to transmit video or audio-conferencing data that is received by many receivers throughout the Internet.

IGMP allows hosts to register as members of a multicast group and receive datagrams addressed to the group. The following sections introduce some aspects of the IP multicast system and the IGMP protocol.

Multicast Addressing

IP multicasting uses a special group of addresses distinct from normal IP addresses. All class D IP addresses are reserved as IP multicast addresses and will never be assigned to individual hosts. Class D addresses are distinguished by the binary value 1110 as the high-order address bits. This means that all IP addresses in the range 224.0.0.0 through 239.255.255.255 are IP multicast addresses.

Each multicast address represents a group of receiver nodes. If a packet is addressed to a multicast address, all nodes in the group will (most likely) receive it. Because IP multicast relies on IP datagrams, it is not totally reliable, and the possiblity exists for some members of a multicast group to receive a datagram while others may not.

Two IP multicast addresses, 224.0.0.0 and 224.0.0.1, are special addresses. The 224.0.0.0 address is not assigned to any multicast group. The 224.0.0.1 address is used to address all nodes participating in IP multicast on the local subnetwork. Other special addresses exist, as shown in Table 14.1.

Datalink Address Mapping

Typical implementations of IP over standard datalink protocols map IP unicast and broadcast addresses to equivalent datalink addressing forms. This is also the case with IP multicast addresses. IP multicast addresses are mapped to 48-bit Ethernet or IEEE 802 addresses by replacing the low-order 23 bits of a special

Table 14.1 Special Multicast Addresses

Address	Description	Reference
224.0.0.0	Base address (reserved)	[RFC1112]
224.0.0.1	All systems on this subnet	[RFC1112]
224.0.0.2	All routers on this subnet	
224.0.0.3	Unassigned	
224.0.0.4	DVMRP routers	[RFC1075]
224.0.0.5	OSPFIGP all routers	[RFC1583]
224.0.0.6	OSPFIGP designated routers	[RFC1583]
224.0.0.7	ST routers	[RFC1190]
224.0.0.8	ST hosts	[RFC1190]
224.0.0.9	RIP2 routers	
224.0.0.10	IGRP routers	
224.0.0.11	Mobile agents	
224.0.0.12–224.0.0.255	Unassigned	
224.0.1.0	VMTP managers group	[RFC1045]
224.0.1.1	Network Time Protocol	[RFC1119]
224.0.1.2	SGI Dogfight	
224.0.1.3	rwhod	
224.0.1.4	VNP	
224.0.1.5	Artificial horizons - aviator	
224.0.1.6	Name Service Server	
224.0.1.7	AUDIONEWS—Audio News Multicast	
224.0.1.8	Sun NIS+ information service	
224.0.1.9	Multicast Transport Protocol	
224.0.1.10	IETF-1-LOW-AUDIO	
224.0.1.11	IETF-1-AUDIO	
224.0.1.12	IETF-1-VIDEO	
224.0.1.13	IETF-2-LOW-AUDIO	
224.0.1.14	IETF-2-AUDIO	
224.0.1.15	IETF-2-VIDEO	
224.0.1.16	MUSIC-SERVICE	

Continued

Table 14.1 Special Multicast Addresses (Continued)

Address	Description	Reference
224.0.1.17	SEANET-TELEMETRY	
224.0.1.18	SEANET-IMAGE	
224.0.1.19	MLOADD	
224.0.1.20	Any private experiment	
224.0.1.21	DVMRP on MOSPF	
224.0.1.22	SVRLOC	
224.0.1.23	XINGTV	
224.0.1.24	microsoft-ds	
224.0.1.25	nbc-pro	
224.0.1.26	nbc-pfn	
224.0.1.27-224.0.1.255	Unassigned	
224.0.2.1	"rwho" group (BSD, unofficial)	
224.0.2.2	SUN RPC PMAPPROC_CALLIT	
224.0.3.000–224.0.3.255	RFE generic service	
224.0.4.000–224.0.4.255	RFE individual conferences	
224.0.5.000–224.0.5.127	CDPD groups	
224.0.5.128–224.0.5.255	Unassigned	
224.0.6.000–224.0.6.127	Cornell ISIS project	
224.0.6.128–224.0.6.255	Unassigned	
224.1.0.0–224.1.255.255	ST multicast groups	[RFC1190]
224.2.0.0–224.2.255.255	Multimedia conference calls	
224.252.0.0–224.255.255.255	DIS transient groups	
232.0.0.0–232.255.255.255	VMTP transient groups	[RFC1045]

multicast datalink address with the 23 low-order bits of the IP multicast address. The special 48-bit datalink multicast address is 1.0.94.0.0.0.

Datalink hardware address filters can be programmed to recognize the multicast addresses corresponding to the multicast groups to which the host currently belongs. Note that not all the significant IP multicast address bits are represented in the equivalent datalink multicast address. Because of this, more than one IP multicast address may map to the same datalink multicast address. This means that host implementations will still have to check the destination addresses of multicast packets to determine if they belong to the addressed group. If not, the IP implementation should discard the packet.

IGMP Basics

Multicast routers use the knowledge of whether hosts on the local subnets to which they are attached are members of given multicast groups, to decide whether to forward IP datagrams addressed to multicast groups. Routers gather their knowledge of group membership using a polling technique.

Multicast routers periodically poll for group membership using the IGMP query message. The query message is addressed to the all-hosts multicast address (224.0.0.1) and carry an IP time-to-live of 1, so all participating multicast hosts on the local subnet receive the query. Hosts respond to the query by generating membership report messages for each group of which they are a member, except the all-hosts group.

The reports are scheduled with a random delay, so the reports from each node don't occur all at once. Each report is addressed to the IP multicast address to which it refers. Other members of the same multicast group monitor the reports returned by other group members and cancel their own reports if another node generates a report before they themselves do. This behavior causes only one report to be generated per multicast group, which is sufficient for the multicast router to determine which groups exist on the local subnet. Figure 14.1 shows the host behavior as a state machine.

RFC 1112 provides more detail about the generation of queries and reports.

Protocol State Machine

Figure 14.1 shows the state machine kept by each host participating in IP multicast. The state machine is implemented on a per-group basis.

The Non-Member state represents groups of which the host is not a member.

The Idle Member state describes groups of which the host is a member when no query has been received.

The host transitions to the Delaying Member state when it is a member of the group and it has scheduled the generation of an IGMP report at some point in the future.

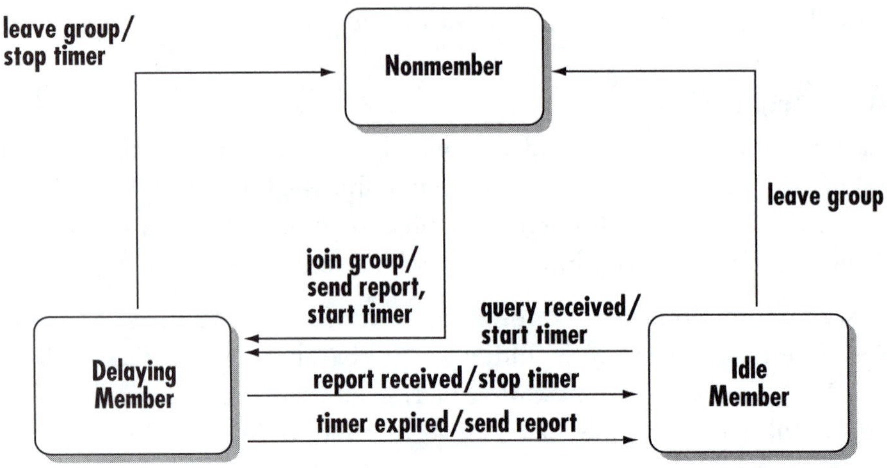

Figure 14.1
IGMP host state machine.

The timer referred to in the figure controls the generation of reports. It is set to a random value when a query is received. If the timer expires before the host receives a report for the same group generated by another node, the host sends a report itself and transitions from the Delaying Member state to the Idle Member state. If the host receives a report before the timer expires, the host stops the timer, cancels the generation of its own report, and transitions from the Delaying Member state to the Idle Member state.

Joining or leaving a group moves the host between the Non-Member state and one of the Member states, as appropriate.

Message Format

Figure 14.2 shows the IGMP message format. IGMP messages are carried in IP datagrams and are identified by IP protocol number 2.

The following is a brief summary of the fields shown in Figure 14.2:

Version The Version field identifies the IGMP protocol version number. The IGMP version described in RFC 1112 is version 1.

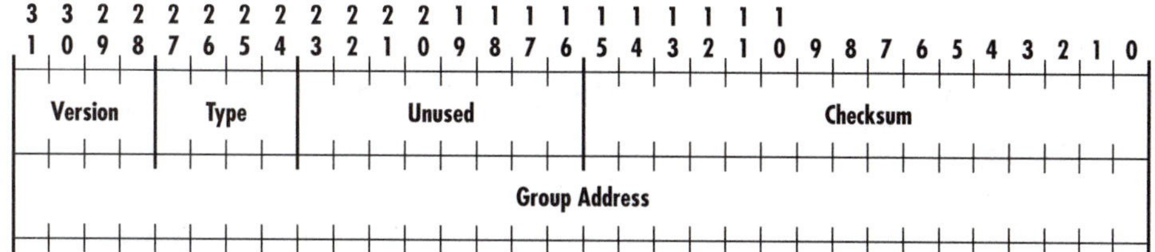

Figure 14.2
IGMP message format.

Type The Type field identifies the type of IGMP message:

- 1 = Host membership query
- 2 = Host membership report

Unused This field is reserved for future use and must be set to 0.

Checksum This field identifies the standard Internet checksum computed over the IGMP message data. The Internet checksum is the one's complement of the one's complement sum of the message data. The checksum field is set to 0 before computing the checksum over the message data.

Group Address In a host membership query message, the Group Address field is set to zero and ignored by receivers. In a host membership report message, the Group Address field is set to the IP group address to which the report refers.

15 Internet Message Access Protocol

Name

Internet Message Access Protocol, Version 4

Abbreviation

IMAP4

Status

Elective Proposed Standard

Specifications

RFC 1730, RFC 1731

Abstract

The Internet Message Access Protocol (IMAP4 or IMAP) allows a client to access and manipulate email messages stored on a remote server. Using IMAP, a client can move mail to and from the server, create remote message folders, and move messages between folders. Whereas the POP3 protocol provides for the simple retrieval of mail, IMAP provides this functionality in addition to a complete system for remote mail filing.

Related Specifications

Format of Electronic Mail Messages (RFC 822), MIME (RFC 1521)

See Also

POP3 (RFC 1725), SMTP (RFC 821)

Description

The Internet Message Access Protocol (IMAP) is a sophisticated protocol for email message management. IMAP includes the basic functionality of POP3, allowing a user to retrieve mail from a remote mailbox, and adds further sophisticated filing, searching, and parsing functionality. IMAP is much more powerful than POP3 and allows the client to manage a set of remote mailboxes on the server, and to move messages between mailboxes and from the client to the server.

IMAP can also search a folder for mail messages that meet a given criteria. All searching is performed on the server itself; the client does not have to download messages just to search them. The IMAP server also includes RFC 822 and MIME knowledge, and can parse messages and return portions of them to the client. The client can use this functionality to determine whether to retrieve the whole message or just a portion that the user might be interested in.

Transport Information

The IMAP4 server listens for connections on well-known TCP port 143.

Protocol States

An IMAP session progresses through a series of states. Figure 15.1 shows the states and the transitions between them. Certain commands can only be issued in certain states, and other commands cause transitions between states. It is important for the client and server to keep track of the current session state to remain synchronized.

Commands and Responses

IMAP commands consist of a short identifier, called a *tag*, followed by the command name, which in turn is followed by one or more parameters, depending

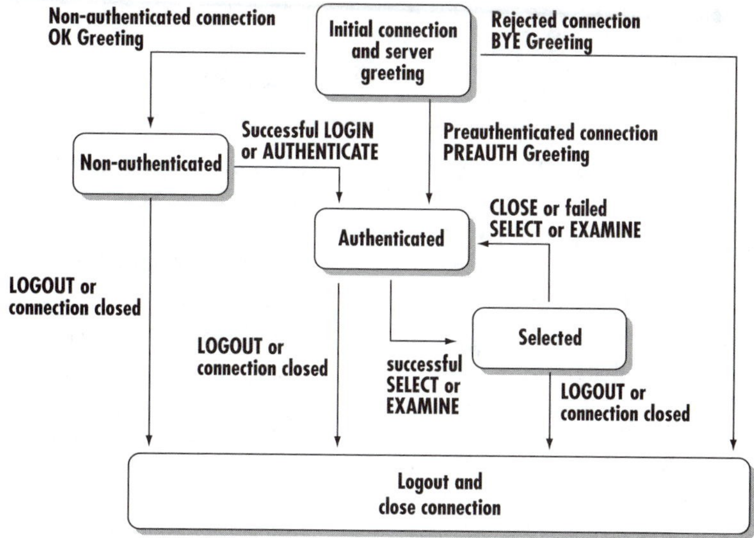

Figure 15.1
The IMAP4 session states.

on the particular command. IMAP allows the client to start a second command before the first command is finished. The tag included with a command is included in the server reply. The tags allow the client to correlate replies with the command that originally generated them.

Sometimes the server generates spontaneous responses that do not simply indicate the success or failure of a command given by the client. These are called *untagged responses* and have "*" as their tag value rather than a tag assigned by the client.

The following sections summarize the IMAP4 commands and their corresponding responses. Note that the IMAP4 command syntax is quite sophisticated. The tables in the following sections supply only summary information. For more complete information about the syntax of a particular command or response, consult the *Formal Syntax* section or see RFC 1730.

Commands

Table 15.1 lists the complete IMAP4 command set. Note that the commands are sorted according to the session state they are appropriate for. Some commands can be sent by the client in all session states while others are only valid in certain session states.

Table 15.1 IMAP4 Commands

Group	Command	Description
All States		
	CAPABILITY	Requests a list of capabilities the server supports; the server returns an untagged response indicating the server capabilities; the only current capability is "IMAP4."
	NOOP	Does nothing; can be used to reset an inactivity timer at the server
	LOGOUT	Tells the server that the client is ending the session; the server returns an untagged "BYE" response
Non-Authenticated State		
	AUTHENTICATE *mechanism-name*	Indicates that the client wants to authenticate using the specified authentication mechanism
	LOGIN *user-name password*	Simple login using a user name and password pair carried in the clear; note that this method is not as secure as using the AUTHENTICATE command
Authenticated State		
	SELECT *mailbox*	Selects a mailbox at the server; before returning the result of the SELECT command, the server returns information about the mailbox as a series of untagged responses
	EXAMINE *mailbox*	Operates identically to the SELECT command, but the mailbox is selected in read-only mode; no changes to the mailbox are permitted
	CREATE *mailbox*	Creates a mailbox
	DELETE *mailbox*	Removes a mailbox from the server
	RENAME *current-name new-name*	Renames a mailbox
	SUBSCRIBE *mailbox*	Adds the mailbox to the server's list of active or subscribed mailboxes, as returned by the LSUB command
	UNSUBSCRIBE *mailbox*	Removes the mailbox from the server's list of active or subscribed mailboxes

Continued

Table 15.1 IMAP4 Commands (Continued)

Group	Command	Description
	LIST *reference mailbox*	Returns a subset list of names available to the user; the *reference* argument is used to provide additional context for the server to perform the search; the *mailbox* argument can contain wildcard characters; see RFC 1730 for more about the use of this command
	LSUB *reference mailbox*	Similar to the LIST command except that the server limits its search to those names added to its subscribed list using the SUBSCRIBE command
	APPEND *mailbox [flags] [date-time] message*	Appends the message to the specified mailbox; if the *flags* or *date-time* parameters are present, the command also sets the appropriate flags and date for the message
Selected State		
	CHECK	Requests a checkpoint of the current mailbox; the exact behavior of this command depends on the server implementation, but in general, servers should flush all mailbox states to disk
	CLOSE	Closes the mailbox; all messages that have the "/Deleted" flag set are removed from the mailbox, and the session returns to the Authenticated State
	EXPUNGE	Causes the removal of all messages in the mailbox that have the "/Deleted" flag set; the server returns a series of untagged EXPUNGE responses to indicate which messages were deleted
	SEARCH *[charset] criteria-list*	Searches the mailbox for messages that meet the specified search criteria; the server returns a list of messages meeting the criteria in an untagged SEARCH response; see RFC 1730 for a complete set of search criteria that may be specified using this command

Continued

Table 15.1 IMAP4 Commands (Continued)

Group	Command	Description
Selected State	FETCH *message-set item-names*	Returns a set of information from the specified message set; example information includes the contents of an individual header line or the complete message; see RFC 1730 for a complete list of item names
	PARTIAL *message item-name first-octet length*	Similar to the FETCH command except that it includes a capability to return only a portion of the information from the specified message set; the *first-octet* and *length* parameters indicate the octets to return from the standard FETCH response
	STORE *message-set item-name value*	Alters flag data associated with a message and optionally returns the new value of the flags
	COPY *message-set mailbox*	Makes a copy of the specified messages in the destination mailbox
	UID *command-name command-arguments*	Indicates that the command specified as a parameter uses unique ID values to specify messages rather than sequence numbers; the *command-name* argument can be a COPY, FETCH, STORE or SEARCH command
	X<*atom*>	All commands beginning with an "X" are experimental or system dependent extensions to the IMAP4 protocol

Responses

Every IMAP command generates an IMAP response. As described previously, each IMAP command contains a tag that is returned in the corresponding IMAP response. Some responses are untagged, however, and may occur at any time. Other responses, while untagged, occur in response to a command but are not the response that signals the completion of the command. For instance, the LIST command may generate a set of untagged LIST responses before the corresponding tagged OK response that completes the command.

Table 15.2 lists the IMAP4 responses. Note that the responses have been sorted into categories. Responses with similar behavior and response syntax are grouped together.

Table 15.2 IMAP4 Responses

Group	Response	Description
Status Responses		Status responses may be tagged or untagged; they may include an optional response code in square brackets following the basic response; the possible response codes are listed in Table 15.3
	OK *[response-code] text*	When tagged, the OK response indicates the successful completion of a previously issued command; the server also uses untagged OK responses to convey informational messages to the client
	NO *[response-code] text*	When tagged, the NO response indicates the unsuccessful completion of a previously issued command; the server also uses untagged NO responses to convey warning messages to the client
	BAD *[response-code] text*	The BAD response indicates a protocol-level error; if tagged, the BAD response indicates a problem with a client command; if untagged, the BAD response indicates an overall problem or serious condition
	PREAUTH *[response-code] text*	The PREAUTH response is always untagged and is one of the possible first responses given when the session begins; the PREAUTH response indicates that the session is already authenticated and there is no need to issue a LOGIN command
	BYE *[response-code] text*	The BYE response indicates that the server is about to end the session and is always untagged; the response may be issued as the result of a LOGOUT command or an unplanned server shutdown
Server and Mailbox Status		Server and mailbox status responses are always untagged
	CAPABILITY *capability-list*	The server issues a CAPABILITY response as the result of a CAPABILITY command; the *capability-list* is a space-separated list of capability names
	LIST *attributes delimiter name*	The server issues LIST responses as the result of a LIST command. The *attributes* lists a set of name attributes; the *delimiter* indicates the character sequence the server uses to separate parts of a hierarchical name; the *name* itself is the name returned by the LIST command

Continued

Table 15.2 IMAP4 Responses (Continued)

Group	Response	Description
	LSUB *attributes delimiter name*	The server issues LSUB responses as the result of an LSUB command; the parameters are the same as those in the LIST command
	SEARCH *message-list*	The server issues a SEARCH response as the result of a SEARCH command; the *message-list* indicates the messages that meet the search criteria; the *message-list* is either a list of message numbers or a list of unique identifiers if the UID command was used to execute the search
	FLAGS *flag-list*	The server issues a FLAGS response as the result of a SELECT or EXAMINE command; the *flag-list* is a parenthesized list of flags that apply to the selected mailbox
Message Status		Message status responses are always untagged; Immediately following the "*" untagged indication, the responses include a number indicating the message sequence number or message count
	EXISTS	The EXISTS response indicates the number of messages in the mailbox and is sent by the server in response to a SELECT or EXAMINE command or if the mailbox size changes on the server as the result of new mail
	RECENT	The RECENT response indicates the number of messages that have arrived in the mailbox since the last SELECT or EXAMINE command was used to select the mailbox; the RECENT response is issued after a SELECT or EXAMINE command when the mailbox size changes
	EXPUNGE	The EXPUNGE response indicates that the specified message has been removed from the mailbox
	FETCH *message-data*	The FETCH response is used to send data to the client; the server sends the FETCH response as the result of a FETCH or STORE command

The Status responses may include an optional response code in square brackets following the response name to convey additional information. Table 15.3 describes the various IMAP4 response codes.

Table 15.3 IMAP4 Optional Status Response Codes

Code	Description
ALERT	The text contains an alert message that must be presented to the user
PARSE	The text contains an RFC 822 or MIME parsing error in a mailbox message
PERMANENTFLAGS	This status code is followed by a parenthesized list of flags that the client may change permanently; see RFC 1730 for more information about this status code
READ-ONLY	The mailbox is selected as read-only, or its access mode has changed since it was selected and is now read-only
READ-WRITE	The mailbox is selected as read-write, or its access mode has changed since it was selected and is now read-write
TRYCREATE	If an APPEND or COPY command fails because the target mailbox doesn't exist, the server may send a TRYCREATE status code to indicate the problem and the remedy—creating the mailbox first may solve the problem
UIDVALIDITY	This status code is followed by a decimal number indicating a unique identifier validity value; see the UID command
UNSEEN	The decimal number following the response code indicates that first message in the mailbox without the \Seen flag set.

Formal Syntax

IMAP4 uses a much more sophisticated syntax for commands and responses than most other Internet protocols. This section describes the formal syntax of the command and responses.

```
address ::=  "(" addr_name SPACE addr_adl SPACE addr_mailbox
     SPACE addr_host ")"

addr_adl  ::=  nstring

addr_host ::=  nstring
     ;; NIL indicates [RFC-822] group syntax

addr_mailbox ::=  nstring
     ;; NIL indicates end of [RFC-822] group; if
     ;; non-NIL and addr_host is NIL, holds
     ;; [RFC-822] group name

addr_name ::=  nstring

alpha  ::=  "A" / "B" / "C" / "D" / "E" / "F" / "G" / "H" /
     "I" / "J" / "K" / "L" / "M" / "N" / "O" / "P" /
```

```
     "Q" / "R" / "S" / "T" / "U" / "V" / "W" / "X" /
     "Y" / "Z" /
     "a" / "b" / "c" / "d" / "e" / "f" / "g" / "h" /
     "i" / "j" / "k" / "l" / "m" / "n" / "o" / "p" /
     "q" / "r" / "s" / "t" / "u" / "v" / "w" / "x" /
     "y" / "z" /
     ;; Case-sensitive

append ::= "APPEND" SPACE mailbox [SPACE flag_list]
     [SPACE date_time] SPACE literal

astring ::= atom / string

atom ::= 1*ATOM_CHAR

ATOM_CHAR ::= <any CHAR except atom_specials>

atom_specials ::= "(" / ")" / "{" / SPACE / CTLs / list_wildcards /
     quoted_specials

authenticate ::= "AUTHENTICATE" SPACE auth_type *(CRLF base64)

auth_type ::= atom

base64 ::= *(4base64_char) [base64_terminal]

base64_char ::= alpha / digit / "+" / "/"

base64_terminal ::= (2base64_char "==") / (3base64_char "=")

body ::= "(" body_type_1part / body_type_mpart ")"

body_extension ::= nstring / number / "(" 1#body_extension ")"
     ;; Future expansion. Client implementations
     ;; MUST accept body_extension fields. Server
     ;; implementations MUST NOT generate
     ;; body_extension fields except as defined by
     ;; future standard or standards-track
     ;; revisions of this specification.

body_ext_1part ::= body_fld_md5 [SPACE 1#body_extension]
     ;; MUST NOT be returned on non-extensible
     ;; "BODY" fetch

body_ext_mpart ::= body_fld_param [SPACE 1#body_extension]]
     ;; MUST NOT be returned on non-extensible
     ;; "BODY" fetch
```

```
body_fields ::= body_fld_param SPACE body_fld_id SPACE
     body_fld_desc SPACE body_fld_enc SPACE
     body_fld_octets

body_fld_desc ::= nstring

body_fld_enc ::= (<"> ("7BIT" / "8BIT" / "BINARY" / "BASE64"/
     "QUOTED-PRINTABLE") <">) / string

body_fld_id ::= nstring

body_fld_lines ::= number

body_fld_md5 ::= nstring

body_fld_octets ::= number

body_fld_param ::= "(" 1#(string string) ")" / nil

body_fld_subtyp ::= string

body_type_1part ::= (body_type_basic / body_type_msg / body_type_text)
      [SPACE body_ext_1part]

body_type_basic ::= (<"> ("APPLICATION" / "AUDIO" / "IMAGE" /
     "MESSAGE" / "VIDEO") <">) / string) SPACE
     body_fld_subtyp SPACE body_fields
     ;; MESSAGE subtype MUST NOT be "RFC822"

body_type_mpart ::= 1*body SPACE body_fld_subtyp
     [SPACE body_ext_mpart]

body_type_msg ::= <"> "MESSAGE" <"> SPACE <"> "RFC822" <"> SPACE
     body_fields SPACE envelope SPACE body SPACE
     body_fld_lines

body_type_text ::= <"> "TEXT" <"> SPACE body_fld_subtyp SPACE
     body_fields SPACE body_fld_lines

capability ::= atom
     ;; Must begin with "X" or be registered with
     ;; IANA as standard or standards-track

capability_data ::= "CAPABILITY" SPACE "IMAP4" [SPACE 1#capability]

CHAR ::= <any 7-bit US-ASCII character except NUL,
     0x01 - 0x7f>
```

```
CHAR8  ::=  <any 8-bit octet except NUL, 0x01 - 0xff>

command ::=  tag SPACE (command_any / command_auth /
     command_nonauth / command_select) CRLF
     ;; Modal based on state

command_any  ::=  "CAPABILITY" / "LOGOUT" / "NOOP" / x_command
     ;; Valid in all states

command_auth ::=  append / create / delete / examine / find / list /
     lsub / rename / select / subscribe / unsubscribe /
     ;; Valid only in Authenticated or Selected state

command_nonauth  ::=  login / authenticate
     ;; Valid only when in Non-Authenticated state

command_select ::=  "CHECK" / "CLOSE" / "EXPUNGE" /
     copy / fetch / partial / store / uid / search
     ;; Valid only when in Selected state

continue_req ::=  "+" SPACE (resp_text / base64)

copy ::=  "COPY" SPACE set SPACE mailbox

CR ::=  <ASCII CR, carriage return, 0x0C>

create  ::=  "CREATE" SPACE mailbox
     ;; Use of INBOX gives a NO error

CRLF ::=  CR LF

CTL  ::=  <any ASCII control character and DEL,
     0x00 - 0x1f, 0x7f>

date ::=  date_text / <"> date_text <">

date_day  ::=  1*2digit
     ;; Day of month

date_day_fixed ::=  (SPACE digit) / 2digit
     ;; Fixed-format version of date_day

date_month  ::=  "Jan" / "Feb" / "Mar" / "Apr" / "May" / "Jun" /
     "Jul" / "Aug" / "Sep" / "Oct" / "Nov" / "Dec"

date_text ::=  date_day "-" date_month "-" (date_year /
     date_year_old)
```

```
date_year ::=  4digit

date_year_old  ::=  2digit
     ;; OBSOLETE, (year - 1900)

date_time ::=  <"> (date_time_new / date_time_old) <">

date_time_new  ::=  date_day_fixed "-" date_month "-" date_year
     SPACE time SPACE zone

date_time_old  ::=  date_day_fixed "-" date_month "-" date_year_old
     SPACE time "-" zone_old
     ;; OBSOLETE

delete  ::=  "DELETE" SPACE mailbox
     ;; Use of INBOX gives a NO error

digit   ::=  "0" / digit_nz

digit_nz  ::=  "1" / "2" / "3" / "4" / "5" / "6" / "7" / "8" / "9"

envelope  ::=  "(" env_date SPACE env_subject SPACE env_from
     SPACE env_sender SPACE env_reply-to SPACE env_to
     SPACE env_cc SPACE env_bcc SPACE env_in-reply-to
     SPACE env_message-id ")"

env_bcc ::=  "(" 1*address ")" / nil

env_cc  ::=  "(" 1*address ")" / nil

env_date  ::=  nstring

env_from  ::=  "(" 1*address ")" / nil

env_in-reply-to  ::=  nstring

env_message-id ::=  nstring

env_reply-to ::=  "(" 1*address ")" / nil

env_sender  ::=  "(" 1*address ")" / nil

env_subject ::=  nstring

env_to  ::=  "(" 1*address ")" / nil

examine ::=  "EXAMINE" SPACE mailbox
```

```
fetch   ::=  "FETCH" SPACE set SPACE ("ALL" / "FULL" /
     "FAST" / fetch_att / "(" 1#fetch_att ")")

fetch_att ::=  "BODY" / "BODYSTRUCTURE" /
     "BODY" [".PEEK"] "[" section "]" / "ENVELOPE" /
     "FLAGS" / "INTERNALDATE" / "UID" /
     "RFC822" (([".TEXT"] [".PEEK"]) / ".SIZE" /
     (".HEADER" [".LINES" [".NOT"] SPACE header_list])

find ::=  "FIND" SPACE ["ALL."] "MAILBOXES" SPACE
     list_mailbox
     ;; OBSOLETE

flag ::=  "\Answered" / "\Flagged" / "\Deleted" /
     "\Seen" / "\Draft" / flag_keyword /
     flag_extension

flag_extension ::=  "\" atom
     ;; Future expansion. Client implementations
     ;; MUST accept flag_extension flags. Server
     ;; implementations MUST NOT generate
     ;; flag_extension flags except as defined by
     ;; future standard or standards-track
     ;; revisions of this specification.

flag_keyword::=  atom

flag_list ::=  "(" #flag ")"

greeting  ::=  "*" SPACE (resp_cond_auth / resp_cond_bye) CRLF

header_line  ::=  astring

header_list  ::=  "(" 1#header_line ")"

LF ::=  <ASCII LF, line feed, 0x0A>

list ::=  "LIST" SPACE mailbox SPACE list_mailbox

list_mailbox::=  1*(ATOM_CHAR / list_wildcards) / string

list_wildcards ::=  "%" / "*"

literal::=  "{" number "}" CRLF *CHAR8
     ;; Number represents the number of CHAR8 octets

login   ::=  "LOGIN" SPACE userid SPACE password
```

```
lsub ::=  "LSUB" SPACE mailbox SPACE list_mailbox

mailbox ::=  "INBOX" / astring
     ;; INBOX is case-insensitive; other names may be
     ;; case-sensitive depending on implementation.

mailbox_data ::=  "FLAGS" SPACE flag_list /
     "LIST" SPACE mailbox_list /
     "LSUB" SPACE mailbox_list /
     "MAILBOX" SPACE text /
     "SEARCH" [SPACE 1#nz_number] /
     number SPACE "EXISTS" / number SPACE "RECENT"

mailbox_list ::=  "(" #("\Marked" / "\Noinferiors" /
     "\Noselect" / "\Unmarked" / flag_extension) ")"
     SPACE (<"> QUOTED_CHAR <"> / nil) SPACE mailbox

message_data ::=  nz_number SPACE ("EXPUNGE" /
     ("FETCH" SPACE msg_fetch) / msg_obsolete)

msg_fetch ::=  "(" 1#("BODY" SPACE body /
     "BODYSTRUCTURE" SPACE body /
     "BODY[" section "]" SPACE nstring /
     "ENVELOPE" SPACE envelope /
     "FLAGS" SPACE "(" #(flag / "\Recent") ")" /
     "INTERNALDATE" SPACE date_time /
     "RFC822" [".HEADER" / ".TEXT"] SPACE nstring /
     "RFC822.SIZE" SPACE number /
     "UID" SPACE uniqueid) ")"

msg_obsolete ::=  "COPY" / ("STORE" SPACE msg_fetch)
     ;; OBSOLETE untagged data responses

nil  ::=  "NIL"

nstring ::=  string / nil

number  ::=  1*digit
     ;; Unsigned 32-bit integer
     ;; (0 <= n < 4,294,967,296)

nz_number ::=  digit_nz *digit
     ;; Non-zero unsigned 32-bit integer
     ;; (0 < n < 4,294,967,296)

partial ::=  "PARTIAL" SPACE nz_number SPACE
     ("BODY" [".PEEK"] "[" section "]" /
```

```
     "RFC822" (([".TEXT"] [".PEEK"]) / ".HEADER")
     SPACE number SPACE number

password  ::=  astring

quoted ::=  <"> *QUOTED_CHAR <">

QUOTED_CHAR ::=  <any TEXT_CHAR except quoted_specials> /
     "\" quoted_specials

quoted_specials  ::=  <"> / "\"

rename ::=  "RENAME" SPACE mailbox SPACE mailbox
     ;; Use of INBOX as a destination gives a NO error

response  ::=  *response_data response_done

response_data  ::=  "*" SPACE (resp_cond_state / resp_cond_bye /
     mailbox_data / message_data / capability_data)
     CRLF

response_done  ::=  response_tagged / response_fatal

response_fatal ::=  "*" SPACE resp_cond_bye CRLF

response_tagged  ::=  tag SPACE resp_cond_state CRLF

resp_cond_auth ::=  ("OK" / "PREAUTH") SPACE resp_text
     ;; Authentication condition

resp_cond_bye  ::=  "BYE" SPACE resp_text
     ;; Server will disconnect condition

resp_cond_state  ::=  ("OK" / "NO" / "BAD") SPACE resp_text
     ;; Status condition

resp_text ::=  ["[" resp_text_code "]" SPACE] (text_mime2 / text)

resp_text_code ::=  "ALERT" / "PARSE" /
     "PERMANENTFLAGS" SPACE "(" #(flag / "\*") ")" /
     "READ-ONLY" / "READ-WRITE" / "TRYCREATE" /
     "UIDVALIDITY" SPACE nz_number /
     "UNSEEN" SPACE nz_number /
     atom [SPACE 1*<any TEXT_CHAR except "]">]

search ::=  "SEARCH" SPACE ["CHARSET" SPACE astring SPACE]
     search_criteria
```

```
     ;; Character set must be registered with IANA
     ;; as a MIME character set

search_criteria  ::=  1#search_key

search_key  ::=  search_new / search_old

search_new  ::=  "DRAFT" /
     "HEADER" SPACE header_line SPACE astring /
     "LARGER" SPACE number / "NOT" SPACE search_key /
     "OR" SPACE search_key SPACE search_key /
     "SENTBEFORE" SPACE date / "SENTON" SPACE date /
     "SENTSINCE" SPACE date / "SMALLER" SPACE number /
     "UID" SPACE set / "UNDRAFT" / set /
     "(" search_criteria ")"
     ;; New in IMAP4

search_old  ::=  "ALL" / "ANSWERED" / "BCC" SPACE astring /
     "BEFORE" SPACE date / "BODY" SPACE astring /
     "CC" SPACE astring / "DELETED" / "FLAGGED" /
     "FROM" SPACE astring /
     "KEYWORD" SPACE flag_keyword / "NEW" / "OLD" /
     "ON" SPACE date / "RECENT" / "SEEN" /
     "SINCE" SPACE date / "SUBJECT" SPACE astring /
     "TEXT" SPACE astring / "TO" SPACE astring /
     "UNANSWERED" / "UNDELETED" / "UNFLAGGED" /
     "UNKEYWORD" SPACE flag_keyword / "UNSEEN"
     ;; Defined in [IMAP2]

section ::=  "0" / nz_number ["." section]

select  ::=  "SELECT" SPACE mailbox

sequence_num ::=  nz_number / "*"
     ;; * is the largest number in use. For message
     ;; sequence numbers, it is the number of messages
     ;; in the mailbox. For unique identifiers, it is
     ;; the unique identifier of the last message in
     ;; the mailbox.

set  ::=  sequence_num / (sequence_num ":" sequence_num) /
     (set "," set)
     ;; Identifies a set of messages. For message
     ;; sequence numbers, these are consecutive
     ;; numbers from 1 to the number of messages in
     ;; the mailbox.
```

```
     ;; Comma delimits individual numbers, colon
     ;; delimits between two numbers inclusive.
     ;; Example: 2,4:7,9,12:* is 2,4,5,6,7,9,12,13,
     ;; 14,15 for a mailbox with 15 messages.

SPACE  ::=  <ASCII SP, space, 0x20>

store  ::=  "STORE" SPACE set SPACE store_att_flags

store_att_flags  ::=  (["+" / "-"] "FLAGS" [".SILENT"]) SPACE
     (flag_list / #flag)

string ::=  quoted / literal

subscribe ::=  ("SUBSCRIBE" SPACE mailbox) / subscribe_obs

subscribe_obs  ::=  "SUBSCRIBE" SPACE "MAILBOX" SPACE mailbox
     ;;OBSOLETE

tag  ::=  1*<any ATOM_CHAR except "+">

text ::=  1*TEXT_CHAR

text_mime2  ::=  "=?" <charset> "?" <encoding> "?"
     <encoded-text> "?="
     ;; Syntax defined in [MIME-2]

TEXT_CHAR ::=  <any CHAR except CR and LF>

time ::=  2digit ":" 2digit ":" 2digit
     ;; Hours minutes seconds

uid  ::=  "UID" SPACE (copy / fetch / search / store)
     ;; Unique identifiers used instead of message
     ;; sequence numbers

uniqueid  ::=  nz_number
     ;; Strictly ascending

unsubscribe ::=  ("UNSUBSCRIBE" SPACE mailbox) / unsubscribe_obs

unsubscribe_obs  ::=  "UNSUBSCRIBE" SPACE "MAILBOX" SPACE mailbox
     ;;OBSOLETE

userid ::=  astring

x_command ::=  "X" atom <experimental command arguments>
```

```
zone ::=  ("+" / "-") 4digit
     ;; Signed four-digit value of hhmm representing
     ;; hours and minutes west of Greenwich (that is,
     ;; (the amount that the given time differs from
     ;; Universal Time). Subtracting the time zone
     ;; from the given time will give the UT form.
     ;; The Universal time zone is "+0000".

zone_old  ::=  "UT" / "GMT" / "Z" /  ;; +0000
     "AST" / "EDT" /  ;; -0400
     "EST" / "CDT" /  ;; -0500
     "CST" / "MDT" /  ;; -0600
     "MST" / "PDT" /  ;; -0700
     "PST" / "YDT" /  ;; -0800
     "YST" / "HDT" /  ;; -0900
     "HST" / "BDT" /  ;; -1000
     "BST" / ;; -1100
     "A" / "B" / "C" / "D" / "E" / "F" /  ;; +1 to +6
     "G" / "H" / "I" / "K" / "L" / "M" /  ;; +7 to +12
     "N" / "O" / "P" / "Q" / "R" / "S" /  ;; -1 to -6
     "T" / "U" / "V" / "W" / "X" / "Y" ;; -7 to -12
     ;; OBSOLETE
```

16 Internet Protocol on Ethernet Networks

Name

Internet Protocol on Ethernet Networks

Abbreviation

IP-E

Status

Standard (STD 41)

Specifications

RFC 894

Abstract

It has been said that the availability of Ethernet was the spark that really lit the networking fire. Ethernet allowed simple, inexpensive local area networks (LANs) to be constructed. IP was one of the first protocols used on the new network. RFC 894 describes the simple encapsulation of IP datagrams in Ethernet framing.

Related Specifications

IP (RFC 791), IGMP (RFC 1112), ARP (RFC 826)

See Also

IP-IEEE (RFC 1042) provides details for running IP over IEEE 802.3 networks using IEEE 802.2 encapsulation.

Comments

Although IP can be run over IEEE 802.3/Ethernet networks using IEEE 802.2 framing (RFC 1042), this approach is not very common. RFC 894 is used much more frequently.

Description

Running IP over Ethernet is very simple. The following sections describe the specifications. This specification is used for all types of standard Ethernets, including 10 Mbps, 100 Mbps, and higher-speed versions.

Framing

IP datagrams are transmitted in standard Ethernet frames. IP datagrams are identified by the use of 0x0800 as the Ethernet type value following the Ethernet Source Address field.

Ethernet frames have a minimum data payload size of 46 octets. If the IP packet is smaller than this size, padding is added to reach the minimum size. The padding is *not* considered part of the IP packet itself.

Ethernet has a maximum data payload size of 1500 octets. IP datagrams may be up to 1500 octets long when encapsulated in Ethernet frames. Longer IP datagrams must be fragmented using IP fragmentation.

Address Mapping

IP addresses can be mapped to 48-bit Ethernet addresses using multiple methods:

- Static Hosts can be provided with a table of mappings.
- The Address Resolution Protocol (ARP) can be used to dynamically map IP addresses to Ethernet addresses.

In practice, most hosts use ARP for dynamic address resolution with the possibility of configuring static ARP cache entries.

The IP broadcast address (255.255.255.255) is mapped to the Ethernet broadcast address (0xFF-FF-FF-FF-FF-FF). RFC 1112 describes the mapping of IP multicast addresses to Ethernet multicast addresses.

Frame Format

Figure 16.1 shows the IP datagram encapsulated in an Ethernet frame.

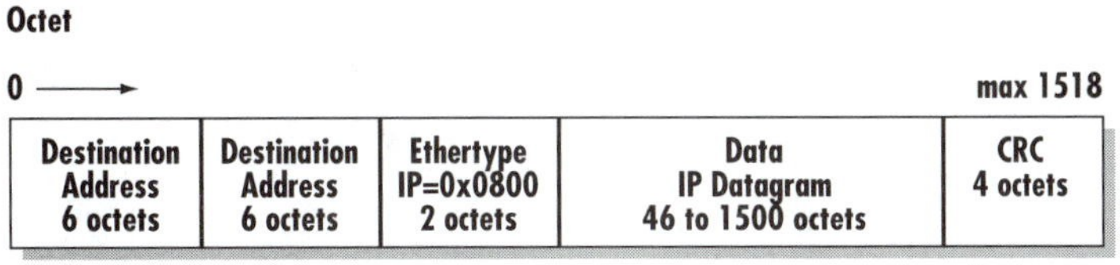

Octet

0 ⟶ max 1518

Destination Address 6 octets	Destination Address 6 octets	Ethertype IP=0x0800 2 octets	Data IP Datagram 46 to 1500 octets	CRC 4 octets

Figure 16.1

IP Over Ethernet Frame Format.

Internet Protocol

Name

Internet Protocol

Abbreviation

IP

Status

Required Standard (STD 5)

Specifications

RFC 791, amended by RFC 950, RFC 919, RFC 922

Abstract

The Internet Protocol (IP) provides for the delivery of data through a set of interconnected packet-switched networks (an internetwork or internet). IP transmits and routes datagrams from sources to destinations based on a fixed-length address. The addressing scheme is independent of any particular datalink network technology, allowing the construction of large internetworks composed of many heterogeneous network and host systems.

Related Specifications

ICMP (RFC 792), IGMP (RFC 1112)

See Also

UDP (RFC 768), TCP (RFC 793)

Comments

The original IP address field size and address allocation scheme have led to a shortage of IP addresses necessary for the large global Internet. IP version 6 (IPv6) has been developed to correct the addressing scheme problems associated with the original version of IP (IPv4).

Description

The Internet Protocol provides for the transmission of datagrams from sources to destinations through a series of interconnected networks. IP provides a global addressing scheme independent of any datalink layer addressing scheme. IP allows intermediate systems to fragment datagrams to allow the transmission of a large datagram over a datalink network that would not otherwise support it. IP does not guarantee delivery of datagrams, the integrity of their payloads, or the order in which they arrive. IP does, however, provide a header error checksum to allow the detection of errors in the IP header itself. A related protocol, ICMP, provides for the reporting of IP errors.

Frame Formats

This section describes the basic IP frame format. A prototypical IP packet is shown in Figure 17.1.

Version

4 bits

The Version field indicates the format of the Internet header. The current version is 4. Note that IPv6 is version 6.

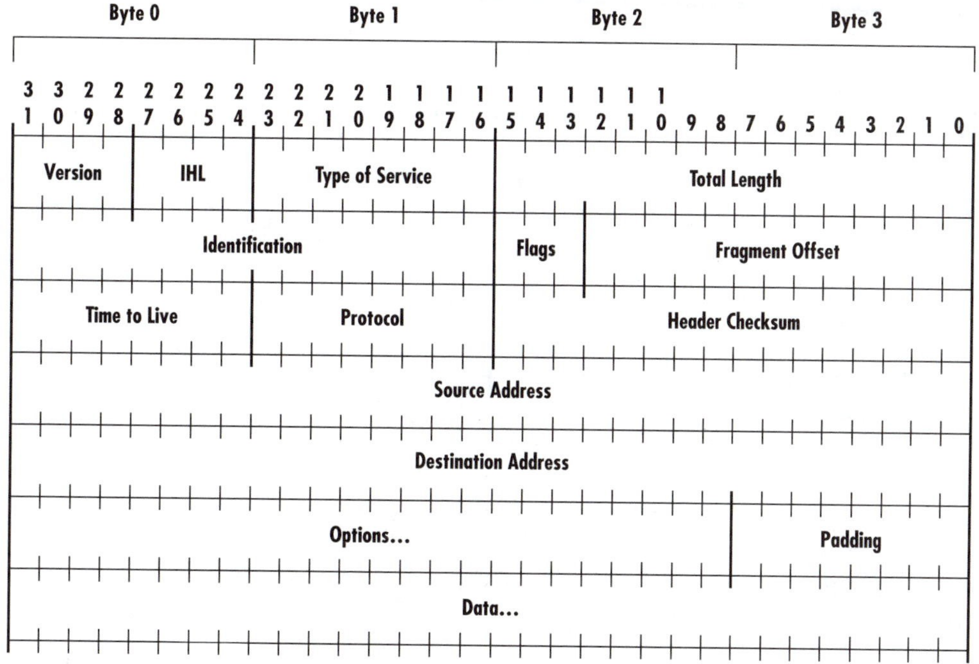

Figure 17.1

The IP frame format.

IHL

4 bits

The IHL (Internet Header Length) field is the length of the Internet header in 32-bit words. The minimum value for a correct header is 5.

Type of Service

8 bits

The Type of Service field indicates the level of service that should be given to the datagram if the traversed routers and datalink networks support such services. Figure 17.2 shows the breakdown of the Type of Service bits.

Bits 7 through 5 indicate the datagram precedence:

- 111 - Network Control
- 110 - Internetwork Control
- 101 - CRITIC/ECP

Figure 17.2
The Type of Service bits.

- 100 - Flash Override
- 011 - Flash
- 010 - Immediate
- 001 - Priority
- 000 - Routine

Bit 4 indicates the desired frame delay: 0 = normal delay, 1 = low delay.

Bit 3 indicates the desired frame throughput: 0 = normal throughput, 1 = high throughput.

Bit 2 indicates the desired frame reliability: 0 = normal reliability, 1 = high reliability.

Bits 1 and 0 are reserved and must be set to 0.

Total Length

16 bits

The Total Length field indicates the total length of the datagram, measured in octets. This value includes all headers and data. The maximum datagram length is 65,535 bytes.

Identification

16 bits

The Indentification field contains a value assigned by the sender to aid in assembling the fragments of a datagram.

Flags

3 bits

The Flags field contains flags controlling fragmentation. The possible Flag bit settings are shown in Figure 17.3.

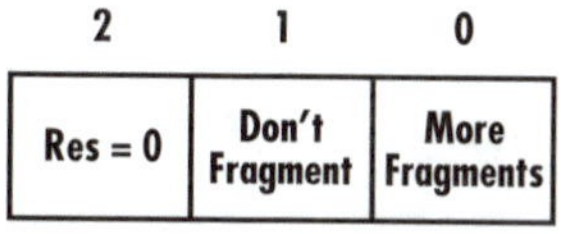

2	1	0
Res = 0	Don't Fragment	More Fragments

Figure 17.3
The flags bits.

Bit 2 is reserved and should be set to 0.

Bit 1: 0 = may fragment this datagram, 1 = don't fragment this datagram.

Bit 0: 0 = last fragment, 1 = more fragments.

Fragment Offset

13 bits

The Fragment Offset field indicates where in the datagram this fragment belongs. The fragment offset is measured in units of eight octets (64 bits). The first fragment has offset zero.

Time to Live

8 bits

The Time to Live field bounds the lifetime of a datagram within an internetwork. Each router that processes a datagram must decrement this field by 1. The datagram is discarded when the field reaches zero. This field would be more appropriately named "Remaining Hop Count."

Protocol

8 bits

The Protocol field indicates the protocol associated with the data in the data portion of the datagram. See Table 17.2 for assigned protocol numbers.

Header Checksum

16 bits

The Header Checksum field represents a checksum computed on the datagram header fields only. The checksum algorithm is: The checksum field is the 16 bit one's complement of the one's complement sum of all 16 bit words in the header. For purposes of computing the checksum, the value of the checksum field is zero.

Source Address

32 bits

This field indicates the datagram source address.

Destination Address

32 bits

This field indicates the datagram destination address.

Options

Variable length

The Option field is variable length. Options are not required to be present.

Options occur in two formats:

- A single octet containing the option type.
- A multi-byte option encoded in type/length/value (TLV) format. In this case, the type and length values are each one octet long and the data may be variable length. The length octet specifies the length of the entire option, including the type octet and the length octet itself.

The option type octet has three fields:

- Copied flag: 1 bit
- Option class: 2 bits
- Option number: 5 bits

The Copied Flag field indicates that this option is copied to all fragment datagrams when fragmentation occurs:

- 0 = not copied
- 1 = copied

Options are divided into four classes:

- 0 = control
- 1 = reserved for future use
- 2 = debugging and measurement
- 3 = reserved for future use

Table 17.1 shows the standard IP options.

Table 17.1 Standard IP Options

Class	Number	Length	Description
0	0	–	End of Option list; this option occupies only one octet; it has no length octet
0	1	–	No Operation; this option occupies only one octet; it has no length octet
0	2	11	Security; used to carry Security, Compartmentation, User Group (TCC), and Handling Restriction Codes compatible with DOD requirements
0	3	var.	Loose Source Routing; used to route the Internet datagram based on information supplied by the source
0	9	var.	Strict Source Routing; used to route the Internet datagram based on information supplied by the source
0	7	var.	Record Route; used to trace the route an Internet datagram takes
0	8	4	Stream Identifier; used to carry the stream identifier
2	4	var.	Internet Timestamp

End of Option List

Type = 0

This option is used as padding at the end of all the options in the datagram when the last option does not end on a 32-bit boundary. This option may be copied on fragmentation, added, or removed, as is appropriate.

No Operation

Type = 1

This option can be used anywhere. It simply specifies that no processing is to be done on this option. The most typical use for a No Operation option is to insert padding between options in the option list to force a following option to begin on a 32-bit boundary. This option may be copied on fragmentation, added, or removed, as is appropriate.

Security

Type = 130

This option was originally designed to carry security information. It is not used on the global Internet. Recent work on IP security has eliminated the need for this option. See RFC 791 for more information about its original use.

Loose Source Route and Record Route
Type = 131

The Loose Source Route and Record Route option is used to supply routing information about the path a datagram should follow and to record the route information.

This option begins with type and length octets followed by a pointer octet. The pointer octet specifies the next source route address to be processed. The pointer offset is relative to the option type octet, and the smallest legal value is 4.

Route data follows the pointer octet and is composed of a sequence of IP addresses, each 32-bits long. If the pointer octet is greater than the option length octet, all the source addresses have been processed and replaced by recorded route addresses. In this case, the IP destination address should be used to route the datagram to its final destination.

If the pointer octet is not greater than the option length, then more routing information remains. When a datagram arrives at the destination specified in the IP header, the receiving IP module overwrites the IP header destination address with the source route address specified by the pointer octet, overwrites the source route specified by the pointer octet with the local address, and increments the pointer octet by 4.

This option indicates a loose source route because an intermediate router is free to choose any path to the next source route address, including routes that pass through multiple intermediate routers. This differs from the strict source route, discussed next.

This option must be copied on fragmentation and must appear in a datagram only once.

Strict Source Route and Record Route
Type = 137

The Strict Source Route and Record Route option functions identically to the Loose Source Route and Record Route option, except that the specified source route is *strict*. This means that the source route specifies the exact route from the source to the destination. Each intermediate router must forward the datagram to the next address in the route through a directly connected network.

This option must be copied on fragmentation and must appear in a datagram only once.

Record Route
Type = 7

The record route option is used to record the route of a datagram. This option functions similarly to the Source Routing options, except that the only the route recording function is used. A pointer octet follows the option type and length octets. The pointer octet is then followed by enough space for the recorded 32-bit IP addresses. This space must be preallocated by the originating host.

As each router processes the datagram, it inserts its own address into the 32-bit field indicated by the pointer octet, and increments the pointer octet by 4. If the pointer octet is equal to the length octet, then no more space remains to record route information. In this case, the datagram is simply forwarded on to the destination with no further processing of this option. If the pointer octet is less than the length octet but not enough space remains to record a full address, the datagram is discarded and an ICMP message can be sent to the source.

The octets used to store the recorded route must be set to zero by the originating host.

This option is *not* copied on fragmentation. It must appear only once and only in the first fragment.

Stream Identifier
Type = 136

This option was originally used to carry SATNET stream identifiers. It is not normally used. See RFC 791 for more information about this option.

Internet Timestamp
Type = 68

This option is used to record the time at which a datagram was processed by an intermediate system. See RFC 791 for more information about this option.

Assigned Internet Protocol Numbers

Table 17.2 shows the currently assigned IP protocol numbers, as specified in the current version of the Internet Assigned Numbers document, RFC 1700. See revisions to RFC 1700 for updates to this list.

Table 17.2 Assigned Internet Protocol Numbers

Decimal	Keyword	Protocol	References
0		Reserved	
1	ICMP	Internet Control Message	RFC 792
2	IGMP	Internet Group Management	RFC 1112
3	GGP	Gateway-to-Gateway	RFC 823
4	IP	IP in IP (Encapsulation)	
5	ST	Stream	RFC 1190
6	TCP	Transmission Control	RFC 793
7	UCL	UCL	
8	EGP	Exterior Gateway Protocol	RFC 888
9	IGP	Any Private Interior Gateway	
10	BBN-RCC-MON	BBN RCC Monitoring	
11	NVP-II	Network Voice Protocol	RFC 741
12	PUP	PUP	
13	ARGUS	ARGUS	
14	EMCON	EMCON	
15	XNET	Cross Net Debugger	
16	CHAOS	Chaos	
17	UDP	User Datagram	RFC 768
18	MUX	Multiplexing	
19	DCN-MEAS	DCN Measurement Subsystems	
20	HMP	Host Monitoring	RFC 869
21	PRM	Packet Radio Measurement	
22	XNS-IDP	XEROX NS IDP	
23	TRUNK-1	Trunk-1	
24	TRUNK-2	Trunk-2	
25	LEAF-1	Leaf-1	
26	LEAF-2	Leaf-2	
27	RDP	Reliable Data Protocol	RFC 908
28	IRTP	Internet Reliable Transaction	RFC 938
29	ISO-TP4	ISO Transport Protocol Class 4	RFC 905
30	NETBLT	Bulk Data Transfer Protocol	RFC 969

Continued

Table 17.2 Assigned Internet Protocol Numbers (Continued)			
Decimal	**Keyword**	**Protocol**	**References**
31	MFE-NSP	MFE Network Services Protocol	
32	MERIT-INP	MERIT Internodal Protocol	
33	SEP	Sequential Exchange Protocol	
34	3PC	Third Party Connect Protocol	
35	IDPR	Inter-Domain Policy Routing Protocol	
36	XTP	XTP	
37	DDP	Datagram Delivery Protocol	
38	IDPR-CMTP	IDPR Control Message Transport Protocol	
39	TP++	TP++ Transport Protocol	
40	IL	IL Transport Protocol	
41	SIP	Simple Internet Protocol	
42	SDRP	Source Demand Routing Protocol	
43	SIP-SR	SIP Source Route	
44	SIP-FRAG	SIP Fragment	
45	IDRP	Inter-Domain Routing Protocol	
46	RSVP	Reservation Protocol	
47	GRE	General Routing Encapsulation	
48	MHRP	Mobile Host Routing Protocol	
49	BNA	BNA	
50	SIPP-ESP	SIPP Encap Security Payload	
51	SIPP-AH	SIPP Authentication Header	
52	I-NLSP	Integrated Net Layer Security TUBA	
53	SWIPE	IP with Encryption	
54	NHRP	NBMA Next Hop Resolution Protocol	
55-60		Unassigned	
61		Any Host Internal Protocol	
62	CFTP	CFTP	
63		Any Local Network	
64	SAT-EXPAK	SATNET and Backroom EXPAK	
65	KRYPTOLAN	Kryptolan	
66	RVD	MIT Remote Virtual Disk Protocol	

Continued

Table 17.2 Assigned Internet Protocol Numbers (Continued)

Decimal	Keyword	Protocol	References
67	IPPC	Internet Pluribus Packet Core	
68		Any Distributed File System	
69	SAT-MON	SATNET Monitoring	
70	VISA	VISA Protocol	
71	IPCV	Internet Packet Core Utility	
72	CPNX	Computer Protocol Network Executive	
73	CPHB	Computer Protocol Heart Beat	
74	WSN	Wang Span Network	
75	PVP	Packet Video Protocol	
76	BR-SAT-MON	Backroom SATNET Monitoring	
77	SUN-ND	SUN ND PROTOCOL-Temporary	
78	WB-MON	WIDEBAND Monitoring	
79	WB-EXPAK	WIDEBAND EXPAK	
80	ISO-IP	ISO Internet Protocol	
81	VMTP	VMTP	
82	SECURE-VMTP	SECURE-VMTP	
83	VINES	VINES	
84	TTP	TTP	
85	NSFNET-IGP	NSFNET-IGP	
86	DGP	Dissimilar Gateway Protocol	
87	TCF	TCF	
88	IGRP	IGRP	
89	OSPFIGP	OSPFIGP	RFC 1583
90	Sprite-RPC	Sprite RPC Protocol	
91	LARP	Locus Address Resolution Protocol	
92	MTP	Multicast Transport Protocol	
93	AX.25	AX.25 Frames	
94	IPIP	IP-within-IP Encapsulation Protocol	
95	MICP	Mobile Internetworking Control Pro.	
96	SCC-SP	Semaphore Communications Sec. Pro.	
97	ETHERIP	Ethernet-within-IP Encapsulation	

Continued

Table 17.2 Assigned Internet Protocol Numbers (Continued)

Decimal	Keyword	Protocol	References
98	ENCAP	Encapsulation Header	RFC 1241
99		Any Private Encryption Scheme	
100	GMTP	GMTP	
101-254		Unassigned	
255		Reserved	

18 Internet Relay Chat

Name

Internet Relay Chat

Abbreviation

IRC

Status

The IETF has classified IRC as experimental, but the protocol is widely implemented and used.

Specifications

RFC 1459

Abstract

Internet Relay Chat (IRC) connects people from around the world into a set of discussion groups, or channels. Users can chat in realtime with other users about whatever happens to be on anyone's mind.

Comments

The version of IRC described in RFC 1459 is fairly old. IRC has evolved steadily since its deployment and many new features have been added on. These newer features are not documented in this chapter.

Description

The IRC system consists of a set of clients and servers. IRC servers join the IRC system and establish a tree structure such that there is only one path from the server to ant other server. There must be no loops in the tree. This allows for messages flooding without having to worry about servers or clients receiving duplicate messages. Clients communicate directly with servers and form the leaves of the IRC tree.

Clients and servers communicate with each other using a set of messages. The messages are used to convey status or actual chat message text. Clients and server return responses to commands to indicate the command result. Subsequent sections describe the various commands and responses.

Transport Information

The official well-known port for IRC connections is TCP port 194. However, many servers operate different, non-standard port numbers.

Table 18.1 IRC Command Set

Command Group	Command	Description
Connection Registration		
	PASS <password>	Sets a connection password
	NICK <nickname> [<hopcount>]	Specifies the nickname the user wants to be known by
	USER <username> <hostname> <servername> <realname>	Indicates the arrival of a new IRC user
	SERVER <servername> <hopcount> <info>	Indicates that a new connection is a server rather than a user
	OPER <user> <password>	Allows a user to gain operator privileges
	QUIT [<Quit message>]	Indicates that a client is quitting

Continued

Table 18.1 IRC Command Set (Continued)

<table>
<tr><th>Command Group</th><th>Command</th><th>Description</th></tr>
<tr><td></td><td>SQUIT <server> <comment></td><td>Indicates that a server is quitting</td></tr>
<tr><td>Channel Operations</td><td></td><td></td></tr>
<tr><td></td><td>JOIN <channel>{,<channel>} [<key>{,<key>}]</td><td>Indicates that a client wants to listen to the specified channels</td></tr>
<tr><td></td><td>PART <channel>{,<channel>}</td><td>Indicates that a client wants to stop listening to the specified channels</td></tr>
<tr><td></td><td>MODE <channel> {[+|-]|o|p|s|i|t|n|b|v} [<limit>] [<user>] [<ban mask>]</td><td>Changes the channel mode</td></tr>
<tr><td></td><td>MODE <nickname> {[+|-]|i|w|s|o}</td><td>Changes the user mode</td></tr>
<tr><td></td><td>TOPIC <channel> [<topic>]</td><td>Changes the channel topic</td></tr>
<tr><td></td><td>NAMES [<channel>{,<channel>}]</td><td>Lists the nicknames of the users in the specified channels; lists all users in the system if no channel is specified</td></tr>
<tr><td></td><td>LIST [<channel>{,<channel>} [<server>]]</td><td>Lists the available channels and their topics; if channel names are specified, only the status of the specified channels is listed</td></tr>
<tr><td></td><td>INVITE <nickname> <channel></td><td>Invites a user to a channel</td></tr>
<tr><td></td><td>KICK <channel> <user> [<comment>]</td><td>Forcibly removes a user from the specified channel</td></tr>
<tr><td>Server Queries and Commands</td><td></td><td></td></tr>
<tr><td></td><td>VERSION [<server>]</td><td>Queries the version number of the directly connected server or a specified server</td></tr>
<tr><td></td><td>STATS [<query> [<server>]]</td><td>Requests statistics from a server</td></tr>
<tr><td></td><td>LINKS [[<remote server>] <server mask>]</td><td>Requests a list of servers known to the server answering the query</td></tr>
<tr><td></td><td>TIME [<server>]</td><td>Queries the local time on the specified server</td></tr>
<tr><td></td><td>CONNECT <target server> [<port> [<remote server>]]</td><td>Forces a server to try to establish a connection with another server; this command is privileged and may only be given by an IRC operator</td></tr>
</table>

Continued

Table 18.1 IRC Command Set (Continued)

Command Group	Command	Description
	TRACE [<server>]	Requests the list of servers that form the route to the specified server
	ADMIN [<server>]	Requests the name of the administrator of the specified server
	INFO [<server>]	Requests miscellaneous information about the specified server
Sending Messages		
	PRIVMSG <receiver>{,<receiver>} <text to be sent>	Sends a private message to a list of receivers
	NOTICE <nickname> <text>	Similar to PRIVMSG, but requires that automatic replies never be sent back to the source of the NOTICE message; used by "bots"
User Queries		
	WHO [<name> [<o>]]	Requests a list of users that match a specified name; the name may be the name of a channel or a user's host, server, real name, or nickname
	WHOIS [<server>] <nickmask> [,<nickmask>[,...]]	Requests information about a list of users
	WHOWAS <nickname> [<count> [<server>]]	Similar to WHOIS but for a user name that no longer exists
Miscellaneous Messages		
	KILL <nickname> <comment>	Causes the user's link to the local server to be terminated; used by servers or by operators when a duplicate nickname is detected
	PING <server1> [<server2>]	Used by servers to verify that a client link is still active; clients must return a PONG message to <server1> as soon as possible
	PONG <daemon> [<daemon2>]	The reply to a PING message
	ERROR <error message>	Used to report a serious error to the operators

Continued

Table 18.1 IRC Command Set (Continued)

Command Group	Command	Description
Optionals		
	AWAY [message]	Specifies a message to automatically send the source of a PRIVMSG command to indicate that the user is away from the terminal; using the command with no parameters indicates that the user is back and removes the automatic reply
	REHASH	Used by an operator to force a server to reread its configuration file
	RESTART	Used by an operator to force a server to restart itself
	SUMMON <user> [<server>]	Sends a message to a user on a host running an IRC server to join IRC
	USERS [<server>]	Returns a list of users logged into the specified server
	WALLOPS <text>	Sends the specified text to all operators currently online
	USERHOST <nickname>{<space> <nickname>}	Takes list of up to five nicknames and returns information about the specified users
	ISON <nickname>{<space> <nickname>}	Given a list of space-separated nicknames, the server returns the nicknames of the users that are presently using IRC

Commands

Table 18.1 lists the command set supported by IRC.

Responses

IRC responses use the same basic message structure as commands (see the *Grammar* section). Responses can be distinguished from commands by the use of a numeric reply code in the <command> portion of the message grammar. Each reply code is a three-digit number. For convenience, reply codes are also given symbolic names. The symbolic names are not used in messages, however, but may be used as symbolic constants when writing IRC client and server programs.

Table 18.2 lists the complete set of IRC reply codes.

Table 18.2 IRC Reply Codes

Category	Code	Symbolic Name
Error Replies		
	401	ERR_NOSUCHNICK
	402	ERR_NOSUCHSERVER
	403	ERR_NOSUCHCHANNEL
	404	ERR_CANNOTSENDTOCHAN
	405	ERR_TOOMANYCHANNELS
	406	ERR_WASNOSUCHNICK
	407	ERR_TOOMANYTARGETS
	409	ERR_NOORIGIN
	411	ERR_NORECIPIENT
	412	ERR_NOTEXTTOSEND
	413	ERR_NOTOPLEVEL
	414	ERR_WILDTOPLEVEL
	421	ERR_UNKNOWNCOMMAND
	422	ERR_NOMOTD
	423	ERR_NOADMININFO
	424	ERR_FILEERROR
	431	ERR_NONICKNAMEGIVEN
	432	ERR_ERRONEUSNICKNAME
	433	ERR_NICKNAMEINUSE
	436	ERR_NICKCOLLISION
	441	ERR_USERNOTINCHANNEL
	442	ERR_NOTONCHANNEL
	443	ERR_USERONCHANNEL
	444	ERR_NOLOGIN
	445	ERR_SUMMONDISABLED
	446	ERR_USERSDISABLED

Continued

Table 18.2 IRC Reply Codes (Continued)

Category	Code	Symbolic Name
	451	ERR_NOTREGISTERED
	461	ERR_NEEDMOREPARAMS
	462	ERR_ALREADYREGISTRED
	463	ERR_NOPERMFORHOST
	464	ERR_PASSWDMISMATCH
	465	ERR_YOUREBANNEDCREEP
	467	ERR_KEYSET
	471	ERR_CHANNELISFULL
	472	ERR_UNKNOWNMODE
	473	ERR_INVITEONLYCHAN
	474	ERR_BANNEDFROMCHAN
	475	ERR_BADCHANNELKEY
	481	ERR_NOPRIVILEGES
	482	ERR_CHANOPRIVSNEEDED
	483	ERR_CANTKILLSERVER
	491	ERR_NOOPERHOST
	501	ERR_UMODEUNKNOWNFLAG
	502	ERR_USERSDONTMATCH
Command Responses		
	300	RPL_NONE
	302	RPL_USERHOST
	303	RPL_ISON
	301	RPL_AWAY
	305	RPL_UNAWAY
	306	RPL_NOWAWAY
	311	RPL_WHOISUSER
	312	RPL_WHOISSERVER
	313	RPL_WHOISOPERATOR
	317	RPL_WHOISIDLE
	318	RPL_ENDOFWHOIS
	319	RPL_WHOISCHANNELS

Continued

Table 18.2 IRC Reply Codes (Continued)

Category	Code	Symbolic Name
	314	RPL_WHOWASUSER
	369	RPL_ENDOFWHOWAS
	321	RPL_LISTSTART
	322	RPL_LIST
	323	RPL_LISTEND
	324	RPL_CHANNELMODEIS
	331	RPL_NOTOPIC
	332	RPL_TOPIC
	341	RPL_INVITING
	342	RPL_SUMMONING
	351	RPL_VERSION
	352	RPL_WHOREPLY
	315	RPL_ENDOFWHO
	353	RPL_NAMREPLY
	366	RPL_ENDOFNAMES
	364	RPL_LINKS
	365	RPL_ENDOFLINKS
	367	RPL_BANLIST
	368	RPL_ENDOFBANLIST
	371	RPL_INFO
	374	RPL_ENDOFINFO
	375	RPL_MOTDSTART
	372	RPL_MOTD
	376	RPL_ENDOFMOTD
	381	RPL_YOUREOPER
	382	RPL_REHASHING
	391	RPL_TIME
	392	RPL_USERSSTART
	393	RPL_USERS
	394	RPL_ENDOFUSERS
	395	RPL_NOUSERS

Continued

Table 18.2 IRC Reply Codes (Continued)

Category	Code	Symbolic Name
	200	RPL_TRACELINK
	201	RPL_TRACECONNECTING
	202	RPL_TRACEHANDSHAKE
	203	RPL_TRACEUNKNOWN
	204	RPL_TRACEOPERATOR
	205	RPL_TRACEUSER
	206	RPL_TRACESERVER
	208	RPL_TRACENEWTYPE
	261	RPL_TRACELOG
	211	RPL_STATSLINKINFO
	212	RPL_STATSCOMMANDS
	213	RPL_STATSCLINE
	214	RPL_STATSNLINE
	215	RPL_STATSILINE
	216	RPL_STATSKLINE
	218	RPL_STATSYLINE
	219	RPL_ENDOFSTATS
	241	RPL_STATSLLINE
	242	RPL_STATSUPTIME
	243	RPL_STATSOLINE
	244	RPL_STATSHLINE
	221	RPL_UMODEIS
	251	RPL_LUSERCLIENT
	252	RPL_LUSEROP
	253	RPL_LUSERUNKNOWN
	254	RPL_LUSERCHANNELS
	255	RPL_LUSERME
	256	RPL_ADMINME
	257	RPL_ADMINLOC1
	258	RPL_ADMINLOC2
	259	RPL_ADMINEMAIL

Grammar

Message Format

```
<message> ::=  [':' <prefix> <SPACE> ] <command> <params> <crlf>
<prefix>  ::=  <servername> | <nick> [ '!' <user> ] [ '@' <host> ]
<command> ::=  <letter> { <letter> } | <number> <number> <number>
<SPACE>   ::=  ' ' { ' ' }
<params>  ::=  <SPACE> [ ':' <trailing> | <middle> <params> ]
<middle>  ::=  <Any *non-empty* sequence of octets not including SPACE or
   NUL or CR or LF, the first of which may not be ':'>
<trailing>  ::=  <Any, possibly *empty*, sequence of octets not including
   NUL or CR or LF>
<crlf>  ::=  CR LF
```

Parameters

```
<target>  ::=  <to> [ "," <target> ]
<to> ::=  <channel> | <user> '@' <servername> | <nick> | <mask>
<channel> ::=  ('#' | '&') <chstring>
<servername>::=  <host>
<host>  ::=  see RFC 952 for details on allowed hostnames
<nick>  ::=  <letter> { <letter> | <number> | <special> }
<mask>  ::=  ('#' | '$') <chstring>
<chstring>  ::=  <any 8bit code except SPACE, BELL, NUL, CR, LF
   and comma (',')>
<user>  ::=  <nonwhite> { <nonwhite> }
<letter>  ::=  'a' ... 'z' | 'A' ... 'Z'
<number>  ::=  '0' ... '9'
<special> ::=  '-' | '[' | ']' | '\' | '`' | '^' | '{' | '}'
<nonwhite>  ::=  <any 8bit code except SPACE (0x20), NUL (0x0), CR (0xd),
   and LF (0xa)>
```

19 MIB-II

Name

Management Information Base for Network Management of TCP/IP-based Internets

Abbreviation

MIB-II

Status

Recommended Standard

Specifications

RFC 1213

Abstract

MIB-II describes a standard MIB used to manage TCP/IP-based Internet entities. MIB-II is the second version of the original MIB (called, simply, MIB-I). Since its creation, MIB-II has become the basic MIB used to manage every TCP/IP-based device in the Internet.

Related Specifications

SNMPv1 (RFC 1157)

See A so

SNMPv2 (RFC 1902, 1903, 1904, 1905, 1906, 1907, 1908)

Comments

Note that MIB-II was originally written for SNMPv1, not SNMPv2, using the original Structure of Management Information (SMI) defined in RFC 1155. The object definitions in this chapter have not been rewritten to be consistent to the changes introduced with the development of SNMPv2. See RFC 1908 for more information about converting RFC 1155-based MIBs to the SNMPv2 version of the SMI.

Description

MIB-II defines 10 groups of management objects. Each group includes objects to manage different TCP/IP protocol entities. For instance, the TCP Group includes counters and tables relating to the operation of the TCP module within an Internet device, and the IP Group includes counters and tables relating to the operation of the IP module.

Although MIB-II is presented as a single set of definitions, managed devices are not required to implement every object in the MIB. Rather, optional functionality is allowed at the object group level. If a managed device implements *any* object in a group, it must implement *every* object in the group; however, the device is not required to implement groups that make no sense for the particular object. For instance, standard Internet hosts do not implement EGP and thus are not required to implement the EGP Group.

Object Definitions

This section presents the formal object definitions that make up MIB-II. Although subsection headings have been inserted into the MIB at appropriate points to make finding a particular section easier, MIB-II is presented in RFC 1213 as a single definition module.

```
RFC1213-MIB DEFINITIONS ::= BEGIN

IMPORTS
        mgmt, NetworkAddress, IpAddress, Counter, Gauge,
                TimeTicks
            FROM RFC1155-SMI
        OBJECT-TYPE
                FROM RFC-1212;

--  This MIB module uses the extended OBJECT-TYPE macro as
--  defined in [14];


--  MIB-II (same prefix as MIB-I)

mib-2      OBJECT IDENTIFIER ::= { mgmt 1 }

-- textual conventions

DisplayString ::=
    OCTET STRING
-- This data type is used to model textual information taken
-- from the NVT ASCII character set.  By convention, objects
-- with this syntax are declared as having
--
--      SIZE (0..255)

PhysAddress ::=
    OCTET STRING
-- This data type is used to model media addresses.  For many
-- types of media, this will be in a binary representation.
-- For example, an Ethernet address would be represented as
-- a string of 6 octets.


-- groups in MIB-II

system       OBJECT IDENTIFIER ::= { mib-2 1 }

interfaces   OBJECT IDENTIFIER ::= { mib-2 2 }

at           OBJECT IDENTIFIER ::= { mib-2 3 }

ip           OBJECT IDENTIFIER ::= { mib-2 4 }

icmp         OBJECT IDENTIFIER ::= { mib-2 5 }
```

```
tcp          OBJECT IDENTIFIER ::= { mib-2 6 }

udp          OBJECT IDENTIFIER ::= { mib-2 7 }

egp          OBJECT IDENTIFIER ::= { mib-2 8 }

-- historical (some say hysterical)
-- cmot      OBJECT IDENTIFIER ::= { mib-2 9 }

transmission OBJECT IDENTIFIER ::= { mib-2 10 }

snmp         OBJECT IDENTIFIER ::= { mib-2 11 }
```

System Group

```
-- the System group

-- Implementation of the System group is mandatory for all
-- systems.  If an agent is not configured to have a value
-- for any of these variables, a string of length 0 is
-- returned.

sysDescr OBJECT-TYPE
    SYNTAX  DisplayString (SIZE (0..255))
    ACCESS  read-only
    STATUS  mandatory
    DESCRIPTION
            "A textual description of the entity.  This value
            should include the full name and version
            identification of the system's hardware type,
            software operating-system, and networking
            software.  It is mandatory that this only contain
            printable ASCII characters."
    ::= { system 1 }

sysObjectID OBJECT-TYPE
    SYNTAX  OBJECT IDENTIFIER
    ACCESS  read-only
    STATUS  mandatory
    DESCRIPTION
            "The vendor's authoritative identification of the
            network management subsystem contained in the
            entity.  This value is allocated within the SMI
            enterprises subtree (1.3.6.1.4.1) and provides an
            easy and unambiguous means for determining 'what
            kind of box' is being managed.  For example, if
            vendor 'Flintstones, Inc.' was assigned the
```

```
                subtree 1.3.6.1.4.1.4242, it could assign the
                identifier 1.3.6.1.4.1.4242.1.1 to its 'Fred
                Router'."
        ::= { system 2 }

sysUpTime OBJECT-TYPE
        SYNTAX  TimeTicks
        ACCESS  read-only
        STATUS  mandatory
        DESCRIPTION
                "The time (in hundredths of a second) since the
                network management portion of the system was last
                re-initialized."
        ::= { system 3 }

sysContact OBJECT-TYPE
        SYNTAX  DisplayString (SIZE (0..255))
        ACCESS  read-write
        STATUS  mandatory
        DESCRIPTION
                "The textual identification of the contact person
                for this managed node, together with information
                on how to contact this person."
        ::= { system 4 }

sysName OBJECT-TYPE
        SYNTAX  DisplayString (SIZE (0..255))
        ACCESS  read-write
        STATUS  mandatory
        DESCRIPTION
                "An administratively-assigned name for this
                managed node.  By convention, this is the node's
                fully-qualified domain name."
        ::= { system 5 }

sysLocation OBJECT-TYPE
        SYNTAX  DisplayString (SIZE (0..255))
        ACCESS  read-write
        STATUS  mandatory
        DESCRIPTION
                "The physical location of this node (e.g.,
                'telephone closet, 3rd floor')."
        ::= { system 6 }

sysServices OBJECT-TYPE
        SYNTAX  INTEGER (0..127)
        ACCESS  read-only
```

```
    STATUS  mandatory
    DESCRIPTION
            "A value which indicates the set of services that
            this entity primarily offers.

            The value is a sum.  This sum initially takes the
            value zero, Then, for each layer, L, in the range
            1 through 7, that this node performs transactions
            for, 2 raised to (L - 1) is added to the sum.  For
            example, a node which performs primarily routing
            functions would have a value of 4 (2^(3-1)).  In
            contrast, a node which is a host offering
            application services would have a value of 72
            (2^(4-1) + 2^(7-1)).  Note that in the context of
            the Internet suite of protocols, values should be
            calculated accordingly:

                 layer  functionality
                     1  physical (e.g., repeaters)
                     2  datalink/subnetwork (e.g., bridges)
                     3  internet (e.g., IP gateways)
                     4  end-to-end  (e.g., IP hosts)
                     7  applications (e.g., mail relays)

            For systems including OSI protocols, layers 5 and
            6 may also be counted."
    ::= { system 7 }
```

Interfaces Group

```
-- the Interfaces group

-- Implementation of the Interfaces group is mandatory for
-- all systems.

ifNumber OBJECT-TYPE
    SYNTAX  INTEGER
    ACCESS  read-only
    STATUS  mandatory
    DESCRIPTION
            "The number of network interfaces (regardless of
            their current state) present on this system."
    ::= { interfaces 1 }


-- the Interfaces table
```

```
-- The Interfaces table contains information on the entity's
-- interfaces.  Each interface is thought of as being
-- attached to a 'subnetwork'.  Note that this term should
-- not be confused with 'subnet' which refers to an
-- addressing partitioning scheme used in the Internet suite
-- of protocols.

ifTable OBJECT-TYPE
    SYNTAX  SEQUENCE OF IfEntry
    ACCESS  not-accessible
    STATUS  mandatory
    DESCRIPTION
            "A list of interface entries.  The number of
            entries is given by the value of ifNumber."
    ::= { interfaces 2 }

ifEntry OBJECT-TYPE
    SYNTAX  IfEntry
    ACCESS  not-accessible
    STATUS  mandatory
    DESCRIPTION
            "An interface entry containing objects at the
            subnetwork layer and below for a particular
            interface."
    INDEX   { ifIndex }
    ::= { ifTable 1 }

IfEntry ::=
    SEQUENCE {
        ifIndex
            INTEGER,
        ifDescr
            DisplayString,
        ifType
            INTEGER,
        ifMtu
            INTEGER,
        ifSpeed
            Gauge,
        ifPhysAddress
            PhysAddress,
        ifAdminStatus
            INTEGER,
        ifOperStatus
            INTEGER,
        ifLastChange
            TimeTicks,
```

```
        ifInOctets
            Counter,
        ifInUcastPkts
            Counter,
        ifInNUcastPkts
            Counter,
        ifInDiscards
            Counter,
        ifInErrors
            Counter,
        ifInUnknownProtos
            Counter,
        ifOutOctets
            Counter,
        ifOutUcastPkts
            Counter,
        ifOutNUcastPkts
            Counter,
        ifOutDiscards
            Counter,
        ifOutErrors
            Counter,
        ifOutQLen
            Gauge,
        ifSpecific
            OBJECT IDENTIFIER
    }

ifIndex OBJECT-TYPE
    SYNTAX  INTEGER
    ACCESS  read-only
    STATUS  mandatory
    DESCRIPTION
            "A unique value for each interface.  Its value
            ranges between 1 and the value of ifNumber.  The
            value for each interface must remain constant at
            least from one re-initialization of the entity's
            network management system to the next re-
            initialization."
    ::= { ifEntry 1 }

ifDescr OBJECT-TYPE
    SYNTAX  DisplayString (SIZE (0..255))
    ACCESS  read-only
    STATUS  mandatory
    DESCRIPTION
            "A textual string containing information about the
```

```
            interface.  This string should include the name of
            the manufacturer, the product name, and the version
            of the hardware interface."
    ::= { ifEntry 2 }

ifType OBJECT-TYPE
    SYNTAX  INTEGER {
                other(1),          -- none of the following
                regular1822(2),
                hdh1822(3),
                ddn-x25(4),
                rfc877-x25(5),
                ethernet-csmacd(6),
                iso88023-csmacd(7),
                iso88024-tokenBus(8),
                iso88025-tokenRing(9),
                iso88026-man(10),
                starLan(11),
                proteon-10Mbit(12),
                proteon-80Mbit(13),
                hyperchannel(14),
                fddi(15),
                lapb(16),
                sdlc(17),
                ds1(18),           -- T-1
                e1(19),            -- european equiv. of T-1
                basicISDN(20),
                primaryISDN(21),   -- proprietary serial
                propPointToPointSerial(22),
                ppp(23),
                softwareLoopback(24),
                eon(25),            -- CLNP over IP [11]
                ethernet-3Mbit(26),
                nsip(27),           -- XNS over IP
                slip(28),           -- generic SLIP
                ultra(29),          -- ULTRA technologies
                ds3(30),            -- T-3
                sip(31),            -- SMDS
                frame-relay(32)
            }
    ACCESS  read-only
    STATUS  mandatory
    DESCRIPTION
            "The type of interface, distinguished according to
            the physical/link protocol(s) immediately 'below'
            the network layer in the protocol stack."
    ::= { ifEntry 3 }
```

```
ifMtu OBJECT-TYPE
    SYNTAX  INTEGER
    ACCESS  read-only
    STATUS  mandatory
    DESCRIPTION
            "The size of the largest datagram which can be
            sent/received on the interface, specified in
            octets.  For interfaces that are used for
            transmitting network datagrams, this is the size
            of the largest network datagram that can be sent
            on the interface."
    ::= { ifEntry 4 }

ifSpeed OBJECT-TYPE
    SYNTAX  Gauge
    ACCESS  read-only
    STATUS  mandatory
    DESCRIPTION
            "An estimate of the interface's current bandwidth
            in bits per second.  For interfaces which do not
            vary in bandwidth or for those where no accurate
            estimation can be made, this object should contain
            the nominal bandwidth."
    ::= { ifEntry 5 }

ifPhysAddress OBJECT-TYPE
    SYNTAX  PhysAddress
    ACCESS  read-only
    STATUS  mandatory
    DESCRIPTION
            "The interface's address at the protocol layer
            immediately 'below' the network layer in the
            protocol stack.  For interfaces which do not have
            such an address (e.g., a serial line), this object
            should contain an octet string of zero length."
    ::= { ifEntry 6 }

ifAdminStatus OBJECT-TYPE
    SYNTAX  INTEGER {
                up(1),        -- ready to pass packets
                down(2),
                testing(3)    -- in some test mode
            }
    ACCESS  read-write
    STATUS  mandatory
    DESCRIPTION
            "The desired state of the interface.  The
            testing(3) state indicates that no operational
```

```
                packets can be passed."
        ::= { ifEntry 7 }

    ifOperStatus OBJECT-TYPE
        SYNTAX  INTEGER {
                    up(1),        -- ready to pass packets
                    down(2),
                    testing(3)    -- in some test mode
                }
        ACCESS  read-only
        STATUS  mandatory
        DESCRIPTION
                "The current operational state of the interface.
                The testing(3) state indicates that no operational
                packets can be passed."
        ::= { ifEntry 8 }

    ifLastChange OBJECT-TYPE
        SYNTAX  TimeTicks
        ACCESS  read-only
        STATUS  mandatory
        DESCRIPTION
                "The value of sysUpTime at the time the interface
                entered its current operational state.  If the
                current state was entered prior to the last re-
                initialization of the local network management
                subsystem, then this object contains a zero
                value."
        ::= { ifEntry 9 }

    ifInOctets OBJECT-TYPE
        SYNTAX  Counter
        ACCESS  read-only
        STATUS  mandatory
        DESCRIPTION
                "The total number of octets received on the
                interface, including framing characters."
        ::= { ifEntry 10 }

    ifInUcastPkts OBJECT-TYPE
        SYNTAX  Counter
        ACCESS  read-only
        STATUS  mandatory
        DESCRIPTION
                "The number of subnetwork-unicast packets
                delivered to a higher-layer protocol."
        ::= { ifEntry 11 }
```

```
ifInNUcastPkts OBJECT-TYPE
    SYNTAX  Counter
    ACCESS  read-only
    STATUS  mandatory
    DESCRIPTION
            "The number of non-unicast (i.e., subnetwork-
            broadcast or subnetwork-multicast) packets
            delivered to a higher-layer protocol."
    ::= { ifEntry 12 }

ifInDiscards OBJECT-TYPE
    SYNTAX  Counter
    ACCESS  read-only
    STATUS  mandatory
    DESCRIPTION
            "The number of inbound packets which were chosen
            to be discarded even though no errors had been
            detected to prevent their being deliverable to a
            higher-layer protocol.  One possible reason for
            discarding such a packet could be to free up
            buffer space."
    ::= { ifEntry 13 }

ifInErrors OBJECT-TYPE
    SYNTAX  Counter
    ACCESS  read-only
    STATUS  mandatory
    DESCRIPTION
            "The number of inbound packets that contained
            errors preventing them from being deliverable to a
            higher-layer protocol."
    ::= { ifEntry 14 }

ifInUnknownProtos OBJECT-TYPE
    SYNTAX  Counter
    ACCESS  read-only
    STATUS  mandatory
    DESCRIPTION
            "The number of packets received via the interface
            which were discarded because of an unknown or
            unsupported protocol."
    ::= { ifEntry 15 }

ifOutOctets OBJECT-TYPE
    SYNTAX  Counter
    ACCESS  read-only
    STATUS  mandatory
```

```
    DESCRIPTION
            "The total number of octets transmitted out of the
            interface, including framing characters."
    ::= { ifEntry 16 }

ifOutUcastPkts OBJECT-TYPE
    SYNTAX  Counter
    ACCESS  read-only
    STATUS  mandatory
    DESCRIPTION
            "The total number of packets that higher-level
            protocols requested be transmitted to a
            subnetwork-unicast address, including those that
            were discarded or not sent."
    ::= { ifEntry 17 }

ifOutNUcastPkts OBJECT-TYPE
    SYNTAX  Counter
    ACCESS  read-only
    STATUS  mandatory
    DESCRIPTION
            "The total number of packets that higher-level
            protocols requested be transmitted to a non-
            unicast (i.e., a subnetwork-broadcast or
            subnetwork-multicast) address, including those
            that were discarded or not sent."
    ::= { ifEntry 18 }

ifOutDiscards OBJECT-TYPE
    SYNTAX  Counter
    ACCESS  read-only
    STATUS  mandatory
    DESCRIPTION
            "The number of outbound packets which were chosen
            to be discarded even though no errors had been
            detected to prevent their being transmitted.  One
            possible reason for discarding such a packet could
            be to free up buffer space."
    ::= { ifEntry 19 }

ifOutErrors OBJECT-TYPE
    SYNTAX  Counter
    ACCESS  read-only
    STATUS  mandatory
    DESCRIPTION
            "The number of outbound packets that could not be
            transmitted because of errors."
    ::= { ifEntry 20 }
```

```
ifOutQLen OBJECT-TYPE
    SYNTAX  Gauge
    ACCESS  read-only
    STATUS  mandatory
    DESCRIPTION
            "The length of the output packet queue (in
            packets)."
    ::= { ifEntry 21 }

ifSpecific OBJECT-TYPE
    SYNTAX  OBJECT IDENTIFIER
    ACCESS  read-only
    STATUS  mandatory
    DESCRIPTION
            "A reference to MIB definitions specific to the
            particular media being used to realize the
            interface.  For example, if the interface is
            realized by an Ethernet, then the value of this
            object refers to a document defining objects
            specific to Ethernet.  If this information is not
            present, its value should be set to the OBJECT
            IDENTIFIER { 0 0 }, which is a syntatically valid
            object identifier, and any conformant
            implementation of ASN.1 and BER must be able to
            generate and recognize this value."
    ::= { ifEntry 22 }
```

Address Translation Group

```
-- the Address Translation group

-- Implementation of the Address Translation group is
-- mandatory for all systems.  Note, however, that this group
-- is deprecated by MIB-II. That is, it is being included
-- solely for compatibility with MIB-I nodes, and will most
-- likely be excluded from MIB-III nodes.  From MIB-II and
-- onwards, each network protocol group contains its own
-- address translation tables.

-- The Address Translation group contains one table which is
-- the union across all interfaces of the translation tables
-- for converting a NetworkAddress (e.g., an IP address) into
-- a subnetwork-specific address.  For lack of a better term,
-- this document refers to such a subnetwork-specific address
-- as a 'physical' address.
```

```
-- Examples of such translation tables are: for broadcast
-- media where ARP is in use, the translation table is
-- equivalent to the ARP cache; or, on an X.25 network where
-- non-algorithmic translation to X.121 addresses is
-- required, the translation table contains the
-- NetworkAddress to X.121 address equivalences.

atTable OBJECT-TYPE
    SYNTAX  SEQUENCE OF AtEntry
    ACCESS  not-accessible
    STATUS  deprecated
    DESCRIPTION
            "The Address Translation tables contain the
            NetworkAddress to 'physical' address equivalences.
            Some interfaces do not use translation tables for
            determining address equivalences (e.g., DDN-X.25
            has an algorithmic method); if all interfaces are
            of this type, then the Address Translation table
            is empty, i.e., has zero entries."
    ::= { at 1 }

atEntry OBJECT-TYPE
    SYNTAX  AtEntry
    ACCESS  not-accessible
    STATUS  deprecated
    DESCRIPTION
            "Each entry contains one NetworkAddress to
            'physical' address equivalence."
    INDEX   { atIfIndex,
              atNetAddress }
    ::= { atTable 1 }

AtEntry ::=
    SEQUENCE {
        atIfIndex
            INTEGER,
        atPhysAddress
            PhysAddress,
        atNetAddress
            NetworkAddress
    }

atIfIndex OBJECT-TYPE
    SYNTAX  INTEGER
    ACCESS  read-write
    STATUS  deprecated
```

```
    DESCRIPTION
            "The interface on which this entry's equivalence
            is effective.  The interface identified by a
            particular value of this index is the same
            interface as identified by the same value of
            ifIndex."
    ::= { atEntry 1 }

atPhysAddress OBJECT-TYPE
    SYNTAX  PhysAddress
    ACCESS  read-write
    STATUS  deprecated
    DESCRIPTION
            "The media-dependent 'physical' address.

            Setting this object to a null string (one of zero
            length) has the effect of invaliding the
            corresponding entry in the atTable object.  That
            is, it effectively dissasociates the interface
            identified with said entry from the mapping
            identified with said entry.  It is an
            implementation-specific matter as to whether the
            agent removes an invalidated entry from the table.
            Accordingly, management stations must be prepared
            to receive tabular information from agents that
            corresponds to entries not currently in use.
            Proper interpretation of such entries requires
            examination of the relevant atPhysAddress object."
    ::= { atEntry 2 }

atNetAddress OBJECT-TYPE
    SYNTAX  NetworkAddress
    ACCESS  read-write
    STATUS  deprecated
    DESCRIPTION
            "The NetworkAddress (e.g., the IP address)
            corresponding to the media-dependent 'physical'
            address."
    ::= { atEntry 3 }
```

IP Group

```
-- the IP group

-- Implementation of the IP group is mandatory for all
-- systems.
```

```
ipForwarding OBJECT-TYPE
    SYNTAX  INTEGER {
                forwarding(1),     -- acting as a gateway
                not-forwarding(2)  -- NOT acting as a gateway
            }
    ACCESS  read-write
    STATUS  mandatory
    DESCRIPTION
            "The indication of whether this entity is acting
            as an IP gateway in respect to the forwarding of
            datagrams received by, but not addressed to, this
            entity.  IP gateways forward datagrams.  IP hosts
            do not (except those source-routed via the host).

            Note that for some managed nodes, this object may
            take on only a subset of the values possible.
            Accordingly, it is appropriate for an agent to
            return a 'badValue' response if a management
            station attempts to change this object to an
            inappropriate value."
    ::= { ip 1 }

ipDefaultTTL OBJECT-TYPE
    SYNTAX  INTEGER
    ACCESS  read-write
    STATUS  mandatory
    DESCRIPTION
            "The default value inserted into the Time-To-Live
            field of the IP header of datagrams originated at
            this entity, whenever a TTL value is not supplied
            by the transport layer protocol."
    ::= { ip 2 }

ipInReceives OBJECT-TYPE
    SYNTAX  Counter
    ACCESS  read-only
    STATUS  mandatory
    DESCRIPTION
            "The total number of input datagrams received from
            interfaces, including those received in error."
    ::= { ip 3 }

ipInHdrErrors OBJECT-TYPE
    SYNTAX  Counter
    ACCESS  read-only
    STATUS  mandatory
```

```
    DESCRIPTION
            "The number of input datagrams discarded due to
            errors in their IP headers, including bad
            checksums, version number mismatch, other format
            errors, time-to-live exceeded, errors discovered
            in processing their IP options, etc."
    ::= { ip 4 }

ipInAddrErrors OBJECT-TYPE
    SYNTAX  Counter
    ACCESS  read-only
    STATUS  mandatory
    DESCRIPTION
            "The number of input datagrams discarded because
            the IP address in their IP header's destination
            field was not a valid address to be received at
            this entity.  This count includes invalid
            addresses (e.g., 0.0.0.0) and addresses of
            unsupported Classes (e.g., Class E).  For entities
            which are not IP gateways and therefore do not
            forward datagrams, this counter includes datagrams
            discarded because the destination address was not
            a local address."
    ::= { ip 5 }

ipForwDatagrams OBJECT-TYPE
    SYNTAX  Counter
    ACCESS  read-only
    STATUS  mandatory
    DESCRIPTION
            "The number of input datagrams for which this
            entity was not their final IP destination, as a
            result of which an attempt was made to find a
            route to forward them to that final destination.
            In entities which do not act as IP gateways, this
            counter will include only those packets which were
            Source-Routed via this entity, and the Source-
            Route option processing was successful."
    ::= { ip 6 }

ipInUnknownProtos OBJECT-TYPE
    SYNTAX  Counter
    ACCESS  read-only
    STATUS  mandatory
    DESCRIPTION
            "The number of locally-addressed datagrams
            received successfully but discarded because of an
```

```
            unknown or unsupported protocol."
    ::= { ip 7 }

ipInDiscards OBJECT-TYPE
    SYNTAX  Counter
    ACCESS  read-only
    STATUS  mandatory
    DESCRIPTION
            "The number of input IP datagrams for which no
            problems were encountered to prevent their
            continued processing, but which were discarded
            (e.g., for lack of buffer space).  Note that this
            counter does not include any datagrams discarded
            while awaiting re-assembly."
    ::= { ip 8 }

ipInDelivers OBJECT-TYPE
    SYNTAX  Counter
    ACCESS  read-only
    STATUS  mandatory
    DESCRIPTION
            "The total number of input datagrams successfully
            delivered to IP user-protocols (including ICMP)."
    ::= { ip 9 }

ipOutRequests OBJECT-TYPE
    SYNTAX  Counter
    ACCESS  read-only
    STATUS  mandatory
    DESCRIPTION
            "The total number of IP datagrams which local IP
            user-protocols (including ICMP) supplied to IP in
            requests for transmission.  Note that this counter
            does not include any datagrams counted in
            ipForwDatagrams."
    ::= { ip 10 }

ipOutDiscards OBJECT-TYPE
    SYNTAX  Counter
    ACCESS  read-only
    STATUS  mandatory
    DESCRIPTION
            "The number of output IP datagrams for which no
            problem was encountered to prevent their
            transmission to their destination, but which were
            discarded (e.g., for lack of buffer space).  Note
            that this counter would include datagrams counted
```

```
          in ipForwDatagrams if any such packets met this
          (discretionary) discard criterion."
    ::= { ip 11 }

ipOutNoRoutes OBJECT-TYPE
    SYNTAX  Counter
    ACCESS  read-only
    STATUS  mandatory
    DESCRIPTION
          "The number of IP datagrams discarded because no
          route could be found to transmit them to their
          destination.  Note that this counter includes any
          packets counted in ipForwDatagrams which meet this
          'no-route' criterion.  Note that this includes any
          datagrams which a host cannot route because all of
          its default gateways are down."
    ::= { ip 12 }

ipReasmTimeout OBJECT-TYPE
    SYNTAX  INTEGER
    ACCESS  read-only
    STATUS  mandatory
    DESCRIPTION
          "The maximum number of seconds which received
          fragments are held while they are awaiting
          reassembly at this entity."
    ::= { ip 13 }

ipReasmReqds OBJECT-TYPE
    SYNTAX  Counter
    ACCESS  read-only
    STATUS  mandatory
    DESCRIPTION
          "The number of IP fragments received which needed
          to be reassembled at this entity."
    ::= { ip 14 }

ipReasmOKs OBJECT-TYPE
    SYNTAX  Counter
    ACCESS  read-only
    STATUS  mandatory
    DESCRIPTION
          "The number of IP datagrams successfully re-
          assembled."
    ::= { ip 15 }
```

```
ipReasmFails OBJECT-TYPE
    SYNTAX  Counter
    ACCESS  read-only
    STATUS  mandatory
    DESCRIPTION
            "The number of failures detected by the IP re-
            assembly algorithm (for whatever reason: timed
            out, errors, etc).  Note that this is not
            necessarily a count of discarded IP fragments
            since some algorithms (notably the algorithm in
            RFC 815) can lose track of the number of fragments
            by combining them as they are received."
    ::= { ip 16 }

ipFragOKs OBJECT-TYPE
    SYNTAX  Counter
    ACCESS  read-only
    STATUS  mandatory
    DESCRIPTION
            "The number of IP datagrams that have been
            successfully fragmented at this entity."
    ::= { ip 17 }

ipFragFails OBJECT-TYPE
    SYNTAX  Counter
    ACCESS  read-only
    STATUS  mandatory
    DESCRIPTION
            "The number of IP datagrams that have been
            discarded because they needed to be fragmented at
            this entity but could not be, e.g., because their
            Don't Fragment flag was set."
    ::= { ip 18 }

ipFragCreates OBJECT-TYPE
    SYNTAX  Counter
    ACCESS  read-only
    STATUS  mandatory
    DESCRIPTION
            "The number of IP datagram fragments that have
            been generated as a result of fragmentation at
            this entity."
    ::= { ip 19 }


-- the IP address table
```

```
-- The IP address table contains this entity's IP addressing
-- information.

ipAddrTable OBJECT-TYPE
    SYNTAX  SEQUENCE OF IpAddrEntry
    ACCESS  not-accessible
    STATUS  mandatory
    DESCRIPTION
            "The table of addressing information relevant to
            this entity's IP addresses."
    ::= { ip 20 }

ipAddrEntry OBJECT-TYPE
    SYNTAX  IpAddrEntry
    ACCESS  not-accessible
    STATUS  mandatory
    DESCRIPTION
            "The addressing information for one of this
            entity's IP addresses."
    INDEX   { ipAdEntAddr }
    ::= { ipAddrTable 1 }

IpAddrEntry ::=
    SEQUENCE {
        ipAdEntAddr
            IpAddress,
        ipAdEntIfIndex
            INTEGER,
        ipAdEntNetMask
            IpAddress,
        ipAdEntBcastAddr
            INTEGER,
        ipAdEntReasmMaxSize
            INTEGER (0..65535)
    }

ipAdEntAddr OBJECT-TYPE
    SYNTAX  IpAddress
    ACCESS  read-only
    STATUS  mandatory
    DESCRIPTION
            "The IP address to which this entry's addressing
            information pertains."
    ::= { ipAddrEntry 1 }

ipAdEntIfIndex OBJECT-TYPE
    SYNTAX  INTEGER
```

```
    ACCESS  read-only
    STATUS  mandatory
    DESCRIPTION
            "The index value which uniquely identifies the
            interface to which this entry is applicable.  The
            interface identified by a particular value of this
            index is the same interface as identified by the
            same value of ifIndex."
    ::= { ipAddrEntry 2 }

ipAdEntNetMask OBJECT-TYPE
    SYNTAX  IpAddress
    ACCESS  read-only
    STATUS  mandatory
    DESCRIPTION
            "The subnet mask associated with the IP address of
            this entry.  The value of the mask is an IP
            address with all the network bits set to 1 and all
            the hosts bits set to 0."
    ::= { ipAddrEntry 3 }

ipAdEntBcastAddr OBJECT-TYPE
    SYNTAX  INTEGER
    ACCESS  read-only
    STATUS  mandatory
    DESCRIPTION
            "The value of the least-significant bit in the IP
            broadcast address used for sending datagrams on
            the (logical) interface associated with the IP
            address of this entry.  For example, when the
            Internet standard all-ones broadcast address is
            used, the value will be 1.  This value applies to
            both the subnet and network broadcast addresses
            used by the entity on this (logical) interface."
    ::= { ipAddrEntry 4 }

ipAdEntReasmMaxSize OBJECT-TYPE
    SYNTAX  INTEGER (0..65535)
    ACCESS  read-only
    STATUS  mandatory
    DESCRIPTION
            "The size of the largest IP datagram which this
            entity can re-assemble from incoming IP fragmented
            datagrams received on this interface."
    ::= { ipAddrEntry 5 }
```

```
-- the IP routing table

-- The IP routing table contains an entry for each route
-- presently known to this entity.

ipRouteTable OBJECT-TYPE
    SYNTAX  SEQUENCE OF IpRouteEntry
    ACCESS  not-accessible
    STATUS  mandatory
    DESCRIPTION
            "This entity's IP Routing table."
    ::= { ip 21 }

ipRouteEntry OBJECT-TYPE
    SYNTAX  IpRouteEntry
    ACCESS  not-accessible
    STATUS  mandatory
    DESCRIPTION
            "A route to a particular destination."
    INDEX   { ipRouteDest }
    ::= { ipRouteTable 1 }

IpRouteEntry ::=
    SEQUENCE {
        ipRouteDest
            IpAddress,
        ipRouteIfIndex
            INTEGER,
        ipRouteMetric1
            INTEGER,
        ipRouteMetric2
            INTEGER,
        ipRouteMetric3
            INTEGER,
        ipRouteMetric4
            INTEGER,
        ipRouteNextHop
            IpAddress,
        ipRouteType
            INTEGER,
        ipRouteProto
            INTEGER,
        ipRouteAge
            INTEGER,
        ipRouteMask
            IpAddress,
```

```
        ipRouteMetric5
            INTEGER,
        ipRouteInfo
            OBJECT IDENTIFIER
    }

ipRouteDest OBJECT-TYPE
    SYNTAX  IpAddress
    ACCESS  read-write
    STATUS  mandatory
    DESCRIPTION
            "The destination IP address of this route.  An
            entry with a value of 0.0.0.0 is considered a
            default route.  Multiple routes to a single
            destination can appear in the table, but access to
            such multiple entries is dependent on the table-
            access mechanisms defined by the network
            management protocol in use."
    ::= { ipRouteEntry 1 }

ipRouteIfIndex OBJECT-TYPE
    SYNTAX  INTEGER
    ACCESS  read-write
    STATUS  mandatory
    DESCRIPTION
            "The index value which uniquely identifies the
            local interface through which the next hop of this
            route should be reached.  The interface identified
            by a particular value of this index is the same
            interface as identified by the same value of
            ifIndex."
    ::= { ipRouteEntry 2 }

ipRouteMetric1 OBJECT-TYPE
    SYNTAX  INTEGER
    ACCESS  read-write
    STATUS  mandatory
    DESCRIPTION
            "The primary routing metric for this route.  The
            semantics of this metric are determined by the
            routing-protocol specified in the route's
            ipRouteProto value.  If this metric is not used,
            its value should be set to -1."
    ::= { ipRouteEntry 3 }

ipRouteMetric2 OBJECT-TYPE
    SYNTAX  INTEGER
```

```
    ACCESS  read-write
    STATUS  mandatory
    DESCRIPTION
            "An alternate routing metric for this route.  The
            semantics of this metric are determined by the
            routing-protocol specified in the route's
            ipRouteProto value.  If this metric is not used,
            its value should be set to -1."
    ::= { ipRouteEntry 4 }

ipRouteMetric3 OBJECT-TYPE
    SYNTAX  INTEGER
    ACCESS  read-write
    STATUS  mandatory
    DESCRIPTION
            "An alternate routing metric for this route.  The
            semantics of this metric are determined by the
            routing-protocol specified in the route's
            ipRouteProto value.  If this metric is not used,
            its value should be set to -1."
    ::= { ipRouteEntry 5 }

ipRouteMetric4 OBJECT-TYPE
    SYNTAX  INTEGER
    ACCESS  read-write
    STATUS  mandatory
    DESCRIPTION
            "An alternate routing metric for this route.  The
            semantics of this metric are determined by the
            routing-protocol specified in the route's
            ipRouteProto value.  If this metric is not used,
            its value should be set to -1."
    ::= { ipRouteEntry 6 }

ipRouteNextHop OBJECT-TYPE
    SYNTAX  IpAddress
    ACCESS  read-write
    STATUS  mandatory
    DESCRIPTION
            "The IP address of the next hop of this route.
            (In the case of a route bound to an interface
            which is realized via a broadcast media, the value
            of this field is the agent's IP address on that
            interface.)"
    ::= { ipRouteEntry 7 }
```

```
ipRouteType OBJECT-TYPE
    SYNTAX  INTEGER {
                other(1),           -- none of the following

                invalid(2),         -- an invalidated route

                                    -- route to directly
                direct(3),          -- connected (sub-)network

                                    -- route to a non-local
                indirect(4)         -- host/network/sub-network
            }
    ACCESS  read-write
    STATUS  mandatory
    DESCRIPTION
            "The type of route.  Note that the values
            direct(3) and indirect(4) refer to the notion of
            direct and indirect routing in the IP
            architecture.

            Setting this object to the value invalid(2) has
            the effect of invalidating the corresponding entry
            in the ipRouteTable object.  That is, it
            effectively dissasociates the destination
            identified with said entry from the route
            identified with said entry.  It is an
            implementation-specific matter as to whether the
            agent removes an invalidated entry from the table.
            Accordingly, management stations must be prepared
            to receive tabular information from agents that
            corresponds to entries not currently in use.
            Proper interpretation of such entries requires
            examination of the relevant ipRouteType object."
    ::= { ipRouteEntry 8 }

ipRouteProto OBJECT-TYPE
    SYNTAX  INTEGER {
                other(1),           -- none of the following

                                    -- non-protocol information,
                                    -- e.g., manually configured
                local(2),           -- entries

                                    -- set via a network
                netmgmt(3),         -- management protocol
```

```
                                -- obtained via ICMP,
                icmp(4),        -- e.g., Redirect

                                -- the remaining values are
                                -- all gateway routing
                                -- protocols
                egp(5),
                ggp(6),
                hello(7),
                rip(8),
                is-is(9),
                es-is(10),
                ciscoIgrp(11),
                bbnSpfIgp(12),
                ospf(13),
                bgp(14)
            }
    ACCESS  read-only
    STATUS  mandatory
    DESCRIPTION
            "The routing mechanism via which this route was
            learned.  Inclusion of values for gateway routing
            protocols is not intended to imply that hosts
            should support those protocols."
    ::= { ipRouteEntry 9 }

ipRouteAge OBJECT-TYPE
    SYNTAX  INTEGER
    ACCESS  read-write
    STATUS  mandatory
    DESCRIPTION
            "The number of seconds since this route was last
            updated or otherwise determined to be correct.
            Note that no semantics of 'too old' can be implied
            except through knowledge of the routing protocol
            by which the route was learned."
    ::= { ipRouteEntry 10 }

ipRouteMask OBJECT-TYPE
    SYNTAX  IpAddress
    ACCESS  read-write
    STATUS  mandatory
    DESCRIPTION
            "Indicate the mask to be logical-ANDed with the
            destination address before being compared to the
            value in the ipRouteDest field.  For those systems
```

```
            that do not support arbitrary subnet masks, an
            agent constructs the value of the ipRouteMask by
            determining whether the value of the correspondent
            ipRouteDest field belong to a class-A, B, or C
            network, and then using one of:

                 mask            network
                 255.0.0.0       class-A
                 255.255.0.0     class-B
                 255.255.255.0   class-C
            If the value of the ipRouteDest is 0.0.0.0 (a
            default route), then the mask value is also
            0.0.0.0.  It should be noted that all IP routing
            subsystems implicitly use this mechanism."
    ::= { ipRouteEntry 11 }

ipRouteMetric5 OBJECT-TYPE
    SYNTAX  INTEGER
    ACCESS  read-write
    STATUS  mandatory
    DESCRIPTION
            "An alternate routing metric for this route.  The
            semantics of this metric are determined by the
            routing-protocol specified in the route's
            ipRouteProto value.  If this metric is not used,
            its value should be set to -1."
    ::= { ipRouteEntry 12 }

ipRouteInfo OBJECT-TYPE
    SYNTAX  OBJECT IDENTIFIER
    ACCESS  read-only
    STATUS  mandatory
    DESCRIPTION
            "A reference to MIB definitions specific to the
            particular routing protocol which is responsible
            for this route, as determined by the value
            specified in the route's ipRouteProto value.  If
            this information is not present, its value should
            be set to the OBJECT IDENTIFIER { 0 0 }, which is
            a syntatically valid object identifier, and any
            conformant implementation of ASN.1 and BER must be
            able to generate and recognize this value."
    ::= { ipRouteEntry 13 }


-- the IP Address Translation table
```

```
-- The IP Address Translation table contains the IpAddress to
-- 'physical' address equivalences.  Some interfaces do not
-- use translation tables for determining address
-- equivalences (e.g., DDN-X.25 has an algorithmic method);
-- if all interfaces are of this type, then the Address
-- Translation table is empty, i.e., has zero entries.

ipNetToMediaTable OBJECT-TYPE
    SYNTAX  SEQUENCE OF IpNetToMediaEntry
    ACCESS  not-accessible
    STATUS  mandatory
    DESCRIPTION
            "The IP Address Translation table used for mapping
            from IP addresses to physical addresses."
    ::= { ip 22 }

ipNetToMediaEntry OBJECT-TYPE
    SYNTAX  IpNetToMediaEntry
    ACCESS  not-accessible
    STATUS  mandatory
    DESCRIPTION
            "Each entry contains one IpAddress to 'physical'
            address equivalence."
    INDEX   { ipNetToMediaIfIndex,
              ipNetToMediaNetAddress }
    ::= { ipNetToMediaTable 1 }

IpNetToMediaEntry ::=
    SEQUENCE {
        ipNetToMediaIfIndex
            INTEGER,
        ipNetToMediaPhysAddress
            PhysAddress,
        ipNetToMediaNetAddress
            IpAddress,
        ipNetToMediaType
            INTEGER
    }

ipNetToMediaIfIndex OBJECT-TYPE
    SYNTAX  INTEGER
    ACCESS  read-write
    STATUS  mandatory
    DESCRIPTION
            "The interface on which this entry's equivalence
            is effective.  The interface identified by a
            particular value of this index is the same
```

```
            interface as identified by the same value of
            ifIndex."
    ::= { ipNetToMediaEntry 1 }

ipNetToMediaPhysAddress OBJECT-TYPE
    SYNTAX  PhysAddress
    ACCESS  read-write
    STATUS  mandatory
    DESCRIPTION
            "The media-dependent 'physical' address."
    ::= { ipNetToMediaEntry 2 }

ipNetToMediaNetAddress OBJECT-TYPE
    SYNTAX  IpAddress
    ACCESS  read-write
    STATUS  mandatory
    DESCRIPTION
            "The IpAddress corresponding to the media-
            dependent 'physical' address."
    ::= { ipNetToMediaEntry 3 }

ipNetToMediaType OBJECT-TYPE
    SYNTAX  INTEGER {
                other(1),        -- none of the following
                invalid(2),      -- an invalidated mapping
                dynamic(3),
                static(4)
            }
    ACCESS  read-write
    STATUS  mandatory
    DESCRIPTION
            "The type of mapping.

            Setting this object to the value invalid(2) has
            the effect of invalidating the corresponding entry
            in the ipNetToMediaTable.  That is, it effectively
            dissasociates the interface identified with said
            entry from the mapping identified with said entry.
            It is an implementation-specific matter as to
            whether the agent removes an invalidated entry
            from the table.  Accordingly, management stations
            must be prepared to receive tabular information
            from agents that corresponds to entries not
            currently in use.  Proper interpretation of such
            entries requires examination of the relevant
            ipNetToMediaType object."
    ::= { ipNetToMediaEntry 4 }
```

```
-- additional IP objects

ipRoutingDiscards OBJECT-TYPE
    SYNTAX  Counter
    ACCESS  read-only
    STATUS  mandatory
    DESCRIPTION
            "The number of routing entries which were chosen
            to be discarded even though they are valid.  One
            possible reason for discarding such an entry could
            be to free up buffer space for other routing
            entries."
    ::= { ip 23 }
```

ICMP Group

```
-- the ICMP group

-- Implementation of the ICMP group is mandatory for all
-- systems.

icmpInMsgs OBJECT-TYPE
    SYNTAX  Counter
    ACCESS  read-only
    STATUS  mandatory
    DESCRIPTION
            "The total number of ICMP messages which the
            entity received.  Note that this counter includes
            all those counted by icmpInErrors."
    ::= { icmp 1 }

icmpInErrors OBJECT-TYPE
    SYNTAX  Counter
    ACCESS  read-only
    STATUS  mandatory
    DESCRIPTION
            "The number of ICMP messages which the entity
            received but determined as having ICMP-specific
            errors (bad ICMP checksums, bad length, etc.)."
    ::= { icmp 2 }

icmpInDestUnreachs OBJECT-TYPE
    SYNTAX  Counter
    ACCESS  read-only
    STATUS  mandatory
    DESCRIPTION
            "The number of ICMP Destination Unreachable
```

```
            messages received."
    ::= { icmp 3 }

icmpInTimeExcds OBJECT-TYPE
    SYNTAX  Counter
    ACCESS  read-only
    STATUS  mandatory
    DESCRIPTION
            "The number of ICMP Time Exceeded messages
            received."
    ::= { icmp 4 }

icmpInParmProbs OBJECT-TYPE
    SYNTAX  Counter
    ACCESS  read-only
    STATUS  mandatory
    DESCRIPTION
            "The number of ICMP Parameter Problem messages
            received."
    ::= { icmp 5 }

icmpInSrcQuenchs OBJECT-TYPE
    SYNTAX  Counter
    ACCESS  read-only
    STATUS  mandatory
    DESCRIPTION
            "The number of ICMP Source Quench messages
            received."
    ::= { icmp 6 }

icmpInRedirects OBJECT-TYPE
    SYNTAX  Counter
    ACCESS  read-only
    STATUS  mandatory
    DESCRIPTION
            "The number of ICMP Redirect messages received."
    ::= { icmp 7 }

icmpInEchos OBJECT-TYPE
    SYNTAX  Counter
    ACCESS  read-only
    STATUS  mandatory
    DESCRIPTION
            "The number of ICMP Echo (request) messages
            received."
    ::= { icmp 8 }
```

```
icmpInEchoReps OBJECT-TYPE
    SYNTAX  Counter
    ACCESS  read-only
    STATUS  mandatory
    DESCRIPTION
            "The number of ICMP Echo Reply messages received."
    ::= { icmp 9 }

icmpInTimestamps OBJECT-TYPE
    SYNTAX  Counter
    ACCESS  read-only
    STATUS  mandatory
    DESCRIPTION
            "The number of ICMP Timestamp (request) messages
            received."
    ::= { icmp 10 }

icmpInTimestampReps OBJECT-TYPE
    SYNTAX  Counter
    ACCESS  read-only
    STATUS  mandatory
    DESCRIPTION
            "The number of ICMP Timestamp Reply messages
            received."
    ::= { icmp 11 }

icmpInAddrMasks OBJECT-TYPE
    SYNTAX  Counter
    ACCESS  read-only
    STATUS  mandatory
    DESCRIPTION
            "The number of ICMP Address Mask Request messages
            received."
    ::= { icmp 12 }

icmpInAddrMaskReps OBJECT-TYPE
    SYNTAX  Counter
    ACCESS  read-only
    STATUS  mandatory
    DESCRIPTION
            "The number of ICMP Address Mask Reply messages
            received."
    ::= { icmp 13 }

icmpOutMsgs OBJECT-TYPE
    SYNTAX  Counter
    ACCESS  read-only
```

```
    STATUS  mandatory
    DESCRIPTION
            "The total number of ICMP messages which this
            entity attempted to send.  Note that this counter
            includes all those counted by icmpOutErrors."
    ::= { icmp 14 }

icmpOutErrors OBJECT-TYPE
    SYNTAX  Counter
    ACCESS  read-only
    STATUS  mandatory
    DESCRIPTION
            "The number of ICMP messages which this entity did
            not send due to problems discovered within ICMP,
            such as a lack of buffers.  This value should not
            include errors discovered outside the ICMP layer,
            such as the inability of IP to route the resultant
            datagram.  In some implementations there may be no
            types of error which contribute to this counter's
            value."
    ::= { icmp 15 }

icmpOutDestUnreachs OBJECT-TYPE
    SYNTAX  Counter
    ACCESS  read-only
    STATUS  mandatory
    DESCRIPTION
            "The number of ICMP Destination Unreachable
            messages sent."
    ::= { icmp 16 }

icmpOutTimeExcds OBJECT-TYPE
    SYNTAX  Counter
    ACCESS  read-only
    STATUS  mandatory
    DESCRIPTION
            "The number of ICMP Time Exceeded messages sent."
    ::= { icmp 17 }

icmpOutParmProbs OBJECT-TYPE
    SYNTAX  Counter
    ACCESS  read-only
    STATUS  mandatory
    DESCRIPTION
            "The number of ICMP Parameter Problem messages
            sent."
    ::= { icmp 18 }
```

```
icmpOutSrcQuenchs OBJECT-TYPE
    SYNTAX  Counter
    ACCESS  read-only
    STATUS  mandatory
    DESCRIPTION
            "The number of ICMP Source Quench messages sent."
    ::= { icmp 19 }

icmpOutRedirects OBJECT-TYPE
    SYNTAX  Counter
    ACCESS  read-only
    STATUS  mandatory
    DESCRIPTION
            "The number of ICMP Redirect messages sent.  For a
            host, this object will always be zero, since hosts
            do not send redirects."
    ::= { icmp 20 }

icmpOutEchos OBJECT-TYPE
    SYNTAX  Counter
    ACCESS  read-only
    STATUS  mandatory
    DESCRIPTION
            "The number of ICMP Echo (request) messages sent."
    ::= { icmp 21 }

icmpOutEchoReps OBJECT-TYPE
    SYNTAX  Counter
    ACCESS  read-only
    STATUS  mandatory
    DESCRIPTION
            "The number of ICMP Echo Reply messages sent."
    ::= { icmp 22 }

icmpOutTimestamps OBJECT-TYPE
    SYNTAX  Counter
    ACCESS  read-only
    STATUS  mandatory
    DESCRIPTION
            "The number of ICMP Timestamp (request) messages
            sent."
    ::= { icmp 23 }

icmpOutTimestampReps OBJECT-TYPE
    SYNTAX  Counter
    ACCESS  read-only
    STATUS  mandatory
```

```
    DESCRIPTION
            "The number of ICMP Timestamp Reply messages
            sent."
    ::= { icmp 24 }

icmpOutAddrMasks OBJECT-TYPE
    SYNTAX  Counter
    ACCESS  read-only
    STATUS  mandatory
    DESCRIPTION
            "The number of ICMP Address Mask Request messages
            sent."
    ::= { icmp 25 }

icmpOutAddrMaskReps OBJECT-TYPE
    SYNTAX  Counter
    ACCESS  read-only
    STATUS  mandatory
    DESCRIPTION
            "The number of ICMP Address Mask Reply messages
            sent."
    ::= { icmp 26 }
```

TCP Group

```
-- the TCP group

-- Implementation of the TCP group is mandatory for all
-- systems that implement the TCP.

-- Note that instances of object types that represent
-- information about a particular TCP connection are
-- transient; they persist only as long as the connection
-- in question.

tcpRtoAlgorithm OBJECT-TYPE
    SYNTAX  INTEGER {
                other(1),    -- none of the following

                constant(2), -- a constant rto
                rsre(3),     -- MIL-STD-1778, Appendix B
                vanj(4)      -- Van Jacobson's algorithm [10]
            }
    ACCESS  read-only
    STATUS  mandatory
    DESCRIPTION
```

```
            "The algorithm used to determine the timeout value
            used for retransmitting unacknowledged octets."
    ::= { tcp 1 }

tcpRtoMin OBJECT-TYPE
    SYNTAX  INTEGER
    ACCESS  read-only
    STATUS  mandatory
    DESCRIPTION
            "The minimum value permitted by a TCP
            implementation for the retransmission timeout,
            measured in milliseconds.  More refined semantics
            for objects of this type depend upon the algorithm
            used to determine the retransmission timeout.  In
            particular, when the timeout algorithm is rsre(3),
            an object of this type has the semantics of the
            LBOUND quantity described in RFC 793."
    ::= { tcp 2 }

tcpRtoMax OBJECT-TYPE
    SYNTAX  INTEGER
    ACCESS  read-only
    STATUS  mandatory
    DESCRIPTION
            "The maximum value permitted by a TCP
            implementation for the retransmission timeout,
            measured in milliseconds.  More refined semantics
            for objects of this type depend upon the algorithm
            used to determine the retransmission timeout.  In
            particular, when the timeout algorithm is rsre(3),
            an object of this type has the semantics of the
            UBOUND quantity described in RFC 793."
    ::= { tcp 3 }

tcpMaxConn OBJECT-TYPE
    SYNTAX  INTEGER
    ACCESS  read-only
    STATUS  mandatory
    DESCRIPTION
            "The limit on the total number of TCP connections
            the entity can support.  In entities where the
            maximum number of connections is dynamic, this
            object should contain the value -1."
    ::= { tcp 4 }

tcpActiveOpens OBJECT-TYPE
    SYNTAX  Counter
```

```
    ACCESS  read-only
    STATUS  mandatory
    DESCRIPTION
            "The number of times TCP connections have made a
            direct transition to the SYN-SENT state from the
            CLOSED state."
    ::= { tcp 5 }

tcpPassiveOpens OBJECT-TYPE
    SYNTAX  Counter
    ACCESS  read-only
    STATUS  mandatory
    DESCRIPTION
            "The number of times TCP connections have made a
            direct transition to the SYN-RCVD state from the
            LISTEN state."
    ::= { tcp 6 }

tcpAttemptFails OBJECT-TYPE
    SYNTAX  Counter
    ACCESS  read-only
    STATUS  mandatory
    DESCRIPTION
            "The number of times TCP connections have made a
            direct transition to the CLOSED state from either
            the SYN-SENT state or the SYN-RCVD state, plus the
            number of times TCP connections have made a direct
            transition to the LISTEN state from the SYN-RCVD
            state."
    ::= { tcp 7 }

tcpEstabResets OBJECT-TYPE
    SYNTAX  Counter
    ACCESS  read-only
    STATUS  mandatory
    DESCRIPTION
            "The number of times TCP connections have made a
            direct transition to the CLOSED state from either
            the ESTABLISHED state or the CLOSE-WAIT state."
    ::= { tcp 8 }

tcpCurrEstab OBJECT-TYPE
    SYNTAX  Gauge
    ACCESS  read-only
    STATUS  mandatory
    DESCRIPTION
```

```
            "The number of TCP connections for which the
            current state is either ESTABLISHED or CLOSE-
            WAIT."
    ::= { tcp 9 }

tcpInSegs OBJECT-TYPE
    SYNTAX  Counter
    ACCESS  read-only
    STATUS  mandatory
    DESCRIPTION
            "The total number of segments received, including
            those received in error.  This count includes
            segments received on currently established
            connections."
    ::= { tcp 10 }

tcpOutSegs OBJECT-TYPE
    SYNTAX  Counter
    ACCESS  read-only
    STATUS  mandatory
    DESCRIPTION
            "The total number of segments sent, including
            those on current connections but excluding those
            containing only retransmitted octets."
    ::= { tcp 11 }

tcpRetransSegs OBJECT-TYPE
    SYNTAX  Counter
    ACCESS  read-only
    STATUS  mandatory
    DESCRIPTION
            "The total number of segments retransmitted - that
            is, the number of TCP segments transmitted
            containing one or more previously transmitted
            octets."
    ::= { tcp 12 }


-- the TCP Connection table

-- The TCP Connection table contains information about this
-- entity's existing TCP connections.

tcpConnTable OBJECT-TYPE
    SYNTAX  SEQUENCE OF TcpConnEntry
    ACCESS  not-accessible
    STATUS  mandatory
```

```
    DESCRIPTION
            "A table containing TCP connection-specific
            information."
    ::= { tcp 13 }

tcpConnEntry OBJECT-TYPE
    SYNTAX  TcpConnEntry
    ACCESS  not-accessible
    STATUS  mandatory
    DESCRIPTION
            "Information about a particular current TCP
            connection.  An object of this type is transient,
            in that it ceases to exist when (or soon after)
            the connection makes the transition to the CLOSED
            state."
    INDEX   { tcpConnLocalAddress,
              tcpConnLocalPort,
              tcpConnRemAddress,
              tcpConnRemPort }
    ::= { tcpConnTable 1 }

TcpConnEntry ::=
    SEQUENCE {
        tcpConnState
            INTEGER,
        tcpConnLocalAddress
            IpAddress,
        tcpConnLocalPort
            INTEGER (0..65535),
        tcpConnRemAddress
            IpAddress,
        tcpConnRemPort
            INTEGER (0..65535)
    }

tcpConnState OBJECT-TYPE
    SYNTAX  INTEGER {
                closed(1),
                listen(2),
                synSent(3),
                synReceived(4),
                established(5),
                finWait1(6),
                finWait2(7),
                closeWait(8),
                lastAck(9),
```

```
                closing(10),
                timeWait(11),
                deleteTCB(12)
            }
    ACCESS  read-write
    STATUS  mandatory
    DESCRIPTION
            "The state of this TCP connection.

            The only value which may be set by a management
            station is deleteTCB(12).  Accordingly, it is
            appropriate for an agent to return a 'badValue'
            response if a management station attempts to set
            this object to any other value.

            If a management station sets this object to the
            value deleteTCB(12), then this has the effect of
            deleting the TCB (as defined in RFC 793) of the
            corresponding connection on the managed node,
            resulting in immediate termination of the
            connection.

            As an implementation-specific option, a RST
            segment may be sent from the managed node to the
            other TCP endpoint (note however that RST segments
            are not sent reliably)."
    ::= { tcpConnEntry 1 }

tcpConnLocalAddress OBJECT-TYPE
    SYNTAX  IpAddress
    ACCESS  read-only
    STATUS  mandatory
    DESCRIPTION
            "The local IP address for this TCP connection.  In
            the case of a connection in the listen state which
            is willing to accept connections for any IP
            interface associated with the node, the value
            0.0.0.0 is used."
    ::= { tcpConnEntry 2 }

tcpConnLocalPort OBJECT-TYPE
    SYNTAX  INTEGER (0..65535)
    ACCESS  read-only
    STATUS  mandatory
    DESCRIPTION
            "The local port number for this TCP connection."
    ::= { tcpConnEntry 3 }
```

```
tcpConnRemAddress OBJECT-TYPE
    SYNTAX  IpAddress
    ACCESS  read-only
    STATUS  mandatory
    DESCRIPTION
            "The remote IP address for this TCP connection."
    ::= { tcpConnEntry 4 }

tcpConnRemPort OBJECT-TYPE
    SYNTAX  INTEGER (0..65535)
    ACCESS  read-only
    STATUS  mandatory
    DESCRIPTION
            "The remote port number for this TCP connection."
    ::= { tcpConnEntry 5 }


-- additional TCP objects

tcpInErrs OBJECT-TYPE
    SYNTAX  Counter
    ACCESS  read-only
    STATUS  mandatory
    DESCRIPTION
            "The total number of segments received in error
            (e.g., bad TCP checksums)."
    ::= { tcp 14 }

tcpOutRsts OBJECT-TYPE
    SYNTAX  Counter
    ACCESS  read-only
    STATUS  mandatory
    DESCRIPTION
            "The number of TCP segments sent containing the
            RST flag."
    ::= { tcp 15 }
```

UDP Group

```
-- the UDP group

-- Implementation of the UDP group is mandatory for all
-- systems which implement the UDP.

udpInDatagrams OBJECT-TYPE
    SYNTAX  Counter
    ACCESS  read-only
```

```
    STATUS  mandatory
    DESCRIPTION
            "The total number of UDP datagrams delivered to
            UDP users."
    ::= { udp 1 }

udpNoPorts OBJECT-TYPE
    SYNTAX  Counter
    ACCESS  read-only
    STATUS  mandatory
    DESCRIPTION
            "The total number of received UDP datagrams for
            which there was no application at the destination
            port."
    ::= { udp 2 }

udpInErrors OBJECT-TYPE
    SYNTAX  Counter
    ACCESS  read-only
    STATUS  mandatory
    DESCRIPTION
            "The number of received UDP datagrams that could
            not be delivered for reasons other than the lack
            of an application at the destination port."
    ::= { udp 3 }

udpOutDatagrams OBJECT-TYPE
    SYNTAX  Counter
    ACCESS  read-only
    STATUS  mandatory
    DESCRIPTION
            "The total number of UDP datagrams sent from this
            entity."
    ::= { udp 4 }


-- the UDP Listener table

-- The UDP listener table contains information about this
-- entity's UDP end-points on which a local application is
-- currently accepting datagrams.

udpTable OBJECT-TYPE
    SYNTAX  SEQUENCE OF UdpEntry
    ACCESS  not-accessible
    STATUS  mandatory
```

```
    DESCRIPTION
            "A table containing UDP listener information."
    ::= { udp 5 }

udpEntry OBJECT-TYPE
    SYNTAX  UdpEntry
    ACCESS  not-accessible
    STATUS  mandatory
    DESCRIPTION
            "Information about a particular current UDP
            listener."
    INDEX   { udpLocalAddress, udpLocalPort }
    ::= { udpTable 1 }

UdpEntry ::=
    SEQUENCE {
        udpLocalAddress
            IpAddress,
        udpLocalPort
            INTEGER (0..65535)
    }

udpLocalAddress OBJECT-TYPE
    SYNTAX  IpAddress
    ACCESS  read-only
    STATUS  mandatory
    DESCRIPTION
            "The local IP address for this UDP listener.  In
            the case of a UDP listener which is willing to
            accept datagrams for any IP interface associated
            with the node, the value 0.0.0.0 is used."
    ::= { udpEntry 1 }

udpLocalPort OBJECT-TYPE
    SYNTAX  INTEGER (0..65535)
    ACCESS  read-only
    STATUS  mandatory
    DESCRIPTION
            "The local port number for this UDP listener."
    ::= { udpEntry 2 }
```

EGP Group

```
-- the EGP group

-- Implementation of the EGP group is mandatory for all
-- systems which implement the EGP.
```

```
egpInMsgs OBJECT-TYPE
    SYNTAX  Counter
    ACCESS  read-only
    STATUS  mandatory
    DESCRIPTION
            "The number of EGP messages received without
            error."
    ::= { egp 1 }

egpInErrors OBJECT-TYPE
    SYNTAX  Counter
    ACCESS  read-only
    STATUS  mandatory
    DESCRIPTION
            "The number of EGP messages received that proved
            to be in error."
    ::= { egp 2 }

egpOutMsgs OBJECT-TYPE
    SYNTAX  Counter
    ACCESS  read-only
    STATUS  mandatory
    DESCRIPTION
            "The total number of locally generated EGP
            messages."
    ::= { egp 3 }

egpOutErrors OBJECT-TYPE
    SYNTAX  Counter
    ACCESS  read-only
    STATUS  mandatory
    DESCRIPTION
            "The number of locally generated EGP messages not
            sent due to resource limitations within an EGP
            entity."
    ::= { egp 4 }


-- the EGP Neighbor table

-- The EGP Neighbor table contains information about this
-- entity's EGP neighbors.

egpNeighTable OBJECT-TYPE
    SYNTAX  SEQUENCE OF EgpNeighEntry
    ACCESS  not-accessible
    STATUS  mandatory
```

```
    DESCRIPTION
            "The EGP Neighbor table."
    ::= { egp 5 }

egpNeighEntry OBJECT-TYPE
    SYNTAX  EgpNeighEntry
    ACCESS  not-accessible
    STATUS  mandatory
    DESCRIPTION
            "Information about this entity's relationship with
            a particular EGP neighbor."
    INDEX   { egpNeighAddr }
    ::= { egpNeighTable 1 }

EgpNeighEntry ::=
    SEQUENCE {
        egpNeighState
            INTEGER,
        egpNeighAddr
            IpAddress,
        egpNeighAs
            INTEGER,
        egpNeighInMsgs
            Counter,
        egpNeighInErrs
            Counter,
        egpNeighOutMsgs
            Counter,
        egpNeighOutErrs
            Counter,
        egpNeighInErrMsgs
            Counter,
        egpNeighOutErrMsgs
            Counter,
        egpNeighStateUps
            Counter,
        egpNeighStateDowns
            Counter,
        egpNeighIntervalHello
            INTEGER,
        egpNeighIntervalPoll
            INTEGER,
        egpNeighMode
            INTEGER,
        egpNeighEventTrigger
            INTEGER
    }
```

```
egpNeighState OBJECT-TYPE
    SYNTAX  INTEGER {
                idle(1),
                acquisition(2),
                down(3),
                up(4),
                cease(5)
            }
    ACCESS  read-only
    STATUS  mandatory
    DESCRIPTION
            "The EGP state of the local system with respect to
            this entry's EGP neighbor.  Each EGP state is
            represented by a value that is one greater than
            the numerical value associated with said state in
            RFC 904."
    ::= { egpNeighEntry 1 }

egpNeighAddr OBJECT-TYPE
    SYNTAX  IpAddress
    ACCESS  read-only
    STATUS  mandatory
    DESCRIPTION
            "The IP address of this entry's EGP neighbor."
    ::= { egpNeighEntry 2 }

egpNeighAs OBJECT-TYPE
    SYNTAX  INTEGER
    ACCESS  read-only
    STATUS  mandatory
    DESCRIPTION
            "The autonomous system of this EGP peer.  Zero
            should be specified if the autonomous system
            number of the neighbor is not yet known."
    ::= { egpNeighEntry 3 }

egpNeighInMsgs OBJECT-TYPE
    SYNTAX  Counter
    ACCESS  read-only
    STATUS  mandatory
    DESCRIPTION
            "The number of EGP messages received without error
            from this EGP peer."
    ::= { egpNeighEntry 4 }

egpNeighInErrs OBJECT-TYPE
    SYNTAX  Counter
```

```
    ACCESS  read-only
    STATUS  mandatory
    DESCRIPTION
            "The number of EGP messages received from this EGP
            peer that proved to be in error (e.g., bad EGP
            checksum)."
    ::= { egpNeighEntry 5 }

egpNeighOutMsgs OBJECT-TYPE
    SYNTAX  Counter
    ACCESS  read-only
    STATUS  mandatory
    DESCRIPTION
            "The number of locally generated EGP messages to
            this EGP peer."
    ::= { egpNeighEntry 6 }

egpNeighOutErrs OBJECT-TYPE
    SYNTAX  Counter
    ACCESS  read-only
    STATUS  mandatory
    DESCRIPTION
            "The number of locally generated EGP messages not
            sent to this EGP peer due to resource limitations
            within an EGP entity."
    ::= { egpNeighEntry 7 }

egpNeighInErrMsgs OBJECT-TYPE
    SYNTAX  Counter
    ACCESS  read-only
    STATUS  mandatory
    DESCRIPTION
            "The number of EGP-defined error messages received
            from this EGP peer."
    ::= { egpNeighEntry 8 }

egpNeighOutErrMsgs OBJECT-TYPE
    SYNTAX  Counter
    ACCESS  read-only
    STATUS  mandatory
    DESCRIPTION
            "The number of EGP-defined error messages sent to
            this EGP peer."
    ::= { egpNeighEntry 9 }

egpNeighStateUps OBJECT-TYPE
    SYNTAX  Counter
```

```
    ACCESS  read-only
    STATUS  mandatory
    DESCRIPTION
            "The number of EGP state transitions to the UP
            state with this EGP peer."
    ::= { egpNeighEntry 10 }

egpNeighStateDowns OBJECT-TYPE
    SYNTAX  Counter
    ACCESS  read-only
    STATUS  mandatory
    DESCRIPTION
            "The number of EGP state transitions from the UP
            state to any other state with this EGP peer."
    ::= { egpNeighEntry 11 }

egpNeighIntervalHello OBJECT-TYPE
    SYNTAX  INTEGER
    ACCESS  read-only
    STATUS  mandatory
    DESCRIPTION
            "The interval between EGP Hello command
            retransmissions (in hundredths of a second).  This
            represents the t1 timer as defined in RFC 904."
    ::= { egpNeighEntry 12 }

egpNeighIntervalPoll OBJECT-TYPE
    SYNTAX  INTEGER
    ACCESS  read-only
    STATUS  mandatory
    DESCRIPTION
            "The interval between EGP poll command
            retransmissions (in hundredths of a second).  This
            represents the t3 timer as defined in RFC 904."
    ::= { egpNeighEntry 13 }

egpNeighMode OBJECT-TYPE
    SYNTAX  INTEGER { active(1), passive(2) }
    ACCESS  read-only
    STATUS  mandatory
    DESCRIPTION
            "The polling mode of this EGP entity, either
            passive or active."
    ::= { egpNeighEntry 14 }

egpNeighEventTrigger OBJECT-TYPE
    SYNTAX  INTEGER { start(1), stop(2) }
```

```
    ACCESS  read-write
    STATUS  mandatory
    DESCRIPTION
            "A control variable used to trigger operator-
            initiated Start and Stop events.  When read, this
            variable always returns the most recent value that
            egpNeighEventTrigger was set to.  If it has not
            been set since the last initialization of the
            network management subsystem on the node, it
            returns a value of 'stop'.

            When set, this variable causes a Start or Stop
            event on the specified neighbor, as specified on
            pages 8-10 of RFC 904.  Briefly, a Start event
            causes an Idle peer to begin neighbor acquisition
            and a non-Idle peer to reinitiate neighbor
            acquisition.  A stop event causes a non-Idle peer
            to return to the Idle state until a Start event
            occurs, either via egpNeighEventTrigger or
            otherwise."
    ::= { egpNeighEntry 15 }


-- additional EGP objects

egpAs OBJECT-TYPE
    SYNTAX  INTEGER
    ACCESS  read-only
    STATUS  mandatory
    DESCRIPTION
            "The autonomous system number of this EGP entity."
    ::= { egp 6 }
```

Transmission Group

```
-- the Transmission group

-- Based on the transmission media underlying each interface
-- on a system, the corresponding portion of the Transmission
-- group is mandatory for that system.

-- When Internet-standard definitions for managing
-- transmission media are defined, the Transmission group is
-- used to provide a prefix for the names of those objects.

-- Typically, such definitions reside in the experimental
-- portion of the MIB until they are "proven", then as a
```

```
-- part of the Internet standardization process, the
-- definitions are accordingly elevated and a new object
-- identifier, under the Transmission group, is defined. By
-- convention, the name assigned is:
--
--     type OBJECT IDENTIFIER    ::= { transmission number }
--
-- where "type" is the symbolic value used for the media in
-- the ifType column of the ifTable object, and "number" is
-- the actual integer value corresponding to the symbol.
```

SNMP Group

```
-- the SNMP group

-- Implementation of the SNMP group is mandatory for all
-- systems which support an SNMP protocol entity.  Some of
-- the objects defined below will be zero-valued in those
-- SNMP implementations that are optimized to support only
-- those functions specific to either a management agent or
-- a management station.  In particular, it should be
-- observed that the objects below refer to an SNMP entity,
-- and there may be several SNMP entities residing on a
-- managed node (e.g., if the node is hosting acting as
-- a management station).

snmpInPkts OBJECT-TYPE
    SYNTAX  Counter
    ACCESS  read-only
    STATUS  mandatory
    DESCRIPTION
            "The total number of Messages delivered to the
            SNMP entity from the transport service."
    ::= { snmp 1 }

snmpOutPkts OBJECT-TYPE
    SYNTAX  Counter
    ACCESS  read-only
    STATUS  mandatory
    DESCRIPTION
            "The total number of SNMP Messages which were
            passed from the SNMP protocol entity to the
            transport service."
    ::= { snmp 2 }

snmpInBadVersions OBJECT-TYPE
    SYNTAX  Counter
```

```
    ACCESS  read-only
    STATUS  mandatory
    DESCRIPTION
            "The total number of SNMP Messages which were
            delivered to the SNMP protocol entity and were for
            an unsupported SNMP version."
    ::= { snmp 3 }

snmpInBadCommunityNames OBJECT-TYPE
    SYNTAX  Counter
    ACCESS  read-only
    STATUS  mandatory
    DESCRIPTION
            "The total number of SNMP Messages delivered to
            the SNMP protocol entity which used a SNMP
            community name not known to said entity."
    ::= { snmp 4 }

snmpInBadCommunityUses OBJECT-TYPE
    SYNTAX  Counter
    ACCESS  read-only
    STATUS  mandatory
    DESCRIPTION
            "The total number of SNMP Messages delivered to
            the SNMP protocol entity which represented an SNMP
            operation which was not allowed by the SNMP
            community named in the message."
    ::= { snmp 5 }

snmpInASNParseErrs OBJECT-TYPE
    SYNTAX  Counter
    ACCESS  read-only
    STATUS  mandatory
    DESCRIPTION
            "The total number of ASN.1 or BER errors
            encountered by the SNMP protocol entity when
            decoding received SNMP Messages."
    ::= { snmp 6 }

-- { snmp 7 } is not used

snmpInTooBigs OBJECT-TYPE
    SYNTAX  Counter
    ACCESS  read-only
    STATUS  mandatory
    DESCRIPTION
            "The total number of SNMP PDUs which were
```

```
            delivered to the SNMP protocol entity and for
            which the value of the error-status field is
            'tooBig'."
    ::= { snmp 8 }

snmpInNoSuchNames OBJECT-TYPE
    SYNTAX  Counter
    ACCESS  read-only
    STATUS  mandatory
    DESCRIPTION
            "The total number of SNMP PDUs which were
            delivered to the SNMP protocol entity and for
            which the value of the error-status field is
            'noSuchName'."
    ::= { snmp 9 }

snmpInBadValues OBJECT-TYPE
    SYNTAX  Counter
    ACCESS  read-only
    STATUS  mandatory
    DESCRIPTION
            "The total number of SNMP PDUs which were
            delivered to the SNMP protocol entity and for
            which the value of the error-status field is
            'badValue'."
    ::= { snmp 10 }

snmpInReadOnlys OBJECT-TYPE
    SYNTAX  Counter
    ACCESS  read-only
    STATUS  mandatory
    DESCRIPTION
            "The total number valid SNMP PDUs which were
            delivered to the SNMP protocol entity and for
            which the value of the error-status field is
            'readOnly'.  It should be noted that it is a
            protocol error to generate an SNMP PDU which
            contains the value 'readOnly' in the error-status
            field, as such this object is provided as a means
            of detecting incorrect implementations of the
            SNMP."
    ::= { snmp 11 }

snmpInGenErrs OBJECT-TYPE
    SYNTAX  Counter
    ACCESS  read-only
    STATUS  mandatory
```

```
    DESCRIPTION
            "The total number of SNMP PDUs which were
            delivered to the SNMP protocol entity and for
            which the value of the error-status field is
            'genErr'."
    ::= { snmp 12 }

snmpInTotalReqVars OBJECT-TYPE
    SYNTAX  Counter
    ACCESS  read-only
    STATUS  mandatory
    DESCRIPTION
            "The total number of MIB objects which have been
            retrieved successfully by the SNMP protocol entity
            as the result of receiving valid SNMP Get-Request
            and Get-Next PDUs."
    ::= { snmp 13 }

snmpInTotalSetVars OBJECT-TYPE
    SYNTAX  Counter
    ACCESS  read-only
    STATUS  mandatory
    DESCRIPTION
            "The total number of MIB objects which have been
            altered successfully by the SNMP protocol entity
            as the result of receiving valid SNMP Set-Request
            PDUs."
    ::= { snmp 14 }

snmpInGetRequests OBJECT-TYPE
    SYNTAX  Counter
    ACCESS  read-only
    STATUS  mandatory
    DESCRIPTION
            "The total number of SNMP Get-Request PDUs which
            have been accepted and processed by the SNMP
            protocol entity."
    ::= { snmp 15 }

snmpInGetNexts OBJECT-TYPE
    SYNTAX  Counter
    ACCESS  read-only
    STATUS  mandatory
    DESCRIPTION
            "The total number of SNMP Get-Next PDUs which have
            been accepted and processed by the SNMP protocol
            entity."
    ::= { snmp 16 }
```

```
snmpInSetRequests OBJECT-TYPE
    SYNTAX  Counter
    ACCESS  read-only
    STATUS  mandatory
    DESCRIPTION
            "The total number of SNMP Set-Request PDUs which
            have been accepted and processed by the SNMP
            protocol entity."
    ::= { snmp 17 }

snmpInGetResponses OBJECT-TYPE
    SYNTAX  Counter
    ACCESS  read-only
    STATUS  mandatory
    DESCRIPTION
            "The total number of SNMP Get-Response PDUs which
            have been accepted and processed by the SNMP
            protocol entity."
    ::= { snmp 18 }

snmpInTraps OBJECT-TYPE
    SYNTAX  Counter
    ACCESS  read-only
    STATUS  mandatory
    DESCRIPTION
            "The total number of SNMP Trap PDUs which have
            been accepted and processed by the SNMP protocol
            entity."
    ::= { snmp 19 }

snmpOutTooBigs OBJECT-TYPE
    SYNTAX  Counter
    ACCESS  read-only
    STATUS  mandatory
    DESCRIPTION
            "The total number of SNMP PDUs which were
            generated by the SNMP protocol entity and for
            which the value of the error-status field is
            'tooBig.'"
    ::= { snmp 20 }

snmpOutNoSuchNames OBJECT-TYPE
    SYNTAX  Counter
    ACCESS  read-only
    STATUS  mandatory
    DESCRIPTION
            "The total number of SNMP PDUs which were
```

```
            generated by the SNMP protocol entity and for
            which the value of the error-status is
            'noSuchName'."
    ::= { snmp 21 }

snmpOutBadValues OBJECT-TYPE
    SYNTAX  Counter
    ACCESS  read-only
    STATUS  mandatory
    DESCRIPTION
            "The total number of SNMP PDUs which were
            generated by the SNMP protocol entity and for
            which the value of the error-status field is
            'badValue'."
    ::= { snmp 22 }

-- { snmp 23 } is not used

snmpOutGenErrs OBJECT-TYPE
    SYNTAX  Counter
    ACCESS  read-only
    STATUS  mandatory
    DESCRIPTION
            "The total number of SNMP PDUs which were
            generated by the SNMP protocol entity and for
            which the value of the error-status field is
            'genErr'."
    ::= { snmp 24 }

snmpOutGetRequests OBJECT-TYPE
    SYNTAX  Counter
    ACCESS  read-only
    STATUS  mandatory
    DESCRIPTION
            "The total number of SNMP Get-Request PDUs which
            have been generated by the SNMP protocol entity."
    ::= { snmp 25 }

snmpOutGetNexts OBJECT-TYPE
    SYNTAX  Counter
    ACCESS  read-only
    STATUS  mandatory
    DESCRIPTION
            "The total number of SNMP Get-Next PDUs which have
            been generated by the SNMP protocol entity."
    ::= { snmp 26 }
```

```
snmpOutSetRequests OBJECT-TYPE
    SYNTAX  Counter
    ACCESS  read-only
    STATUS  mandatory
    DESCRIPTION
            "The total number of SNMP Set-Request PDUs which
            have been generated by the SNMP protocol entity."
    ::= { snmp 27 }

snmpOutGetResponses OBJECT-TYPE
    SYNTAX  Counter
    ACCESS  read-only
    STATUS  mandatory
    DESCRIPTION
            "The total number of SNMP Get-Response PDUs which
            have been generated by the SNMP protocol entity."
    ::= { snmp 28 }

snmpOutTraps OBJECT-TYPE
    SYNTAX  Counter
    ACCESS  read-only
    STATUS  mandatory
    DESCRIPTION
            "The total number of SNMP Trap PDUs which have
            been generated by the SNMP protocol entity."
    ::= { snmp 29 }

snmpEnableAuthenTraps OBJECT-TYPE
    SYNTAX  INTEGER { enabled(1), disabled(2) }
    ACCESS  read-write
    STATUS  mandatory
    DESCRIPTION
            "Indicates whether the SNMP agent process is
            permitted to generate authentication-failure
            traps.  The value of this object overrides any
            configuration information; as such, it provides a
            means whereby all authentication-failure traps may
            be disabled.

            Note that it is strongly recommended that this
            object be stored in non-volatile memory so that it
            remains constant between re-initializations of the
            network management system."
    ::= { snmp 30 }

END
```

20 Multipurpose Internet Mail Extensions

Name

Multipurpose Internet Mail Extensions

Abbreviation

MIME

Status

Elective Draft Standard

Specifications

RFC 1521, RFC 1522

Abstract

The MIME RFCs provide extensions to the electronic mail format defined in RFC 822. These extensions add many new features to Internet mail and provide a general-purpose framework for defining new Internet mail services. In particular MIME enables:

- A standard method for the encoding and attachment of binary content to mail messages.

- A general framework for multipart mail messages containing heterogeneous body parts with possibly recursive structures.
- The ability to identify the type of content associated with a mail body part.
- A set of standard body part types, allowing standardized interpretation of body parts.

Related Specifications

Format of Electronic Mail Messages (RFC 822)

See Also

SMTP (RFC 821), SMTP-EXT (RFC 1869), HTTP (currently at the stage of being an Internet Draft; no RFC number yet)

Comments

The MIME RFCs are currently undergoing a revision. Check the Internet Drafts archive (**ftp://ftp.isi.edu/internet-drafts**) for more recent versions of these documents.

Description

To provide its services, MIME extends the format of Internet mail defined in RFC 822 to include type tagging of body parts, multipart messages, and the standardized encoding of non-ASCII content. Using these basic services, MIME allows the transport of rich information content through the Internet mail system. Because the upgrade of the entire Internet mail system to support these features was not feasible, MIME messages are formatted to appear as standard RFC 822 messages to those systems that do not understand MIME. Only the ultimate source and destination need to implement the MIME standards to be able to generate and interpret MIME messages.

MIME messages often contain file attachments and other non-ASCII data. Because RFC 822 specifies that all characters in mail messages must be ASCII characters, an encoding algorithm must be used to convert the binary data to ASCII characters. MIME defines two types of encoding: Quoted-Printable and BASE64. The following sections describe each of these encoding techniques.

Quoted-Printable Encoding

The Quoted-Printable encoding is designed for content that largely consists of ASCII characters, but still contains some non-ASCII characters. An example of this would be a message written using the ISO-8859-1 character set which includes Scandinavian characters. Although most of the characters would be ASCII, some would be 8-bit characters and would have to be encoded. A Quoted-Printable encoded message received by a non-MIME mail user will still be mostly readable, a property not shared by the BASE64 encoding technique.

The Quoted-Printable encoding is designed to keep the characters that fall within the ASCII character range intact while encoding the others. Quoted-Printable encoding uses five rules to accomplish this:

- Rule 1: Any octet, except those indicating a line break, may be represented by "=" followed by two hexadecimal characters representing the octet's value. All hexadecimal characters must be uppercase.
- Rule 2: Octets with values in the range of 33 through 60 inclusive and 62 through 126 inclusive, may be represented as the ASCII characters that correspond to those values.
- Rule 3: Octets with values 9 and 32 may be represented by ASCII horizontal tab (HT) and space, respectively, except when these octets appear at the end of a line of text. All such octets must be encoded using Rule #1. The reason for this rule is that some Internet message transport agents (MTAs) are known to remove trailing white space characters from the ends of message lines. While this is not harmful for text messages, the effect on a binary message can be severe.
- Rule 4: A line break in the body must be represented using the standard RFC 822 line break convention of a carriage return (CR) followed by a line feed (LF).
- Rule 5: The Quoted-Printable encoding format requires that lines not exceed 76 characters, not including the trailing CRLF sequence. If lines greater than this length must be sent, "soft" line breaks must be inserted into the data and then removed by the receiver. A soft line break appears as an equals sign ("=") followed by the CRLF sequence.

The formal grammar for the Quoted-Printable encoding is:

```
quoted-printable := ([*(ptext / SPACE / TAB) ptext] ["="] CRLF)
     ; Maximum line length of 76 characters excluding CRLF
```

```
ptext   := octet /<any ASCII character except "=", SPACE, or TAB>
     ; characters not listed as "mail-safe" in Appendix B
     ; are also not recommended.

octet   := "=" 2(DIGIT / "A" / "B" / "C" / "D" / "E" / "F")
     ; octet must be used for characters > 127, =, SPACE, or TAB,
     ; and is recommended for any characters not listed in
     ; Appendix B as "mail-safe".
```

BASE64 Encoding

The BASE64 encoding technique is used to encode arbitrary binary information that need not be understood by humans before decoding. The BASE64 algorithm is relatively simple and results in a consistent data expansion factor of 33 percent.

The BASE64 algorithm encodes groups of three octets (24 bits) as four encoded characters. A 65 character subset of ASCII is used to represent six original data bits in the encoded data.

The encoding algorithm first groups three octets into a 24-bit string. The 24-bit string is then broken into four 6-bit groups. The first group contains the high-order bits of the first original octet. The second group contains the low-order bits of the first original octet and the high-order bits of the second original octet. The third group contains the low-order bits of the second original octet and the high-order bits of the third original octet. The final, fourth group contains the low-order bits of the third original octet.

The groups are encoded using the alphabet shown in Table 20.1.

The "=" character is not used to encode data, but rather to act as padding when the original data is not an even multiple of 24-bits. In this case, the last encoding group is padded with zero bits for the purpose of encoding, and "=" characters are added to the final encoded output octets to mark characters that do not contain any original data. There are three possibilities:

- The last encoding group contains eight original data bits. The final output group contains two encoded characters followed by two "=" characters.
- The last encoding group contains 16 original data bits. The final output group contains three encoded characters followed by one "=" character.
- The last encoding group contains 24 original data bits. The final output group contains four encoded characters with no additional padding.

Table 20.1 BASE64 Alphabet

Value	Encoding	Value	Encoding	Value	Encoding	Value	Encoding
0	A	17	R	34	i	51	z
1	B	18	S	35	j	52	0
2	C	19	T	36	k	53	1
3	D	20	U	37	l	54	2
4	E	21	V	38	m	55	3
5	F	22	W	39	n	56	4
6	G	23	X	40	o	57	5
7	H	24	Y	41	p	58	6
8	I	25	Z	42	q	59	7
9	J	26	a	43	r	60	8
10	K	27	b	44	s	61	9
11	L	28	c	45	t	62	+
12	M	29	d	46	u	63	/
13	N	30	e	47	v		
14	O	31	f	48	w	(pad)	=
15	P	32	g	49	x		
16	Q	33	h	50	y		

All characters not included in the BASE64 alphabet are ignored during decoding. This allows the encoder to insert CRLF sequences into the encoded output stream to keep the line lengths containing encoded data small.

MIME Content Types

This section describes the basic MIME content types and lists additional types that have been defined.

The Text Content Type

The Text content type is used to identify body parts that contain text. The "text/plain" type/subtype pair identifies raw text with no formatting information. Lines of text are simply terminated with CRLF sequences. The Text type has one optional parameter, "charset", which identifies the character set used to encode the text.

The default character set is "us-ascii". MIME defines the default body part type as "text/plain" with a character set of "us-ascii". This is compatible with standard RFC 822 messages.

The Text type is defined by the following grammar:

```
text-type := "text" "/" text-subtype [";" "charset" "=" charset]

text-subtype := "plain" / extension-token

charset := "us-ascii"/ "iso-8859-1"/ "iso-8859-2"/ "iso-8859-3"
     / "iso-8859-4"/ "iso-8859-5"/ "iso-8859-6"/ "iso-8859-7"
     / "iso-8859-8" / "iso-8859-9" / extension-token
     ; case insensitive
```

The Multipart Content Type

The Multipart content type is used to describe body parts that consist of one or more sub-body parts. Various subtypes of the Multipart type describe the general relationship between the sub-body parts, if any.

Each individual sub-body part is separated from the others by a line of text called an *encapsulation boundary*. The encapsulation boundary is specified by the "boundary" parameter in the multipart Content-Type header field.

Multipart bodies must be encoded using Content-Transfer-Encodings of "7bit", "8bit", or "binary".

Boundaries are indicated by two leading hyphen characters ("-") on a line, followed by the boundary string specified in the boundary parameter. Boundaries separate each of the body parts, with the last boundary appearing followed by two additional hyphen characters.

Note that the CRLF sequence appearing immediately before an encapsulation boundary is logically part of the boundary itself. This allows a boundary to appear on a line by itself while still allowing the previous body part to *not* end with a CRLF pair.

A multipart body part is defined by the following grammar:

```
multipart-body := preamble 1*encapsulation
     close-delimiter epilogue

encapsulation  := delimiter body-part CRLF
```

```
delimiter := "--" boundary CRLF  ; taken from Content-Type field.
        ; There must be no space
        ; between "--" and boundary.

close-delimiter  := "--" boundary "--" CRLF  ; Again, no space by "--",

preamble  := discard-text;  to be ignored upon receipt.

epilogue  := discard-text;  to be ignored upon receipt.

discard-text := *(*text CRLF)

body-part := <"message" as defined in RFC 822,
     with all header fields optional, and with the
     specified delimiter not occurring anywhere in
     the message body, either on a line by itself
     or as a substring anywhere. Note that the
     semantics of a part differ from the semantics
     of a message, as described in the text.>

boundary  := 0*69<bchars> bcharsnospace

bchars  := bcharsnospace / " "

bcharsnospace  := DIGIT / ALPHA / "'" / "(" / ")" / "+" /"_"
     / "," / "-" / "." / "/" / ":" / "=" / "?"
```

The following is a sample multipart message:

```
Date: Sun, 20 Aug 95 19:15:53 pdt
From: Dave Roberts <dave@droberts.com>
To: dave@droberts.com
Subject: Multipart Example
Message-ID: <082095191553.0@droberts.com>
MIME-Version: 1.0
X-Mail-Agent: Mail Client
X-Mail-Agent: From the book, "Developing for the Internet with WinSock"
X-Mail-Agent: By Dave Roberts
Content-Type: multipart/mixed;
    boundary="=_ Boundary KTwEv,JE?148K4Gac"


--=_ Boundary KTwEv,JE?148K4Gac
Content-Type: text/plain; charset=us-ascii
Content-Transfer-Encoding: 7bit
```

```
This is an sample multipart message.  The first part contains a
text body part and the second contains a binary file attachment.


--=_ Boundary KTwEv,JE?148K4Gac
Content-Type: application/octet-stream
Content-Transfer-Encoding: base64
```


```
W21lbnVdDQptZW51aXRlbT13aW5jZCwgV2luZG93cyB3LONEDQptZW51aXRlbT1kb3Nj
ZCwgRE9TIHcvQ0QgDQptZW51aXRlbT13aW5kb3dzLCBXaW5kb3dzDQptZW51aXRlbT1k
b3MsIERPUUw0KbWVudWRlZmF1bHQ9d2luY2QsMjANCg0KW2NvbW1vblONCkRPUz1ISUdI
LFVNQg0KREVWSUNFPUM6XHdpbmRvd3NcSElNRU0uU1lTIC9OZXN0bWVtOm9mZg0KREVW
SUNFPUM6XHdpbmRvd3NcRU1NMzg2LkVYRSBSQUONCkJVRkZFUlM9NDAsMA0KZmlsZXM9
NTANCkxBU1REUklWRT1aDQpGQ0JTPTE2LDANClNIRUxMPUM6XERPU1xDT01NQU5ELkNP
TSBDOlxET1NcIC9lOjEwMjQgL3ANCnJlbSBERVZJQ0U9QzpcRUlERTIzMDBcRUlERTIz
MDAuU1lTDQpERVZJQ0VISUdIPUM6XERPU1xBTlNJLlNZUw0KREVWSUNFSElHSD1DOlxE
T1NcU0VUVkVSLkVYRQ0KU1RBQ0tTPTksMjU2DQpbZG9zXQ0KW3dpbmRvd3NdDQpbZG9z
Y2RdDQpSRU0gKiogRnV0dXJlIERvbWFpbiBQb3dlclNDU0khIHY0LjAgU3VwcG9ydCAq
Kg0KREVWSUNFSElHSD1DOlxQV1JTQ1NJIVxEQ0FNOTUwLkVYRSAvQ0EwMCA1IA0KREVW
SUNFSElHSD1DOlxQV1JTQ1NJIVxBU1BJRkNBTS5TWVMgLOQgLO8gDQpERVZJQ0VISUdI
PUM6XFBXU1NDU0khXEZEQ0QuU1lTIC9EOk1TQ0QwMDAxDQpSRU0gKioqKioqKiBFbmQg
UG93ZXJTQ1NJISB2NC4wIFN1cHBvcnQgKioqKioqKg0KW3dpbmNkXQ0KUkVNICoqIEZ1
dHVyZSBEb21haW4gUG93ZXJTQ1NJISB2NC4wIFN1cHBvcnQgKioNCkRFVklDRUhJR0g9
QzpcUFdSU0NTSSFcRENBTTk1MC5FWEUgL0NBMDAgNSANCkRFVklDRUhJR0g9QzpcUFdS
U0NTSSFcQVNQSUZDQU0uU1lTIC9EIC9PIA0KREVWSUNFSElHSD1DOlxQV1JTQ1NJIVxG
RENELlNZUyAvRDpNU0NEMDAwMQ0KUkVNICoqKioqKiogRW5kIFBvd2VyU0NTSSEgdjQu
MCBTdXBwb3J0ICoqKioqKioNCltjb21tb25dDQpkZXZpY2U9Yzpcd2luZG93c1xpZnNo
bHAuc3lzDQo=
```


```
--=_ Boundary KTwEv,JE?148K4Gac--
```

The Multipart type has several subtypes:

- "mixed". The body parts have no set relationship with one another.
- "alternative". The body parts are alternative versions of the same content. The receiving system displays the most "rich" body part that it can. The body parts appear in order from least rich to most rich.
- "digest". A Multipart/digest contains a series of RFC 822 messages. Within the digest, the default MIME type is changed to message/rfc822 rather than the typical text/plain.
- "parallel". The body parts are meant to be displayed at the same time. Typical examples of this might include an image type displayed in parallel with an audio type that describes the image.

The Multipart Content-Type header field is defined by the following grammar:

```
multipart-type := "multipart" "/" multipart-subtype
     ";" "boundary" "=" boundary
multipart-subtype := "mixed" / "parallel" / "digest"
     / "alternative" / extension-token
```

The Message Content Type

The Message content type is used to identify messages. The Message type defines the following subtypes:

- "rfc822". The body is another RFC 822 (or MIME) message.
- "partial". The body part contains a portion of a large message that has been divided into smaller messages, presumably to subvert a maximum size restriction of an intermediate MTA.
- "external-body". The body part contains information about how to retrieve the actual message body, rather than the information itself. Several different access methods are supported, as described by the "access-type" parameter: FTP, ANON-FTP, TFTP, AFS, LOCAL-FILE, and MAIL-SERVER.

The Message Content-Type header field is defined by the following grammar:

```
message-type := "message" "/" message-subtype

message-subtype  := "rfc822"
     / "partial" 2#3partial-param
     / "external-body" 1*external-param
     / extension-token

partial-param  := (";" "id" "=" value)
     /  (";" "number" "=" 1*DIGIT)
     /  (";" "total" "=" 1*DIGIT)
     ; id & number required; total  required  for  last part

external-param := (";" "access-type" "=" atype)
     / (";" "expiration" "=" date-time)
     ; Note that date-time is quoted
     / (";" "size" "=" 1*DIGIT)
     / (";"  "permission"  "="  ("read"  /  "read-write"))
     ; Permission is case-insensitive
     / (";" "name" "="  value)
     / (";" "site" "=" value)
     / (";" "dir" "=" value)
```

```
     / (";" "mode" "=" value)
     / (";" "server" "=" value)
     / (";" "subject" "=" value)
     ; access-type required;others required based on access-type

atype   := "ftp" / "anon-ftp" / "tftp" / "local-file"
     / "afs" / "mail-server" / extension-token
     ; Case-insensitive
```

The Application Content Type

The Application content type is used to describe content associated with an application program. The Application content type defines two subtypes:

- "octet-stream". The body contains raw binary data. Typically, this is a file attachment.
- "postscript". The body contains Postscript language data.

The Application Content-Type header field is defined by the following grammar:

```
application-type := "application" "/" application-subtype

application-subtype := ("octet-stream" *stream-param)
   / "postscript" / extension-token

stream-param := (";" "type" "=" value)
   / (";" "padding" "=" padding)

padding := "0" / "1" /  "2" /  "3" / "4" / "5" / "6" / "7"
```

The Image Content Type

The Image content type is used to encode image data. The subtype identifies the specific image format.

The Image Content-Type header field is defined by the following grammar:

```
image-type   := "image" "/" ("gif" / "jpeg" / extension-token)
```

The Audio Content Type

The Audio content type describes audio data content. RFC 1521 defines one type of audio subtype: "basic". Basic audio defines ISDN 8-bit, single channel, mu-law encoded audio at a sample rate of 8000 Hz.

The Audio Content-Type header field is defined by the following grammar:

```
audio-type   := "audio" "/" ("basic" / extension-token)
```

The Video Content Type

The Video content type describes video data, including synchronized audio.

The Video Content-Type header field is defined by the following grammar:

```
video-type   := "video" "/" ("mpeg" / extension-token)
```

Experimental Types

MIME allows private or experimental types to be used. MIME reserves all type names beginning with "X-" for experimental types. These types must be used between parties understanding their use.

Grammar

The following sections describe the additional header fields and grammar changes to RFC 822 used by MIME. Note that the MIME grammar is incomplete by itself. The MIME grammar references productions contained in the RFC 822 grammar.

MIME-Version Header

All MIME messages include a MIME-Version header field. In addition to describing the version of MIME used to compose the message, the presence of the MIME-Version header is an assertion that the message corresponds to the MIME formatting conventions and is not simply an older RFC 822 message.

The MIME-Version header field has the following format:

```
version := "MIME-Version" ":" 1*DIGIT "." 1*DIGIT
```

The current MIME version is 1.0.

Content-Type Header

MIME describes the message content type using a Content-Type header field. The actual type information is formatted as a type/subtype pairing, and may have optional parameters that provide additional information about the content.

The Content-Type header is defined by the following grammar:

```
content := "Content-Type"  ":"  type  "/"  subtype  *(";"
      parameter)
     ; case-insensitive matching of type and subtype

type := "application"     / "audio"
     / "image"            / "message"
     / "multipart"  / "text"
     / "video"            / extension-token
     ; All values case-insensitive

extension-token  := x-token / iana-token

iana-token  := <a publicly-defined extension token,
     registered with IANA, as specified in
     appendix E>

x-token := <The two characters "X-" or "x-" followed, with
     no intervening white space, by any token>

subtype := token ; case-insensitive

parameter := attribute "=" value

attribute := token   ; case-insensitive

value  := token / quoted-string

token  := 1*<any (ASCII) CHAR except SPACE, CTLs,
     or tspecials>

tspecials := "(" / ")" / "<" / ">" / "@"
     /  "," / ";" / ":" / "\" / <">
     /  "/" / "[" / "]" / "?" / "="
     ; Must be in quoted-string,
     ; to use within parameter values
```

Content-Transfer-Encoding Header

The Content-Transfer-Encoding header field is used to describe the encoding that has been applied to a particular body part. Typically, this encoding has been applied because the body part consists of non-ASCII data that must be encoded to be able to be sent through the Internet mail system.

The Content-Transfer-Encoding header field is defined by the following grammar:

```
encoding  := "Content-Transfer-Encoding" ":" mechanism

mechanism := "7bit"  ;  case-insensitive
   / "quoted-printable"
   / "base64"
   / "8bit"
   / "binary"
   / x-token
```

Content-ID Header Field

MIME allows individual body parts to contain a Content-ID field. This field is conceptually identical to the Message-ID field in RFC 822. Like the Message-ID field, the Content-ID field must be globally unique. The Content-ID field allows separate body parts within a message to reference each other.

The Content-ID header field is defined by the following grammar:

```
id := "Content-ID" ":" msg-id
```

Content-Description Header Field

The Content-Description header field allows a MIME user agent to provide a description of a body part. The receiving user agent can present the description to the user in summary form before decoding the full body part. For instance, a body part of type image might provide a text description of the image.

The Content-Description header field is defined by the following grammar:

```
description  := "Content-Description" ":" *text
```

Alphabetized Grammar

This section contains the complete list of grammar productions from RFC 1521. The productions have been alphabetized for easy reference:

```
application-subtype := ("octet-stream" *stream-param)
     / "postscript" / extension-token

application-type := "application" "/" application-subtype

attribute := token   ; case-insensitive
```

```
atype   := "ftp" / "anon-ftp" / "tftp" / "local-file"
     / "afs" / "mail-server" / extension-token
     ; case-insensitive

audio-type   := "audio" "/" ("basic" / extension-token)

body-part := <"message" as defined in RFC 822,
     with all header fields optional, and with the
     specified delimiter not occurring anywhere in
     the message body, either on a line by itself
     or as a substring anywhere.>

boundary   := 0*69<bchars> bcharsnospace

bchars   := bcharsnospace / " "

bcharsnospace   := DIGIT / ALPHA / "'" / "(" / ")" / "+"  / "_"
     / "," / "-" / "." / "/" / ":" / "=" / "?"

charset := "us-ascii" / "iso-8859-1" / "iso-8859-2"/ "iso-8859-3"
     / "iso-8859-4" / "iso-8859-5" /  "iso-8859-6" / "iso-8859-7"
     / "iso-8859-8" / "iso-8859-9" / extension-token
     ; case insensitive

close-delimiter   := "--" boundary "--" CRLF;Again,no space by "--",

content := "Content-Type"  ":" type "/" subtype  *(";" parameter)
     ; case-insensitive matching of type and subtype

delimiter := "--" boundary CRLF  ;taken from Content-Type field.
     ; There must be no space
     ; between "--" and boundary.

description  := "Content-Description" ":" *text

discard-text := *(*text CRLF)

encapsulation  := delimiter body-part CRLF

encoding  := "Content-Transfer-Encoding" ":" mechanism

epilogue  := discard-text;  to be ignored upon receipt.

extension-token   := x-token / iana-token

external-param := (";" "access-type" "=" atype)
     / (";" "expiration" "=" date-time)
```

```
          ; Note that date-time is quoted
          / (";" "size" "=" 1*DIGIT)
          / (";"  "permission"  "="  ("read" / "read-write"))
          ; Permission is case-insensitive
          / (";" "name" "="  value)
          / (";" "site" "=" value)
          / (";" "dir" "=" value)
          / (";" "mode" "=" value)
          / (";" "server" "=" value)
          / (";" "subject" "=" value)
          ;access-type required; others required based on access-type

iana-token   :=<a publicly-defined extension token,
          registered with IANA, as specified in
          appendix E>

id :="Content-ID" ":" msg-id

image-type   :="image" "/" ("gif" / "jpeg" / extension-token)

mechanism :="7bit"  ;  case-insensitive
          / "quoted-printable"
          / "base64"
          / "8bit"
          / "binary"
          / x-token

message-subtype   :="rfc822"
          / "partial" 2#3partial-param
          / "external-body" 1*external-param
          / extension-token

message-type :="message" "/" message-subtype

multipart-body :=preamble 1*encapsulation close-delimiter epilogue

multipart-subtype :="mixed" / "parallel" / "digest"
          / "alternative" / extension-token

multipart-type :="multipart" "/" multipart-subtype
          ";" "boundary" "=" boundary

octet   :="=" 2(DIGIT / "A" / "B" / "C" / "D" / "E" / "F")
          ; octet must be used for characters > 127, =, SPACE, or TAB,
          ; and is recommended for any characters not listed in
          ; Appendix B as "mail-safe".

padding :="0" / "1" /  "2" /  "3" / "4" / "5" / "6" / "7"
```

```
parameter := attribute "=" value

partial-param  := (";" "id" "=" value)
     /  (";" "number" "=" 1*DIGIT)
     /  (";" "total" "=" 1*DIGIT)
     ; id & number required;total required for last part

preamble  := discard-text       ;  to  be  ignored upon receipt.

ptext   := octet / <any ASCII character except "=", SPACE,  or TAB>
     ; characters not listed as "mail-safe" in Appendix B
     ; are also not recommended.

quoted-printable := ([*(ptext / SPACE /  TAB)  ptext]  ["="] CRLF)
     ; Maximum line length of 76 characters excluding CRLF

stream-param := (";" "type" "=" value)
     / (";" "padding" "=" padding)

subtype := token  ; case-insensitive

text-subtype := "plain" / extension-token

text-type := "text" "/" text-subtype [";" "charset" "=" charset]

token   := 1*<any  (ASCII) CHAR except SPACE, CTLs, or tspecials>

tspecials := "(" / ")" / "<" / ">" / "@"
     /  "," / ";" / ":" / "\" / <">
     /  "/" / "[" / "]" / "?" / "="
     ; Must be in quoted-string,
     ; to use within parameter values

type := "application"     /  "audio"   ; case-insensitive
     / "image"            / "message"
     / "multipart"  / "text"
     / "video"            / extension-token
     ; All values case-insensitive

value   := token / quoted-string

version := "MIME-Version" ":" 1*DIGIT "." 1*DIGIT

video-type  := "video" "/" ("mpeg" / extension-token)

x-token := <The two characters "X-" or "x-" followed, with no
     intervening white space, by any token>
```

21 Network News Transfer Protocol

Name

Network News Transfer Protocol

Abbreviation

NNTP

Status

Elective Proposed Standard

Specifications

RFC 977

Abstract

The Network News Transfer Protocol (NNTP) provides for the reading and posting of news articles between clients and servers and for the transmission of news articles between peer servers. NNTP is a simple, text-based protocol similar in many respects to SMTP.

Related Specifications

Standard for Interchange of USENET Messages (RFC 1036)

Transport Information

The NNTP server listens on well-known TCP port 119

Commands and Responses

NNTP is a text-based, line-oriented protocol. The NNTP client, whether a user agent or another peer server, sends commands to the server and the server sends back responses.

Commands consist of short command names followed by optional parameters which depend on the particular command. All commands are given as a single line of text followed by a CRLF line termination sequence.

Responses consist of a three-digit numeric response code followed by a text message. The numeric response code is suitable for driving the client protocol state machine, and the text message can be shown to a human in the event of an error. Some responses include return values. Where these occur, they are placed between the response code and the text. All responses consist of a single line of text followed by a CRLF line-termination sequence.

Many commands require the server to send back additional text, such as article headers or bodies. In these cases, the server sends back a response line and then follows with lines of article text. Each line of text is terminated with a CRLF sequence. The end of the text is identified by a single line containing a single period character followed by CRLF. This line is not part of the text itself. All lines beginning with a period are "dot stuffed" to ensure that the receiver does not mistake them for the end-of-message line. Dot stuffing adds a leading period to all lines that begin with a period. The receiver, after checking for the end-of-message indication, removes all leading periods from message lines.

In some cases, the NNTP client must send text to the server, such as when the client posts a message. After sending a command to the server, the server will reply with an intermediate reply code indicating that the client should then send the message text. After receiving the intermediate reply, the client sends the message followed by the end-of-message indication. The client performs the dot stuffing algorithm for all lines of text sent to the server. When the server receives the end-of-message indication, it returns a final response to the client indicating the success or failure of the overall operation.

Response Codes

The response codes returned by the server consist of three numeric digits. Each digit conveys meaning to the client.

The first digit of the response broadly indicates the success, failure, or progress of the previous command. Table 21.1 shows the interpretations of the response code first digit.

The second digit in the code indicates the function response category. Table 21.2 shows the interpretations of the response code's second digit.

NNTP defines several general response codes. These codes are not specific to any one command, but may be returned as the result of a connection, failure, or other unusual condition. Table 21.3 shows the general NNTP response codes.

Table 21.4 shows the full list of NNTP response codes.

Table 21.1 NNTP Response Codes—First Digit

Code	Description
1xx	Informative message
2xx	Command ok
3xx	Command ok so far, send the rest of it
4xx	Command was correct, but couldn't be performed for some reason
5xx	Command unimplemented, or incorrect, or a serious program error occurred

Table 21.2 NNTP Response Codes—Second Digit

Code	Description
x0x	Connection, setup, and miscellaneous messages
x1x	Newsgroup selection
x2x	Article selection
x3x	Distribution functions
x4x	Posting
x8x	Nonstandard (private implementation) extensions
x9x	Debugging output

Table 21.3 General NNTP Response Codes
Codes
100 help text
190-199 debug output
200 server ready - posting allowed
201 server ready - no posting allowed
400 service discontinued
500 command not recognized
501 command syntax error
502 access restriction or permission denied
503 program fault - command not performed

Table 21.4 Complete Set of NNTP Response Codes
Codes
100 help text follows
199 debug output
200 server ready - posting allowed
201 server ready - no posting allowed
202 slave status noted
205 closing connection - goodbye!
211 n f l s group selected
215 list of newsgroups follows
220 n <a> article retrieved - head and body follow
221 n <a> article retrieved - head follows
222 n <a> article retrieved - body follows
223 n <a> article retrieved - request text separately
224 data follows
230 list of new articles by message-id follows
231 list of new newsgroups follows
235 article transferred ok
240 article posted ok
335 send article to be transferred. End with <CR-LF>.<CR-LF>

Continued

Table 21.4 Complete Set of NNTP Response Codes (Continued)
Codes
340 send article to be posted. End with <CR-LF>.<CR-LF>
400 service discontinued
411 no such newsgroup
412 no newsgroup has been selected
420 no current article has been selected
421 no next article in this group
422 no previous article in this group
423 no such article number in this group
430 no such article found
435 article not wanted - do not send it
436 transfer failed - try again later
437 article rejected - do not try again
440 posting not allowed
441 posting failed
500 command not recognized
501 command syntax error
502 access restriction or permission denied
503 program fault - command not performed

Commands

NNTP specifies 15 commands that a client can use to interact with the server. These commands are shown in Table 21.5. Each command is described in a subsequent section.

Table 21.5 NNTP Commands

Commands					
ARTICLE	BODY	GROUP	HEAD	HELP	IHAVE
LAST	LIST	NEWGROUPS	NEWNEWS	NEXT	POST
QUIT	SLAVE	STAT	XOVER		

ARTICLE

The ARTICLE command is used to request the server to return an article to the client. The command takes either a message ID or an article index number as its parameter.

The format for this command is:

```
ARTICLE <message-id>
ARTICLE [nnn]
```

The possible responses to the command are:

```
220 n <a> article retrieved - head and body follow
```
(where n = article number, and <a> = message-id)
```
221 n <a> article retrieved - head follows
222 n <a> article retrieved - body follows
223 n <a> article retrieved - request text separately
412 no newsgroup has been selected
420 no current article has been selected
423 no such article number in this group
430 no such article found
```

BODY

The BODY command is virtually identical to the ARTICLE command but requests that only the message body be returned by the server.

GROUP

The GROUP command selects the current newsgroup for the session and returns information about the first and last article numbers in the group along with an estimate of the total number of articles in the group.

The server maintains a "current article pointer" for the current newsgroup in the current session. The GROUP commands sets this pointer to the first article in the group.

The format for this command is:

```
GROUP ggg
```

The possible responses to the command are:

```
211 n f l s group selected
```

(where, n = estimated number of articles in group, f = first article number in the group, l = last article number in the group, and s = name of the group)

```
411 no such newsgroup
```

HEAD

The HEAD command is virtually identical to the ARTICLE command but requests that only the message headers be returned by the server.

HELP

The HELP command provides a summary of the commands implemented by this server. The help text is returned as textual data following the response line and is terminated with a line containing a single period.

The format for this command is:

```
HELP
```

The only possible response to the command is:

```
100 help text follows
```

IHAVE

The IHAVE command is used by other servers when exchanging articles with another server. The IHAVE command tells the server that the client has an article with the specified message ID.

If the server wants the client to send it the article, it sends back a positive intermediate response code. The client then sends the article, and the server responds with a final response code.

If the server already has the specified article or it does not wish to receive the article, the server responds with a negative initial reply code to the IHAVE command.

The format for this command is:

```
IHAVE <messageid>
```

The possible responses to the command are:

```
235 article transferred ok
335 send article to be transferred. End with <CR-LF>.<CR-LF>
435 article not wanted - do not send it
436 transfer failed - try again later
437 article rejected - do not try again
```

LAST

The LAST command moves the current article pointer to the previous article in the newsgroup. If the pointer is already at the first article, it is not moved.

The format for this command is:

```
LAST
```

The possible responses to the command are:

```
223 n a article retrieved - request text separately
```

(where n = article number, and a = unique article id)

```
412 no newsgroup selected
420 no current article has been selected
422 no previous article in this group
```

LIST

The LIST command requests the server to return a list of valid newsgroups. The list is returned as text following the initial response line. Each group is provided as a line of text using the format

```
groupname last first p
```

where *groupname* is the name of the group, *last* is the article number of the last article in the group, *first* is the article number of the first article in the group, and *p* is either "y" or "n" and indicates whether this server allows posting to this newsgroup.

The format for this command is:

```
LIST
```

The only possible response to the command is:

```
215 list of newsgroups follows
```

NEWGROUPS

The NEWSGROUPS command asks the server to return a list of groups created since a specified date and time. The returned list is formatted as for the LIST command.

The format for this command is

```
NEWGROUPS date time [GMT] [<distributions>]
```

where *date* and *time* are specified in YYMMDD and HHMMSS format. The server interprets the data and time as local time, unless the GMT token is included. The optional *distributions* parameter specifies a list of newsgroup distributions in angle brackets. Only groups belonging to the specified distributions will be listed.

The only possible response to the command is:

```
231 list of new newsgroups follows
```

NEWNEWS

The NEWNEWS command requests the server to return the message IDs of articles received in the specified newsgroups since the specified date. The message IDs are returned one per line and are terminated with a line consisting of a single period.

The format for this command is:

```
NEWNEWS newsgroups date time [GMT] [<distribution>]
```

The *newsgroups* parameter specifies the newsgroups in which the client is interested. Multiple group names may be specified, separated by a comma. If multiple names are specified, there should be no space characters between the names and commas. The asterisk ("*") character can be used to specify a wildcard match of a portion of the newsgroup name. All the groups selected by the wildcard criteria will be searched. An exclamation point at the start of a group name indicates negation of the group specified. Note that a group name may use both an exclamation point and an asterisk character indicating that all the groups matching the wildcard should *not* be searched.

The *date* and *time* fields are specified in YYMMDD and HHMMSS format. The optional "GMT" token indicates the date and time are relative to GMT.

The optional *distribution* parameter indicates a list of distribution groups, separated by commas. If specified, only articles that contain at least one of the specified distribution groups in their Newsgroups header will be returned.

The only possible response to the command is:

```
230 list of new articles by message-id follows
```

NEXT

The NEXT command is used to move the current article pointer to the next article in the current newsgroup. If no more articles remain following the current article, the server returns an error and the pointer is not advanced.

The format for this command is:

```
NEXT
```

The possible responses to the command are:

```
223 n a article retrieved - request text separately
```
(where n = article number, and a = unique article id)
```
412 no newsgroup selected
420 no current article has been selected
421 no next article in this group
```

POST

The POST command is used by clients to post new articles to the server. If the server allows posting, it will respond with a positive intermediate reply code and request that the client send the article text followed by a single line containing a period. When transfer of the article text is complete, the server will send back a final reply code indicating the success or failure of the overall operation.

If the server does not allow posting, it will respond with an initial negative reply code to the POST command.

The format for this command is:

```
POST
```

The possible responses to the command are:

```
240 article posted ok
340 send article to be posted. End with <CR-LF>.<CR-LF>
440 posting not allowed
441 posting failed
```

Note that when the client initially connects with the server, the server will send one of the following responses as its initial greeting. The client should note the response to avoid repeated failed posting attempts:

```
200 server ready - posting allowed
201 server ready - no posting allowed
```

QUIT

The QUIT command indicates that the client is ready to terminate the session. The server sends a single response line and then closes the connection.

The format for this command is:

```
QUIT
```

The only possible responses for this command is:

```
205 closing connection - goodbye!
```

SLAVE

The SLAVE command is used to inform the server that the client is another slave server rather than an interactive client. This command allows the server to prioritize this session appropriately. For instance, the session may be given lower priority than interactive clients.

The format for this command is:

```
SLAVE
```

The only possible responses for this command is:

```
202 slave status noted
```

STAT

The STAT command is identical to the ARTICLE command except that no text is returned. The STAT command is typically used to set the current article pointer to the indicated article when selecting articles by message number rather than by message ID.

XOVER

The XOVER command is not described in RFC 977. Rather, it is a de facto standard extension command implemented by many popular NNTP servers and user agents. The XOVER command is used to access a database of article header information called the News Overview (NOV) database. This idea was first implemented by Geoff Collyer.

The XOVER command increases the performance of news readers by retrieving the header information for a group of articles using a single command rather than repeated HEAD/NEXT commands.

The XOVER command is issued after a newsgroup is selected with the GROUP command.

The header information is returned as a multi-line response following the initial response line, terminated with a line containing a single period. The information for each article is returned on a single summary line using the following format:

```
Artid|Subject|From|Date|Message-Id|References|Bytecount|Linecount| _
  Optional-Header: Stuff
```

The "|" character represents a tab character (US-ASCII character 9). Before generating the summary line, the server takes the information field from each header indicated and converts all tab characters and CRLF sequences to spaces.

None of the fields in the summary, except the optional headers, include the header names. Only the data portion of the header is returned. Optional headers are configured as a local site option. If configured, the optional headers appear after the required headers. Optional headers include the header name to allow the client to determine which header is returned.

The returned fields are:

Artid The article number on the server

Subject The Subject header text

From The From header text

Date The Date header text

Message-ID The Message-ID

References The References header text

Bytecount The article byte count

Linecount The article line count

Optional-Header Any optional header configured locally including the header field name

The format for this command is:

```
XOVER article1[-article2]
```

where *article1* < *article2*. If *article2* is not specified, all the headers from *article1* to the end of the group are returned.

The possible responses to this command are:

```
224 data follows
412 no newsgroup has been selected
500 command not recognized
```

If the "500 command not recognized" reply is returned, the server does not support the XOVER extension and standard NNTP or other nonstandard extensions mechanisms must be used to retrieve article headers.

22 Post Office Protocol

Name

Post Office Protocol, Version 3

Abbreviation

POP3

Status

Elective Draft Standard

Specifications

RFC 1725

Abstract

The Post Office Protocol (POP3) allows a client to retrieve mail from a remote server mailbox. This protocol is commonly used by personal computers, which are powered off at various times, to retrieve mail from a permanent SMTP host. The SMTP host holds messages for the client until the client empties its mailbox. This allows the client to be disconnected for a time without generating SMTP delivery errors.

Related Specifications

SMTP (RFC 821), IMAP4 (RFC 1730)

Comments

POP3 is a simple, widely implemented protocol. Unfortunately, it only allows a client to retrieve mail from a server. The IMAP4 protocol provides the same service as POP3, but also provides for the bi-directional movement of messages and allows the management of remote mailboxes.

Description

POP3 implements a simple, line-oriented, ASCII-based request response protocol. The client sends commands to the server, which then sends responses back to the client. The following sections describe the exact commands and the response format.

Transport Information

The POP3 server listens on well-known TCP port 110.

Commands and Responses

POP3 commands consist of short keywords, followed by optional parameters sent as a single line of text, followed by <CRLF>. The protocol uses only a small number of commands, as shown in Table 22.1. Each of the commands and the appropriate responses are described in the following sections.

Responses to POP3 commands may take two forms: single-line responses and multi-line responses. Single-line responses first indicate the success or failure of the command and then provide additional information that may be suitable for humans to read or machines to parse. The basic POP3 success and failure codes are "+OK" and "-ERR". Any additional information that appears on the line following the basic codes is described with the appropriate command.

Multi-line POP3 responses consist of a single-line response followed by additional lines of information appropriate to the command that invoked the response. The multi-line response is terminated with a line containing a single period character followed by <CRLF>. This final line is not considered part of the response.

Table 22.1 POP3 Commands

Command Name	Valid States	Description
USER name	Authorization	Indicates the POP3 user (mail drop) name
PASS string	Authorization	Indicates the user password
STAT	Transaction	Requests the server to return the number of messages in the mail drop and the size of the mail drop in octets
LIST [msg]	Transaction	Requests the server to return information about the size of a given message or all messages if the *msg* parameter is not supplied
RETR msg	Transaction	Requests the server to send the client the full message indicated by the *msg* parameter
DELE msg	Transaction	Requests the server to delete the indicated message; the actual deletion only occurs when the session enters the Update state
NOOP	Transaction	Does nothing other than force the server to generate a positive reply
RSET	Transaction	Requests that the server reset all deletion indications
QUIT	Authorization, Update	Quits the session; the server enters the Update state and deletes all marked messages before quitting
APOP name digest	Authorization	Optional
TOP msg n	Transaction	Requests the server to return the first *n* lines of the message body of message *msg* (optional)
UIDL [msg]	Transaction	Returns a unique ID string for the requested message or all messages if *msg* is not specified (optional)

Any lines of the multi-line response that begin with a period have an additional period inserted before the first character. This ensures that the client does not confuse them for the termination line. The client removes a leading period from all lines which are not the termination line. This process is called *dot stuffing.*

USER

The USER command is given to identify the user or mail drop name to the server. This command is sent after the server identifies itself with a one-line positive greeting, while the session is in Authorization state #1.

The possible responses to the USER command are:

+OK user is known

-ERR user is unknown

PASS

The PASS command specifies the user password corresponding to the user name given in the USER command. If the password agrees with the given user name, the server attempts to acquire an exclusive lock on the mail drop. This ensures that all index numbers used in the POP3 session are not affected by incoming mail. If the PASS command succeeds, the session enters the Transaction state.

The possible responses by the server to the PASS command are:

+OK mail drop locked

-ERR incorrect password

-ERR could not lock mail drop

STAT

The STAT command requests the server to provide statistics about the mail drop. The server response indicates the number of messages in the mail drop and the size of the mail drop in octets.

The format of the response is:

+OK *nn mm*

where *nn* is the number of messages in the mail drop and *mm* is the size of the mail drop in octets. No other information should be returned in the response.

LIST

The LIST command requests the server to provide size information about individual messages in the mail drop. If the optional *msg* parameter is given, the server response is a single line. If no individual message is specified, information about each message in the mailbox is returned in a multi-line response.

If the LIST command specifies a message, but the message has been marked for deletion, the server returns an error. The LIST command does not specify an individual message. Information about deleted messages is not provided in the multi-line response.

If the LIST command specifies a message, the format of the response is:

+OK *msg size*

-ERR no such message

where *msg* is the specified message number, and *size* is the size of the message in octets.

If the command does not specify a message, the format of the response is:

+OK scan listing follows

msg-1 size-1

msg-2 size-2

...

Each line of the multi-line response contains a single message-number-size tuple.

RETR

The RETR command asks the server to send the client the contents of a message. The mandatory *msg* parameter specifies the message to be retrieved. If the specified message exists and has not been marked for deletion, the server returns the message as a multi-line response.

The possible responses to the RETR command are:

+OK message follows

-ERR no such message

DELE

The DELE command instructs the server to mark the specified message for deletion. The *msg* parameter is mandatory. The server does not actually delete the message when the client issues the DELE command. The message is only deleted when the POP3 session enters the Update state. The RSET command can be issued to clear all pending deletions.

The possible responses to the DELE command are:

+OK message deleted

-ERR no such message

NOOP

The NOOP command simply requests the server to respond with a positive reply.

The only possible response to the NOOP command is:

+OK

RSET

The RSET command is used to clear the state of all messages currently marked for deletion. The session remains in the Transaction state, but no messages will be deleted unless additional DELE commands are given before the session transitions to the Update state.

The only possible response to the RSET command is:

+OK

QUIT

The QUIT command is used to terminate a session. If the QUIT command is given while the session is still in the Authentication state, the server simply responds to the command and closes the connection without entering the Update state. If the QUIT command is given from the Transaction state, the server enters the Update state, deletes all messages marked for deletion, removes the lock on the mail drop, sends a response, and closes the connection.

The only possible response to the QUIT command is:

+OK

APOP

The APOP command is an optional command used to authenticate users with the server. With the typical USER/PASS command sequence, the user's password is sent in the clear with the PASS command and is subject to eavesdropping: therefore, it's not very secure. The APOP command allows a much better authentication.

A POP server implementing the APOP authentication scheme will include a timestamp in its initial greeting. The timestamp is surrounded by the < and > symbols, using the message ID format specified in RFC 822. The contents of the timestamp are not very important, but the server must ensure that the contents are different every time the initial greeting is sent to a client. For example, a server might use the following format:

```
<process-ID.clock@hostname>
```

where *process-ID* is the server's process ID on its host, and *clock* is some information derived from the local clock.

A client wishing to use the APOP authentication parses the timestamp from the initial greeting, appends its shared password to the timestamp text (including the angle brackets), and computes the MD5 hash function over this resulting string. The client then sends an APOP command with its user name and the MD5 digest expressed as hexadecimal digits. All alphabetic characters in the digest are sent using lowercase.

When the server receives the APOP command, it computes the same MD5 digest using the same timestamp and its version of the shared secret key. If the digest sent by the client matches the one computed by the server, the client is authenticated, the server locks the mail drop, and the session enters the Transaction state.

The possible responses to the APOP command are:

+OK mailbox locked and ready

-ERR permission denied

TOP

The TOP command is used to request the server to return just a few lines from a message without returning the entire message. This command is useful in cases where the client might be a mobile computer using a slow dial up connection. Rather than retrieve all messages automatically, client software might first get a summary listing of each of the available messages, retrieve all the short messages, and then present the first few lines of each large message. If the user wants to retrieve a large message after viewing the first few lines, the client software can then perform the task. This prevents the user from having to retrieve large messages without knowing what they are.

The two required parameters to the TOP command are the message number (*msg*) and the number of lines of body text to return (*n*). The server returns all the RFC 822 header lines, the line separating the headers from the body, and *n* lines of body text. The message lines are returned in a multi-line response following the initial response line.

The possible responses to the TOP command are:

+OK top of message follows

-ERR no such message

UIDL

The UIDL command asks the server to report a unique message ID string for each message in the mail drop. This ID is guaranteed to be unique and consistent for the message across mail sessions, as compared to message index numbers, which change from session to session as messages are deleted and added to the mail drop. The client can use the message ID strings returned by the UIDL command to identify messages in later sessions. The message ID string is composed of ASCII characters in the range 0x21 to 0x7E.

The UIDL command takes an optional message number, *msg*, as its only parameter. If the message number is specified, the response is a single-line response containing "+OK" followed by the message number and the message ID string. If the UIDL command does not specify a message, the message ID strings for all the messages in the mail drop are returned in a multi-line response. Each line of the multi-line response after the initial line contains a message number followed by a message ID string. Messages marked for deletion are not included in the listing.

The possible responses to the UIDL command are:

+OK

-ERR no such message

Protocol State Machine

Figure 22.1 shows the session state machine for the POP3 protocol.

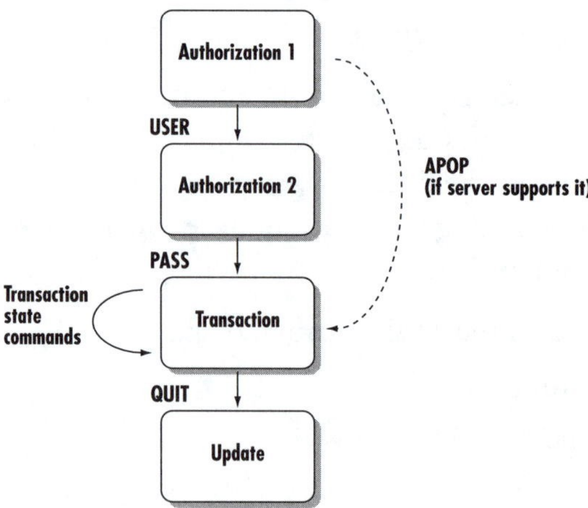

Figure 22.1

The POP3 session state machine.

23 Quote of the Day Protocol

Name

Quote of the Day Protocol

Abbreviation

QUOTE or COOKIE

Status

Elective Standard (STD 23)

Specifications

RFC 865

Abstract

The Quote of the Day Protocol provides a simple service that gives out famous quotes or bits of advice. Because of this dispensing of good tidbits, the service is often nicknamed the "Cookie Service". While somewhat practical, the service provides more use as a diagnostic tool.

Comments

Many servers no longer run the Quote service.

Description

The QUOTE service is very similar to the DAYTIME service described in RFC 867, except it returns famous quotes rather than the current date and time. The QUOTE service is provided for both TCP and UDP clients.

In the TCP case, the server waits for a connection. As soon as a connection is established, the server sends a text string containing a quote and closes the connection. The client does not need to send any data; data that is sent is ignored by the server.

In the UDP case, the client simply sends the server a UDP datagram. The server throws away the client datagram and returns a second datagram containing the quote text.

The format of the quote data is minimally defined. RFC 865 suggests that it be less than 512 characters. The server should limit the character set to the printing ASCII characters, space, carriage return, and line feed.

Transport Information

The QUOTE server listens on well-known TCP port 17 and UDP port 17.

24 Registered MIME Types

Name

Registered MIME Types

Abbreviation

-NA-

Status

This chapter contains types that have been registered with the Internet Assigned Numbers Authority (IANA) and some unregistered types that are in common use.

Specifications

The most current listing of registered MIME types is available online at **ftp://ftp.isi.edu/in-notes/iana/assignments/media-types.**

In addition to the formal list of types registered with the IANA, many other types are commonly used on the Internet. The MIME FAQ contains a list of such types. The current list is described in a following section. For the current version of the MIME FAQ, see **ftp://rtfm.mit.edu/pub/usenet-by-group/news.answers/mail/mime-faq/**.

Abstract

RFC 1521 provides an extensible framework for extended Internet mail service. MIME provides a method of tagging each portion of a message with a type. MIME allows the definition and registration of new types to describe specific types of new content. The Internet Assigned Numbers Authority (IANA) is responsible for cataloging the registered MIME types.

Related Specifications

RFC 1521 (MIME)

Comments

It is important to note that registration of a type in no way indicates endorsement by the IETF or IANA.

Registered MIME Types

The following MIME types are registered with the IANA and are taken from the current MIME FAQ, again, located at **ftp://ftp.isi.edu/in-notes/iana/assignments/media-types**.

Consult the Media Types document or the MIME FAQ for up-to-date information about currently registered MIME types.

You should note that the Media Types document contains some out-of-date information—some of the references are older or difficult to find.

Application Types

type: application/activemessage
see: **ftp://ftp.isi.edu/in-notes/iana/assignments/media-types/application/activemessage**

type: application/andrew-inset
see: **ftp://ftp.isi.edu/in-notes/iana/assignments/media-types/application/andrew-inset**

type: application/applefile
see: RFC 1740

see: **ftp://ftp.isi.edu/in-notes/iana/assignments/media-types/application/applefile**

type: application/atomicmail
see: **ftp://ftp.isi.edu/in-notes/iana/assignments/media-types/application/atomicmail**

type: application/cals-1840
see: RFC 1895
see: **ftp://ftp.isi.edu/in-notes/iana/assignments/media-types/application/cals-1840**

type: application/commonground
see: **ftp://ftp.isi.edu/in-notes/iana/assignments/media-types/application/commonground**

type: application/cybercash
see: RFC 1898
see: **ftp://ftp.isi.edu/in-notes/iana/assignments/media-types/application/cybercash**

type: application/dec-dx
see: **ftp://ftp.isi.edu/in-notes/iana/assignments/media-types/application/dec-dx**

type: application/dca-rft
see: **ftp://ftp.isi.edu/in-notes/iana/assignments/media-types/application/dca-rft**

type: application/eshop
see: **ftp://ftp.isi.edu/in-notes/iana/assignments/media-types/application/eshop**

type: application/iges
see: **ftp://ftp.isi.edu/in-notes/iana/assignments/media-types/application/iges**

type: application/mac-binhex40
see: **ftp://ftp.isi.edu/in-notes/iana/assignments/media-types/application/mac-binhex40**

type: application/macwriteii
see: **ftp://ftp.isi.edu/in-notes/iana/assignments/media-types/application/macwriteii**

type: application/mathematica
see: **ftp://ftp.isi.edu/in-notes/iana/assignments/media-types/application/mathematica**

type: application/msword
see: **ftp://ftp.isi.edu/in-notes/iana/assignments/media-types/application/msword**

type: application/news-message-id
see: **ftp://ftp.isi.edu/in-notes/iana/assignments/media-types/application/news-message-id**

type: application/news-transmission
see: **ftp://ftp.isi.edu/in-notes/iana/assignments/media-types/application/news-transmission**

type: application/octet-stream
see: RFC 1521
see: **ftp://ftp.isi.edu/in-notes/iana/assignments/media-types/application/octet-stream**

type: application/oda
see: RFC 1494
see: **ftp://ftp.isi.edu/in-notes/iana/assignments/media-types/application/oda**

type: application/pdf
see: **ftp://ftp.isi.edu/in-notes/iana/assignments/media-types/application/pdf**

type: application/postscript
see: RFC 1521
see: news:comp.lang.postscript
see: **ftp://ftp.isi.edu/in-notes/iana/assignments/media-types/application/postscript**

type: application/remote-printing
see: RFC 1528
see: **ftp://ftp.isi.edu/in-notes/iana/assignments/media-types/application/remote-printing**

type: application/riscos
see: **ftp://ftp.isi.edu/in-notes/iana/assignments/media-types/application/riscos**

type: application/rtf
see: **ftp://indri.primate.wisc.edu/pub/RTF/RTF-Spec.rtf**
see: **ftp://indri.primate.wisc.edu/pub/RTF/RTF-Spec.hqx**
see: **ftp://ftp.isi.edu/in-notes/iana/assignments/media-types/application/rtf**

type: application/sgml
see: RFC 1874
comment: no corresponding media-types file at ISI

type: application/slate
see: **ftp://ftp.isi.edu/in-notes/iana/assignments/media-types/application/slate**

type: application/wita
see: **ftp://ftp.isi.edu/in-notes/iana/assignments/media-types/application/wita**

type: application/wordperfect5.1
see: **ftp://ftp.isi.edu/in-notes/iana/assignments/media-types/application/wordperfect5.1**

type: application/x400-bp
see: RFC 1494
see: **ftp://ftp.isi.edu/in-notes/iana/assignments/media-types/application/x400-bp**

type: application/zip
see: **ftp://ftp.isi.edu/in-notes/iana/assignments/media-types/application/zip**

Audio Types

type: audio/basic
see: RFC 1521
see: **ftp://ftp.isi.edu/in-notes/iana/assignments/media-types/audio/basic**

type: audio/32kadpcm
see: RFC 1911
see: **ftp://ftp.isi.edu/in-notes/iana/assignments/media-types/audio/32kadpcm**

Image Types

type: image/cgm
see: **ftp://ftp.isi.edu/in-notes/iana/assignments/media-types/image/cgm**

type: image/g3fax
see: RFC 1494
see: **ftp://ftp.isi.edu/in-notes/iana/assignments/media-types/image/g3fax**

type: image/gif
see: RFC 1521
see: **ftp://ftp.isi.edu/in-notes/iana/assignments/media-types/image/gif**

type: image/ief
see: RFC 1314
see: **ftp://ftp.isi.edu/in-notes/iana/assignments/media-types/image/ief**

type: image/jpeg
see: RFC 1521
see: **ftp://ftp.isi.edu/in-notes/iana/assignments/media-types/image/jpeg**

type: image/naplps
see: **ftp://ftp.isi.edu/in-notes/iana/assignments/media-types/image/naplps**

type: image/tiff
see: RFC 1314
see: RFC 1528
see: **ftp://ftp.isi.edu/in-notes/iana/assignments/media-types/image/tiff**

Message Types

type: message/external-body
see: RFC 1521
see: **ftp://ftp.isi.edu/in-notes/iana/assignments/media-types/message/external-body**

type: message/news
see: RFC 1036
see: **ftp://ftp.isi.edu/in-notes/iana/assignments/media-types/message/news**

type: message/partial
see: RFC 1521
see: **ftp://ftp.isi.edu/in-notes/iana/assignments/media-types/message/partial**

type: message/rfc822
see: RFC 1521
see: RFC 822
see: **ftp://ftp.isi.edu/in-notes/iana/assignments/media-types/message/rfc822**

Multipart Types

type: multipart/alternative
see: RFC 1521
see: **ftp://ftp.isi.edu/in-notes/iana/assignments/media-types/multipart/alternative**

type: multipart/appledouble
see: RFC 1740
see: **ftp://ftp.isi.edu/in-notes/iana/assignments/media-types/multipart/appledouble**

type: multipart/digest
see: RFC 1521
see: **ftp://ftp.isi.edu/in-notes/iana/assignments/media-types/multipart/digest**

type: multipart/form-data
see: RFC 1867
see: **ftp://ftp.isi.edu/in-notes/iana/assignments/media-types/multipart/form-data**

type: multipart/header-set
see: **ftp://ftp.isi.edu/in-notes/iana/assignments/media-types/multipart/header-set**

type: multipart/mixed
see: RFC 1521
see: **ftp://ftp.isi.edu/in-notes/iana/assignments/media-types/multipart/mixed**

type: multipart/parallel
see: RFC 1521
see: **ftp://ftp.isi.edu/in-notes/iana/assignments/media-types/multipart/parallel**

type: multipart/related
see: RFC 1872

type: multipart/report
see: RFC 1892
see: **ftp://ftp.isi.edu/in-notes/iana/assignments/media-types/multipart/report**

type: multipart/voice-message
see: RFC 1911
see: **ftp://ftp.isi.edu/in-notes/iana/assignments/media-types/multipart/voice-message**

Text Types

type: text/enriched
see: RFC 1896
see: **ftp://ftp.isi.edu/in-notes/iana/assignments/media-types/text/enriched**

type: text/plain
see: RFC 1521
see: **ftp://ftp.isi.edu/in-notes/iana/assignments/media-types/text/plain**

type: text/richtext
see: RFC 1341 (obs.)
see: **ftp://ftp.isi.edu/in-notes/iana/assignments/media-types/text/richtext**
comments: obsolete—see text/enriched instead

type: text/sgml
see: RFC 1874
see: **ftp://ftp.isi.edu/in-notes/iana/assignments/media-types/text/sgml**

type: text/tab-separated-values
see: **ftp://ftp.isi.edu/in-notes/iana/assignments/media-types/text/tab-separated-values**

Video Types

type: video/mpeg
see: RFC 1521
see: **ftp://ftp.isi.edu/in-notes/iana/assignments/media-types/video/mpeg**

type: video/quicktime
see: **ftp://ftp.isi.edu/in-notes/iana/assignments/media-types/video/quicktime**

Unregistered MIME Types in Common Use

The following list of types commonly appear in MIME messages but are not registered with the IANA. The following list is taken from the current version of the MIME FAQ.

Application Types

type: application/green-commerce
for: commercial transactions
see: **http://www.fv.com/pubdocs/agc-spec.txt**

type: application/ms-tnef
from: Microsoft
for: Microsoft Exchange

type: application/pgp
from: PGP
for: Pretty Good Privacy
see: section 3.3 of the MIME FAQ

type: application/safe-tcl
for: enabled-mail
see: multipart/enabled-mail

type: application/x-aiff
from: Z-Mail
for: AIFF audio data

type: application/x-bcpio
from: MHonArc
for: bcpio data

type: application/x-bitmap
from: Z-Mail
for: X11 bitmaps

type: application/x-cpio
from: MHonArc
for: cpio archives

type: application/x-csh
from: MHonArc
for: csh scripts

type: application/x-dvi
from: MHonArc
for: TeX DVI data

type: application/x-framemaker
from: Z-Mail
for: FrameMaker documents

type: application/x-gtar
from: MHonArc
for: GNU tar archives

type: application/x-hdf
from: MHonArc
for: hdf data

type: application/x-inventor
from: Z-Mail
for: Inventor files

type: application/x-island-draw
from: Z-Mail
for: IslandDraw files

type: application/x-island-paint
from: Z-Mail
for: IslandPaint files

type: application/x-island-write
from: Z-Mail
for: IslandWrite files

type: application/x-jot
from: Z-Mail
for: Jot documents

type: application/x-latex
from: MHonArc
for: LaTeX documents

type: application/x-macbinhex40
from: TCP/Connect II
for: Mac BinHex 4.0
comment: see application/macbinhex40

type: application/x-metamail-patch
from: metamail
for: patches to metamail

type: application/x-mif
from: MHonArc
for: Frame MIF documents

type: application/x-movie
from: Z-Mail
for: MoviePlayer documents

type: application/x-ms-tnef
from: Worldtalk
for: proprietary "tunneling" type for MS Exchange

type: application/x-netcdf
from: MHonArc
for: netcdf data

type: application/x-patch
from: { unknown }
for: miscellaneous source code patches
see: patch(1)

type: application/x-sgi
from: Z-Mail
for: SGI ImageWorks documents

type: application/x-sh
from: MHonArc
for: sh scripts
comments: obvious security problem

type: application/x-shar
from: MHonArc
for: shell archives
comments: obvious security problem

type: application/x-showcase
from: Z-Mail
for: Showcase documents

type: application/x-sv4cpio
from: MHonArc
for: SVR4 cpio archives

type: application/x-sv4crc
from: MHonArc
for: SVR4 crc data

type: application/x-tar
from: MHonArc
for: tar archives

type: application/x-tcl
from: MHonArc
for: tcl programs
comments: obvious security problem

type: application/x-tex
from: MHonArc
for: TeX documents

type: application/x-texinfo
from: MHonArc
for: GNU texinfo documents

type: application/x-troff
from: MHonArc
for: plain troff documents

type: application/x-troff-man
from: MHonArc
for: troff -man documents

type: application/x-troff-me
from: MHonArc
for: troff -me documents

type: application/x-troff-ms
from: MHonArc
for: troff -ms documents

type: application/x-ustar
from: MHonArc
for: ustar data

type: application/x-wais-source
from: MHonArc
for: WAIS sources

type: application/x-wingz
from: Z-Mail
for: Wingz documents

type: application/x-xpm1
from: Z-Mail
for: OL pixmap files

type: application/x-wt-stf
from: Worldtalk
for: proprietary "tunneling" type for Worldtalk

type: application/x-zm-fax
from: Z-Mail
for: Z-Fax documents

Audio Types

type: audio/x-aiff
from: MHonArc
for: AIFF audio data

type: audio/x-wav
from: MHonArc
for: WAV audio data

type: audio/x-macaudio
from: Iride
for: *not* sampled Macintosh audio

type: audio/x-next
from: MH 6.8
for: self-describing SunOS/NeXT audio data
see: **ftp://ftp.ics.uci.edu/mh/contrib/multimedia/mhn-tutorial.ps**
comment: suggested by MH 6.8 docs

Image Types

type: image/x-cmu-raster
from: MHonArc
for: CMU raster data

type: image/x-fits
for: FITS files

type: image/x-macpict
from: TCP/Connect II
from: Iride
for: Macintosh PICT

type: image/x-pbm
from: MHonArc
for: portable bit map data

type: image/x-pgm
from: MHonArc
for: PGM data

type: image/x-pict
from: MHonArc
for: Macintosh PICT data

type: image/x-pnm
from: MHonArc

type: image/x-portable-anymap
from: MHonArc

type: image/x-portable-bitmap
from: MHonArc

type: image/x-portable-graymap
from: MHonArc

type: image/x-portable-pixmap
from: MHonArc

type: image/x-ppm
from: MHonArc

type: image/x-rgb
from: MHonArc

type: image/x-xbitmap
from: MHonArc
for: in-lines into the HTML

type: image/x-xbm
from: MHonArc
for: in-lines into the HTML

type: image/x-xpixmap
from: MHonArc

type: image/x-xpm
from: MHonArc

type: image/x-xwd
from: MHonArc

type: image/x-xwindowdump
from: MHonArc
for: X window dump

Multipart Types

type: multipart/enabled-mail
see: section 7.2 of the MIME FAQ - "Safe-TCL (Enabled Mail)"
see: **ftp://ftp.bellcore.com/pub/nsb/st/em-model.txt**
see: **ftp://ftp.bellcore.com/pub/nsb/st/safe-tcl.txt**

type: multipart/encrypted
see: RFC 1847

type: multipart/signed
see: RFC 1847

Text Types

type: text/html
see: RFC 1866

type: text/unknown
from: Worldtalk

type: text/x-html
from: MHonArc
comment: see type text/html

type: text/x-setext
from: MHonArc
for: setext

type: text/x-usenet-faq
for: Ohio State WWW FAQ documents

Video Types

type: video/x-msvideo
from: MHonArc: Microsoft video data

type: video/x-sgi-movie
from: MHonArc: SGI movie data

25 Reverse Address Resolution Protocol

Name

Reverse Address Resolution Protocol

Abbreviation

RARP

Status

Standard (STD 38)

Specifications

RFC 903

Abstract

Where the Address Resolution Protocol (ARP) provides a method of mapping protocol addresses to hardware addresses, the Reverse Address Resolution Protocol (RARP) allows a node to learn its protocol address given its local hardware address.

Related Specifications

ARP (RFC 826)

Description

RARP is commonly used by diskless workstations during boot time. When first started, a diskless workstation does not know its protocol address, but does have its local hardware address available. RARP allows the node to ask an unspecified server to provide its protocol address. Typically, only one node on a local link provides RARP support. For example, the server node runs RARP and all the diskless client nodes use the RARP support at boot time.

Frame Formats

RARP uses the same frame formats specified by ARP, but defines a few new constants for the various fields. These constants are shown in Table 25.1.

Ethernet headers (this portion of the frame is replaced appropriately for other datalink protocols):

48 bits: Destination address, broadcast for *ares_op$REQUEST_REVERSE*, unicast for *ares_op$REPLY_REVERSE*.

48 bits: Source address.

16 bits: Ethernet protocol type = *ether_type$REVERSE_ARP*.

Ethernet packet data:

16 bits: (*ar$hrd*) Hardware address space. For example, *ares_hrd$Ethernet*.

16 bits: (*ar$pro*) Protocol address space. For Ethernet hardware, this is from the set of type fields *ether_typ$<protocol>* (0x0800 for IP—see RFC 1700 for more Ethernet protocol types).

Table 25.1 RARP Protocol Constants

Constant Name	Value
ether_type$REVERSE_ARP	0x8035
ares_op$REQUEST_REVERSE	3
ares_op$REPLY_REVERSE	4
ares_hrd$Ethernet	1

8 bits: (*ar$hln*) Byte length of each hardware address (Ethernet = 6 or 2).

8 bits: (*ar$pln*) Byte length of each protocol address (IPv4 = 4).

16 bits: (*ar$op*) Operation code—*ares_op$REQUEST_REVERSE* or *ares_op$REPLY_REVERSE.*

n bytes: (*ar$sha*) Hardware address of sender of this packet (*n* = *ar$hln*).

m bytes: (*ar$spa*) Protocol address of sender of this packet (*m* = *ar$pln*).

n bytes: (*ar$tha*) Hardware address of target of this packet (if known).

m bytes: (*ar$tpa*) Protocol address of target.

The frame fields are filled in a bit differently when using RARP than when using ARP. The *arhrd, arpro, ar$hln,* and *ar$pln* fields are used equivalently, but the address fields are not.

When *ar$op* = *ares_op$REQUEST_REVERSE,* the sender fills in:

ar$sha The hardware address of the sender of this packet.

ar$spa Undefined.

ar$tha The target hardware address. If the requesting node wants to learn its own protocol address (the usual case), then this field will be set to the same value as *ar$sha,* the local hardware address.

ar$tpa Undefined.

When *ar$op* = *ares_op$REPLY_REVERSE,* the sender fills in:

ar$sha The hardware address of the sender of this packet (the responder to the request).

ar$spa The protocol address of the sender of this packet (the responder to the request).

ar$tha The target hardware address. This is the same value as in the request packet.

ar$tpa The protocol address of the target. This is the value the requesting node was looking for.

Note that RARP uses a different Ethertype value than does ARP. This difference highlights the fact that although their names are similar, RARP and ARP are really different protocols. Nodes supporting ARP do not have to support RARP.

26 Simple Mail Transfer Protocol

Name

Simple Mail Transfer Protocol

Abbreviation

SMTP

Status

Recommended Standard (STD 10)

Specifications

RFC 821

Abstract

The Simple Mail Transfer Protocol (SMTP) provides a method to exchange electronic mail messages. The SMTP protocol exchange is very simple, as suggested by the protocol name.

Related Specifications

SMTP-EXT (RFC 1869), Format of Electronic Mail Messages (MAIL, RFC 822), MIME (RFC 1521)

See Also

POP3 (RFC 1725), IMAP4 (RFC 1730)

Comments

RFC 821 and RFC 822 are currently being updated by the IETF in the "DRUMS" (Detailed Revision and Update of Messaging Standards) working group. The charter of this group is to produce an updated RFC that clarifies the ambiguities of RFC 821 and RFC 822 and attempts to document some existing practice of Internet mail implementations. See the Internet Drafts distribution site (**ftp://ftp.isi.edu/internet-drafts/**) for more information about DRUMS working group documents.

Description

An SMTP client wishing to exchange mail with an SMTP server contacts the server on the well-known service port. The SMTP protocol is a simple ASCII, line-oriented command/response protocol. Each command is a simple command name followed by some parameters, depending on the command. Responses consist of a three-digit numeric code followed by a string explaining the response. The numeric code is easily processed by the client software, and the error string can be passed on for human interpretation, if so desired.

After contacting the server, the client waits for a simple greeting message from the server. When the client receives the message, it sends a HELO command identifying itself. Further commands identify the recipients of a message and transfer the message data itself.

SMTP is capable of transferring multiple messages during a given session. Each message can be independently addressed and need not be related to the other messages sent during the session. This capability allows an SMTP client to exchange a set of messages in a single batch with the SMTP server, leading to more efficient communication.

Transport Information

SMTP uses well-known TCP port 25.

Commands

SMTP commands consist of short command names followed by parameters, depending on the individual command. Commands are sent as a single line of ASCII text and are terminated with a carriage return followed by a line feed (<CRLF>). None of the command names are case sensitive, though the information conveyed as parameters may be case sensitive (such as mailbox names). The various SMTP commands are shown in Table 26.1.

HELO

The HELO command is used to inform the server of the client's identity. The client sends its fully qualified domain name to the server as the parameter to the HELO command. The server informs the client of its identity in the initial greeting message. This command is sent only once per session.

MAIL

The MAIL command is used to initiate a message transfer. The MAIL command tells the server the reverse path that the message has taken from the source

Table 26.1 SMTP Commands

SMTP Commands	Optional/Required
HELO <SP> <domain> <CRLF>	Required
MAIL <SP> FROM:<reverse-path> <CRLF>	Required
RCPT <SP> TO:<forward-path> <CRLF>	Required
DATA <CRLF>	Required
RSET <CRLF>	Required
SEND <SP> FROM:<reverse-path> <CRLF>	Optional
SOML <SP> FROM:<reverse-path> <CRLF>	Optional
SAML <SP> FROM:<reverse-path> <CRLF>	Optional
VRFY <SP> <string> <CRLF>	Optional
EXPN <SP> <string> <CRLF>	Optional
HELP [<SP> <string>] <CRLF>	Optional
NOOP <CRLF>	Required
QUIT <CRLF>	Required
TURN <CRLF>	Optional

to this point in the mail relay process. This information is conveyed "out of band." The information appears as part of the MAIL command rather than in the message headers. An SMTP server must preserve this out-of-band information separately from the message itself to be able to relay it to the next SMTP on the way to final delivery.

Note that in the modern Internet, the reverse path is rarely an actual path, but is typically just the fully qualified domain name of the original sender.

RCPT

The RCPT command follows the MAIL command in a typical SMTP exchange. The RCPT command specifies one of the message addressees. If a message must be sent to multiple addressees, multiple RCPT commands can be given in sequence.

As with the MAIL command, the forward path given in the RCPT command in the modern Internet is rarely an actual path. Typically, it is just the fully qualified destination of the message.

DATA

Once all the message recipients have been specified using RCPT commands, actual data transfer can begin. The client sends the server the DATA command to inform it that it is about to send the message. Once the server indicates that it is ready for the data transfer, the client sends the RFC 822 message data line by line.

When all the message data has been sent, the client sends a single line consisting of a single period followed by <CRLF>. The server then sends a reply code indicating whether the transfer was successful.

The client should perform a process known as "dot stuffing" to ensure that the server does not mistake a single line consisting of a period in the actual message text for the end of message indication. For all lines beginning with a period in the actual message text, the client inserts a leading period before the line is sent. After checking for a line containing the end-of-message indication, the server removes a leading period from a message line before storing it.

RSET

The RSET command specifies that the current mail transfer should be aborted. All in-process transfers are aborted. All data is discarded, and all tables and states are cleared. After this command is issued, the state of the client and server should be equivalent to the state right after the HELO command is issued.

SEND

This command is used in place of the MAIL command and indicates that the message text should be displayed directly on the addressed user's terminal. This paradigm was useful for the environment in which SMTP was first developed, but is rarely used today.

SOML

The SOML command is used instead of the MAIL command and specifies that the message should be sent either to the addressed user's terminal if the user is currently logged in, or to the user's mailbox for later retrieval if the user is not currently logged in. As with the SEND command, this command is not typically used today.

SAML

The SAML command is used instead of the MAIL command and specifies that the message should be sent to the addressed user's terminal, if the user is currently logged in. In any case, the message is also copied to the mailboxes of all the recipients. As with the SEND command, this command is not typically used today.

VRFY

The VRFY command is used by the client to verify a user name with the server. Given a string, the server responds with a positive reply code if it knows of the user or with a negative reply code if it does not.

EXPN

The EXPN command is used to ask the server to confirm its knowledge of a mailing list alias and to return the list of members, if so. If the server does not know of the list, it sends a negative reply code. If the server does know of the list, it sends a multi-line reply with a positive reply code. Each line contains the address of a member of the list.

HELP

The HELP command is used to request help from the server. This command is typically used to query the commands the server supports and can be used by a human to get additional information about the server. HELP is typically not used by automated client software.

NOOP

The NOOP command may be sent at any time and has no effect on any processing done in the SMTP session. The NOOP command simply requests that the server respond with a positive reply code.

QUIT

The QUIT command is used to tell the server that the client is ending the session. Upon receipt of this command, the server responds with a positive reply code and closes the TCP connection. The client should end a session with a QUIT command rather than simply closing the connection itself.

TURN

The TURN command is used to reverse the role of the client and the server. This reversal is useful in some cases where contact between clients and servers is infrequent. After sending all mail in one direction, the client issues the TURN command to become the server. All mail needing to be sent in the reverse direction is then sent by the new client.

When the server issues the TURN command, the client can either refuse or accept it. If it refuses the TURN command, the server sends back a negative reply code and all roles remain as they were previously. If the server sends a positive reply code, the client and server then reverse roles. The session state is then reset to what it would be when a client and server first open a connection. After receiving the positive reply code from the TURN command, the new server sends an initial greeting message. The new client then sends a HELO command and the session proceeds as normal.

This command is rarely used in the modern Internet. The efficiency gain this command allows is small and is typically not worth the implementation cost.

Responses

SMTP systems return a response to each command sent by the client. The responses consist of a three-digit numeric code followed by a string suitable for a human to read. The numeric code is easily interpreted by client software to drive the SMTP session state machine.

In some cases, a multi-line response may be given. Each line of a multi-line response is similar to a single-line response. It consists of a reply code, followed

Table 26.2 SMTP Reply Code—First Digit

First Digit	Meaning
1yz	Positive Preliminary Reply
2yz	Positive Completion Reply
3yz	Positive Intermediate Reply
4yz	Transient Negative Completion Reply
5yz	Permanent Negative Completion Reply

by a hyphen character (rather than a space), followed by the reply text. The last line of the reply is identical to a single-line reply (a reply code, followed by a space, followed by the reply text).

The first digit of the reply code indicates the general success or failure of the command. The first digit interpretations are listed in Table 26.2.

The second digit of the reply code specifies the general category of the response. The second digit interpretations are listed in Table 26.3.

The final digit of an SMTP reply code is used to distinguish between replies that would otherwise have the same two initial digits. For example, the 250 and 251 reply codes are each generated to show the success of a RCPT command, but they indicate slightly different variations of the success of the command.

The complete list of SMTP replies is shown in Table 26.4.

Of course, not all commands return the same reply codes. Table 26.5 lists the codes that each command may return.

Table 26.3 SMTP Reply Code—Second Digit

Second Digit	Meaning
x0z	Syntax
x1z	Information
x2z	Connections
x3z	Reserved
x4z	Reserved
x5z	Mail System

Table 26.4 SMTP Reply Codes

211 System status, or system help reply
214 Help message
220 <domain> Service ready
221 <domain> Service closing transmission channel
250 Requested mail action okay, completed
251 User not local; will forward to <forward-path>
354 Start mail input; end with <CRLF>.<CRLF>
421 <domain> Service not available, closing transmission channel
450 Requested mail action not taken: mailbox unavailable
451 Requested action aborted: local error in processing
452 Requested action not taken: insufficient system storage
500 Syntax error, command unrecognized
501 Syntax error in parameters or arguments
502 Command not implemented
503 Bad sequence of commands
504 Command parameter not implemented
550 Requested action not taken: mailbox unavailable
551 User not local; please try <forward-path>
552 Requested mail action aborted: exceeded storage allocation
553 Requested action not taken: mailbox name not allowed
554 Transaction failed

Table 26.5 Possible Replies for Each Command

Command	**Reply Codes (Success, Failure, Error, Information)**
CONNECTION ESTABLISHMENT	S: 220 F: 421
HELO	S: 250 E: 500, 501, 504, 421
MAIL	S: 250 F: 552, 451, 452 E: 500, 501, 421

Continued

Table 26.5 Possible Replies for Each Command (Continued)

Command	Reply Codes (Success, Failure, Error, Information)
RCPT	E: 500, 501, 503, 421 F: 550, 551, 552, 553, 450, 451, 452 E: 500, 501, 503, 421
DATA	I: 354 -> data -> S: 250 F: 552, 554, 451, 452 F: 451, 554 E: 500, 501, 503, 421
RSET	S: 250 E: 500, 501, 504, 421
SEND	S: 250 F: 552, 451, 452 E: 500, 501, 502, 421
SOML	S: 250 F: 552, 451, 452 E: 500, 501, 502, 421
SAML	S: 250 F: 552, 451, 452 E: 500, 501, 502, 421
VRFY	S: 250, 251 F: 550, 551, 553 E: 500, 501, 502, 504, 421
EXPN	S: 250 F: 550 E: 500, 501, 502, 504, 421
HELP	S: 211, 214 E: 500, 501, 502, 504, 421
NOOP	S: 250 E: 500, 421
QUIT	S: 221 E: 500
TURN	S: 250 F: 502 E: 500, 503

Grammar

The following grammar specifies the syntax of the various SMTP command parameters.

```
<reverse-path> ::= <path>
<forward-path> ::= <path>
<path> ::= "<" [ <a-d-l> ":" ] <mailbox> ">"
<a-d-l> ::= <at-domain> | <at-domain> "," <a-d-l>
<at-domain> ::= "@" <domain>
<domain> ::=  <element> | <element> "." <domain>
<element> ::= <name> | "#" <number> | "[" <dotnum> "]"
<mailbox> ::= <local-part> "@" <domain>
<local-part> ::= <dot-string> | <quoted-string>
<name> ::= <a> <ldh-str> <let-dig>
<ldh-str> ::= <let-dig-hyp> | <let-dig-hyp> <ldh-str>
<let-dig> ::= <a> | <d>
<let-dig-hyp> ::= <a> | <d> | "-"
<dot-string> ::= <string> | <string> "." <dot-string>
<string> ::= <char> | <char> <string>
<quoted-string> ::=  """ <qtext> """
<qtext> ::=  "\" <x> | "\" <x> <qtext> | <q> | <q> <qtext>
<char> ::= <c> | "\" <x>
<dotnum> ::= <snum> "." <snum> "." <snum> "." <snum>
<number> ::= <d> | <d> <number>
<CRLF> ::= <CR> <LF>
<CR> ::= The carriage return character (ASCII code 13).
<LF> ::= The line feed character (ASCII code 10).
<SP> ::= the space character (ASCII code 32).
<snum> ::= One, two, or three digits representing a decimal integer
         value in the range 0 through 255.
<a> ::= Any one of the 52 alphabetic characters A through Z in uppercase
         and a through z in lowercase.
<c> ::= Any one of the 128 ASCII characters, but not any <special> or <SP>.
<d> ::= Any one of the ten digits 0 through 9.
<q> ::= Any one of the 128 ASCII characters except <CR>, <LF>,
         quote ("), or backslash (\).
<x> ::= Any one of the 128 ASCII characters (no exceptions).
<special> ::= "<" | ">" | "(" | ")" | "[" | "]" | "\" | "." | "," | ";"
         | ":" | "@"  """ | the control characters (ASCII codes 0 through
         31 inclusive and 127)
```

When a server receives a message, either to relay or for final delivery, it prepends a "Received" header to the message. The Received header indicates the name of the relay, the method of transport, and the time the message was received by each mail relay. These headers can be used by administrators to diagnose mail problems. When a server receives a message for final delivery, it prepends a "Return-Path" header to the message specifying the path back to the sender. The timestamp line and the return path line are formally defined as follows:

```
<return-path-line> ::= "Return-Path:" <SP><reverse-path><CRLF>
<time-stamp-line> ::= "Received:" <SP> <stamp> <CRLF>
<stamp> ::= <from-domain> <by-domain> <opt-info> ";" <daytime>
<from-domain> ::= "FROM" <SP> <domain> <SP>
<by-domain> ::= "BY" <SP> <domain> <SP>
<opt-info> ::= [<via>] [<with>] [<id>] [<for>]
<via> ::= "VIA" <SP> <link> <SP>
<with> ::= "WITH" <SP> <protocol> <SP>
<id> ::= "ID" <SP> <string> <SP>
<for> ::= "FOR" <SP> <path> <SP>
<link> ::= The standard names for links are registered with the Network
  Information Center.
<protocol> ::= The standard names for protocols are registered with the
  Network Information Center.
<daytime> ::= <SP> <date> <SP> <time>
<date> ::= <dd> <SP> <mon> <SP> <yy>
<time> ::= <hh> ":" <mm> ":" <ss> <SP> <zone>
<dd> ::= The one or two decimal integer day of the month in the range 1 to 31.
<mon> ::= "JAN" | "FEB" | "MAR" | "APR" | "MAY" | "JUN" | "JUL" |
  "AUG" | "SEP" | "OCT" | "NOV" | "DEC"
<yy> ::= The two decimal integer year of the century in the range 00 to 99.
<hh> ::= The two decimal integer hour of the day in the range 00 to 24.
<mm> ::= The two decimal integer minute of the hour in the range 00 to 59.
<ss> ::= The two decimal integer second of the minute in the range 00 to 59.
<zone> ::= "UT" for Universal Time (the default) or other time zone
  designator (as in RFC 822).
```

27 Simple Network Management Protocol, Version 2

Name

Simple Network Management Protocol, Version 2

Abbreviation

SNMPv2

Status

Elective Draft Standard

Specifications

Different parts of SNMPv2 are defined in several different RFCs, including RFCs 1902, 1903, 1904, 1905, 1906, 1907, and 1908. RFC 1901 provides a nice summary of the contents of the other documents. RFCs 1909 and 1910 describe experimental extensions to the basic SNMPv2 framework.

Abstract

The Simple Network Management Protocol (SNMP) has rapidly become the standard management framework. The original version of SNMP, SNMPv1, lacked capabilities that allowed it to scale to enterprise-wide proportions. The latest version of SNMP, SNMPv2, provides these capabilities. SNMPv2 is mostly compatible with SNMPv1. RFC 1908 describes the changes necessary for SNMPv1 and SNMPv2 to coexist in the same environment.

Related Specifications

ASN.1 is described in:

> Information processing systems - Open Systems Interconnection - Specification of Abstract Syntax Notation One (ASN.1), International Organization for Standardization. International Standard 8824, (December, 1987).

The ASN.1 basic encoding rules (BER) are described in:

> Information processing systems - Open Systems Interconnection - Specification of Basic Encoding Rules for Abstract Syntax Notation One (ASN.1), International Organization for Standardization. International Standard 8825, (December, 1987).

See Also

SNMPv1 is described by RFCs 1155, 1157, and 1212.

Numerous RFCs describe particular management information bases (MIBs). See Internet Official Protocol Standards (currently RFC 1920) for more information about defined MIBs, the RFCs in which they are described, and their current standardization status.

Two of the most popular MIBs are MIB-II, described in RFC 1213, and ETHER-MIB, described in RFC 1643.

Comments

This chapter describes only SNMPv2. Although SNMPv2 is very new, it is clear that the Internet community will move quickly to implement it. In the interest of keeping this material as current as possible, I've made the choice to describe SNMPv2 rather than SNMPv1.

Description

SNMPv2 describes the protocols and object definitions necessary to remotely manage network equipment and entities.

Each entity under management contains an agent that is responsible for accessing management information. The agent implements the management protocols, receives management requests, and returns objects from the entity's management information base.

A network manager uses a network management station to send requests to each entity agent. Using the protocol requests, the network manager can query and set object values in the remote entity. Object queries can be used to monitor the remote entity, while setting object values can reconfigure the remote entity.

The remote agent can also be configured to send notifications of state changes to a *notification sink.* This functionality can be used to alert a network manager to a critical state change without the manager having to continually query the remote entity for its state.

Management information is structured as a set of *managed objects.* The set of objects implemented by an entity is termed a *management information base* (MIB). MIB modules are described using a subset of OSI's Abstract Syntax Notation One (ASN.1) called the Structure of Management Information (SMI).

Note that most of SNMPv2 is described using ASN.1. Because of this, the majority of this chapter is devoted to these ASN.1 definitions. See the *Object Definitions* section for the SMI and protocol data unit (PDU) definitions.

Transport Information

SNMPv2 agents typically listen for PDUs on well-known UDP port 161. Notification sinks typically listen for PDUs on well-known UDP port 162.

Note that SNMPv2 also defines mappings to other transport protocols in addition to UDP. See RFC 1906 for more information about the other transport mappings.

Object Definitions

Structure of Management Information

RFC 1902 defines the Structure of Management Information for SNMPv2. This structure describes the subset of ASN.1 used to encode SNMPv2 objects and provides basic definitions for use in other MIBs and object descriptions. The following module provides a set of basic definitions used in other SNMPv2 modules. Note that this module replaces the SNMPv1 SMI defined in RFC 1155.

```
SNMPv2-SMI DEFINITIONS ::= BEGIN


-- the path to the root

org             OBJECT IDENTIFIER ::= { iso 3 }
dod             OBJECT IDENTIFIER ::= { org 6 }
internet        OBJECT IDENTIFIER ::= { dod 1 }

directory       OBJECT IDENTIFIER ::= { internet 1 }

mgmt            OBJECT IDENTIFIER ::= { internet 2 }
mib-2           OBJECT IDENTIFIER ::= { mgmt 1 }
transmission    OBJECT IDENTIFIER ::= { mib-2 10 }

experimental    OBJECT IDENTIFIER ::= { internet 3 }

private         OBJECT IDENTIFIER ::= { internet 4 }
enterprises     OBJECT IDENTIFIER ::= { private 1 }

security        OBJECT IDENTIFIER ::= { internet 5 }

snmpV2          OBJECT IDENTIFIER ::= { internet 6 }

-- transport domains
snmpDomains     OBJECT IDENTIFIER ::= { snmpV2 1 }

-- transport proxies
snmpProxys      OBJECT IDENTIFIER ::= { snmpV2 2 }

-- module identities
snmpModules     OBJECT IDENTIFIER ::= { snmpV2 3 }


-- definitions for information modules

MODULE-IDENTITY MACRO ::=
BEGIN
    TYPE NOTATION ::=
                  "LAST-UPDATED" value(Update UTCTime)
                  "ORGANIZATION" Text
                  "CONTACT-INFO" Text
                  "DESCRIPTION" Text
                  RevisionPart

    VALUE NOTATION ::=
```

```
                value(VALUE OBJECT IDENTIFIER)

    RevisionPart ::=
                Revisions
              | empty
    Revisions ::=
                Revision
              | Revisions Revision
    Revision ::=
                "REVISION" value(Update UTCTime)
                "DESCRIPTION" Text

    -- uses the NVT ASCII character set
    Text ::= """" string """"
END


OBJECT-IDENTITY MACRO ::=
BEGIN
    TYPE NOTATION ::=
                "STATUS" Status
                "DESCRIPTION" Text
                ReferPart

    VALUE NOTATION ::=
                value(VALUE OBJECT IDENTIFIER)

    Status ::=
                "current"
              | "deprecated"
              | "obsolete"

    ReferPart ::=
              "REFERENCE" Text
            | empty

    Text ::= """" string """"
END


-- names of objects

ObjectName ::=
    OBJECT IDENTIFIER

NotificationName ::=
    OBJECT IDENTIFIER
```

```
-- syntax of objects

ObjectSyntax ::=
    CHOICE {
        simple
            SimpleSyntax,

          -- note that SEQUENCEs for conceptual tables and
          -- rows are not mentioned here...

        application-wide
            ApplicationSyntax
    }


-- built-in ASN.1 types

SimpleSyntax ::=
    CHOICE {
        -- INTEGERs with a more restrictive range
        -- may also be used
        integer-value               -- includes Integer32
            INTEGER (-2147483648..2147483647),

        -- OCTET STRINGs with a more restrictive size
        -- may also be used
        string-value
            OCTET STRING (SIZE (0..65535)),

        objectID-value
            OBJECT IDENTIFIER
    }


-- indistinguishable from INTEGER, but never needs more than
-- 32-bits for a two's complement representation
Integer32 ::=
    [UNIVERSAL 2]
        IMPLICIT INTEGER (-2147483648..2147483647)


-- application-wide types

ApplicationSyntax ::=
    CHOICE {
        ipAddress-value
```

```
            IpAddress,

        counter-value
            Counter32,

        timeticks-value
            TimeTicks,

        arbitrary-value
            Opaque,

        big-counter-value
            Counter64,

        unsigned-integer-value  -- includes Gauge32
            Unsigned32
    }

-- in network-byte order
-- (this is a tagged type for historical reasons)
IpAddress ::=
    [APPLICATION 0]
        IMPLICIT OCTET STRING (SIZE (4))

-- this wraps
Counter32 ::=
    [APPLICATION 1]
        IMPLICIT INTEGER (0..4294967295)

-- this doesn't wrap
Gauge32 ::=
    [APPLICATION 2]
        IMPLICIT INTEGER (0..4294967295)

-- an unsigned 32-bit quantity
-- indistinguishable from Gauge32
Unsigned32 ::=
    [APPLICATION 2]
        IMPLICIT INTEGER (0..4294967295)

-- hundredths of seconds since an epoch
TimeTicks ::=
    [APPLICATION 3]
        IMPLICIT INTEGER (0..4294967295)

-- for backward-compatibility only
Opaque ::=
    [APPLICATION 4]
```

```
        IMPLICIT OCTET STRING

-- for counters that wrap in less than one hour with only 32 bits
Counter64 ::=
    [APPLICATION 6]
        IMPLICIT INTEGER (0..18446744073709551615)


-- definition for objects

OBJECT-TYPE MACRO ::=
BEGIN
    TYPE NOTATION ::=
                  "SYNTAX" Syntax
                  UnitsPart
                  "MAX-ACCESS" Access
                  "STATUS" Status
                  "DESCRIPTION" Text
                  ReferPart
                  IndexPart
                  DefValPart

    VALUE NOTATION ::=
                  value(VALUE ObjectName)

    Syntax ::=
                  type(ObjectSyntax)
                | "BITS" "{" Kibbles "}"
    Kibbles ::=
                  Kibble
                | Kibbles "," Kibble
    Kibble ::=
                 identifier "(" nonNegativeNumber ")"

    UnitsPart ::=
                  "UNITS" Text
                | empty

    Access ::=
                  "not-accessible"
                | "accessible-for-notify"
                | "read-only"
                | "read-write"
                | "read-create"

    Status ::=
                  "current"
                | "deprecated"
```

```
                  | "obsolete"

    ReferPart ::=
                    "REFERENCE" Text
                  | empty

    IndexPart ::=
                    "INDEX"    "{" IndexTypes "}"
                  | "AUGMENTS" "{" Entry      "}"
                  | empty
    IndexTypes ::=
                    IndexType
                  | IndexTypes "," IndexType
    IndexType ::=
                    "IMPLIED" Index
                  | Index
    Index ::=
                      -- use the SYNTAX value of the
                      -- correspondent OBJECT-TYPE invocation
                    value(Indexobject ObjectName)
    Entry ::=
                      -- use the INDEX value of the
                      -- correspondent OBJECT-TYPE invocation
                    value(Entryobject ObjectName)

    DefValPart ::=
                    "DEFVAL" "{" value(Defval Syntax) "}"
                  | empty

    -- uses the NVT ASCII character set
    Text ::= """" string """"
END


-- definitions for notifications

NOTIFICATION-TYPE MACRO ::=
BEGIN
    TYPE NOTATION ::=
                    ObjectsPart
                    "STATUS" Status
                    "DESCRIPTION" Text
                    ReferPart

    VALUE NOTATION ::=
                    value(VALUE NotificationName)
```

```
    ObjectsPart ::=
                  "OBJECTS" "{" Objects "}"
                | empty
    Objects ::=
                  Object
                | Objects "," Object
    Object ::=
                  value(Name ObjectName)

    Status ::=
                  "current"
                | "deprecated"
                | "obsolete"

    ReferPart ::=
                "REFERENCE" Text
              | empty

    -- uses the NVT ASCII character set
    Text ::= """" string """"
END

-- definitions of administrative identifiers

zeroDotZero     OBJECT-IDENTITY
    STATUS      current
    DESCRIPTION
            "A value used for null identifiers."
    ::= { 0 0 }

END
```

Textual Conventions

When defining MIB objects, it is often convenient for a new data type to represent values with slightly different semantics than the existing data type. Often, the new data type is simply a variation of the older data type. These new types are called *textual conventions.* RFC 1903 contains a number of textual conventions based on the RFC 1902 SMI that are used in SNMPv2 object defintions.

```
SNMPv2-TC DEFINITIONS ::= BEGIN

IMPORTS
    ObjectSyntax, TimeTicks
        FROM SNMPv2-SMI;
```

```
-- definition of textual conventions

TEXTUAL-CONVENTION MACRO ::=
BEGIN
    TYPE NOTATION ::=
                  DisplayPart
                  "STATUS" Status
                  "DESCRIPTION" Text
                  ReferPart
                  "SYNTAX" Syntax

    VALUE NOTATION ::=
                  value(VALUE Syntax)

    DisplayPart ::=
                  "DISPLAY-HINT" Text
                | empty

    Status ::=
                  "current"
                | "deprecated"
                | "obsolete"

    ReferPart ::=
                  "REFERENCE" Text
                | empty

    -- uses the NVT ASCII character set
    Text ::= """" string """"

    Syntax ::=
                  type(ObjectSyntax)
                | "BITS" "{" Kibbles "}"
    Kibbles ::=
                  Kibble
                | Kibbles "," Kibble
    Kibble ::=
                  identifier "(" nonNegativeNumber ")"

END


DisplayString ::= TEXTUAL-CONVENTION
    DISPLAY-HINT "255a"
```

```
    STATUS       current
    DESCRIPTION
            "Represents textual information taken from the NVT ASCII
            character set, as defined in pages 4, 10-11 of RFC 854.

            To summarize RFC 854, the NVT ASCII repertoire specifies:

              - the use of character codes 0-127 (decimal)

              - the graphics characters (32-126) are interpreted as
                US ASCII

              - NUL, LF, CR, BEL, BS, HT, VT and FF have the special
                meanings specified in RFC 854

              - the other 25 codes have no standard interpretation

              - the sequence 'CR LF' means newline

              - the sequence 'CR NUL' means carriage-return

              - an 'LF' not preceded by a 'CR' means moving to the
                same column on the next line.

              - the sequence 'CR x' for any x other than LF or NUL is
                illegal. (Note that this also means that a string may
                end with either 'CR LF' or 'CR NUL', but not with CR.)

            Any object defined using this syntax may not exceed 255
            characters in length."
    SYNTAX       OCTET STRING (SIZE (0..255))


PhysAddress ::= TEXTUAL-CONVENTION
    DISPLAY-HINT "1x:"
    STATUS       current
    DESCRIPTION
            "Represents media- or physical-level addresses."
    SYNTAX       OCTET STRING


MacAddress ::= TEXTUAL-CONVENTION
    DISPLAY-HINT "1x:"
    STATUS       current
    DESCRIPTION
            "Represents an 802 MAC address represented in the
```

```
            'canonical' order defined by IEEE 802.1a, i.e., as if it
            were transmitted least significant bit first, even though
            802.5 (in contrast to other 802.x protocols) requires MAC
            addresses to be transmitted most significant bit first."
    SYNTAX       OCTET STRING (SIZE (6))


TruthValue ::= TEXTUAL-CONVENTION
    STATUS       current
    DESCRIPTION
            "Represents a boolean value."
    SYNTAX       INTEGER { true(1), false(2) }

TestAndIncr ::= TEXTUAL-CONVENTION
    STATUS       current
    DESCRIPTION
            "Represents integer-valued information used for atomic
            operations. When the management protocol is used to specify
            that an object instance having this syntax is to be
            modified, the new value supplied via the management protocol
            must precisely match the value presently held by the
            instance. If not, the management protocol set operation
            fails with an error of 'inconsistentValue'. Otherwise, if
            the current value is the maximum value of 2^31-1 (2147483647
            decimal), then the value held by the instance is wrapped to
            zero; otherwise, the value held by the instance is
            incremented by one. (Note that regardless of whether the
            management protocol set operation succeeds, the variable-
            binding in the request and response PDUs are identical.)

            The value of the ACCESS clause for objects having this
            syntax is either 'read-write' or 'read-create'. When an
            instance of a columnar object having this syntax is created,
            any value may be supplied via the management protocol.

            When the network management portion of the system is re-
            initialized, the value of every object instance having this
            syntax must either be incremented from its value prior to
            the re-initialization, or (if the value prior to the re-
            initialization is unknown) be set to a pseudo-randomly
            generated value."
    SYNTAX       INTEGER (0..2147483647)


AutonomousType ::= TEXTUAL-CONVENTION
    STATUS       current
    DESCRIPTION
```

```
            "Represents an independently extensible type identification
            value. It may, for example, indicate a particular sub-tree
            with further MIB definitions, or define a particular type of
            protocol or hardware."
    SYNTAX       OBJECT IDENTIFIER


InstancePointer ::= TEXTUAL-CONVENTION
    STATUS       obsolete
    DESCRIPTION
            "A pointer to either a specific instance of a MIB object or
            a conceptual row of a MIB table in the managed device. In
            the latter case, by convention, it is the name of the
            particular instance of the first accessible columnar object
            in the conceptual row.

            The two uses of this textual convention are replaced by
            VariablePointer and RowPointer, respectively."
    SYNTAX       OBJECT IDENTIFIER


VariablePointer ::= TEXTUAL-CONVENTION
    STATUS       current
    DESCRIPTION
            "A pointer to a specific object instance. For example,
            sysContact.0 or ifInOctets.3."
    SYNTAX       OBJECT IDENTIFIER


RowPointer ::= TEXTUAL-CONVENTION
    STATUS       current
    DESCRIPTION
            "Represents a pointer to a conceptual row. The value is the
            name of the instance of the first accessible columnar object
            in the conceptual row.

            For example, ifIndex.3 would point to the 3rd row in the
            ifTable (note that if ifIndex were not-accessible, then
            ifDescr.3 would be used instead)."
    SYNTAX       OBJECT IDENTIFIER


RowStatus ::= TEXTUAL-CONVENTION
    STATUS       current
    DESCRIPTION
            "The RowStatus textual convention is used to manage the
            creation and deletion of conceptual rows, and is used as the
            value of the SYNTAX clause for the status column of a
```

conceptual row (as described in Section 7.7.1 of [2].)

The status column has six defined values:

- 'active', which indicates that the conceptual row is available for use by the managed device;

- 'notInService', which indicates that the conceptual row exists in the agent, but is unavailable for use by the managed device (see NOTE below);

- 'notReady', which indicates that the conceptual row exists in the agent, but is missing information necessary in order to be available for use by the managed device;

- 'createAndGo', which is supplied by a management station wishing to create a new instance of a conceptual row and to have its status automatically set to active, making it available for use by the managed device;

- 'createAndWait', which is supplied by a management station wishing to create a new instance of a conceptual row (but not make it available for use by the managed device); and,

- 'destroy', which is supplied by a management station wishing to delete all of the instances associated with an existing conceptual row.

Whereas five of the six values (all except 'notReady') may be specified in a management protocol set operation, only three values will be returned in response to a management protocol retrieval operation: 'notReady', 'notInService' or 'active'. That is, when queried, an existing conceptual row has only three states: it is either available for use by the managed device (the status column has value 'active'); it is not available for use by the managed device, though the agent has sufficient information to make it so (the status column has value 'notInService'); or, it is not available for use by the managed device, and an attempt to make it so would fail because the agent has insufficient information (the state column has value 'notReady').

NOTE WELL

This textual convention may be used for a MIB table, irrespective of whether the values of that table's conceptual rows are able to be modified while it is active, or whether its conceptual rows must be taken out of service in order to be modified. That is, it is the responsibility of the DESCRIPTION clause of the status column to specify whether the status column must not be 'active' in order for the value of some other column of the same conceptual row to be modified. If such a specification is made, affected columns may be changed by an SNMP set PDU if the RowStatus would not be equal to 'active' either immediately before or after processing the PDU. In other words, if the PDU also contained a varbind that would change the RowStatus value, the column in question may be changed if the RowStatus was not equal to 'active' as the PDU was received, or if the varbind sets the status to a value other than 'active'.

Also note that whenever any elements of a row exist, the RowStatus column must also exist.

To summarize the effect of having a conceptual row with a status column having a SYNTAX clause value of RowStatus, consider the following state diagram:

```
                                       STATE
               +--------------+-----------+-------------+-------------
               |      A       |     B     |      C      |      D
               |              |status col.|status column|
               |status column |    is     |      is     |status column
    ACTION     |does not exist| notReady  | notInService|  is active
---------------+--------------+-----------+-------------+-------------
set status     |noError    ->D|inconsist- |inconsistent-|inconsistent-
column to      |      or      |   entValue|        Value|        Value
createAndGo    |inconsistent- |           |             |
               |         Value|           |             |
---------------+--------------+-----------+-------------+-------------
set status     |noError  see 1|inconsist- |inconsistent-|inconsistent-
column to      |      or      |   entValue|        Value|        Value
createAndWait  |wrongValue    |           |             |
---------------+--------------+-----------+-------------+-------------
set status     |inconsistent- |inconsist- |noError      |noError
column to      |         Value|   entValue|             |
active         |              |           |             |
               |              |     or    |             |
               |              |           |             |
```

```
              |             |see 2    ->D|          ->D|          ->D
--------------+-------------+-----------+------------+------------
set status    |inconsistent-|inconsist- |noError     |noError   ->C
column to     |        Value|  entValue |            |
notInService  |             |           |            |
              |             |    or     |            |     or
              |             |           |            |
              |             |see 3   ->C|         ->C|wrongValue
--------------+-------------+-----------+------------+------------
set status    |noError      |noError    |noError     |noError
column to     |             |           |            |
destroy       |          ->A|        ->A|         ->A|          ->A
--------------+-------------+-----------+------------+------------
set any other |see 4        |noError    |noError     |see 5
column to some|             |           |            |
value         |             |     see 1 |         ->C|          ->D
--------------+-------------+-----------+------------+------------
```

(1) goto B or C, depending on information available to the agent.

(2) if other variable bindings included in the same PDU, provide values for all columns which are missing but required, then return noError and goto D.

(3) if other variable bindings included in the same PDU, provide values for all columns which are missing but required, then return noError and goto C.

(4) at the discretion of the agent, the return value may be either:

> inconsistentName: because the agent does not choose to create such an instance when the corresponding RowStatus instance does not exist, or
>
> inconsistentValue: if the supplied value is inconsistent with the state of some other MIB object's value, or
>
> noError: because the agent chooses to create the instance.

If noError is returned, then the instance of the status column must also be created, and the new state is B or C, depending on the information available to the agent. If inconsistentName or inconsistentValue is returned, the row remains in state A.

(5) depending on the MIB definition for the column/table, either noError or inconsistentValue may be returned.

NOTE: Other processing of the set request may result in a response other than noError being returned, e.g., wrongValue, noCreation, etc.

Conceptual Row Creation

There are four potential interactions when creating a conceptual row: selecting an instance-identifier which is not in use; creating the conceptual row; initializing any objects for which the agent does not supply a default; and, making the conceptual row available for use by the managed device.

Interaction 1: Selecting an Instance-Identifier

The algorithm used to select an instance-identifier varies for each conceptual row. In some cases, the instance-identifier is semantically significant, e.g., the destination address of a route, and a management station selects the instance-identifier according to the semantics.

In other cases, the instance-identifier is used solely to distinguish conceptual rows, and a management station without specific knowledge of the conceptual row might examine the instances present in order to determine an unused instance-identifier. (This approach may be used, but it is often highly sub-optimal; however, it is also a questionable practice for a naive management station to attempt conceptual row creation.)

Alternately, the MIB module which defines the conceptual row might provide one or more objects which provide assistance in determining an unused instance-identifier. For example, if the conceptual row is indexed by an integer-value, then an object having an integer-valued SYNTAX clause might be defined for such a purpose, allowing a management station to issue a management protocol retrieval operation. In order to avoid unnecessary collisions between competing management stations, 'adjacent' retrievals of this object should be different.

Finally, the management station could select a pseudo-random number to use as the index. In the event that this index was already in use and an inconsistentValue was returned in response to the management protocol set operation, the management station should simply select a new pseudo-random number and retry the operation.

A MIB designer should choose between the two latter algorithms based on the size of the table (and therefore the efficiency of each algorithm). For tables in which a large number of entries are expected, it is recommended that a MIB object be defined that returns an acceptable index for creation. For tables with small numbers of entries, it is recommended that the latter pseudo-random index mechanism be used.

Interaction 2: Creating the Conceptual Row

Once an unused instance-identifier has been selected, the management station determines if it wishes to create and activate the conceptual row in one transaction or in a negotiated set of interactions.

Interaction 2a: Creating and Activating the Conceptual Row

The management station must first determine the column requirements, i.e., it must determine those columns for which it must or must not provide values. Depending on the complexity of the table and the management station's knowledge of the agent's capabilities, this determination can be made locally by the management station. Alternately, the management station issues a management protocol get operation to examine all columns in the conceptual row that it wishes to create. In response, for each column, there are three possible outcomes:

- a value is returned, indicating that some other management station has already created this conceptual row. We return to interaction 1.

- the exception 'noSuchInstance' is returned, indicating that the agent implements the object-type associated with this column, and that this column in at least one conceptual row would be accessible in the MIB view used by the retrieval were it to exist. For those columns to which the agent provides read-create access, the 'noSuchInstance' exception tells the management station that it should supply a value for this column when the conceptual row is to be created.

- the exception 'noSuchObject' is returned, indicating that the agent does not implement the object-type associated with this column or that there is no conceptual row for which this column would be accessible in the MIB view used by the retrieval. As such, the management station can not issue any management protocol set operations to create an instance of this column.

Once the column requirements have been determined, a management protocol set operation is accordingly issued. This operation also sets the new instance of the status column to 'createAndGo'.

When the agent processes the set operation, it verifies that it has sufficient information to make the conceptual row available for use by the managed device. The information available to the agent is provided by two sources: the management protocol set operation which creates the conceptual row, and, implementation-specific defaults supplied by the agent (note that an agent must provide implementation-specific defaults for at least those objects which it implements as read-only). If there is sufficient information available, then the conceptual row is created, a 'noError' response is returned, the status column is set to 'active', and no further interactions are necessary (i.e., interactions 3 and 4 are skipped). If there is insufficient information, then the conceptual row is not created, and the set operation fails with an error of 'inconsistentValue'. On this error, the management station can issue a management protocol retrieval operation to determine if this was because it failed to specify a value for a required column, or, because the selected instance of the status column already existed. In the latter case, we return to interaction 1. In the former case, the management station can re-issue the set operation with the additional information, or begin interaction 2 again using 'createAndWait' in order to negotiate creation of the conceptual row.

NOTE WELL

Regardless of the method used to determine the column requirements, it is possible that the management station might deem a column necessary when, in fact, the agent will not allow that particular columnar instance to be created or written. In this case, the management protocol set operation will fail with an error such as 'noCreation' or 'notWritable'. In this case, the management station decides whether it needs to be able to set a value for that particular columnar instance. If not, the management station re-issues the management protocol set operation, but without setting a value for that particular columnar instance; otherwise, the management station aborts the row creation algorithm.

Interaction 2b: Negotiating the Creation of the Conceptual Row

The management station issues a management protocol set operation which sets the desired instance of the status column to 'createAndWait'. If the agent is unwilling to process a request of this sort, the set operation fails with an error of 'wrongValue'. (As a consequence, such an agent must be prepared to accept a single management protocol set operation, i.e., interaction 2a above, containing all of the columns indicated by its column requirements.) Otherwise, the conceptual row is created, a 'noError' response is returned, and the status column is immediately set to either 'notInService' or 'notReady', depending on whether it has sufficient information to make the conceptual row available for use by the managed device. If there is sufficient information available, then the status column is set to 'notInService'; otherwise, if there is insufficient information, then the status column is set to 'notReady'. Regardless, we proceed to interaction 3.

Interaction 3: Initializing non-defaulted Objects

The management station must now determine the column requirements. It issues a management protocol get operation to examine all columns in the created conceptual row. In the response, for each column, there are three possible outcomes:

- a value is returned, indicating that the agent implements the object-type associated with this column and had sufficient information to provide a value. For those columns to which the agent provides read-create access (and for which the agent allows their values to be changed after their creation), a value return tells the management station that it may issue additional management protocol set operations, if it desires, in

```
     order to change the value associated with this column.

     - the exception 'noSuchInstance' is returned,
     indicating that the agent implements the object-type
     associated with this column, and that this column in at
     least one conceptual row would be accessible in the MIB
     view used by the retrieval were it to exist. However,
     the agent does not have sufficient information to
     provide a value, and until a value is provided, the
     conceptual row may not be made available for use by the
     managed device. For those columns to which the agent
     provides read-create access, the 'noSuchInstance'
     exception tells the management station that it must
     issue additional management protocol set operations, in
     order to provide a value associated with this column.

     - the exception 'noSuchObject' is returned, indicating
     that the agent does not implement the object-type
     associated with this column or that there is no
     conceptual row for which this column would be
     accessible in the MIB view used by the retrieval. As
     such, the management station can not issue any
     management protocol set operations to create an
     instance of this column.

If the value associated with the status column is
'notReady', then the management station must first deal with
all 'noSuchInstance' columns, if any. Having done so, the
value of the status column becomes 'notInService', and we
proceed to interaction 4.

Interaction 4: Making the Conceptual Row Available

Once the management station is satisfied with the values
associated with the columns of the conceptual row, it issues
a management protocol set operation to set the status column
to 'active'. If the agent has sufficient information to
make the conceptual row available for use by the managed
device, the management protocol set operation succeeds (a
'noError' response is returned). Otherwise, the management
protocol set operation fails with an error of
'inconsistentValue'.


                         NOTE WELL
```

```
     A conceptual row having a status column with value
     'notInService' or 'notReady' is unavailable to the
     managed device. As such, it is possible for the
     managed device to create its own instances during the
     time between the management protocol set operation
     which sets the status column to 'createAndWait' and the
     management protocol set operation which sets the status
     column to 'active'. In this case, when the management
     protocol set operation is issued to set the status
     column to 'active', the values held in the agent
     supersede those used by the managed device.

If the management station is prevented from setting the
status column to 'active' (e.g., due to management station
or network failure) the conceptual row will be left in the
'notInService' or 'notReady' state, consuming resources
indefinitely. The agent must detect conceptual rows that
have been in either state for an abnormally long period of
time and remove them. It is the responsibility of the
DESCRIPTION clause of the status column to indicate what an
abnormally long period of time would be. This period of
time should be long enough to allow for human response time
(including 'think time') between the creation of the
conceptual row and the setting of the status to 'active'.
In the absense of such information in the DESCRIPTION
clause, it is suggested that this period be approximately 5
minutes in length. This removal action applies not only to
newly-created rows, but also to previously active rows which
are set to, and left in, the notInService state for a
prolonged period exceeding that which is considered normal
for such a conceptual row.


                  Conceptual Row Suspension

When a conceptual row is 'active', the management station
may issue a management protocol set operation which sets the
instance of the status column to 'notInService'. If the
agent is unwilling to do so, the set operation fails with an
error of 'wrongValue'. Otherwise, the conceptual row is
taken out of service, and a 'noError' response is returned.
It is the responsibility of the DESCRIPTION clause of the
status column to indicate under what circumstances the
status column should be taken out of service (e.g., in order
for the value of some other column of the same conceptual
row to be modified).
```

```
                              Conceptual Row Deletion

            For deletion of conceptual rows, a management protocol set
            operation is issued which sets the instance of the status
            column to 'destroy'. This request may be made regardless of
            the current value of the status column (e.g., it is possible
            to delete conceptual rows which are either 'notReady',
            'notInService' or 'active'.)  If the operation succeeds,
            then all instances associated with the conceptual row are
            immediately removed."


    SYNTAX       INTEGER {
                     -- the following two values are states:
                     -- these values may be read or written
                     active(1),
                     notInService(2),

                     -- the following value is a state:
                     -- this value may be read, but not written
                     notReady(3),

                     -- the following three values are
                     -- actions: these values may be written,
                     --   but are never read
                     createAndGo(4),
                     createAndWait(5),
                     destroy(6)
                 }


TimeStamp ::= TEXTUAL-CONVENTION
    STATUS       current
    DESCRIPTION
            "The value of the sysUpTime object at which a specific
            occurrence happened. The specific occurrence must be
            defined in the description of any object defined using this
            type."
    SYNTAX       TimeTicks


TimeInterval ::= TEXTUAL-CONVENTION
    STATUS       current
    DESCRIPTION
            "A period of time, measured in units of 0.01 seconds."
    SYNTAX       INTEGER (0..2147483647)
```

```
DateAndTime ::= TEXTUAL-CONVENTION
    DISPLAY-HINT "2d-1d-1d,1d:1d:1d.1d,1a1d:1d"
    STATUS       current
    DESCRIPTION
            "A date-time specification.

            field  octets  contents                  range
            ----  ------  --------                  ----
              1      1-2   year                      0..65536
              2       3    month                     1..12
              3       4    day                       1..31
              4       5    hour                      0..23
              5       6    minutes                   0..59
              6       7    seconds                   0..60
                           (use 60 for leap-second)
              7       8    deci-seconds              0..9
              8       9    direction from UTC        '+' / '-'
              9      10    hours from UTC            0..11
             10      11    minutes from UTC          0..59

            For example, Tuesday May 26, 1992 at 1:30:15 PM EDT would be
            displayed as:

                            1992-5-26,13:30:15.0,-4:0

            Note that if only local time is known, then timezone
            information (fields 8-10) is not present."
    SYNTAX       OCTET STRING (SIZE (8 | 11))


StorageType ::= TEXTUAL-CONVENTION
    STATUS       current
    DESCRIPTION
            "Describes the memory realization of a conceptual row. A
            row which is volatile(2) is lost upon reboot. A row which
            is either nonVolatile(3), permanent(4) or readOnly(5), is
            backed up by stable storage. A row which is permanent(4)
            can be changed but not deleted. A row which is readOnly(5)
            cannot be changed nor deleted.

            If the value of an object with this syntax is either
            permanent(4) or readOnly(5), it cannot be modified.
            Conversely, if the value is either other(1), volatile(2) or
            nonVolatile(3), it cannot be modified to be permanent(4) or
```

```
            readOnly(5).

            Every usage of this textual convention is required to
            specify the columnar objects which a permanent(4) row must
            at a minimum allow to be writable."
    SYNTAX       INTEGER {
                     other(1),        -- eh?
                     volatile(2),     -- e.g., in RAM
                     nonVolatile(3),  -- e.g., in NVRAM
                     permanent(4),    -- e.g., partially in ROM
                     readOnly(5)      -- e.g., completely in ROM
                 }


TDomain ::= TEXTUAL-CONVENTION
    STATUS       current
    DESCRIPTION
          "Denotes a kind of transport service.

          Some possible values, such as snmpUDPDomain, are defined in
          'Transport Mappings for Version 2 of the Simple Network
          Management Protocol (SNMPv2)'."
    SYNTAX       OBJECT IDENTIFIER


TAddress ::= TEXTUAL-CONVENTION
    STATUS       current
    DESCRIPTION
          "Denotes a transport service address.

          For snmpUDPDomain, a TAddress is 6 octets long, the initial 4
          octets containing the IP-address in network-byte order and the
          last 2 containing the UDP port in network-byte order. Consult
          'Transport Mappings for Version 2 of the Simple Network
          Management Protocol (SNMPv2)' for further information on
          snmpUDPDomain."
    SYNTAX       OCTET STRING (SIZE (1..255))

END
```

PDU Definitions

RFC 1905 describes the protocol data units (PDUs) exchanged by SNMPv2 entities (agents and managers). Unlike many other Internet protocols, SNMP describes the PDUs using ASN.1 and the SMI rather than as static message format drawings.

```
SNMPv2-PDU DEFINITIONS ::= BEGIN

IMPORTS
    ObjectName, ObjectSyntax, Integer32
        FROM SNMPv2-SMI;


-- protocol data units

PDUs ::=
    CHOICE {
        get-request
            GetRequest-PDU,

        get-next-request
            GetNextRequest-PDU,

        get-bulk-request
            GetBulkRequest-PDU,

        response
            Response-PDU,

        set-request
            SetRequest-PDU,

        inform-request
            InformRequest-PDU,

        snmpV2-trap
            SNMPv2-Trap-PDU,

        report
            Report-PDU,
    }


-- PDUs

GetRequest-PDU ::=
    [0]
        IMPLICIT PDU

GetNextRequest-PDU ::=
    [1]
```

```
        IMPLICIT PDU

Response-PDU ::=
    [2]
        IMPLICIT PDU

SetRequest-PDU ::=
    [3]
        IMPLICIT PDU

-- [4] is obsolete

GetBulkRequest-PDU ::=
    [5]
        IMPLICIT BulkPDU

InformRequest-PDU ::=
    [6]
        IMPLICIT PDU

SNMPv2-Trap-PDU ::=
    [7]
        IMPLICIT PDU

--   Usage and precise semantics of Report-PDU are not presently
--   defined. Any SNMP administrative framework making use of
--   this PDU must define its usage and semantics.
Report-PDU ::=
    [8]
        IMPLICIT PDU

max-bindings
    INTEGER ::= 2147483647

PDU ::=
    SEQUENCE {
        request-id
            Integer32,

        error-status            -- sometimes ignored
            INTEGER {
                noError(0),
                tooBig(1),
                noSuchName(2),   -- for proxy compatibility
                badValue(3),     -- for proxy compatibility
                readOnly(4),     -- for proxy compatibility
                genErr(5),
```

```
                noAccess(6),
                wrongType(7),
                wrongLength(8),
                wrongEncoding(9),
                wrongValue(10),
                noCreation(11),
                inconsistentValue(12),
                resourceUnavailable(13),
                commitFailed(14),
                undoFailed(15),
                authorizationError(16),
                notWritable(17),
                inconsistentName(18)
            },

        error-index             -- sometimes ignored
            INTEGER (0..max-bindings),

        variable-bindings   -- values are sometimes ignored
            VarBindList
    }


BulkPDU ::=                     -- MUST be identical in
    SEQUENCE {                  -- structure to PDU
        request-id
            Integer32,

        non-repeaters
            INTEGER (0..max-bindings),

        max-repetitions
            INTEGER (0..max-bindings),

        variable-bindings       -- values are ignored
            VarBindList
    }


-- variable binding

VarBind ::=
    SEQUENCE {
        name
            ObjectName,

        CHOICE {
            value
```

```
                ObjectSyntax,

            unSpecified           -- in retrieval requests
                    NULL,

                                  -- exceptions in responses
            noSuchObject[0]
                    IMPLICIT NULL,

            noSuchInstance[1]
                    IMPLICIT NULL,

            endOfMibView[2]
                    IMPLICIT NULL
        }
    }


-- variable-binding list

VarBindList ::=
    SEQUENCE (SIZE (0..max-bindings)) OF
        VarBind


END
```

Transport Mappings

SNMPv2 can be used with a number of different transport protocols. Although UDP is the most popular transport protocol, IPX, DDP, and OSI can also be used. RFC 1906 contains a number of additional transport mapping definitions.

```
SNMPv2-TM DEFINITIONS ::= BEGIN

IMPORTS
    OBJECT-IDENTITY, snmpDomains, snmpProxys
        FROM SNMPv2-SMI
    TEXTUAL-CONVENTION
        FROM SNMPv2-TC;

-- SNMPv2 over UDP over IPv4

snmpUDPDomain  OBJECT-IDENTITY
    STATUS     current
    DESCRIPTION
            "The SNMPv2 over UDP transport domain. The corresponding
            transport address is of type SnmpUDPAddress."
```

```
    ::= { snmpDomains 1 }

SnmpUDPAddress ::= TEXTUAL-CONVENTION
    DISPLAY-HINT "1d.1d.1d.1d/2d"
    STATUS       current
    DESCRIPTION
            "Represents a UDP address:

               octets   contents        encoding
                1-4     IP-address      network-byte order
                5-6     UDP-port        network-byte order
            "
    SYNTAX       OCTET STRING (SIZE (6))


-- SNMPv2 over OSI

snmpCLNSDomain OBJECT-IDENTITY
    STATUS     current
    DESCRIPTION
            "The SNMPv2 over CLNS transport domain. The corresponding
            transport address is of type SnmpOSIAddress."
    ::= { snmpDomains 2 }

snmpCONSDomain OBJECT-IDENTITY
    STATUS     current
    DESCRIPTION
            "The SNMPv2 over CONS transport domain. The corresponding
            transport address is of type SnmpOSIAddress."
    ::= { snmpDomains 3 }

SnmpOSIAddress ::= TEXTUAL-CONVENTION
    DISPLAY-HINT "*1x:/1x:"
    STATUS       current
    DESCRIPTION
            "Represents an OSI transport-address:

               octets   contents          encoding
                  1     length of NSAP    'n' as an unsigned-integer
                                            (either 0 or from 3 to 20)
               2..(n+1) NSAP               concrete binary representation
               (n+2)..m TSEL               string of (up to 64) octets
            "
    SYNTAX       OCTET STRING (SIZE (1 | 4..85))
```

```
-- SNMPv2 over DDP

snmpDDPDomain  OBJECT-IDENTITY
    STATUS     current
    DESCRIPTION
            "The SNMPv2 over DDP transport domain. The corresponding
            transport address is of type SnmpNBPAddress."
    ::= { snmpDomains 4 }

SnmpNBPAddress ::= TEXTUAL-CONVENTION
    STATUS       current
    DESCRIPTION
            "Represents an NBP name:

                 octets        contents          encoding
                    1          length of object  'n' as an unsigned
integer
                  2..(n+1)     object            string of (up to 32)
octets
                   n+2         length of type    'p' as an unsigned
integer
              (n+3)..(n+2+p)   type              string of (up to 32)
octets
                  n+3+p        length of zone    'q' as an unsigned
integer
            (n+4+p)..(n+3+p+q) zone              string of (up to 32)
octets

            For comparison purposes, strings are case-insensitive All
            strings may contain any octet other than 255 (hex ff)."
    SYNTAX       OCTET STRING (SIZE (3..99))


-- SNMPv2 over IPX

snmpIPXDomain  OBJECT-IDENTITY
    STATUS     current
    DESCRIPTION
            "The SNMPv2 over IPX transport domain. The corresponding
            transport address is of type SnmpIPXAddress."
    ::= { snmpDomains 5 }

SnmpIPXAddress ::= TEXTUAL-CONVENTION
    DISPLAY-HINT "4x.1x:1x:1x:1x:1x:1x.2d"
    STATUS       current
    DESCRIPTION
```

```
        "Represents an IPX address:

           octets   contents           encoding
            1-4     network-number     network-byte order
            5-10    physical-address   network-byte order
           11-12    socket-number      network-byte order
        "
    SYNTAX       OCTET STRING (SIZE (12))


-- for proxy to SNMPv1 (RFC 1157)

rfc1157Proxy   OBJECT IDENTIFIER ::= { snmpProxys 1 }

rfc1157Domain  OBJECT-IDENTITY
    STATUS     current
    DESCRIPTION
        "The transport domain for SNMPv1 over UDP. The
        corresponding transport address is of type SnmpUDPAddress."
    ::= { rfc1157Proxy 1 }

--  ::= { rfc1157Proxy 2 }          this OID is obsolete


END
```

Message Formats

See the *PDU Definitions* section shown previously.

28 SMTP Service Extensions

Name

SMTP Service Extensions

Abbreviation

SMTP-EXT or ESMTP

Status

Recommended Standard (STD 10)

Specifications

RFC 1869, RFC 1870, RFC 1891

Abstract

SMTP-EXT specifies a general framework for extending SMTP with new commands and capabilities. SMTP-EXT does this in a way that maintains compatibility between older SMTP clients and servers. If either the client or the server doesn't support SMTP-EXT, an SMTP session will use the older SMTP capabilities.

Related Specifications

SMTP (RFC 821), SMTP Service Extensions for Message Size (RFC 1870), SMTP Service Extension for Delivery Status Notifications (RFC 1891)

See Also

Format of Electronic Mail Messages (MAIL, RFC 822), MIME (RFC 1521), POP3 (RFC 1725), IMAP4 (RFC 1730)

Comments

A few SMTP service extensions have been put on the standards track. A few others have been proposed and are available as Internet Drafts.

Description

SMTP states that the first command in a SMTP session must be the HELO command. SMTP-EXT amends RFC 821 to also allow the EHLO command. The EHLO command informs the server that the client understands SMTP-EXT and queries the server for the list of extensions that it supports.

If the server does not support SMTP-EXT (that is, it is a simple SMTP server), it thinks the client issued an invalid command and responds with an error reply code. In this case, the client may proceed with a standard SMTP HELO command and use all the facilities defined in RFC 821.

If the server understands the EHLO command (that is, the server implements SMTP-EXT), it will respond with a multi-line 250 reply code, as defined in the grammar later in this chapter. The first line of the reply is the typical response that would have been sent for a HELO command by a standard SMTP server. The following lines specify an extended SMTP keyword followed by optional parameters, depending on the particular keyword. The keywords specify the various SMTP extensions that the server supports.

The IANA maintains a list of currently defined SMTP-EXT keywords.

Transport Information

SMTP-EXT uses the same well-known TCP port as SMTP, 25.

Commands

This section describes the basic set of extension mechanisms SMTP-EXT uses to add functionality to SMTP.

Initial Extension Set

RFC 1869 defines an initial set of SMTP-EXT services and keywords. The initial set consists of all the optional commands described in RFC 821. An SMTP-EXT server that implements these commands should report them using the EHLO command mechanism. The initial set of services is shown in Table 28.1.

Message Size Extension

RFC 1870 defines the first SMTP-EXT extension service beyond the optional commands specified in RFC 821. The initial service extension allows a client to convey the size of a message to a server before the message is sent. This advance information allows the server to refuse to accept the message *before* the entire message data is sent to the server. The refusal may either be temporary (the server doesn't currently have enough storage space, for example) or permanent (the server administrator has implemented a policy that the server will not accept messages above a given size, for example).

This extension is valuable because the use of MIME to encode large body parts is resulting in more large messages traversing the Internet. The ability to refuse to accept a lengthy message allows a client and server to terminate a message exchange that cannot possibly succeed before the entire message data is sent to the server, preventing the waste of valuable bandwidth.

Table 28.1 Initial SMTP-EXT Services

Service Extension	EHLO Keyword	Parameters	Verb	Added Behavior
Send	SEND	none	SEND	defined in RFC 821
Send or Mail	SOML	none	SOML	defined in RFC 821
Send and Mail	SAML	none	SAML	defined in RFC 821
Expand	EXPN	none	EXPN	defined in RFC 821
Help	HELP	none	HELP	defined in RFC 821
Turn	TURN	none	TURN	defined in RFC 821

The name of the extension is "Message Size Declaration." The EHLO keyword is SIZE. The keyword may be followed by one optional parameter specified like this:

```
size-param ::= [1*DIGIT]
```

The optional parameter specifies the maximum size messages this server is allowed to accept as an overall policy. A value of 0 specifies that the server has no set maximum size. If the parameter is omitted, the client cannot deduce anything about an overall policy that may be in effect.

The MAIL command is allowed to have an extra parameter, SIZE. The parameter value is specified by the following grammar:

```
size-value ::= 1*20DIGIT
```

The decimal size specified by the client should include all the characters of the message, including CRLF line terminators (counted as two characters). The size does not include the final termination line consisting of a single period followed by CRLF, nor does it include the dots added by the SMTP "dot-stuffing" algorithm.

The specified message size need not be exact, but will ideally be greater than or equal to the true message size.

When a server encounters a MAIL command with a SIZE parameter, it should check the message size against the fixed maximum size allowed by the server and against the current maximum size allowed by the current set of available server resources. The message size extension defines two reply codes that may be given in response to a MAIL command if the specified message size exceeds these limits:

- 452: insufficient system storage
- 552: message size exceeds fixed maximum message size

The 452 reply code indicates to the client that the message size exceeds the current system resources, but that the situation may be temporary. The client is encouraged to try the transfer at a later time. The 552 reply code indicates that the situation is permanent and, barring any changes by the administrator, the transfer can never succeed.

When the client receives either of these replies, it should send either a RSET command, to attempt a different message transfer, or QUIT command, to terminate the session.

Note that the receipt of a 250 reply code to the MAIL command does not guarantee that the message transfer will succeed. There are many reasons why the transfer may still fail, and a client must not count on the success of the transfer.

The size extension also allows the generation of 452 and 552 reply codes in response to RCPT commands. This allows the server to control the delivery of messages based on sizes associated with individual users.

Delivery Status Notification Extension

RFC 1891 defines an SMTP-EXT extension for delivery status notifications. Delivery status notifications (DSNs) are automated messages sent to the originator of a message to positively inform the sender whether the message was delivered or not. In the past, such notifications were often generated by servers in an ad-hoc manner, and they lacked a consistent format. For more information about DSNs, see RFC 1892, RFC 1893, and RFC 1894.

The extension specified in RFC 1891 allows a client to request the generation of DSNs or specifically suppress their generation. Suppression of DSNs is particularly helpful for automated mailing lists that cannot process delivery failure notifications. The generation of deliver failure notifications in such cases simply causes an added burden on the Internet mail system that could otherwise be avoided.

The official name of this extension is "Deliver Status Notification." The EHLO keyword is DSN and does not specify any additional parameters.

The extension specifies two optional parameters for the RCPT command:

- NOTIFY
- ORCPT

The extension also specifies two optional parameters for the MAIL command:

- RET
- ENVID

The values associated with the ORCPT and ENVID parameters may contain characters that are not allowed in the SMTP-EXT "esmtp-value" grammar definition. Because of this restriction, values associated with these parameters are encoded using "xtext." Xtext is defined as:

```
xtext   = *( xchar / hexchar )
xchar   = Any ASCII character between "!" (33) and "~" (126) inclusive,
  except for "+" and "=".
; "hexchar"s are intended to encode octets that cannot appear
; as ASCII characters within an esmtp-value.
hexchar= ASCII "+" immediately followed by two upper case hexadecimal digits
```

When encoding an octet sequence as xtext:

- Any ASCII character between "!" and "~" inclusive, except for "+" and "=", MAY be encoded as itself. (A character in this range *may* instead be encoded as a "hexchar," at the implementor's discretion.)
- ASCII characters that fall outside the range above must be encoded as "hexchar."

The NOTIFY parameter specifies when DSNs should be generated for the particular recipient specified by the RCPT command. The NOTIFY parameter value is specified as:

```
notify-esmtp-value = "NEVER" / 1#notify-list-element
notify-list-element = "SUCCESS" / "FAILURE" / "DELAY"
```

The ORCPT parameter specifies the original recipient address for the message. The following grammar defines the ORCPT parameter value:

```
orcpt-parameter = "ORCPT=" original-recipient-address
original-recipient-address = addr-type ";" xtext
addr-type = atom
```

The ORCPT parameter may be up to 500 characters long. See RFC 1891 for more information about the use of the ORCPT parameter.

The RET parameter of the MAIL command specifies whether the original message should be returned with a failed DSN. The RET parameter can specify one of the following values:

- FULL The full message should be returned with the DSN.
- HDRS Only the message headers should be returned with the DSN.

If no RET command appears, the system generating the DSN may include the original message or the message headers at its discretion.

The ENVID parameter specifies an envelope identifier that is transferred along with the message and returned in any DSNs. The identifier is used only by the originating system for its own purposes. In particular, it can be used to match DSNs with the original message that generated the DSN. The identifier is specified by the following grammar and may be up to 100 characters long.

```
envid-parameter = "ENVID=" xtext
```

Responses

See RFC 821 for the list of SMTP responses. SMTP-EXT responses are identical to SMTP responses.

Grammar

The grammar for the SMTP-EXT server response to the EHLO command is:

```
ehlo-ok-rsp ::=  "250" domain [ SP greeting ] CR LF
     / ( "250-" domain [ SP greeting ] CR LF
     *( "250-" ehlo-line CR LF )
     "250" SP ehlo-line CR LF )
; the usual HELO chit-chat
greeting  ::=  1*<any character other than CR or LF>
ehlo-line ::=  ehlo-keyword *( SP ehlo-param )
ehlo-keyword::=  (ALPHA / DIGIT) *(ALPHA / DIGIT / "-")
; syntax and values depend on ehlo-keyword
ehlo-param  ::=  1*<any CHAR excluding SP and all control characters
  (US ASCII 0-31 inclusive)>
ALPHA   ::=  <any one of the 52 alphabetic characters (A through Z in
  upper case, and, a through z in lower case)>
DIGIT   ::=  <any one of the 10 numeric characters (0 through 9)>
CR ::=  <the carriage-return character (ASCII decimal code 13)>
LF ::=  <the line-feed character (ASCII decimal code 10)>
SP ::=  <the space character (ASCII decimal code 32)>
```

SMTP-EXT anticipates that a number of extensions will require added parameters for the MAIL and RCPT commands defined in RFC 821. SMTP-EXT extends the RFC 821 grammar for these commands to allow for these added parameters. The new grammar is:

```
esmtp-cmd ::= inner-esmtp-cmd [SP esmtp-parameters] CR LF
esmtp-parameters ::= esmtp-parameter *(SP esmtp-parameter)
```

```
esmtp-parameter ::= esmtp-keyword ["=" esmtp-value]
esmtp-keyword ::= (ALPHA / DIGIT) *(ALPHA / DIGIT / "-")
; syntax and values depend on esmtp-keyword
esmtp-value ::= 1*<any CHAR excluding "=", SP, and all control characters
  (US ASCII 0-31 inclusive)>
; The following commands are extended to accept extended parameters.
inner-esmtp-cmd ::= ("MAIL FROM:" reverse-path) / ("RCPT TO:" forward-path)
```

SMTP-EXT defines the protocol name ESMTP for use in "Received" header lines added to messages. This protocol name, rather than simply SMTP, should be used when ESMTP extensions are used to send a message. This requires no modifications to the grammar specified in RFC 821.

TELNET

Name

TELNET

Abbreviation

TELNET

Status

Recommended Standard (STD 8)

Specifications

RFC 854 and RFC 855 define the basic TELNET specification. Various TELNET options are defined in numerous other RFCs. See Table 29.5 for a listing of standard TELNET options and their associated RFCs.

Abstract

The TELNET protocol allows a remote user to access remote computers as if the user were directly attached to a local terminal. TELNET defines the concept of a network virtual terminal (NVT) and specifies how two virtual terminals interact using a bi-directional character stream. This bi-directional character stream is typically made available using a standard TCP connection. The TELNET specification allows the two endpoints to negotiate a set of optional functionality beyond that provided by the basic specification. Most of the actual TELNET protocol centers around the definition of the option negotiation protocol.

Comments

The TELNET protocol is used for more than simple terminal applications. For instance, the control connection of an FTP session uses the TELNET protocol to allow the client and server to exchange FTP commands and replies. Many other protocols use the basic NVT concept defined in the TELNET RFCs, even if they don't use the entire TELNET protocol.

Description

The Network Virtual Terminal

The TELNET protocol uses the concept of a network virtual terminal (NVT) to help model the connection between the two TELNET entities. Conceptually, both ends of a TELNET connection use an NVT, although in real applications, the server side of the connection is usually a login process rather than a TELNET terminal emulation application.

The standard NVT provides the baseline functionality for a TELNET connection when no options have been negotiated. Both TELNET endpoints must implement the basic NVT concept and not rely on the use of options to provide additional functionality. There is no requirement that a host understand any options that another host might otherwise require.

The NVT is a bi-directional character device. Conceptually, it consists of a keyboard and a printer. Characters inbound from the remote NVT are printed on the local printer for display to the user. Characters typed on the keyboard are sent to the remote NVT and are optionally printed on the local printer to provide local echoing. Local echo may be turned off using option negotiation and provided instead by the remote NVT process.

The NVT has an unspecified width and page length. It is capable of reproducing the printable US-ASCII character codes (codes 32 through 126). Of the remaining US-ASCII control codes (0 through 31 and 127) and the 8-bit codes (128 through 255), the few codes described in Table 29.1 have meaning to the NVT.

Table 29.1 US-ASCII Control Code Meanings for the NVT

Name	US-ASCII Code	Description
NULL (NUL)	0	No operation
Line Feed (LF)	10	Moves the printer to the next print line, keeping the same horizontal position
Carriage Return (CR)	13	Moves the printer to the left margin of the current line

In addition to the basic control codes shown in Table 29.1, the TELNET protocol defines standard meanings to the control codes, shown in Table 29.2, but does not require that an NVT implement these behaviors.

TELNET Commands

In addition to the standard US-ASCII control codes, the TELNET specification defines additional generic commands. These commands are not assigned character codes in the US-ASCII character set, but rather are signaled using the in-band TELNET signaling protocol. Table 29.3 lists the additional TELNET commands.

A TELNET command is signaled to the remote NVT by inserting the IAC indication followed by the command code into the outbound data stream. Command codes that are not preceded by the IAC code are interpreted as data characters, not commands. To communicate the IAC code value itself as data rather than as the IAC indication, insert two consecutive IAC codes.

Table 29.2 Optional US-ASCII Control Codes Meanings for the NVT

Name	US-ASCII Code	Description
BELL (BEL)	7	Produces an audible or visible signal but doe not alter the current print position
Back Space (BS)	8	Moves the print position one character toward the left margin
Horizontal Tab (HT)	9	Moves the print position to the next horizontal tab stop
Vertical Tab (VT)	11	Moves the print position to the next vertical tab stop
Form Feed (FF)	12	Moves the print position to the top of the next page without altering the current horizontal position

Table 29.3 TELNET Commands

Name	Code	Description
SE	240	End of subnegotiation parameters (see the *Subnegotiation* section)
NOP	241	No operation
Data Mark	242	The data stream portion of a Synch; this should always be accompanied by a TCP Urgent notification
Break	243	The equivalent of the Break or Attention key
Interrupt Process	244	Suspends, interrupts, aborts, or terminates the remote process
Abort Output	245	Requests that the remote process run to completion but not continue to produce output
Are You There	246	Requests the remote NVT to send back some printable evidence that it is still connected; this is often just the string "Yes"
Erase Character	247	Tells the remote NVT to delete that last character from the data stream
Erase Line	248	Tells the remote NVT to delete the last line of characters (back to, but not including, the last CRLF sequence)
Go Ahead	249	The GA signal
SB	250	Indicates that what follows is subnegotiation of the indicated option (see the *Subnegotiation* section)
WILL (option code)	251	Indicates the desire to begin performing, or confirmation that you are now performing, the indicated option
WON'T (option code)	252	Indicates the refusal to perform, or continue performing, the indicated option
DO (option code)	253	Indicates the request that the other party perform, or confirmation that you are expecting the other party to perform, the indicated option
DON'T (option code)	254	Indicates the demand that the other party stop performing, or confirmation that you are no longer expecting the other party to perform, the indicated option
IAC	255	Interpret as Command indication; two IAC codes in a row signal the actual data value 255

Option Negotiation

Either NVT may try to negotiate optional functionality using the TELNET option negotiation protocol. Optional functionality may increase the capabilities of the basic NVT or disable some of the default NVT processing (local echo, for instance). A local NVT may request the remote NVT to either enable or disable a functionality, or it can inform the remote NVT that the local NVT

Table 29.4 Option Negotiation Commands

Command	Possible Responses	Description
WILL		Indicates an offer to the remote NVT to perform some functionality
	DO	Indicates that the remote NVT agrees to the WILL offer
	DON'T	Indicates that the remote NVT disagrees to the WILL offer
WON'T		Indicates an offer to the remote NVT to not perform some functionality
	DO	Indicates that the remote NVT disagrees to the WON'T offer
	DON'T	Indicates that the remote NVT agrees to the WON'T offer
DO		Requests that the remote NVT perform some functionality
	WILL	Indicates that the remote NVT agrees to the DO request
	WON'T	Indicates that the remote NVT disagrees to the DO request
DON'T		Requests that the remote NVT not perform some functionality
	WILL	Indicates that the remote NVT disagrees to the DON'T request
	WON'T	Indicates that the remote NVT agrees to the DON'T request

wishes to enable or disable a functionality. Table 29.4 describes the requests and the possible responses. Note that the responses are requests in themselves. If the two NVTs both generate requests at the same time, the commands will act as replies to themselves rather than creating a command-response loop.

To send a command, the local NVT inserts an IAC code, followed by a WILL/WON'T/DO/DON'T code, followed by an option code into the outgoing data stream. This is often represented by:

```
IAC verb option
```

Where *verb* is one of WILL, WON'T, DO, or DON'T, and *option* is one of the standard option codes shown in Table 29.5.

Subnegotiation

Some TELNET options can't be negotiated by the simple exchange of WILL, WON'T, DO, DON'T command but may also require additional parameters. The TELNET subnegotiation process allows the exchange of these parameters.

The subnegotiation begins after the two parties first agree to discuss the option. That is, the parties first exchange WILL, WON'T, DO, DON'T commands and responses to reach agreement that they both support the basic option, and that they agree that it should be enabled or disabled at this time. Once basic agreement has been reached, subnegotiation begins.

Either side sends subnegotiation commands to the other, as defined by the protocol defined by the option itself. The basic exchange of subnegotiation parameters is represented by the following sequence:

```
IAC SB option parameters IAC SE
```

where *option* is the option code and *parameters* is a sequence of one or more data bytes as defined by the option. The subnegotiation command ends with the IAC SE sequence. If the *parameters* data needs to include a data byte of 255, it must be represented as two consecutive IAC command codes, as in the normal TELNET data stream.

Standard Options

Many standard TELNET options have been defined. The currently registered standard TELNET options are listed in Table 29.5. Note that most TELNET implementations implement only a small subset of the total set of standard options. Each of the RFCs that define the various options provide more information about the semantics of the option and any subnegotiation parameters that must be exchanged.

Table 29.5 Standard TELNET Options

Option Code	Name	References
0	Binary Transmission	[RFC856]
1	Echo	[RFC857]
2	Reconnection	[NIC50005]
3	Suppress Go Ahead	[RFC858]
4	Approx Message Size Negotiation	[ETHERNET]
5	Status	[RFC859]
6	Timing Mark	[RFC860]
7	Remote Controlled Trans and Echo	[RFC726]
8	Output Line Width	[NIC50005]
9	Output Page Size	[NIC50005]
10	Output Carriage-Return Disposition	[RFC652]
11	Output Horizontal Tab Stops	[RFC653]
12	Output Horizontal Tab Disposition	[RFC654]

Continued

Table 29.5 Standard TELNET Options (Continued)

Option Code	Name	References
13	Output Formfeed Disposition	[RFC655]
14	Output Vertical Tabstops	[RFC656]
15	Output Vertical Tab Disposition	[RFC657]
16	Output Linefeed Disposition	[RFC657]
17	Extended ASCII	[RFC698]
18	Logout	[RFC727]
19	Byte Macro	[RFC735]
20	Data Entry Terminal	[RFC1043,RFC732]
22	SUPDUP	[RFC736,RFC734]
22	SUPDUP Output	[RFC749]
23	Send Location	[RFC779]
24	Terminal Type	[RFC1091]
25	End of Record	[RFC885]
26	TACACS User Identification	[RFC927]
27	Output Marking	[RFC933]
28	Terminal Location Number	[RFC946]
29	Telnet3270 Regime	[RFC1041]
30	X.3 PAD	[RFC1053]

RFC 1409 defines the TELNET Authentication Option (option 37). This option allows the use of an authentication algorithm to authenticate the user with the TELNET server. Table 29.6 lists the possible authentication algorithm types.

References

[ETHERNET] "The Ethernet, A Local Area Network: Data Link Layer and Physical Layer Specification", AA-K759B-TK, Digital Equipment Corporation, Maynard, MA. Also as: "The Ethernet - A Local Area Network", Version 1.0, Digital Equipment Corporation, Intel Corporation, Xerox Corporation, September 1980. And: "The Ethernet, A Local Area Network: Data Link Layer and Physical Layer Specifications", Digital, Intel and Xerox, November 1982. And: XEROX, "The Ethernet, A Local Area Network: Data Link Layer and Physical Layer Specification", X3T51/80-50, Xerox Corporation, Stamford, CT., October 1980.

Table 29.6 TELNET Authentication Types

Type	Description	Reference
0	NULL	[RFC1409]
1	KERBEROS_V4	[RFC1409]
2	KERBEROS_V5	[RFC1409]
3	SPX	[RFC1409]
4-5	Unassigned	
6	RSA	[RFC1409]
7-9	Unassigned	
10	LOKI	[RFC1409]
11	SSA	

[NIC50005] DDN Protocol Handbook, "Telnet Reconnection Option", "Telnet Output Line Width Option", "Telnet Output Page Size Option", NIC 50005, December 1985.

Transport Information

The TELNET server awaits remote login connections on well-known TCP port 23.

30 Transmission Control Protocol

Name

Transmission Control Protocol

Abbreviation

TCP

Status

Required Standard (STD 7)

Specifications

RFC 793

Abstract

The Transmission Control Protocol (TCP) provides for the reliable delivery of data between two computer systems. TCP provides a bi-directional byte-stream connection between the two systems.

Related Specifications

IP (RFC 791)

See Also

UDP (RFC 768)

Comments

This section has been updated to include some corrections to the original specification described in RFC 1122 (STD 3), "Requirements for Internet hosts—Communication Layers."

Description

TCP provides a reliable, bi-directional data stream between two hosts. TCP uses an underlying, unreliable datagram service, IP, to move data between the systems. TCP then provides reliability and error control mechanisms on top of this underlying datagram service to model its own stream connection. TCP detects lost or corrupted data and provides for the retransmission of the data to the receiver until the receiver acknowledges that it has received it correctly.

Protocol State Machine

Figure 30.1 shows the basic TCP state machine. The state machine is implemented in each TCP symmetrically. The various user events, such as OPEN and CLOSE, are mapped to appropriate application programming interfaces (APIs), such as BSD sockets.

The arrow leading from SYN-Sent to SYN-Received has been labeled with "Send SYN, ACK" according to the correction described in RFC 1122. Section 4.2.2.8 of that document describes some additional state transitions that may be possible. The additional transitions have not been included here.

Frame Formats

Figure 30.2 shows the prototypical TCP frame format. The various fields in the TCP header are described further in the following sections.

Source Port

16 bits

This field indicates the source port number.

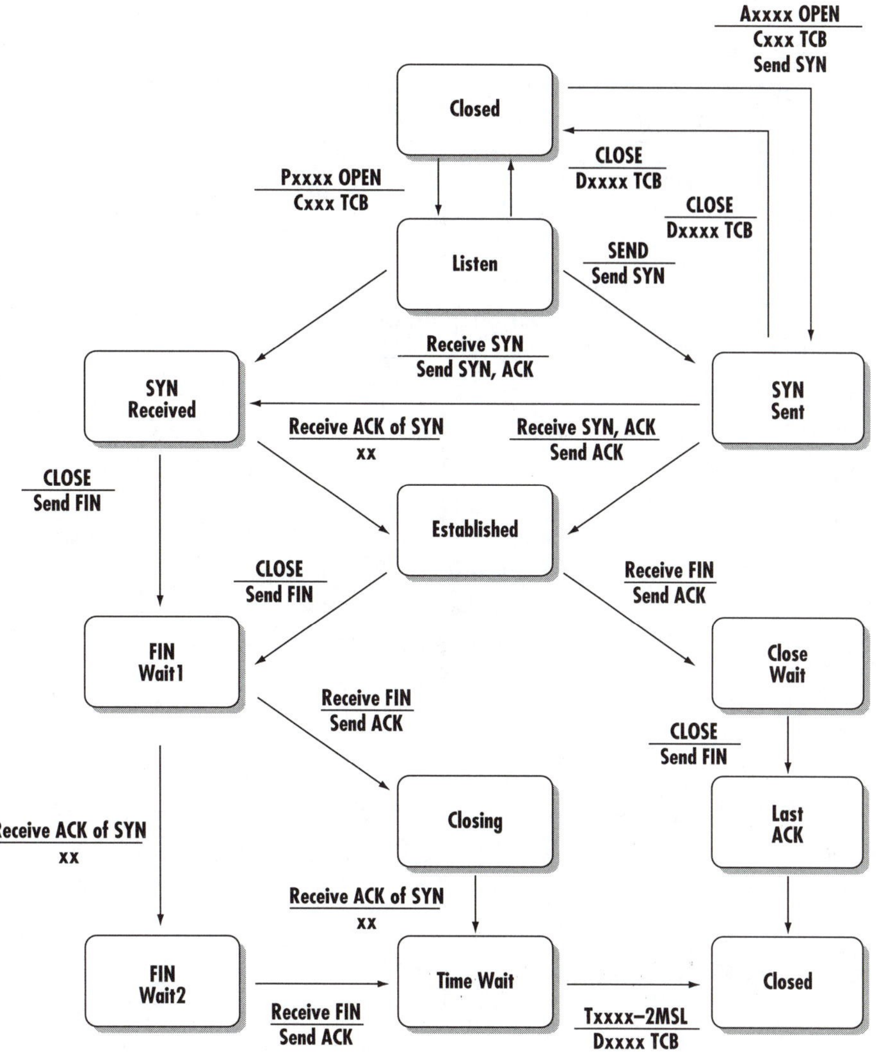

Figure 30.1

The TCP state machine.

Destination Port

16 bits

This field indicates the destination port number.

Sequence Number

32 bits

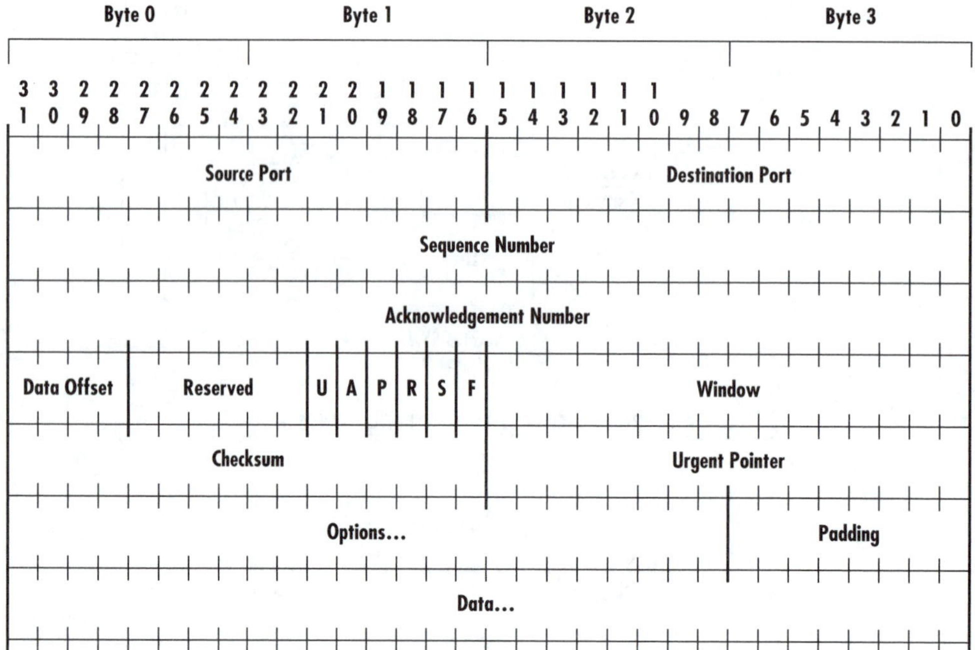

Figure 30.2

The TCP frame format.

This field indicates the sequence number of the first data octet in the current segment. If the SYN flag is set (see Table 30.1), then the Sequence Number field contains the initial sequence number (ISN) and the first data octet is ISN + 1.

Acknowledgment Number

32 bits

If the ACK flag is set (see Table 30.1), this field contains the next sequence number the sender of this segment is expecting to receive. Once a connection is established, the ACK flag is always set and this field is always valid.

Data Offset

4 bits

This field specifies the length of the TCP header, measured in 32-bit words. The value in this field specifies where the data begins.

Reserved

6 bits

This field is reserved for future use, and must be zero.

Control Flags

6 bits

The control flag descriptions are shown in Table 30.1.

Window

16 bits

This field indicates the number of data octets, beginning with the one indicated in the Acknowledgment field, that the sender of this segment is willing to accept.

Checksum

16 bits

The Checksum field is computed by calculating the 16-bit one's complement of the one's complement sum of all the 16-bit words in the header and data. If the data contains an odd number of octets, the last 16-bit word is formed by padding the last data octet with a zero on right. The pad is not transmitted with the data. While computing the checksum, the Checksum field itself is set to zero. In addition to the TCP header and data, the checksum calculation also includes a "pseudo-header," shown in Figure 30.3, formed from some fields contained in the IP header. The pseudo-header protects TCP from misrouted segments. Conceptually, the header is prepended to the TCP header before checksum calculation.

Table 30.1 Control Flag Descriptions

Abbreviation	Name	Description
U	URG	Urgent pointer significant
A	ACK	Acknowledgment field significant
P	PSH	Push function
R	RST	Resets the connection
S	SYN	Synchronizes sequence numbers
F	FIN	No more data from sender

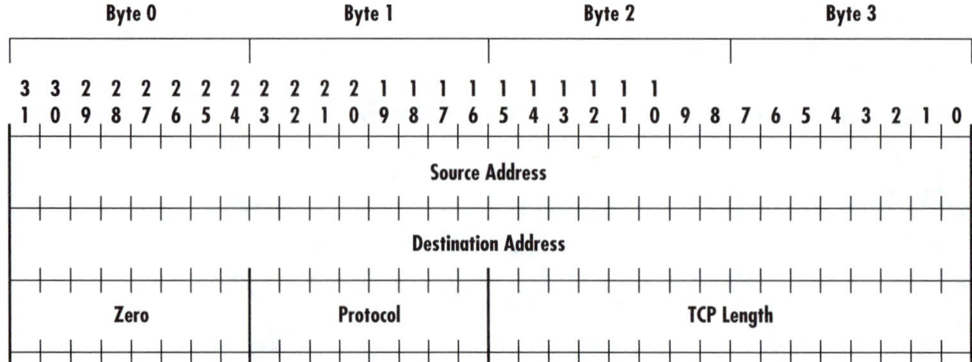

Figure 30.3
The TCP pseudo-header used for checksum calculations.

The TCP Length includes the length of the TCP header and the segment data. It does not include the length of the pseudo-header.

Urgent Pointer

16 bits

This field is added to the sequence number of this segment to form the Urgent Pointer. The Urgent Pointer specifies the sequence number of the last octet of urgent data. This field is significant only when the URG flag is set. Note that RFC 793, section 3.1, specifies the urgent pointer as pointing to the octet following the urgent data. This error was corrected by RFC 1122, section 4.2.2.4.

Options

Variable length

Options occur after the TCP header, but before the actual TCP data. Options are octet aligned and have one of two types:

- A single octet containing the option type.
- A multi-byte option encoded in type/length/value (TLV) format. In this case, the type and length values are each one octet long and the data may be variable length. The length octet specifies the length of the entire option, including the type octet and the length octet itself.

The option data may be shorter than the Data Offset field would indicate. In such cases, the additional octets are padding and must be filled with zero.

Table 30.2 TCP Options

Kind	Length	Meaning
0	–	End of Option List
1	–	No-Operation
2	4	Maximum Segment Size

Table 30.2 shows the defined TCP options.

End of Option List
Kind = 0

This option is used to mark the end of the option list in cases where the option list does not occupy all the data specified by the Data Offset field. This option is not required. If the total length of the option list is exactly equal to the length specified by the Data Offset field, no padding is needed and this option is not used.

No Operation
Kind = 1

This option does not require processing. It is used to insert padding between individual options—to align a following option to a 32-bit boundary, for instance.

Maximum Segment Size
Kind = 2

This option is used to specify the maximum receive segment size of the sender of this option. This option must only be sent when SYN is also sent. If no Maximum Segment Size option is sent, any segment size is allowed. The Maximum Segment Size is specified in a 16-bit value following the option kind and length octets.

31 Trivial File Transfer Protocol

Name

Trivial File Transfer Protocol

Abbreviation

TFTP

Status

Elective Standard (STD 33)

Specifications

RFC 1350, RFC 1782, RFC 1783, RFC 1784

Abstract

The Trivial File Transfer Protocol (TFTP) is a very simple file transfer protocol used in cases where the extensive functionality and complexity of FTP is not needed. TFTP is designed to be small and easy to implement. TFTP uses UDP transport rather than TCP. For all of these reasons, TFTP is ideally suited for retrieving the boot images of diskless workstations. The protocol is small enough to be included in a boot ROM. In fact, TFTP can easily be pair with BOOTP or DHCP to provide a plug-and-play diskless workstation.

Related Specifications

UDP (RFC 768)

See Also

FTP (RFC 959), BOOTP (RFC 951, RFC 1497, RFC 1542), DHCP (RFC 1541, RFC 1533)

Comments

TFTP is not a high-performance protocol. Because of the simple, one-at-a-time packet transmission and loss recovery mechanism, the protocol performance is very sensitive to the path delay between the client and server. Although the block size option defined in RFC 1783 improves performance considerably, TFTP is still best-suited to moving files between hosts on the same, or very nearly the same, LAN segment.

Description

TFTP is much simpler than the full-blown FTP. TFTP transfers files as a sequence of 512-byte fixed-length blocks of data using UDP datagrams. Because UDP is unreliable, TFTP uses a lock-step acknowledgment scheme to confirm the reception of each data block. The sender must wait for the acknowledgment of the previous data block before sending the next data block. If the sender fails to receive an acknowledgment for a timeout period after transmitting a data block, the block is retransmitted.

Error recovery is very simple: Most errors cause the transfer to fail, and failed transfers must be restarted from the beginning.

TFTP does not implement the extensive variations of data typing and transfer modes of standard FTP. Rather, TFTP supports only two modes: *netascii* and *octet.* Netascii mode is used to transfer text files in ASCII format, while octet mode is used to transfer binary files. No other modes are defined (RFC 1350 deprecates the use of *mail* mode, which was described in earlier versions of TFTP).

Basic Protocol

A TFTP client initiates the session by sending either a read request packet (RRQ) or write request packet (WRQ) to the TFTP server. If no errors occur, the TFTP server responds with an acknowledgment packet (ACK) for a WRQ or the first packet of data (DATA) for a RRQ.

Each TFTP data packet is assigned a block number. Block numbers start at 1 and increase consecutively. Each acknowledgment sent by the receiver contains the block number of the corresponding data packet. Since the WRQ contains no data, the acknowledgment sent by the server indicates data block 0 in this special case.

Note that all TFTP packets, except duplicate acknowledgment packets and errors, are acknowledged by the receiver. The next data packet in sequence serves as the acknowledgment of the previous acknowledgment packet. Timers are used to retransmit unacknowledged packets. Interestingly, RFC 1350 does not specify recommended timeout values.

Once the session has been established, data and acknowledgment packets are exchanged by the sender and receiver until the file has been transferred or an error occurs. Because each TFTP data packet contains a fixed number of bytes (512 by default, but this can be increased using the TFTP block size option defined in RFC 1783), the receiver can recognize the end of the transfer by a data block containing fewer than 512 bytes of data (or fewer bytes than the negotiated block size).

Option Negotiation

RFC 1782 describes an extension to the original TFTP protocol that provides for simple option negotiation. The protocol works as follows:

1. The client includes options in the RRQ or WRQ packets sent to the server.
2. If the server understands the options, it responds with a OACK packet indicating the negotiated values of the options. The OACK packet includes the names and values corresponding to all the options the server recognized. Any options that the server does not include in the OACK packet are unrecognized by the server and the client must assume default values for those options.

   If the server does not understand the options, it responds with DATA or ACK as per the original TFTP protocol. Note that some servers may view the options added to a RRQ or WRQ packet as an error and return an error packet. In this case, the client may send another RRQ or WRQ packet without options, assuming that the server does not support option negotiation.

3. The client acknowledges the OACK packet to the server using either an ACK or a DATA packet. An ACK is sent if the client originally started the session with a RRQ packet. The ACK indicates an acknowledgment for block 0, since no data has yet been sent. This is similar to the host response to a WRQ packet. The client sends a DATA packet if it originally started the session with a WRQ packet. If the client finds an option in the OACK packet that it did not request, or for some reason the options values returned from the server are not acceptable, the client returns an ERROR packet indicating error code 8, option negotiation error.

Options

RFC 1783 describes the TFTP block size option. This option uses the option name "blksize." The option value is a number in the range 8 to 65464, inclusive. The server may return an equal or smaller block size than that specified by the client. If the client rejects the value returned by the server, it sends an ERROR packet to the server, aborting the transfer.

RFC 1784 describes two options for negotiating the TFTP timeout value and for specifying the total size of the transferred file.

The timeout option is named "timeout" and specifies a timeout value in seconds, from 1 to 255. If the server accepts the client's timeout value, it acknowledges the request with an OACK.

The transfer size option is named "tsize" and specifies the total file size in octets. In WRQ packets, the file size is specified by the client. In RRQ packets, the client specifies 0 and the server fills in the correct value in the returned OACK packet. If the specified size is too large, either the client or the server may choose to abort the transfer by sending an ERROR packet. Table 31.1 encapsulates the options and their values.

Table 31.1 TFTP Options

Option Name	Value
blksize	Block size in number of octets between 8 and 65464, inclusive
timeout	Timeout value in seconds between 1 and 255, inclusive
tsize	Total file transfer size in octets; the size must be a positive number

Transport Information

The TFTP client initially contacts the TFTP server on well-known UDP port 69. The TFTP server then chooses another port for the connection and sends its reply using this port. The client port and the new server port are then used for the remainder of the TFTP session. Only RRQs and WRQs should be sent to port 69. Once the session ports are established, clients and servers should discard any received datagrams that do not have the correct source addresses.

Packet Formats

TFTP defines five packet types, as shown in Table 31.2. Each TFTP packet includes a TFTP opcode as its first two bytes, which allows the TFTP receiver to distinguish packet types. The format of each TFTP packet is described in more detail in the subsequent sections.

Read and Write Request Packets

The format of the RRQ and WRQ packets is shown in Table 31.3. Note that RFC 1350 only defines the Opcode, Filename, and Mode fields. The Option and Value fields are defined as extensions to the basic TFTP protocol in RFC 1782.

Data Packet

The format of a data packet is shown in Table 31.4.

Acknowledgment Packet

Table 31.5 shows the format of a TFTP acknowledgment packet.

Table 31.2 TFTP Packet Types

Opcode	Description
1	Read request (RRQ)
2	Write request (WRQ)
3	Data (DATA)
4	Acknowledgment (ACK)
5	Error (ERROR)
6	Option acknowledgment (OACK); defined in RFC 1782

Table 31.3 TFTP Read and Write Request Packet Format

Field	Octet Length	Description
Opcode	2	Contains the opcode for RRQ (1) or WRQ (2)
Filename	n	A variable-length, null-terminated NVT-ASCII string containing the file name to read or write; note that the file name may be case sensitive depending on the file system used by the server
Mode	n	A variable-length, null-terminated string describing the file transfer mode. Only two modes are allowed: netascii or octet; the mode string is not case sensitive, and any combination of upper or lowercase letters is acceptable
Option 1	n	The first option name represented as a variable-length, null-terminated, NVT ASCII string; the field is not case sensitive
Value 1	n	The value for the first option, represented as a variable-length, null-terminated, NVT-ASCII string
Option n	n	Repeated names for second and subsequent options
Value n	n	Repeated values for second and subsequent options

Table 31.4 TFTP Data Packet Format

Field	Octet Length	Description
Opcode	2	Contains 3 for data packets
Block Number	2	Contains the sequence number for the current data packet; sequence numbers start at 1 and increase consecutively
Data	n	Contains a full block of data (512 bytes by default), or less than a full block if this is the last data packet in the transfer

Table 31.5 TFTP Acknowledgment Packet Format

Field	Octet Length	Description
Opcode	2	Contains 4 for acknowledgment packets
Block Number	2	Contains the block number from the data packet being acknowledged, or 0 if this packet acknowledges a WRQ packet

Error Packet

Table 31.6 shows the format of a TFTP error packet. Error packets terminate the session and are not acknowledged or retransmitted if lost.

Table 31.7 shows the various TFTP error codes that may populate the Error Code field of the error packet.

Option Acknowledgment

Table 31.8 shows the format of an option acknowledgment packet defined in RFC 1782. Note that some options may allow the server to respond with a different option value than that proposed by the client. Whether this makes sense is described in the individual option definition. The option acknowledgment allows the server to return the value of the acknowledged option to support such options.

Table 31.6 TFTP Error Packet Format

Field	Octet Length	Description
Opcode	2	Contains 5 for error packets
Error Code	2	A code indicating the cause of the error
Error Message	n	A variable-length, null-terminated string containing a human-readable error message; the string should use characters from the NVT-ASCII character set

Table 31.7 TFTP Error Codes

Code	Description
0	Undefined; the error message may indicate more if it is present
1	File not found
2	Access violation
3	Disk full or allocation exceeded
4	Illegal TFTP operation
5	Unknown source port number
6	File already exists
7	No such user
8	Option negotiation error (defined in RFC 1782)

Table 31.8 TFTP Option Acknowledgment Packet Format

Field	Octet Length	Description
Opcode	2	Contains 6 for OACK packets
Option 1	n	The first option acknowledgment given as a variable-length, null-terminated NVT-ASCII string; this is the same string as in the option request
Value 1	n	The acknowledged value of the first option given as a variable-length, null-terminated NVT-ASCII string; this value may or may not be the same value sent for this option by the client
Option n	n	Second and subsequent option names
Value n	n	Second and subsequent option values

32 USENET Article Format

Name

Standard for Interchange of USENET Messages

Abbreviation

none

Status

none

Specifications

RFC 1036

Abstract

RFC 1036 specifies the format of USENET articles exchanged using NNTP and other protocols (notably UUCP). Although similar to RFC 822 mail messages, USENET news articles must include some additional headers, and USENET allows slightly different formats for some headers such as the date header.

Related Specifications

NNTP (RFC 977)

See Also

Format of Electronic Mail Messages (RFC 822)

Comments

RFC 1036 describes some additional information about the transmission of USENET articles using UUCP. This information is not included in this chapter.

Description

USENET, also known as network news, articles follow a format very similar to the electronic mail message format described in RFC 822. News articles have the same basic structure as RFC 822 messages: a block of headers, followed by a single blank line, followed by the article body. Header lines also follow the same basic RFC 822 format: a header name followed by a colon, followed by a space, followed by the header data.

The similarity between news articles and mail messages starts to diverge at this point, however. News articles have their own set of required and optional headers. Some of the headers are similar to equivalent RFC 822 headers while others are generated specifically for network news articles and not for electronic mail messages.

Table 32.1 summarizes the network news headers.

From

The From header specifies the electronic mail address of the person who the article is from. In general, this field is formatted identically to the From field in RFC 822, with a few restrictions.

RFC 822 allows header fields to contain comments enclosed in parentheses. A common Internet custom is to include the full name of the person sending the message in a comment following the email address. RFC 1036 specifies that if a comment is present following the electronic mail address, it *must* be a person's full name.

Following RFC 822 and the previous restriction, the following three formats are possible for RFC 1036 From headers:

From: fred@example.com

From: fred@example.com (Fred)

From: Fred <fred@example.com>

Table 32.1 Network News Header Fields

Header Field	Optional/Required	Description
From	Required	Identifies the electronic mail address of the person sending the message
Date	Required	Indicates the date and time the message was sent
Newsgroups	Required	Indicates the names of the newsgroups to which the message belongs
Subject	Required	Indicates the subject of the message
Message-ID	Required	Specifies a globally unique identifier for the message
Path	Required	Identifies the sequence of hosts through which the message has passed to reach its current location
Followup-To	Optional	Indicates a list of newsgroups to which follow-up messages should be posted
Expires	Optional	Indicates the date and time at which the message should expire
Reply-To	Optional	Identifies the electronic mail address of the person to which electronic mail replies should be sent
Sender	Optional	Identifies the electronic mail address of the person actually submitting the article to the network, if different than that specified in the From header
References	Optional	Specifies a list of message IDs to which the current article is a follow-up
Control	Optional	Indicates an original USENET control message
Distribution	Optional	Limits the scope of an article distribution to a less than world-wide audience
Keywords	Optional	Displays a list of keywords describing the contents of the message
Summary	Optional	Provides a short summary of the message
Approved	Optional	Used by a moderator to approve messages posted to a moderated newsgroup
Lines	Optional	Supplies a count of the number of lines in the body of a message
Xref	Optional	Cross references the groups an article belongs to; this field is used only locally and should not be exchanged between hosts
Organization	Optional	A string indicating the organization associated with the poster or the original posting host

Date

The Date header specifies the date and time the article first entered the news system. The date format used in the news system is less restrictive than that specified in RFC 822. In general, systems should generate RFC 822 compatible dates and accept all the date formats that they can.

In particular, systems should generate and accept dates of the form:

Wdy, DD Mon YY HH:MM:SS TIMEZONE

Systems should also be capable of recognizing this form:

Wdy Mon DD HH:MM:SS YYYY

which is generated by some older news software.

Newsgroups

The Newsgroups header specifies a comma-separated list of newsgroup names to which the article belongs. Systems should ignore any group name that appears to be invalid. In fact, the group name may be valid, but the local server may not receive it for various reasons.

Subject

The Subject header specifies the article subject. If the article is a follow up to a previous article, the Subject header should begin with "Re:" followed by the previous subject line (although follow ups to follow ups should only use a single "Re:").

Message-ID

The Message-ID header specifies a unique message identifier that can be used to reference the article in various contexts. In particular, message IDs are used in NNTP to specify particular articles for retrieval and are used in the References header field to specify the article a follow-up article refers to.

The Message-ID header has the same format as that specified in RFC 822:

```
<unique@full_domain_name>
```

The *unique* portion of the message ID should contain any string that is guaranteed to be unique for the message at the particular host name specified by *full_domain_name.*

Path

The Path header specifies the path the article took to reach the current system. Each time an article is forwarded from one host to another, the receiving host adds its name to the list specified in the Path header. Any characters except letters, digits, periods, and hyphens may be used to separate host names. These characters are used for host names themselves.

A host adds its name to the left side, or front, of the path. That is, if the current path specified for an article is "A!X!Y!Z", then when host A passes the message to host B, host B will modify the Path header to specify "B!A!X!Y!Z".

Followup-To

The Followup-To header is used to specify the newsgroups to which follow-up articles are directed. This header has the same format as the Newsgroups header. When a follow up article is constructed, a news user agent will typically copy the Followup-To header contents to the new Newsgroups header.

Expires

The Expires header specifies the suggested expiration date and time for the message. The field should contain a valid date, in the same format as the Date header. Receiving systems can use this date to help with message expirations. The date can be used to ensure that stale information is purged after its useful life or to ensure that a long-lived article (typically something like a monthly FAQ article) is not removed prematurely.

The exact behavior of a news system acting on the Expires header is system dependent. Some systems may obey the header rigidly, others may use it as a guideline, and still others may ignore it altogether.

Reply-To

The Reply-To header functions identically to the RFC 822 header of the same name. This header specifies the email address of the person to whom electronic mail replies should be directed. This is often the same address specified in the From header, but may reflect a different mailbox name if the user receives mail on a different system than that used to post news articles.

If the Reply-To header is present, the specified address should be used instead of the address in the From field. If no Reply-To header is present, reply mail should be sent to the address in the From header. In no case should mail be sent to the address specified in the Sender header.

Sender

The Sender field specifies the true sender if the message is different than that specified by the From header. For instance, a corporate CEO might draft a press release and give it to another employee for posting in a newsgroup. In this case, the From header would specify the email address of the CEO, the Sender header would specify the email address of the employee, and the Reply-To header might specify the address of someone in the public relations department assigned to handle responses to the press release.

References

The References header is used in follow-up messages to specify the original articles to which the current article is responding. If the original article had no References header itself (that is, it was an original article and not a follow up), then the References header for the follow up should include the message ID of the original article. If the original article contains a References header, the message IDs from the original article should be copied to the new follow up with the message ID of the original article appended to the list.

All message ID strings should include the < and > characters surrounding the unique strings.

Control

The Control header identifies the article as a USENET control message. This header is described in more detail in RFC 1036.

Distribution

The Distribution header specifies a comma-separated list of groups similar to the Newsgroups header. The Distribution header is used to limit the distribution of an article to those systems that also receive the distributions specified on the Distribution line. For instance, if a particular article was only applicable geographically, then the distribution line could be used to specify a distribution that would keep the article local.

Keywords

The Keywords header specifies a list of keywords pertaining to the article. This can be used by a user agent to search for an article.

Summary

The Summary header gives a short summary of the article and can be used in addition to the Subject header to allow a user to select the article for viewing.

Approved

The Approved header is used by newsgroup moderators to indicate that the article has been approved for transmission by the moderator. This header contains the email address of the moderator.

Lines

The Lines header specifies the number of lines in the message body as a decimal integer, which is helpful for users in determining whether to download a large article using a slower transmission link.

Xref

The Xref field is used for local indexing and storage of the article. It is described in more detail in RFC 1036.

Organization

The Organization field is used to specify the organization to which the sender (or the machine the sender used to originally post the article) belongs.

33 User Datagram Protocol

Name

User Datagram Protocol

Abbreviation

UDP

Status

Recommended Standard (STD 6)

Specifications

RFC 768

Abstract

The User Datagram Protocol (UDP) provides a small set of application-oriented features on top of the basic datagram infrastructure provided by the Internet Protocol (IP).

Related Specifications

IP (RFC 791)

See Also

TCP (RFC 793)

Description

UDP provides little more than a thin multiplexing and data-integrity layer on top of IP. In particular, UDP provides port addressing information to allow delivery of UDP datagrams to the correct application process on the receiving host and a checksum covering the UDP data to detect data corruption. UDP does not, however, provide any sequencing or datagram loss protection services. Applications needing these services should use the Transmission Control Protocol (TCP).

Frame Formats

Figure 33.1 shows the basic UDP format. The following sections describe each of the UDP fields in more detail.

Source Port

This field is optional. If used, it indicates the port on the source host from which this UDP datagram was sent. If the port number is not used, it should be set to zero.

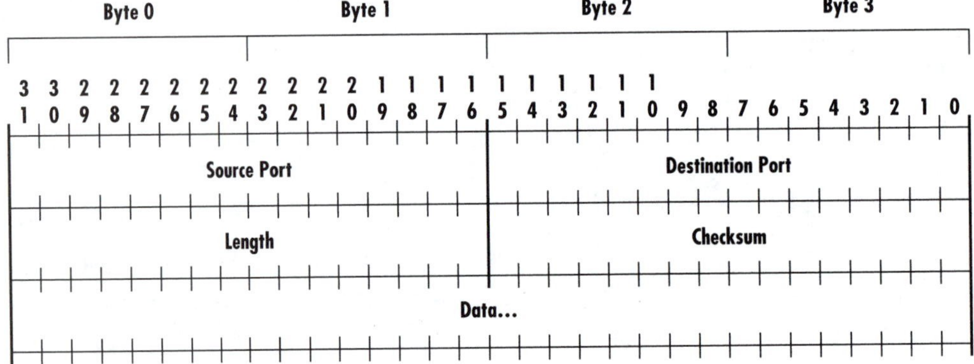

Figure 33.1

The UDP frame format.

Destination Port

This field indicates the destination port number at the host to which this datagram is addressed.

Length

The Length field indicates the length of this UDP datagram in octets. The Length field includes the length of the UDP header. The minimum value of the length field is 8.

Checksum

The Checksum field stores the standard Internet checksum. The checksum is the 16-bit one's complement of the one's complement sum of a pseudo-header composed of fields from the IP header, the UDP header, and the UDP data. If the data is an odd octet length, a zero-byte is added as padding for the checksum computation.

If the calculated checksum is zero, it is transmitted as all ones (-0 in one's complement arithmetic). If the Checksum field is zero, it indicates that the source host did not compute a checksum. In this case, the receiver should always accept the datagram. Setting the Checksum field to zero is sometimes done for datagrams sent to hosts on the local network when such networks already use an error-detection code at the data-link layer. In some cases, this approach can greatly improve performance.

The UDP pseudo-header has the format shown in Figure 33.2.

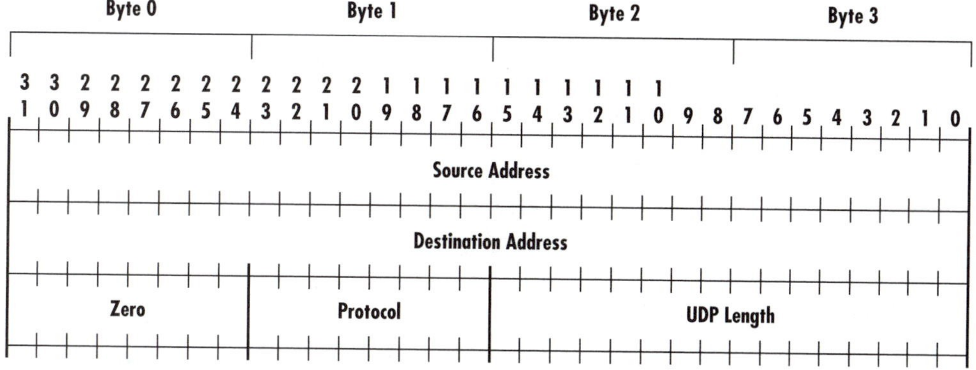

Figure 33.2

The UDP pseudo-header format.

The Source and Destination addresses are standard 32-bit IP addresses. The Protocol field is the IP protocol number for UDP (17). The UDP Length field contains the length of the UDP datagram in octets.

34 Well-Known Ports

Name

Well-Known Ports

Status

The well-known ports are listed in the Assigned Numbers standard (STD 2) document.

Specifications

Well-known ports are registered with the IANA and are published periodically as part of the Assigned Numbers document, currently RFC 1700. The most recent version of the well-known port numbers section of the Assigned Numbers document is located at **ftp://ftp.isi.edu/in-notes/iana/assignments/port-numbers**.

Abstract

The Internet Assigned Numbers Authority (IANA) is responsible for the registration of well-known port numbers for Internet protocols. Periodically, IANA publishes this list as part of the Assigned Numbers RFC.

Related Specifications

TCP (RFC 793), UDP (RFC 768)

Description

The TCP and UDP port number spaces are divided into three sections:

- Well-known ports (0 through 1023)
- Registered ports (1024 through 49151)
- Dynamic or private ports (49152 through 65535)

The first section, well-known ports, is controlled by the IANA. Ports in this range are assigned to well-known (and sometimes not-so-well-known) Internet services. In general, well-known services are assigned the same port number for both TCP and UDP service, even if the service is not available using both TCP and UDP, because it simplifies administration and eliminates confusion. Table 34.1 shows the registered well-known TCP and UDP ports.

The IANA provides a registration service for the second section of ports. Although IANA does not control the use of ports in this section, it provides the registration service to help the Internet community document the use of ports in this range for common network services. Ports in this section can be used by anyone, but services that become popular should be registered with the IANA. Consult the current Assigned Numbers document or **ftp://ftp.isi.edu/in-notes/iana/assignments/port-numbers** for more information about services using port numbers in this range.

The third section of port addresses, dynamic or private ports, is not administered or controlled in any way. Ports in this range are typically used dynamically by client software rather than assigned to servers.

> *+9: The current Assigned Numbers document and **ftp://ftp.isi.edu/in-notes/iana/assignments/port-numbers** contains some additional ports that are not included in Table 34.1. See these sources for more information about a particular well-known port.*

Table 34.1 TCP and UDP Well-Known Port Numbers

Service Name	Port	Description
	0/tcp	Reserved
	0/udp	Reserved
tcpmux	1/tcp	TCP Port Service Multiplexer

Continued

Table 34.1 TCP and UDP Well-Known Port Numbers (Continued)

Service Name	Port	Description
tcpmux	1/udp	TCP Port Service Multiplexer
compressnet	2/tcp	Management utility
compressnet	2/udp	Management utility
compressnet	3/tcp	Compression process
compressnet	3/udp	Compression process
	4/tcp	Unassigned
	4/udp	Unassigned
rje	5/tcp	Remote Job Entry
rje	5/udp	Remote Job Entry
	6/tcp	Unassigned
	6/udp	Unassigned
echo	7/tcp	Echo
echo	7/udp	Echo
	8/tcp	Unassigned
	8/udp	Unassigned
discard	9/tcp	Discard
discard	9/udp	Discard
	10/tcp	Unassigned
	10/udp	Unassigned
systat	11/tcp	Active users
systat	11/udp	Active users
	12/tcp	Unassigned
	12/udp	Unassigned
daytime	13/tcp	Daytime
daytime	13/udp	Daytime
	14/tcp	Unassigned
	14/udp	Unassigned
	15/tcp	Unassigned [was netstat]
	15/udp	Unassigned
	16/tcp	Unassigned
	16/udp	Unassigned

Continued

Table 34.1 TCP and UDP Well-Known Port Numbers (Continued)

Service Name	Port	Description
qotd	17/tcp	Quote of the Day
qotd	17/udp	Quote of the Day
msp	18/tcp	Message Send Protocol
msp	18/udp	Message Send Protocol
chargen	19/tcp	Character Generator
chargen	19/udp	Character Generator
ftp-data	20/tcp	File transfer [Default Data]
ftp-data	20/udp	File transfer [Default Data]
ftp	21/tcp	File transfer [Control]
ftp	21/udp	File Transfer [Control]
ssh	22/tcp	SSH Remote Login Protocol
ssh	22/udp	SSH Remote Login Protocol
telnet	23/tcp	Telnet
telnet	23/udp	Telnet
	24/tcp	Any private mail system
	24/udp	Any private mail system
smtp	25/tcp	Simple Mail Transfer
smtp	25/udp	Simple Mail Transfer
	26/tcp	Unassigned
	26/udp	Unassigned
nsw-fe	27/tcp	NSW User System FE
nsw-fe	27/udp	NSW User System FE
	28/tcp	Unassigned
	28/udp	Unassigned
msg-icp	29/tcp	MSG ICP
msg-icp	29/udp	MSG ICP
	30/tcp	Unassigned
	30/udp	Unassigned
msg-auth	31/tcp	MSG authentication

Continued

Table 34.1 TCP and UDP Well-Known Port Numbers (Continued)

Service Name	Port	Description
msg-auth	31/udp	MSG authentication
	32/tcp	Unassigned
	32/udp	Unassigned
dsp	33/tcp	Display Support Protocol
dsp	33/udp	Display Support Protocol
	34/tcp	Unassigned
	34/udp	Unassigned
	35/tcp	Any private printer server
	35/udp	Any private printer server
	36/tcp	Unassigned
	36/udp	Unassigned
time	37/tcp	Time
time	37/udp	Time
rap	38/tcp	Route Access Protocol
rap	38/udp	Route Access Protocol
rlp	39/tcp	Resource Location Protocol
rlp	39/udp	Resource Location Protocol
	40/tcp	Unassigned
	40/udp	Unassigned
graphics	41/tcp	Graphics
graphics	41/udp	Graphics
nameserver	42/tcp	Host Name Server
nameserver	42/udp	Host Name Server
nicname	43/tcp	Who Is
nicname	43/udp	Who Is
mpm-flags	44/tcp	MPM FLAGS Protocol
mpm-flags	44/udp	MPM FLAGS Protocol
mpm	45/tcp	Message Processing Module [recv]
mpm	45/udp	Message Processing Module [recv]
mpm-snd	46/tcp	MPM [default send]

Continued

Table 34.1 TCP and UDP Well-Known Port Numbers (Continued)

Service Name	Port	Description
mpm-snd	46/udp	MPM [default send]
ni-ftp	47/tcp	NI FTP
ni-ftp	47/udp	NI FTP
auditd	48/tcp	Digital Audit Daemon
auditd	48/udp	Digital Audit Daemon
bbn-login	49/tcp	Login Host Protocol (TACACS)
bbn-login	49/udp	Login Host Protocol (TACACS)
re-mail-ck	50/tcp	Remote Mail Checking Protocol
re-mail-ck	50/udp	Remote Mail Checking Protocol
la-maint	51/tcp	IMP Logical Address Maintenance
la-maint	51/udp	IMP Logical Address Maintenance
xns-time	52/tcp	XNS Time Protocol
xns-time	52/udp	XNS Time Protocol
domain	53/tcp	Domain Name Server
domain	53/udp	Domain Name Server
xns-ch	54/tcp	XNS Clearinghouse
xns-ch	54/udp	XNS Clearinghouse
isi-gl	55/tcp	ISI Graphics Language
isi-gl	55/udp	ISI Graphics Language
xns-auth	56/tcp	XNS Authentication
xns-auth	56/udp	XNS Authentication
	57/tcp	Any private terminal access
	57/udp	Any private terminal access
xns-mail	58/tcp	XNS Mail
xns-mail	58/udp	XNS Mail
	59/tcp	Any private file service
	59/udp	Any private file service
	60/tcp	Unassigned
	60/udp	Unassigned
ni-mail	61/tcp	NI MAIL
ni-mail	61/udp	NI MAIL
acas	62/tcp	ACA Services

Continued

Table 34.1 TCP and UDP Well-Known Port Numbers (Continued)

Service Name	Port	Description
acas	62/udp	ACA Services
whois++	63/tcp	whois++
whois++	63/udp	whois++
covia	64/tcp	Communications Integrator (CI)
covia	64/udp	Communications Integrator (CI)
tacacs-ds	65/tcp	TACACS-Database Service
tacacs-ds	65/udp	TACACS-Database Service
sql*net	66/tcp	Oracle SQL*NET
sql*net	66/udp	Oracle SQL*NET
bootps	67/tcp	Bootstrap Protocol Server
bootps	67/udp	Bootstrap Protocol Server
bootpc	68/tcp	Bootstrap Protocol Client
bootpc	68/udp	Bootstrap Protocol Client
tftp	69/tcp	Trivial File Transfer
tftp	69/udp	Trivial File Transfer
gopher	70/tcp	Gopher
gopher	70/udp	Gopher
netrjs-1	71/tcp	Remote Job Service
netrjs-1	71/udp	Remote Job Service
netrjs-2	72/tcp	Remote Job Service
netrjs-2	72/udp	Remote Job Service
netrjs-3	73/tcp	Remote Job Service
netrjs-3	73/udp	Remote Job Service
netrjs-4	74/tcp	Remote Job Service
netrjs-4	74/udp	Remote Job Service
	75/tcp	Any private dial out service
	75/udp	Any private dial out service
deos	76/tcp	Distributed External Object Store
deos	76/udp	Distributed External Object Store
	77/tcp	Any private RJE service
	77/udp	Any private RJE service

Continued

Table 34.1 TCP and UDP Well-Known Port Numbers (Continued)

Service Name	Port	Description
vettcp	78/tcp	vettcp
vettcp	78/udp	vettcp
finger	79/tcp	Finger
finger	79/udp	Finger
http	80/tcp	World Wide Web HTTP
http	80/udp	World Wide Web HTTP
www-http	80/tcp	World Wide Web HTTP
www-http	80/udp	World Wide Web HTTP
hosts2-ns	81/tcp	HOSTS2 Name Server
hosts2-ns	81/udp	HOSTS2 Name Server
xfer	82/tcp	XFER Utility
xfer	82/udp	XFER Utility
mit-ml-dev	83/tcp	MIT ML Device
mit-ml-dev	83/udp	MIT ML Device
ctf	84/tcp	Common Trace Facility
ctf	84/udp	Common Trace Facility
mit-ml-dev	85/tcp	MIT ML Device
mit-ml-dev	85/udp	MIT ML Device
mfcobol	86/tcp	Micro Focus Cobol
mfcobol	86/udp	Micro Focus Cobol
	87/tcp	Any private terminal link
	87/udp	Any private terminal link
kerberos	88/tcp	Kerberos
kerberos	88/udp	Kerberos
su-mit-tg	89/tcp	SU/MIT Telnet Gateway
su-mit-tg	89/udp	SU/MIT Telnet Gateway
dnsix	90/tcp	DNSIX Securit Attribute Token Map
dnsix	90/udp	DNSIX Securit Attribute Token Map
mit-dov	91/tcp	MIT Dover Spooler
mit-dov	91/udp	MIT Dover Spooler
npp	92/tcp	Network Printing Protocol

Continued

Table 34.1 TCP and UDP Well-Known Port Numbers (Continued)

Service Name	Port	Description
npp	92/udp	Network Printing Protocol
dcp	93/tcp	Device Control Protocol
dcp	93/udp	Device Control Protocol
objcall	94/tcp	Tivoli Object Dispatcher
objcall	94/udp	Tivoli Object Dispatcher
supdup	95/tcp	SUPDUP
supdup	95/udp	SUPDUP
dixie	96/tcp	DIXIE Protocol Specification
dixie	96/udp	DIXIE Protocol Specification
swift-rvf	97/tcp	Swift Remote Virtural File Protocol
swift-rvf	97/udp	Swift Remote Virtural File Protocol
tacnews	98/tcp	TAC News
tacnews	98/udp	TAC News
metagram	99/tcp	Metagram Relay
metagram	99/udp	Metagram Relay
newacct	100/tcp	[unauthorized use]
hostname	101/tcp	NIC Host Name Server
hostname	101/udp	NIC Host Name Server
iso-tsap	102/tcp	ISO-TSAP Class 0
iso-tsap	102/udp	ISO-TSAP Class 0
gppitnp	103/tcp	Genesis Point-to-Point Trans Net
gppitnp	103/udp	Genesis Point-to-Point Trans Net
acr-nema	104/tcp	ACR-NEMA Digital Imag. & Comm. 300
acr-nema	104/udp	ACR-NEMA Digital Imag. & Comm. 300
csnet-ns	105/tcp	Mailbox Name Nameserver
csnet-ns	105/udp	Mailbox Name Nameserver
3com-tsmux	106/tcp	3COM-TSMUX
3com-tsmux	106/udp	3COM-TSMUX
rtelnet	107/tcp	Remote Telnet Service
rtelnet	107/udp	Remote Telnet Service
snagas	108/tcp	SNA Gateway Access Server

Continued

Table 34.1 TCP and UDP Well-Known Port Numbers (Continued)

Service Name	Port	Description
snagas	108/udp	SNA Gateway Access Server
pop2	109/tcp	Post Office Protocol - Version 2
pop2	109/udp	Post Office Protocol - Version 2
pop3	110/tcp	Post Office Protocol - Version 3
pop3	110/udp	Post Office Protocol - Version 3
sunrpc	111/tcp	SUN Remote Procedure Call
sunrpc	111/udp	SUN Remote Procedure Call
mcidas	112/tcp	McIDAS Data Transmission Protocol
mcidas	112/udp	McIDAS Data Transmission Protocol
auth	113/tcp	Authentication Service
auth	113/udp	Authentication Service
audionews	114/tcp	Audio News Multicast
audionews	114/udp	Audio News Multicast
sftp	115/tcp	Simple File Transfer Protocol
sftp	115/udp	Simple File Transfer Protocol
ansanotify	116/tcp	ANSA REX Notify
ansanotify	116/udp	ANSA REX Notify
uucp-path	117/tcp	UUCP Path Service
uucp-path	117/udp	UUCP Path Service
sqlserv	118/tcp	SQL Services
sqlserv	118/udp	SQL Services
nntp	119/tcp	Network News Transfer Protocol
nntp	119/udp	Network News Transfer Protocol
cfdptkt	120/tcp	CFDPTKT
cfdptkt	120/udp	CFDPTKT
erpc	121/tcp	Encore Expedited Remote Pro.Call
erpc	121/udp	Encore Expedited Remote Pro.Call
smakynet	122/tcp	SMAKYNET
smakynet	122/udp	SMAKYNET
ntp	123/tcp	Network Time Protocol
ntp	123/udp	Network Time Protocol

Continued

Table 34.1 TCP and UDP Well-Known Port Numbers (Continued)

Service Name	Port	Description
ansatrader	124/tcp	ANSA REX Trader
ansatrader	124/udp	ANSA REX Trader
locus-map	125/tcp	Locus PC-Interface Net Map Ser
locus-map	125/udp	Locus PC-Interface Net Map Ser
unitary	126/tcp	Unisys Unitary Login
unitary	126/udp	Unisys Unitary Login
locus-con	127/tcp	Locus PC-Interface Conn Server
locus-con	127/udp	Locus PC-Interface Conn Server
gss-xlicen	128/tcp	GSS X License Verification
gss-xlicen	128/udp	GSS X License Verification
pwdgen	129/tcp	Password Generator Protocol
pwdgen	129/udp	Password Generator Protocol
cisco-fna	130/tcp	cisco FNATIVE
cisco-fna	130/udp	cisco FNATIVE
cisco-tna	131/tcp	cisco TNATIVE
cisco-tna	131/udp	cisco TNATIVE
cisco-sys	132/tcp	cisco SYSMAINT
cisco-sys	132/udp	cisco SYSMAINT
statsrv	133/tcp	Statistics Service
statsrv	133/udp	Statistics Service
ingres-net	134/tcp	INGRES-NET Service
ingres-net	134/udp	INGRES-NET Service
loc-srv	135/tcp	Location Service
loc-srv	135/udp	Location Service
profile	136/tcp	PROFILE Naming System
profile	136/udp	PROFILE Naming System
netbios-ns	137/tcp	NETBIOS Name Service
netbios-ns	137/udp	NETBIOS Name Service
netbios-dgm	138/tcp	NETBIOS Datagram Service
netbios-dgm	138/udp	NETBIOS Datagram Service
netbios-ssn	139/tcp	NETBIOS Session Service

Continued

Table 34.1 TCP and UDP Well-Known Port Numbers (Continued)

Service Name	Port	Description
netbios-ssn	139/udp	NETBIOS Session Service
emfis-data	140/tcp	EMFIS Data Service
emfis-data	140/udp	EMFIS Data Service
emfis-cntl	141/tcp	EMFIS Control Service
emfis-cntl	141/udp	EMFIS Control Service
bl-idm	142/tcp	Britton-Lee IDM
bl-idm	142/udp	Britton-Lee IDM
imap2	143/tcp	Interim Mail Access Protocol v2
imap2	143/udp	Interim Mail Access Protocol v2
news	144/tcp	NewS
news	144/udp	NewS
uaac	145/tcp	UAAC Protocol
uaac	145/udp	UAAC Protocol
iso-tp0	146/tcp	ISO-IP0
iso-tp0	146/udp	ISO-IP0
iso-ip	147/tcp	ISO-IP
iso-ip	147/udp	ISO-IP
cronus	148/tcp	CRONUS-SUPPORT
cronus	148/udp	CRONUS-SUPPORT
aed-512	149/tcp	AED 512 Emulation Service
aed-512	149/udp	AED 512 Emulation Service
sql-net	150/tcp	SQL-NET
sql-net	150/udp	SQL-NET
hems	151/tcp	HEMS
hems	151/udp	HEMS
bftp	152/tcp	Background File Transfer Program
bftp	152/udp	Background File Transfer Program
sgmp	153/tcp	SGMP
sgmp	153/udp	SGMP
netsc-prod	154/tcp	NETSC
netsc-prod	154/udp	NETSC

Continued

Table 34.1 TCP and UDP Well-Known Port Numbers (Continued)

Service Name	Port	Description
netsc-dev	155/tcp	NETSC
netsc-dev	155/udp	NETSC
sqlsrv	156/tcp	SQL Service
sqlsrv	156/udp	SQL Service
knet-cmp	157/tcp	KNET/VM Command/Message Protocol
knet-cmp	157/udp	KNET/VM Command/Message Protocol
pcmail-srv	158/tcp	PCMail Server
pcmail-srv	158/udp	PCMail Server
nss-routing	159/tcp	NSS-Routing
nss-routing	159/udp	NSS-Routing
sgmp-traps	160/tcp	SGMP-TRAPS
sgmp-traps	160/udp	SGMP-TRAPS
snmp	161/tcp	SNMP
snmp	161/udp	SNMP
snmptrap	162/tcp	SNMPTRAP
snmptrap	162/udp	SNMPTRAP
cmip-man	163/tcp	CMIP/TCP Manager
cmip-man	163/udp	CMIP/TCP Manager
cmip-agent	164/tcp	CMIP/TCP Agent
smip-agent	164/udp	CMIP/TCP Agent
xns-courier	165/tcp	Xerox
xns-courier	165/udp	Xerox
s-net	166/tcp	Sirius Systems
s-net	166/udp	Sirius Systems
namp	167/tcp	NAMP
namp	167/udp	NAMP
rsvd	168/tcp	RSVD
rsvd	168/udp	RSVD
send	169/tcp	SEND
send	169/udp	SEND
print-srv	170/tcp	Network PostScript

Continued

Table 34.1 TCP and UDP Well-Known Port Numbers (Continued)

Service Name	Port	Description
print-srv	170/udp	Network PostScript
multiplex	171/tcp	Network Innovations Multiplex
multiplex	171/udp	Network Innovations Multiplex
cl/1	172/tcp	Network Innovations CL/1
cl/1	172/udp	Network Innovations CL/1
xyplex-mux	173/tcp	Xyplex
xyplex-mux	173/udp	Xyplex
mailq	174/tcp	MAILQ
mailq	174/udp	MAILQ
vmnet	175/tcp	VMNET
vmnet	175/udp	VMNET
genrad-mux	176/tcp	GENRAD-MUX
genrad-mux	176/udp	GENRAD-MUX
xdmcp	177/tcp	X Display Manager Control Protocol
xdmcp	177/udp	X Display Manager Control Protocol
nextstep	178/tcp	NextStep Window Server
NextStep	178/udp	NextStep Window Server
bgp	179/tcp	Border Gateway Protocol
bgp	179/udp	Border Gateway Protocol
ris	180/tcp	Intergraph
ris	180/udp	Intergraph
unify	181/tcp	Unify
unify	181/udp	Unify
audit	182/tcp	Unisys Audit SITP
audit	182/udp	Unisys Audit SITP
ocbinder	183/tcp	OCBinder
ocbinder	183/udp	OCBinder
ocserver	184/tcp	OCServer
ocserver	184/udp	OCServer
remote-kis	185/tcp	Remote-KIS
remote-kis	185/udp	Remote-KIS

Continued

Table 34.1 TCP and UDP Well-Known Port Numbers (Continued)

Service Name	Port	Description
kis	186/tcp	KIS Protocol
kis	186/udp	KIS Protocol
aci	187/tcp	Application Communication Interface
aci	187/udp	Application Communication Interface
mumps	188/tcp	Plus Five's MUMPS
mumps	188/udp	Plus Five's MUMPS
qft	189/tcp	Queued File Transport
qft	189/udp	Queued File Transport
gacp	190/tcp	Gateway Access Control Protocol
cacp	190/udp	Gateway Access Control Protocol
prospero	191/tcp	Prospero Directory Service
prospero	191/udp	Prospero Directory Service
osu-nms	192/tcp	OSU Network Monitoring System
osu-nms	192/udp	OSU Network Monitoring System
srmp	193/tcp	Spider Remote Monitoring Protocol
srmp	193/udp	Spider Remote Monitoring Protocol
irc	194/tcp	Internet Relay Chat Protocol
irc	194/udp	Internet Relay Chat Protocol
dn6-nlm-aud	195/tcp	DNSIX Network Level Module Audit
dn6-nlm-aud	195/udp	DNSIX Network Level Module Audit
dn6-smm-red	196/tcp	DNSIX Session Mgt Module Audit Redir
dn6-smm-red	196/udp	DNSIX Session Mgt Module Audit Redir
dls	197/tcp	Directory Location Service
dls	197/udp	Directory Location Service
dls-mon	198/tcp	Directory Location Service Monitor
dls-mon	198/udp	Directory Location Service Monitor
smux	199/tcp	SMUX
smux	199/udp	SMUX
src	200/tcp	IBM System Resource Controller
src	200/udp	IBM System Resource Controller
at-rtmp	201/tcp	AppleTalk Routing Maintenance

Continued

Table 34.1 TCP and UDP Well-Known Port Numbers (Continued)

Service Name	Port	Description
at-rtmp	201/udp	AppleTalk Routing Maintenance
at-nbp	202/tcp	AppleTalk Name Binding
at-nbp	202/udp	AppleTalk Name Binding
at-3	203/tcp	AppleTalk Unused
at-3	203/udp	AppleTalk Unused
at-echo	204/tcp	AppleTalk Echo
at-echo	204/udp	AppleTalk Echo
at-5	205/tcp	AppleTalk Unused
at-5	205/udp	AppleTalk Unused
at-zis	206/tcp	AppleTalk Zone Information
at-zis	206/udp	AppleTalk Zone Information
at-7	207/tcp	AppleTalk Unused
at-7	207/udp	AppleTalk Unused
at-8	208/tcp	AppleTalk Unused
at-8	208/udp	AppleTalk Unused
qmtp	209/tcp	The Quick Mail Transfer Protocol
qmtp	209/udp	The Quick Mail Transfer Protocol
z39.50	210/tcp	ANSI Z39.50
z39.50	210/udp	ANSI Z39.50
914c/g	211/tcp	Texas Instruments 914C/G Terminal
914c/g	211/udp	Texas Instruments 914C/G Terminal
anet	212/tcp	ATEXSSTR
anet	212/udp	ATEXSSTR
ipx	213/tcp	IPX
ipx	213/udp	IPX
vmpwscs	214/tcp	VM PWSCS
vmpwscs	214/udp	VM PWSCS
softpc	215/tcp	Insignia Solutions
softpc	215/udp	Insignia Solutions
CAIlic	216/tcp	Computer Associates Int'l License Server
CAIlic	216/udp	Computer Associates Int'l License Server

Continued

Table 34.1 TCP and UDP Well-Known Port Numbers (Continued)

Service Name	Port	Description
dbase	217/tcp	dBASE Unix
dbase	217/udp	dBASE Unix
mpp	218/tcp	Netix Message Posting Protocol
mpp	218/udp	Netix Message Posting Protocol
uarps	219/tcp	Unisys ARPs
uarps	219/udp	Unisys ARPs
imap3	220/tcp	Interactive Mail Access Protocol v3
imap3	220/udp	Interactive Mail Access Protocol v3
fln-spx	221/tcp	Berkeley rlogind with SPX auth
fln-spx	221/udp	Berkeley rlogind with SPX auth
rsh-spx	222/tcp	Berkeley rshd with SPX auth
rsh-spx	222/udp	Berkeley rshd with SPX auth
cdc	223/tcp	Certificate Distribution Center
cdc	223/udp	Certificate Distribution Center
	224-241	Reserved
	242/tcp	Unassigned
	242/udp	Unassigned
sur-meas	243/tcp	Survey Measurement
sur-meas	243/udp	Survey Measurement
	244/tcp	Unassigned
	244/udp	Unassigned
link	245/tcp	LINK
link	245/udp	LINK
dsp3270	246/tcp	Display Systems Protocol
dsp3270	246/udp	Display Systems Protocol
	247-255	Reserved
	256-343	Unassigned
pdap	344/tcp	Prospero Data Access Protocol
pdap	344/udp	Prospero Data Access Protocol
pawserv	345/tcp	Perf Analysis Workbench
pawserv	345/udp	Perf Analysis Workbench

Continued

Table 34.1 TCP and UDP Well-Known Port Numbers (Continued)

Service Name	Port	Description
zserv	346/tcp	Zebra server
zserv	346/udp	Zebra server
fatserv	347/tcp	Fatmen Server
fatserv	347/udp	Fatmen Server
csi-sgwp	348/tcp	Cabletron Management Protocol
csi-sgwp	348/udp	Cabletron Management Protocol
	349-370	Unassigned
clearcase	371/tcp	Clearcase
clearcase	371/udp	Clearcase
ulistserv	372/tcp	Unix Listserv
ulistserv	372/udp	Unix Listserv
legent-1	373/tcp	Legent Corporation
legent-1	373/udp	Legent Corporation
legent-2	374/tcp	Legent Corporation
legent-2	374/udp	Legent Corporation
hassle	375/tcp	Hassle
hassle	375/udp	Hassle
nip	376/tcp	Amiga Envoy Network Inquiry Proto
nip	376/udp	Amiga Envoy Network Inquiry Proto
tnETOS	377/tcp	NEC Corporation
tnETOS	377/udp	NEC Corporation
dsETOS	378/tcp	NEC Corporation
dsETOS	378/udp	NEC Corporation
is99c	379/tcp	TIA/EIA/IS-99 modem client
is99c	379/udp	TIA/EIA/IS-99 modem client
is99s	380/tcp	TIA/EIA/IS-99 modem server
is99s	380/udp	TIA/EIA/IS-99 modem server
hp-collector	381/tcp	hp performance data collector
hp-collector	381/udp	hp performance data collector
hp-managed-node	382/tcp	hp performance data managed node
hp-managed-node	382/udp	hp performance data managed node

Continued

Table 34.1 TCP and UDP Well-Known Port Numbers (Continued)

Service Name	Port	Description
hp-alarm-mgr	383/tcp	hp performance data alarm manager
hp-alarm-mgr	383/udp	hp performance data alarm manager
arns	384/tcp	A Remote Network Server System
arns	384/udp	A Remote Network Server System
ibm-app	385/tcp	IBM Application
ibm-app	385/tcp	IBM Application
asa	386/tcp	ASA Message Router Object Def.
asa	386/udp	ASA Message Router Object Def.
aurp	387/tcp	Appletalk Update-Based Routing Pro.
aurp	387/udp	Appletalk Update-Based Routing Pro.
unidata-ldm	388/tcp	Unidata LDM Version 4
unidata-ldm	388/udp	Unidata LDM Version 4
ldap	389/tcp	Lightweight Directory Access Protocol
ldap	389/udp	Lightweight Directory Access Protocol
uis	390/tcp	UIS
uis	390/udp	UIS
synotics-relay	391/tcp	SynOptics SNMP Relay Port
synotics-relay	391/udp	SynOptics SNMP Relay Port
synotics-broker	392/tcp	SynOptics Port Broker Port
synotics-broker	392/udp	SynOptics Port Broker Port
dis	393/tcp	Data Interpretation System
dis	393/udp	Data Interpretation System
embl-ndt	394/tcp	EMBL Nucleic Data Transfer
embl-ndt	394/udp	EMBL Nucleic Data Transfer
netcp	395/tcp	NETscout Control Protocol
netcp	395/udp	NETscout Control Protocol
netware-ip	396/tcp	Novell Netware over IP
netware-ip	396/udp	Novell Netware over IP
mptn	397/tcp	Multi Protocol Trans. Net.
mptn	397/udp	Multi Protocol Trans. Net.
kryptolan	398/tcp	Kryptolan

Continued

Table 34.1 TCP and UDP Well-Known Port Numbers (Continued)

Service Name	Port	Description
kryptolan	398/udp	Kryptolan
iso-tsap-c2	399/tcp	ISO Transport Class 2 Non-Control over TCP
iso-tsap-c2	399/udp	ISO Transport Class 2 Non-Control over TCP
work-sol	400/tcp	Workstation Solutions
work-sol	400/udp	Workstation Solutions
ups	401/tcp	Uninterruptible Power Supply
ups	401/udp	Uninterruptible Power Supply
genie	402/tcp	Genie Protocol
genie	402/udp	Genie Protocol
decap	403/tcp	decap
decap	403/udp	decap
nced	404/tcp	nced
nced	404/udp	nced
ncld	405/tcp	ncld
ncld	405/udp	ncld
imsp	406/tcp	Interactive Mail Support Protocol
imsp	406/udp	Interactive Mail Support Protocol
timbuktu	407/tcp	Timbuktu
timbuktu	407/udp	Timbuktu
prm-sm	408/tcp	Prospero Resource Manager Sys. Man.
prm-sm	408/udp	Prospero Resource Manager Sys. Man.
prm-nm	409/tcp	Prospero Resource Manager Node Man.
prm-nm	409/udp	Prospero Resource Manager Node Man.
decladebug	410/tcp	DECLadebug Remote Debug Protocol
decladebug	410/udp	DECLadebug Remote Debug Protocol
rmt	411/tcp	Remote MT Protocol
rmt	411/udp	Remote MT Protocol
synoptics-trap	412/tcp	Trap Convention Port
synoptics-trap	412/udp	Trap Convention Port
smsp	413/tcp	SMSP
smsp	413/udp	SMSP

Continued

Table 34.1 TCP and UDP Well-Known Port Numbers (Continued)

Service Name	Port	Description
infoseek	414/tcp	InfoSeek
infoseek	414/udp	InfoSeek
bnet	415/tcp	BNet
bnet	415/udp	BNet
silverplatter	416/tcp	Silverplatter
silverplatter	416/udp	Silverplatter
onmux	417/tcp	Onmux
onmux	417/udp	Onmux
hyper-g	418/tcp	Hyper-G
hyper-g	418/udp	Hyper-G
ariel1	419/tcp	Ariel
ariel1	419/udp	Ariel
smpte	420/tcp	SMPTE
smpte	420/udp	SMPTE
ariel2	421/tcp	Ariel
ariel2	421/udp	Ariel
ariel3	422/tcp	Ariel
ariel3	422/udp	Ariel
opc-job-start	423/tcp	IBM Operations Planning and Control Start
opc-job-start	423/udp	IBM Operations Planning and Control Start
opc-job-track	424/tcp	IBM Operations Planning and Control Track
opc-job-track	424/udp	IBM Operations Planning and Control Track
icad-el	425/tcp	ICAD
icad-el	425/udp	ICAD
smartsdp	426/tcp	smartsdp
smartsdp	426/udp	smartsdp
svrloc	427/tcp	Server Location
svrloc	427/udp	Server Location
ocs_cmu	428/tcp	OCS_CMU
ocs_cmu	428/udp	OCS_CMU
ocs_amu	429/tcp	OCS_AMU

Continued

Table 34.1 TCP and UDP Well-Known Port Numbers (Continued)

Service Name	Port	Description
ocs_amu	429/udp	OCS_AMU
utmpsd	430/tcp	UTMPSD
utmpsd	430/udp	UTMPSD
utmpcd	431/tcp	UTMPCD
utmpcd	431/udp	UTMPCD
iasd	432/tcp	IASD
iasd	432/udp	IASD
nnsp	433/tcp	NNSP
nnsp	433/udp	NNSP
mobileip-agent	434/tcp	MobileIP-Agent
mobileip-agent	434/udp	MobileIP-Agent
mobilip-mn	435/tcp	MobilIP-MN
mobilip-mn	435/udp	MobilIP-MN
dna-cml	436/tcp	DNA-CML
dna-cml	436/udp	DNA-CML
comscm	437/tcp	comscm
comscm	437/udp	comscm
dsfgw	438/tcp	dsfgw
dsfgw	438/udp	dsfgw
dasp	439/tcp	dasp Thomas Obermair
dasp	439/udp	dasp tommy@inlab.m.eunet.de
sgcp	440/tcp	sgcp
sgcp	440/udp	sgcp
decvms-sysmgt	441/tcp	decvms-sysmgt
decvms-sysmgt	441/udp	decvms-sysmgt
cvc_hostd	442/tcp	cvc_hostd
cvc_hostd	442/udp	cvc_hostd
https	443/tcp	https MCom
https	443/udp	https MCom
snpp	444/tcp	Simple Network Paging Protocol
snpp	444/udp	Simple Network Paging Protocol

Continued

Table 34.1 TCP and UDP Well-Known Port Numbers (Continued)

Service Name	Port	Description
microsoft-ds	445/tcp	Microsoft-DS
microsoft-ds	445/udp	Microsoft-DS
ddm-rdb	446/tcp	DDM-RDB
ddm-rdb	446/udp	DDM-RDB
ddm-dfm	447/tcp	DDM-RFM
ddm-dfm	447/udp	DDM-RFM
ddm-byte	448/tcp	DDM-BYTE
ddm-byte	448/udp	DDM-BYTE
as-servermap	449/tcp	AS Server Mapper
as-servermap	449/udp	AS Server Mapper
tserver	450/tcp	TServer
tserver	450/udp	TServer
sfs-smp-net	451/tcp	Cray Network Semaphore server
sfs-smp-net	451/udp	Cray Network Semaphore server
sfs-config	452/tcp	Cray SFS config server
sfs-config	452/udp	Cray SFS config server
creativeserver	453/tcp	CreativeServer
creativeserver	453/udp	CreativeServer
contentserver	454/tcp	ContentServer
contentserver	454/udp	ContentServer
creativepartnr	455/tcp	CreativePartnr
creativepartnr	455/udp	CreativePartnr
macon-tcp	456/tcp	macon-tcp
macon-udp	456/udp	macon-udp
scohelp	457/tcp	scohelp
scohelp	457/udp	scohelp
appleqtc	458/tcp	Apple QuickTime
appleqtc	458/udp	Apple QuickTime
ampr-rcmd	459/tcp	ampr-rcmd
ampr-rcmd	459/udp	ampr-rcmd
skronk	460/tcp	skronk

Continued

Table 34.1 TCP and UDP Well-Known Port Numbers (Continued)

Service Name	Port	Description
skronk	460/udp	skronk
datasurfsrv	461/tcp	DataRampSrv
datasurfsrv	461/udp	DataRampSrv
datasurfsrvsec	462/tcp	DataRampSrvSec
datasurfsrvsec	462/udp	DataRampSrvSec
alpes	463/tcp	alpes
alpes	463/udp	alpes
kpasswd	464/tcp	kpasswd
kpasswd	464/udp	kpasswd
ssmtp	465/tcp	ssmtp
ssmtp	465/udp	ssmtp
digital-vrc	466/tcp	digital-vrc
digital-vrc	466/udp	digital-vrc
mylex-mapd	467/tcp	mylex-mapd
mylex-mapd	467/udp	mylex-mapd
photuris	468/tcp	proturis
photuris	468/udp	proturis
rcp	469/tcp	Radio Control Protocol
rcp	469/udp	Radio Control Protocol
scx-proxy	470/tcp	scx-proxy
scx-proxy	470/udp	scx-proxy
mondex	471/tcp	Mondex
mondex	471/udp	Mondex
ljk-login	472/tcp	ljk-login
ljk-login	472/udp	ljk-login
hybrid-pop	473/tcp	hybrid-pop
hybrid-pop	473/udp	hybrid-pop
tn-tl-w1	474/tcp	tn-tl-w1
tn-tl-w2	474/udp	tn-tl-w2
tcpnethaspsrv	475/tcp	tcpnethaspsrv
tcpnethaspsrv	475/tcp	tcpnethaspsrv

Continued

Table 34.1 TCP and UDP Well-Known Port Numbers (Continued)

Service Name	Port	Description
tn-tl-fd1	476/tcp	tn-tl-fd1
tn-tl-fd1	476/udp	tn-tl-fd1
ss7ns	477/tcp	ss7ns
ss7ns	477/udp	ss7ns
spsc	478/tcp	spsc
spsc	478/udp	spsc
iafserver	479/tcp	iafserver
iafserver	479/udp	iafserver
iafdbase	480/tcp	iafdbase
iafdbase	480/udp	iafdbase
ph	481/tcp	Ph service
ph	481/udp	Ph service
bgs-nsi	482/tcp	bgs-nsi
bgs-nsi	482/udp	bgs-nsi
ulpnet	483/tcp	ulpnet
ulpnet	483/udp	ulpnet
integra-sme	484/tcp	Integra Software Management Environment
integra-sme	484/udp	Integra Software Management Environment
powerburst	485/tcp	Air Soft Power Burst
powerburst	485/udp	Air Soft Power Burst
avian	486/tcp	avian
avian	486/udp	avian
saft	487/tcp	saft
saft	487/udp	saft
gss-http	488/tcp	gss-http
gss-http	488/udp	gss-http
nest-protocol	489/tcp	nest-protocol
nest-protocol	489/udp	nest-protocol
micom-pfs	490/tcp	micom-pfs
micom-pfs	490/udp	micom-pfs
go-login	491/tcp	go-login

Continued

Table 34.1 TCP and UDP Well-Known Port Numbers (Continued)

Service Name	Port	Description
go-login	491/udp	go-login
ticf-1	492/tcp	Transport Independent Convergence for FNA
ticf-1	492/udp	Transport Independent Convergence for FNA
ticf-2	493/tcp	Transport Independent Convergence for FNA
ticf-2	493/udp	Transport Independent Convergence for FNA
pov-ray	494/tcp	POV-Ray
pov-ray	494/udp	POV-Ray
intecourier	495/tcp	intecourier
intecourier	495/udp	intecourier
pim-rp-disc	496/tcp	PIM-RP-DISC
pim-rp-disc	496/udp	PIM-RP-DISC
dantz	497/tcp	dantz
dantz	497/udp	dantz
siam	498/tcp	siam
siam	498/udp	siam
iso-ill	499/tcp	ISO ILL Protocol
iso-ill	499/udp	ISO ILL Protocol
isakmp	500/tcp	isakmp
isakmp	500/udp	isakmp
stmf	501/tcp	SMTF
stmf	501/udp	SMTF
asa-appl-proto	502/tcp	asa-appl-proto
asa-appl-proto	502/udp	asa-appl-proto
intrinsa	503/tcp	Intrinsa
intrinsa	503/udp	Intrinsa
citadel	504/tcp	citadel
citadel	504/udp	citadel
mailbox-lm	505/tcp	mailbox-lm
mailbox-lm	505/udp	mailbox-lm
ohimsrv	506/tcp	ohimsrv
ohimsrv	506/udp	ohimsrv

Continued

Table 34.1 TCP and UDP Well-Known Port Numbers (Continued)

Service Name	Port	Description
crs	507/tcp	crs
crs	507/udp	crs
xvttp	508/tcp	xvttp
xvttp	508/udp	xvttp
snare	509/tcp	snare
snare	509/udp	snare
fcp	510/tcp	FirstClass Protocol
fcp	510/udp	FirstClass Protocol
mynet-as	511/tcp	mynet-as
mynet-as	511/udp	mynet-as
exec	512/tcp	Remote process execution; authentication performed using passwords and Unix login names
biff	512/udp	Used by mail system to notify users of new mail received; currently receives messages only from processes on the same machine
login	513/tcp	Remote login a la telnet; automatic authentication performed based on privileged port numbers and distributed databases that identify "authentication domains"
who	513/udp	Maintains databases showing who's logged into machines on a local net and the load average of the machine
cmd	514/tcp	Like exec, but automatic authentication is performed as for login server
syslog	514/udp	
printer	515/tcp	spooler
printer	515/udp	spooler
	516/tcp	Unassigned
	516/udp	Unassigned
talk	517/tcp	Like tenex link, but across machine; unfortunately, talk doesn't use the link protocol (this is actually just a rendezvous port from which a tcp connection is established)
talk	517/udp	Like tenex link, but across machine; unfortunately, talk doesn't use the link protocol (this is actually just a rendezvous port from which a tcp connection is established)
ntalk	518/tcp	

Continued

Table 34.1 TCP and UDP Well-Known Port Numbers (Continued)

Service Name	Port	Description
ntalk	518/udp	
utime	519/tcp	unixtime
utime	519/udp	unixtime
efs	520/tcp	Extended file name server
router	520/udp	Local routing process (on site); uses variant of Xerox NS routing information protocol
ripng	521/tcp	ripng
ripng	521/udp	ripng
	522-524	Unassigned
timed	525/tcp	timeserver
timed	525/udp	timeserver
tempo	526/tcp	newdate
tempo	526/udp	newdate
	527-529	Unassigned
courier	530/tcp	rpc
courier	530/udp	rpc
conference	531/tcp	chat
conference	531/udp	chat
netnews	532/tcp	readnews
netnews	532/udp	readnews
netwall	533/tcp	For emergency broadcasts
netwall	533/udp	For emergency broadcasts
	534-538	Unassigned
apertus-ldp	539/tcp	Apertus Technologies Load Determination
apertus-ldp	539/udp	Apertus Technologies Load Determination
uucp	540/tcp	uucpd
uucp	540/udp	uucpd
uucp-rlogin	541/tcp	uucp-rlogin
uucp-rlogin	541/udp	uucp-rlogin
	542/tcp	Unassigned
	542/udp	Unassigned

Continued

Table 34.1 TCP and UDP Well-Known Port Numbers (Continued)

Service Name	Port	Description
klogin	543/tcp	
klogin	543/udp	
kshell	544/tcp	krcmd
kshell	544/udp	krcmd
appleqtcsrvr	545/tcp	appleqtcsrvr
appleqtcsrvr	545/udp	appleqtcsrvr
dhcpv6-client	546/tcp	DHCPv6 Client
dhcpv6-client	546/udp	DHCPv6 Client
dhcpv6-server	547/tcp	DHCPv6 Server
dhcpv6-server	547/udp	DHCPv6 Server
	548/tcp	Unassigned
	548/udp	Unassigned
	549/tcp	Unassigned
	549/udp	Unassigned
new-rwho	550/tcp	new-who
new-rwho	550/udp	new-who
cybercash	551/tcp	cybercash
cybercash	551/udp	cybercash
deviceshare	552/tcp	deviceshare
deviceshare	552/udp	deviceshare
pirp	553/tcp	pirp
pirp	553/udp	pirp
	554/tcp	Unassigned
	554/udp	Unassigned
dsf	555/tcp	
dsf	555/udp	
remotefs	556/tcp	rfs server
remotefs	556/udp	rfs server
openvms-sysipc	557/tcp	openvms-sysipc
openvms-sysipc	557/udp	openvms-sysipc
sdnskmp	558/tcp	SDNSKMP

Continued

Table 34.1 TCP and UDP Well-Known Port Numbers (Continued)

Service Name	Port	Description
sdnskmp	558/udp	SDNSKMP
teedtap	559/tcp	TEEDTAP
teedtap	559/udp	TEEDTAP
rmonitor	560/tcp	rmonitord
rmonitor	560/udp	rmonitord
monitor	561/tcp	
monitor	561/udp	
chshell	562/tcp	chcmd
chshell	562/udp	chcmd
snews	563/tcp	snews
snews	563/udp	snews
9pfs	564/tcp	plan 9 file service
9pfs	564/udp	plan 9 file service
whoami	565/tcp	whoami
whoami	565/udp	whoami
streettalk	566/tcp	streettalk
streettalk	566/udp	streettalk
banyan-rpc	567/tcp	banyan-rpc
banyan-rpc	567/udp	banyan-rpc
ms-shuttle	568/tcp	microsoft shuttle
ms-shuttle	568/udp	microsoft shuttle
ms-rome	569/tcp	microsoft rome
ms-rome	569/udp	microsoft rome
meter	570/tcp	demon
meter	570/udp	demon
meter	571/tcp	udemon
meter	571/udp	udemon
sonar	572/tcp	sonar
sonar	572/udp	sonar
banyan-vip	573/tcp	banyan-vip
banyan-vip	573/udp	banyan-vip

Continued

Table 34.1 TCP and UDP Well-Known Port Numbers (Continued)

Service Name	Port	Description
ftp-agent	574/tcp	FTP Software Agent System
ftp-agent	574/udp	FTP Software Agent System
vemmi	575/tcp	VEMMI
	576-599	Unassigned
ipcserver	600/tcp	Sun IPC server
ipcserver	600/udp	Sun IPC server
urm	606/tcp	Cray Unified Resource Manager
urm	606/udp	Cray Unified Resource Manager
nqs	607/tcp	nqs
nqs	607/udp	nqs
sift-uft	608/tcp	Sender-Initiated/Unsolicited File Transfer
sift-uft	608/udp	Sender-Initiated/Unsolicited File Transfer
npmp-trap	609/tcp	npmp-trap
npmp-trap	609/udp	npmp-trap
npmp-local	610/tcp	npmp-local
npmp-local	610/udp	npmp-local
npmp-gui	611/tcp	npmp-gui
npmp-gui	611/udp	npmp-gui
	612-632	Unassigned
servstat	633/tcp	Service Status update (Sterling Software)
servstat	633/udp	Service Status update (Sterling Software)
ginad	634/tcp	ginad
ginad	634/udp	ginad
	635-665	Unassigned
mdqs	666/tcp	
mdqs	666/udp	
doom	666/tcp	Doom Id Software
doom	666/udp	Doom Id Software
disclose	667/tcp	Campaign contribution disclosures - SDR Technologies
disclose	667/udp	Campaign contribution disclosures - SDR Technologies
	668-703	Unassigned

Continued

Table 34.1 TCP and UDP Well-Known Port Numbers (Continued)

Service Name	Port	Description
elcsd	704/tcp	errlog copy/server daemon
elcsd	704/udp	errlog copy/server daemon
entrustmanager	709/tcp	EntrustManager
entrustmanager	709/udp	EntrustManager
netviewdm1	729/tcp	IBM NetView DM/6000 Server/Client
netviewdm1	729/udp	IBM NetView DM/6000 Server/Client
netviewdm2	730/tcp	IBM NetView DM/6000 send/tcp
netviewdm2	730/udp	IBM NetView DM/6000 send/tcp
netviewdm3	731/tcp	IBM NetView DM/6000 receive/tcp
netviewdm3	731/udp	IBM NetView DM/6000 receive/tcp
netgw	741/tcp	netGW
netgw	741/udp	netGW
netrcs	742/tcp	Network based Rev. Cont. Sys.
netrcs	742/udp	Network based Rev. Cont. Sys.
flexlm	744/tcp	Flexible License Manager
flexlm	744/udp	Flexible License Manager
fujitsu-dev	747/tcp	Fujitsu Device Control
fujitsu-dev	747/udp	Fujitsu Device Control
ris-cm	748/tcp	Russell Info Sci Calendar Manager
ris-cm	748/udp	Russell Info Sci Calendar Manager
kerberos-adm	749/tcp	kerberos administration
kerberos-adm	749/udp	kerberos administration
rfile	750/tcp	
loadav	750/udp	
pump	751/tcp	
pump	751/udp	
qrh	752/tcp	
qrh	752/udp	
rrh	753/tcp	
rrh	753/udp	

Continued

Table 34.1 TCP and UDP Well-Known Port Numbers (Continued)

Service Name	Port	Description
tell	754/tcp	send
tell	754/udp	send
nlogin	758/tcp	
nlogin	758/udp	
con	759/tcp	
con	759/udp	
ns	760/tcp	
ns	760/udp	
rxe	761/tcp	
rxe	761/udp	
quotad	762/tcp	
quotad	762/udp	
cycleserv	763/tcp	
cycleserv	763/udp	
omserv	764/tcp	
omserv	764/udp	
webster	765/tcp	
webster	765/udp	
phonebook	767/tcp	phone
phonebook	767/udp	phone
vid	769/tcp	
vid	769/udp	
cadlock	770/tcp	
cadlock	770/udp	
rtip	771/tcp	
rtip	771/udp	
cycleserv2	772/tcp	
cycleserv2	772/udp	
submit	773/tcp	
notify	773/udp	
rpasswd	774/tcp	

Continued

Table 34.1 TCP and UDP Well-Known Port Numbers (Continued)

Service Name	Port	Description
acmaint_dbd	774/udp	
entomb	775/tcp	
acmaint_transd	775/udp	
wpages	776/tcp	
wpages	776/udp	
wpgs	780/tcp	
wpgs	780/udp	
concert	786/tcp	Concert
concert	786/udp	Concert
	787-799	Unassigned
mdbs_daemon	800/tcp	
mdbs_daemon	800/udp	
device	801/tcp	
device	801/udp	
	802-887	Unassigned
accessbuilder	888/tcp	AccessBuilder
accessbuilder	888/udp	AccessBuilder
	889-994	Unassigned
spop3	995/tcp	SSL based POP3
spop3	995/udp	SSL based POP3
vsinet	996/tcp	vsinet
vsinet	996/udp	vsinet
maitrd	997/tcp	
maitrd	997/udp	
busboy	998/tcp	
puparp	998/udp	
garcon	999/tcp	
applix	999/udp	Applix ac
puprouter	999/tcp	
puprouter	999/udp	
cadlock	1000/tcp	

Continued

Table 34.1 TCP and UDP Well-Known Port Numbers (Continued)

Service Name	Port	Description
ock	1000/udp	
	1001-1022	Unassigned
	1023/tcp	Reserved
	1023/udp	Reserved

Getting Updated Information

The best way to get updated information between revisions of the paper copy of this book is through electronic distribution mechanisms. One of the best things about the Internet standards process is that all RFCs and in-process Internet Drafts are freely available online. The following sections describe how to retrieve RFCs and Internet Drafts over the Internet.

RFCs

Internet protocols are documented using the Internet Request for Comment format, or RFC. RFCs can be retrieved electronically from Internet sites using the File Transfer Protocol (FTP). You can retrieve RFCs from the following location:

```
ftp://ds.internic.net/rfc/
```

This directory holds all the available RFCs in ASCII text format. Each RFC is named "rfcXXXX.txt", where "XXXX" is the RFC number. Some RFCs are also available in Adobe Postscript format. In such cases the filename is "rfcXXXX.ps". RFCs are always available in text format. When a Postscript version exists, it augments the text version and typically provides some added value, such as enhanced figures.

RFCs are never reissued. Once an RFC number is assigned to a document, the document is archived and is permanently stable. This does not mean that the information contained in the RFC does not change, however. Protocols are updated and new RFCs are published to describe the updates or to make obsolete earlier RFCs that describe the protocol.

Whenever you are working on a project, never assume you have the latest RFC that describes a given protocol. Updates may have occurred since you last checked. You can always find the latest RFC to describe a given protocol using the RFC index:

```
ftp://ds.internic.net/rfc/rfc-index.txt
```

The entries in the index describing the older versions of a protocol are updated with information like, "Obsoleted by RFCxxxx", or, "Updated by RFCxxxx", to alert you to a new RFC that describes the protocol.

Internet Drafts

Internet Drafts are documents with pre-RFC status. They are working documents used to describe the current version of an in-design protocol. Some Internet Drafts are developed by IETF working groups. Others are written by individuals wanting to propose a new protocol.

Because Internet Drafts are works in-progress, they are highly dynamic. Revisions and updates can occur weekly or monthly with some hot topics. The reader is always encouraged to retrieve the latest copy of the draft.

Internet drafts can be retrieved from:

```
ftp://ftp.isi.edu/internet-drafts/
```

The Internet Standards Process

It has been said that the Internet has no leadership; that it is simply a chaotic collection of independent personalities cooperating to create a global phenomenon. While there is some truth to that statement, it is also true that the Internet was developed using a fairly rigorous standards process. To put the matter simply, networks require interoperability. Interoperability requires open specifications that developers can implement. Specifications need some sort of legitimate body to endorse them and refine them over time. There is too much incentive for individual implementers to add proprietary features to protocols in such a way that nothing is interoperable any more.

This appendix looks at the Internet standards process. It describes the bodies involved with the development of Internet standards and the states through which protocols progress on their way toward standardization. It is important to understand this process so that implementers and users can make decisions about which protocols to implement, purchase, and use. Developers want to ensure that they are implementing required protocols. Users may base purchase or deployment decisions based on the predicted standardization of a protocol.

Bodies Involved with Internet Standards

There are many bodies involved with the development of Internet standards. Here are some of the most important ones.

The Internet Society (ISOC)

The Internet Society is an international organization created to promote the development and deployment of Internet technologies and applications. The society provides an important function: it is the pseudo-governing body for a collection of multinational, ungoverned, cooperating systems. The society promotes cooperation and coordination between individuals, corporations, and other bodies which develop, build, maintain, administer, and use parts of the Internet.The Internet Society's principal purpose is to develop and evolve Internet technologies and applications and ensure their availability to the world.

Specific Internet Society goals include[1]:

- Development, maintenance, evolution, and dissemination of standards for the Internet and its internetworking technologies and applications
- Growth and evolution of the Internet architecture
- Maintenance and evolution of effective administrative processes necessary for operation of the global Internet and internets
- Education and research related to the Internet and internetworking
- Harmonization of actions and activities at international levels to facilitate the development and availability of the Internet
- Collection and dissemination of information related to the Internet and internetworking, including histories and archives
- Assisting technologically developing countries, areas, and peoples in implementing and evolving their Internet infrastructure and use
- Liaison with other organizations, governments, and the general public for coordination, collaboration, and education in effecting the above purposes

Internet Architecture Board (IAB)

The IAB is chartered by the Internet Society Trustees. The IAB is responsible for technical oversight of the Internet architecture and protocols. The IAB approves appointments to the Internet Engineering Steering Group (IESG), from the nominations put forth from the Internet Engineering Task Force (IETF) nominating committee. The IAB also serves as the body to which decisions of the IESG can be appealed.

[1] These are taken directly from the Internet Society's "Frequently Asked Questions" document which can be found on the world-wide-web at: http://www.isoc.org.

The IAB provides advice and guidance to the Board of Trustees and Officers of the Internet Society. The IAB can convene panels, hold hearings, and investigate topics to acquire technical information in order to help guide ISOC activities and directions.

The IAB charter is described in detail in RFC 1601.

Internet Engineering Steering Group (IESG)

The Internet Engineering Steering Group is responsible for the management of IETF (see following section) activities and the Internet Standards process. The IESG administers the standards process according to the rules prescribed by the Internet Society. The IESG is responsible for the entry of protocol documents onto the "standards track," and for their eventual approval as Internet Standards. The IESG is composed of the IETF area directors and chairperson.

Internet Engineering Task Force (IETF)

The Internet Engineering Task Force is the principal body responsible for the development and engineering of Internet protocols. The IETF is not part of the Internet Society. Rather, it is a loosely-organized collection of engineers, researchers, academics, and associated hangers-on who make technical contributions toward Internet technologies.

The IETF is composed of a series of working groups, each grouped with others into a defined area of responsibility. Each area director coordinates activities within the particular area and holds a seat on the IESG.

Anyone with time and interest can attend IETF meetings and participate in the Internet Standards process. Details about upcoming IETF meetings can be found on the IETF web page http://www.ietf.org.

Internet Research Task Force (IRTF)

The Internet Research Task Force (IRTF) is a sister body to the IETF, though it is chartered by the IAB and is part of the Internet Society. The IRTF examines technical topics that are too uncertain, too advanced, or not well enough understood to be the subject of IETF working groups. The existence of the IRTF ensures that such issues are investigated, even though immediate standardization of the technology is not imminent. When the IRTF has progressed on a technology to the point where standardization can occur, the technology is taken up in the IETF and standardized according to the Internet standardization process.

Internet Documents

Internet standards require documentation. There are two important types of Internet standards documentation: Internet Drafts and RFCs. Each serves a distinct purpose. This section describes the function of each document type.

Internet Drafts

During the development of a protocol standard, there is a need for a great deal of peer review and commenting. Originally, RFC documents served this purpose. They were, literally, Requests for Comments. When the ARPANET (Advanced Research Projects Agency Network, the forerunner of the Internet) was just beginning, people invented protocols to serve their needs and documented them in RFCs so that others could learn about them and generate feedback for later versions of the protocol. This process worked quite well when the Internet was in its formative stages and most of the protocols were evolving rapidly.

There were a couple of problems with this scheme, however. First, RFCs would be updated from time to time, rather than reissue the same document with the same RFC number, a new number would be assigned to the new document. This ensured that one could always determine which document was the latest version of the protocol. It also had the unfortunate side effect of "polluting" the RFC numbering space with many outdated versions of protocols. Protocols that were evolving rapidly went through several RFC numbers in quick succession.

Second, originally it was the case that just about anybody could issue an RFC. It was a fairly informal process, as "Request for Comments" suggests. As the Internet grew, the protocols specified by RFCs started to take on a greater significance. They were referenced as authoritative specifications.

Clearly, if RFCs were "authoritative," there was a need for a non-authoritative document that would serve the purpose originally served by RFCs: to serve as the basis for discussion and comment on evolving protocols.

The Internet Draft was defined to serve this role. Internet Drafts are pre-RFC documents that contain rapidly changing information. They document the work of IETF working groups or the efforts of individuals. Anybody can write an Internet Draft and issue it for comment.

Because of the unconstrained role an Internet Draft plays in the Internet standards process, it is important to put them into perspective. Internet Drafts have no formal status as authoritative Internet standards documents. Internet Drafts have a maximum lifetime of six months. If, after this period, they are not issued as RFCs, they are deleted from the main Internet Draft distribution server (ftp://ftp.isi.edu/internet-drafts). Because of their volatility, they should not be cited in RFCs or other documents and vendors should not claim compliance to them.

In this book, every effort has been made to avoid material from Internet Drafts. In some cases, however, this has been unavoidable. Where an important protocol is currently undergoing standardization and the only documentation is from an Internet Draft, I have included material from the draft rather than leave the protocol undocumented. In such cases, however, I have indicated that the material is from an Internet Draft. Readers who are depending on the material for important decisions should always consult the latest copy of the draft or the corresponding RFC, if the document has been issued as such after this book went to press.

RFCs

Requests for Comment, or RFCs, document Internet standard protocols. As described in the previous section, they originally served to document existing protocols and to stimulate discussion on evolving protocols. They have since taken on a much more authoritative role.

Though all Internet standards are RFCs, not all RFCs are Internet standards. For instance, all the original RFCs still retain their status as modern RFCs. In some cases, RFCs document protocols that were in wide use at some point in time, but are now largely obsolete (the official classification is "Historic"). In other cases, they document protocols that were experimental and were never widely implemented or adopted. In still other cases, they serve as informational documents that describe the current state of a particular technology or a best current practice (BCP) for deploying or using a particular protocol. Finally, some are just humorous; the IETF has a grand tradition of issuing RFCs for seasonal holidays around Christmas time and April Fool's Day (see RFC 748, RFC 968, RFC 1097, RFC 1607, RFC 1776, etc.—I particularly like the TELNET Subliminal Message Option described in RFC 1097).

In general RFCs are separated into two groups: standards-track and non-standards-track. The issuance of an RFC is not enough to qualify a protocol for standardization. However, even a standards-track protocol that has not yet reached the

Standard state (see the next section) has much more legitimacy than an Internet Draft. As such, pre-standard RFCs are suitable for citations in other documents. Because they are RFCs, they will never be deleted, even if they fail to reach the Standard state for some reason.

Protocol States

This issuance of an RFC describing a protocol is not enough for that protocol to be called a standard. The IETF has a very rigorous qualification process for the creation of Internet standards. This process is the IETF standards track. Each RFC is issued a protocol state to indicate where it is in the standards process or whether it is outside the standards track. The IESG approves the initial state assigned to a new RFC, and any state changes as a protocol is advanced along the standards track.

The IETF standards track process requires multiple interoperable implementations of a protocol to exist, and to have been tested together, before a protocol is advanced to the Standard state. This ensures that protocols can be implemented and gives the implementers a chance to suggest refinements to the protocol before it has achieved Standard status.

The following sections describe each of the possible states an RFC might have associated with it.

Proposed Standard

This is the first step on the standards track. A Proposed Standard designation marks a protocol as important and worthy of standardization by the IESG. At this point, major design choices have been made and the protocol has been widely reviewed by technical experts. Although stable, further implementation experience will probably reveal refinements which should be included in the design.

There is no commitment from the IESG to advance the protocol beyond the Proposed Standard state. If implementation experience reveals serious flaws in the protocol, it may be retracted entirely and assigned an Informational or Experimental state. If the flaws are smaller, it may remain the Proposed Standard state while the flaws are a eliminated.

Draft Standard

The second step along the standards track is the Draft Standard state. When a Proposed Standard protocol has at least two independent, interoperable implementations and is of great utility, the IESG may promote the protocol to the Draft Standard state. If the protocol had changes made to it as the result of operational testing, it may be reissued with a different RFC number. If no changes were made, the IESG will simply change the state associated with the original RFC.

Although the Draft Standard state confers a great deal of confidence in the protocol, it is still a step on the way to full standardization. For instance, the protocol may suffer from pathological behavior when it is scaled to global proportions. This behavior may not have been seen in the small number of implementations required to advance the protocol to the Draft Standard state.

In spite of this caveat, the Draft Standard state usually indicates a protocol that will eventually become a Standard. As such, it is reasonable for vendors to implement Draft Standard protocols. In fact, this is basically required because without a large number of implementations and experience, it will be hard to promote the protocol to the Standard state.

Standard

This is the final state on the standards track. A protocol that has been widely implemented and received significant operational testing is a candidate for the Standard state. When a Draft Standard protocol has received enough testing, it will be advanced to the Standard state by the IESG.

Informational

The Informational state is used to describe protocols or information that, while deserving of being published in an RFC, should not be on the standards track. This might include proprietary protocol specifications or algorithms used in many different protocols.

Experimental

The Experimental state describes a non-standards track protocol that is not intended for operational use. This designation may be given to a protocol by the IESG because the technology used to implement the protocol is still being researched or because the effects of the deployment of the protocol cannot be accurately predicted.

In some cases, Experimental protocols may move to the standards track when the technology is better understood. In other cases, Experimental protocols simply die off as better alternatives are found or the need for them ceases to exist.

Vendors should not implement Experimental protocols unless they are participating in the IETF experiment. In this case, they should coordinate with the other experimenters to share implementation and deployment experience.

Historic

Sometimes protocols outlive their usefulness. A better solution to the problem might be found, or the need for the protocol may diminish. In such cases, the IESG will classify the protocol as *Historic*. Vendors should not implement historic protocols unless there is a compelling reason to do so (servicing the customer base that still relies on the Historic protocol, for instance).

Protocol Status

In addition to a standardization state, each protocol is assigned a protocol status. The status indicates whether a protocol must, should, or may be implemented to ensure interoperability with other nodes on the Internet. Five status levels are defined: Required, Recommended, Elective, Limited Use, and Not Recommended. These status levels are described in the following sections.

Required

All systems must implement Required protocols. The Required status is assigned to protocols like IP and ICMP that are used as the basis for almost every other protocol in the Internet and without which an Internet host would not be able to communicate with any other Internet host. Very few protocols are Required.

Recommended

Recommended protocols should be implemented by all Internet hosts unless there is some compelling reason not to do so. Most general-purpose hosts desire the functionality provided by Recommended protocols. Examples of Recommended protocols include TCP, IP, TELNET, and SMTP. In some cases, however, a special purpose host might not implement a given protocol. A network monitoring system, for example, might not need email services and would thus not implement SMTP functionality.

Elective

The Elective status describes protocols that are useful to some hosts but not to others. A host may implement the protocol if it needs the services described by the protocols. In general, the Elective status suggests that if a host requires this functionality, it should implement the functionality using this protocol. Examples of elective protocols are the TFTP, TIME, and POP3 protocols.

Limited Use

The Limited Use status describes protocols that are for limited use. Experimental protocols are often assigned the Limited Use status.

Not Recommended

The Not Recommended status describes protocols that should not be implemented unless there is a good reason to do so. Often, a protocol with this status is a Historic protocol and other, better alternatives exist to provide the required functionality.

Future Reading

You can find more information about the Internet standards process and the various bodies involved with Internet standards in RFC 1601, 1602, and 1160. Information about the ISOC, IAB, and IETF can be found online at:

- http://www.isoc.org
- http://www.iab.org
- http://www.ietf.org

Glossary

The Internet can present a bewildering array of technical terms, acronyms, and references to standards documents. This glossary should help you make sense of the confusion.

ARP Address Resolution Protocol. A protocol to resolve data link addresses (Ethernet addresses, for example) from network addresses (IP addresses, for example). See RFC 826.

ASN.1 Abstract Syntax Notation One. ASN.1 is an abstract syntax notation developed by the International Standards Organization to describe data structures in a machine-independent fashion. ASN.1 is used to describe SNMP-managed objects, message formats, and other data structures. See ISO International Standard 8824 and *BER*.

BASE64 A technique for encoding 8-bit binary data using a 64-character subset of US-ASCII suitable for transmission through most electronic mail systems. BASE64 is similar in function to the UUENCODE format but is less susceptible to corruption when intermediate systems do not use the US-ASCII character set. BASE64 encoding is most often used with MIME email messages. See *UUENCODE* and *MIME*.

BER Basic Encoding Rules. A set of rules for encoding abstract ASN.1 syntax into a concrete format that can be passed between machines. See ISO International Standard 8825 and *ASN.1*.

body part A distinct section of a MIME message. Each MIME body part contains information that identifies the body part type and contents. See RFC 1521.

BOOTP Bootstrap Protocol. A simple protocol that allows a client node to obtain its IP address, the IP address of its host server, and the name of its boot image file. BOOTP can be used to boot a diskless workstation. See RFC 951.

broadcast A method of a packet addressing where all nodes receive the packet. The local IP subnet broadcast address is 255.255.255.255.

cookie See *QUOTE* or *magic cookie.*

CSMA/CD Carrier Sense Multiple Access with Collision Detection. A medium access control method. Nodes wishing to transmit listen to the medium until they find it is not busy (carrier sense) and then transmit. If two nodes transmit at the same time, they detect the collision (collision detection), back off a random amount of time, and then retry.

DAYTIME Daytime Protocol. See RFC 867.

DHCP Dynamic Host Configuration Protocol. See RFC 1541.

DNS Domain Name System. A distributed database system primarily used to map host names to IP addresses (the system actually allows the retrieval of many parameters associated with a given host name, of which an IP address is the most common parameter used by the client host). See RFC 1034 and RFC 1035.

dot stuffing A technique used to transmit text messages between systems in many Internet protocols, where the end of a message is signaled by a line containing a single period character. In the dot stuffing algorithm, the transmitter prepends a period to every line of text that begins with a period itself. The receiver removes every leading period from all lines it receives. This prevents the receiver from mistaking a line containing a single period that is part of the message text with the actual end-of-message indication. This technique is used with protocols such as SMTP, POP3, and NNTP.

dotted decimal A method of writing multiple octet data values. Each octet is represented as a decimal number in the range 0 to 255, inclusive, and is separated from the following octets by a period character. For instance, the hexadecimal value 0x80FF1105 can be represented as 128.255.17.5 in dotted decimal format.

DSAP Destination service access point. SAPs are used in IEEE 802 LLC and together with the addressing information specify the source and destination on a particular node. The DSAP is the identifier assigned to the network destination in a node. See *SSAP* and *SNAP.*

ECHO The Echo protocol. A simple protocol that returns all data sent to is. See RFC 862.

ESMTP Extended SMTP. See *SMTP-EXT.*

Ethernet A common local area networking protocol using a logical bus topology and the CSMA/CD medium access control method. See RFC 894 for the specification for running IP over Ethernet networks.

Ethertype A set of protocol types used in Ethernet. Ethertypes are used in many other protocols to identify the network layer protocol associated with a piece of data. For instance, the SNAP encapsulation header used in IP over IEEE networks uses Ethertype values. See *SNAP.*

FINGER The Finger protocol. A protocol that allows a client to find out information about a user of a remote server. See RFC 1288.

frame The common name for a layer 2 PDU. Ethernet and IEEE 802 PDUs are called frames. Note that layer 2 PDUs are often incorrectly called packets. See *PDU* and *packet.*

FTP File Transfer Protocol. A sophisticated protocol that provides for the transfer of files between systems. FTP provides many data format options that deal with heterogeneous systems. See RFC 959. A simple file transfer protocol is provided by the Trivial File Transfer Protocol. See *TFTP.*

gateway Another word for a router. The word gateway was originally used in many RFCs but has become a bit obsolete recently. The term is now often used to describe application layer gateways between two dissimilar application protocols (an SMTP to X.400 mail gateway, for instance). See *router.*

HTML Hypertext Markup Language. A hypertext markup language used in documents on the World Wide Web. See RFC 1866 and *WWW.*

HTTP Hypertext Transfer Protocol. A protocol used to transfer hypertext and other documents are the World Wide Web. See *WWW.*

IAB Internet Architecture Board. The board chartered by the Internet Society to oversee the Internet architecture and the development of Internet protocols.

IANA Internet Assigned Numbers Authority. The IANA registers all the important protocol numbers, types, and identifiers used in various Internet protocols. Periodically, the IANA publishes the current set of this information as the Assigned Numbers document. The current Assigned Numbers document is RFC 1700.

IEEE 802.3 IEEE 802.3 is the formally standardized version of Ethernet. Although there are some differences between Ethernet version 2 and IEEE 802.3, they are minor and all common hardware is capable of supporting both standards. The only meaningful difference is the use of Ethernet version 2 versus IEEE 802.2 framing. See RFC 1042 for the specification for running IP over IEEE 802.3 networks using IEEE 802.2 framing.

IEEE 802.5 A common local area networking protocol using a logical ring topology with a token passing medium access control method. Also commonly known as Token Ring or IBM Token Ring. See RFC 1042 for the specification for running IP over IEEE 802.5 networks using IEEE 802.2 framing.

IEEE Institute of Electrical and Electronics Engineers. A professional society of electrical engineers and computer scientists that sponsors a number of technical standards groups.

IESG Internet Engineering Steering Group. The IESG is composed of the area directors of the IETF and is responsible for the management of the IETF and the Internet standards process.

IETF Internet Engineering Task Force. The technical group responsible for the development of mainstream Internet protocols. The IETF is composed of a set of working groups that meet periodically to develop new protocols and enhance old protocols.

IGMP The Internet Group Management Protocol. IGMP is used to manage the membership of IP multicast groups. See RFC 1112.

IMAP Internet Message Access Protocol. A protocol providing message access and remote filing capabilities. IMAP is similar to the POP3 protocol in concept, but provides greatly enhanced functionality. See RFC 1730.

Internet Draft A pre-standard working document used to publish a protocol when development work is still progressing. Most Internet protocols are first published as Internet Drafts until they reach a stable design point and are then published as RFCs.

IP The Internet Protocol. The basic network-layer datagram protocol on which the entire Internet is based. See RFC 791.

IRC Internet Relay Chat. A world-wide, multi-user chat protocol. See RFC 1459.

IRTF Internet Research Task Force. A task force similar to the IETF but responsible for research into protocols and technology that is currently not "mainstream" enough for the work of the IETF.

ISOC Internet Society. The ISOC is an international organization created to promote the development and deployment of Internet technologies and applications.

LLC Logical Link Control. A sub-layer of the data link layer in the OSI 7-layer model. IEEE 802.2 LLC is used on IEEE 802 networks.

magic cookie A special value used to identify the format of a piece of data.

Mbps Megabits per second.

MD5 Message Digest 5. A cryptographic hashing algorithm used to generate digital signatures. This algorithm is used in many parts of the Internet security architecture.

MIME Multipurpose Internet Mail Extensions. A set of extensions to the old Internet mail format (RFC 822) that allows for the standardized transmission of binary and type-tagged information in the Internet mail system. See RFC 1521.

MTU Maximum Transfer Unit. The maximum packet size that can be transmitted across a given data link.

multicast A form of addressing where the destination address specifies a group of hosts rather than a single host or all hosts. Hosts join multicast groups using the Internet Group Management Protocol (IGMP). See *IGMP*.

network byte order The order in which multi-byte fields are transmitted on a network. Network byte order is big-endian. The first transmitted byte of a multi-byte quantity is the high-order byte.

NNTP Network News Transport Protocol. The basic protocol used to exchange network news article between multiple news servers and between news servers and clients. See RFC 977.

NVT ASCII The subset and interpretation of the US-ASCII character set defined in the TELNET protocol (RFC 854). NVT ASCII is the character set used by a TELNET NVT.

NVT Network Virtual Terminal. The abstract virtual terminal used as the endpoints of TELNET communications.

octet Another word for an 8-bit byte. Typically *octet* and *byte* are interchangeable but octet was specifically created to avoid ambiguity when dealing with machines using byte sizes other than 8 bits.

packet The common name for a layer 3 PDU. IP datagrams are often called packets. Note that layer 2 PDUs are often called packets as well but are more properly called frames. See *PDU* and *frame.*

PDU Protocol data unit. A unit of information at any given level of the 7-layer OSI protocol stack. Layer 3 PDUs are often called *packets* while layer 2 PDUs are often called *frames.*

POP3 Post Office Protocol, Version 3. POP3 allows a client to retrieve email messages from a remote mailbox on a server machine. See RFC 1725.

port The addressing information used by the transport layer to associate incoming data and connections with different processes running on a single host.

PPP Point-to-point protocol. A data link protocol using a simple bi-directional serial connection such as a serial cable or modem connection.

QUOTE Quote of the Day Protocol. A protocol that allows a client to retrieve a famous quote or other bit of wisdom from a remote server. See RFC 865.

quoted printable An encoding format used in the MIME protocol. Quoted Printable encoding leaves most characters in the US-ASCII character set unchanged but encodes other characters. Quote Printable messages are often decipherable for users without MIME-enable mail user agents because so much of the text remains US-ASCII. See RFC 1521.

RARP Reverse Address Resolution Protocol. A protocol that allows a node to determine its own IP address given its data link hardware address. This protocol was often used by diskless workstations. See RFC 903.

RFC Request for Comments. An document used to disseminate descriptions of protocols or other information related to the Internet. Many RFCs are published to document the protocol development work of the IETF.

RIF Routing Information Field. A field in the IEEE 802.5 header for storing source routing information.

router A network layer device responsible for forwarding datagrams from one network to another. Routers typically run a routing protocol from which they determine the optimal datagram route to its final destination.

SMI Structure of Management Information. A set of ASN.1 objects that define the syntax of SNMP MIBs. See RFC 1155.

SMTP Simple Mail Transfer Protocol. The protocol used to send mail between Internet hosts. See RFC 821.

SMTP-EXT SMTP Extensions. A set of protocol changes to the original SMTP that provide an extensible framework for enhanced SMTP features. The extensions are compatible with the original SMTP and are only invoked when both client and server are SMTP-EXT aware. See RFC 1869.

SNAP Subnetwork Access Protocol. SNAP specifies a method of encapsulating IP datagrams and ARP messages on IEEE 802 networks. SNAP encapsulation is identified by the DSAP and SSAP fields of the IEEE 802 header containing 0xAA. See RFC 1042.

SNMP Simple Network Management Protocol. The network management protocol used on the Internet. See RFC 1157 and *SNMPv2.*

SNMPv2 The second revision of the Simple Network Management Protocol. The second revision adds features that allow the protocol to scale to enterprise-wide proportions. See RFCs 1902, 1903, 1904, 1905, 1906, 1907, and 1908.

SSAP Source service access point. SAPs are used in IEEE 802 LLC and together with the addressing information specify the source and destination on a particular node. The SSAP is the identifier assigned to the network source in a node. See *SSAP* and *SNAP.*

TCP Transmission Control Protocol. The basic transport protocol in the Internet protocol suite that provides a reliable, connection oriented, bi-directional byte stream between two Internet nodes. See RFC 793.

TELNET The TELNET protocol. The common virtual terminal protocol used on the Internet. TELNET describes the concept of a network virtual terminal and provides for the negotiation of session options to add to the basic NVT functionality. See RFC 854 and 855, *NVT,* and *NVT-ASCII.*

TFTP Trivial File Transfer Protocol. A simple file transfer protocol based on UDP transport. TFTP is small and simple enough to be embedded in boot ROMs. TFTP is commonly used with BOOTP and is used to retrieve the kernel image of a diskless workstation at boot time. See RFC 1350 and *BOOTP.*

time-to-live A field in the IP header that is decremented by each IP entity that handles a datagram. When the time-to-live field reaches zero, the datagram is discarded. The time-to-live field puts an upper bound on a datagram lifetime and prevents a datagram from looping forever when a transient routing loop is established.

UDP User Datagram Protocol. UDP provides datagram service at the transport level. UDP runs on top of IP and provides simple port demultiplexing and error detection services. See RFC 768.

unicast A form of addressing where the destination address specifies a single host rather than a group of hosts (multicast) or all hosts (broadcast).

UUENCODE A form of encoding used to convert binary data into a printable format consisting of ASCII characters. The UUENCODE format was a popular format before the introduction of MIME and BASE64 encoding but has since become less popular. BASE64 encoding, while similar to UUENCODE encoding, performs better when a message is handled by a system that does not use the ASCII character set. See *BASE64* and *MIME.*

well known port A port number permanently assigned to be the server port for standard Internet services. Servers wait for clients to connect to them at their well known port address. For instance, SMTP servers are assigned the well known port 25.

Index

D

I

K

L

M

N

O

U

V

W

X

Y

Z